3D User Interfaces with Java 3

3D User Interfaces with Java 3D

JON BARRILLEAUX

MANNING

Greenwich
(74° w. long.)

For online information and ordering of this and other Manning books,
go to www.manning.com. The publisher offers discounts on this book
when ordered in quantity. For more information, please contact:

Special Sales Department
Manning Publications Co.
32 Lafayette Place   Fax: (203) 661-9018
Greenwich, CT 06830   email: orders@manning.com

Manning Publications Co.   Copyeditors: Kevin Walzer
32 Lafayette Place   Lori Jareo
Greenwich, CT 06830   Typesetter: Tony Roberts
                                Cover designer: Leslie Haimes
                          Developmental editor: Ben Kovitz

Printed in the United States of America
1 2 3 4 5 6 7 8 9 10 – VHG – 03 02 01 00

To Michelle and Francois, the loves of my life,
and to my parents for all their sacrifices

brief contents

Part 4   Java 3D framework and examples   283

contents

Part 4 Java 3D framework and examples 283

15 Why a framework? 285

16 Framework utilities 298

introduction

This book takes a practical approach to providing real-world solutions for real-world problems in 3D user interface (UI) development. Although its emphasis is on next-generation business needs, such as mass customization and online sales, much of what this book offers has broad applicability to 3D user interfaces in other pursuits such as scientific visualization and gaming. Applications and their use of 3D are approached realistically. The book assumes an everyday user without a lot of time to learn a complicated application. From this perspective, Java 3D is introduced as a platform for 3D application development, with a series of examples demonstrating how to implement advanced 3D UI techniques. One could say that this book presents a roadmap from Java 3D to "Swing 3D."

WHAT THIS BOOK OFFERS

Patterns, techniques, and framework

This book describes patterns and terminology useful for classifying 3D user interfaces and offers 3D techniques and a software framework to implement them. Applications are the top level of design abstraction, techniques are the middle level, and the framework—the code—is at the bottom. Numerous Java 3D examples demonstrate the 3D UI techniques and help you to get started on the journey down the road to "Swing 3D."

The 3D techniques introduced early in the book are general in nature and not specific to a particular software language or 3D graphics platform. They take a fresh approach to the problem of highly interactive 3D user interfaces. Some build on trends that have developed in non-3D and web-based applications, such as drag-and-drop and web-like navigation. Others try to impart a natural feel to 3D user interfaces, through cues, suggestive dynamics, and visual feedback. Many rely on computer-intensive techniques such as fine-grained mouseover and collision detection that, until recently, put them beyond the reach of common personal computers.

The software framework presented later in the book, implemented in Java 3D, demonstrates many of the 3D UI techniques. It offers concrete examples of how to implement 3D user interfaces that form the basis of easy-to-use applications. More importantly, it provides you with the means for incorporating these techniques into your own applications.

Java 3D

To make the examples concrete and the techniques immediately usable requires selection of a 3D platform. The clear choice was Java 3D. Java 3D is an up-and-coming extension to Java that had its first full release in December 1998, but was available long before that in a series of solid beta versions. The same widespread appeal for using Java also applies to Java 3D, not the least of which is the promise of platform independence.

Java 3D offers tight integration with the rest of the Java environment, which is useful for developing substantial 3D applications. It was also designed with the intent of speed and flexibility. It should have broad appeal and an air of familiarity to many because it evolved out of the better parts of Open Inventor, OpenGL, DirectX, and Virtual Reality Modeling Language (VRML). The expected long-term benefits of Java 3D more than make up for its short-term growing pains, which in the broader picture are surprisingly few.

Although not intended as a full-blown tutorial, this book includes a good introduction to programming in Java 3D. Emphasis is on the more practical aspects of using Java 3D as a medium for implementing the user interface techniques described in this book. To help you get started, a set of Java 3D classes is provided that serves as an introductory application framework and the foundation for the book's 3D UI examples.

Real solutions for real problems

I identified many of the 3D techniques described in this book while working on e-commerce and other end-user applications. A common goal in this work was to develop 3D applications for use by the common user rather than by trained specialists. The need for this work grew out of the realization that traditional windows-based, CAD-inspired approaches to 3D applications were not readily adaptable for utilization by the casual user. The advent of the web and its democratic nature further highlighted the shortcomings of conventional 3D user interface approaches.

The appeal of web applications is that they are easy to navigate, visually compelling, and generally take a "learn as you go" approach to user training, with extensive dynamic visual feedback. Exploration of the application is fostered by the user's ability to "back up" or "go home" if they find themselves lost, something that is often impossible to do in windows-based applications, 3D or otherwise. Applying such concepts as these to 3D applications should help provide the necessary paradigm shift to make 3D viable and user-friendly for next-generation applications.

Some developers have already recognized the benefits of this approach. Games and child education programs were early adopters of visually compelling, easy-to-use 3D user interfaces. This book tries to apply this philosophy to new business-oriented applications that might not consider 3D as beneficial, and to traditional 3D applications that are seeking broader appeal through more intuitive user interfaces.

A fresh(er) approach to 3D user interfaces

The concepts and techniques described in this book try to take a fresh—or at least a fresher—approach to designing 3D user interfaces. Many take advantage of the immense performance available in recent desktop computer systems to impart a more intuitive feel to the user interface. One of the major failings of 3D applications has been the lack of intuitive navigation that people use in exploring the real world, and the lack of intuitive feel that people have in manipulating real objects. Devices developed for Virtual Reality (VR) such as force feedback, data gloves, head-mounted displays, and 3D mice address some of these shortcomings, but are not widely available. Their general lack of performance and robustness is also an issue.

This book offers techniques that, without resorting to exotic interface devices, impart some of the natural feel we have in the real world. They rely on cues and sensory substitution to suggest tactile feedback. Other techniques provide the user with dynamic in-scene guidance in how to make things happen. These techniques take advantage of computer-intensive operations such as proximity detection, dynamics modeling, and a lavish use of mouseover visual feedback.

Of course, too much realism can get in the way of the task at hand, such as having to use the virtual stairs in order to move virtual furniture from one floor of a virtual building to another in a space planning application. The techniques and guidelines described here try to strike a balance between the competing needs of interactive realism and user effectiveness.

A premise of this book is that a good 3D user interface should make the dimensionality of the interface fade into the application woodwork while making the user's job more natural and easy. In other words, the developer and the computer will have to work harder to make 3D just another part of a well-integrated, easy-to-use application. The fact that an application uses 3D instead of 2D, video, or the theory of relativity is immaterial to users so long as they can get their job done with minimal effort and frustration. This is in keeping with the notion that 3D is not an end unto itself. 3D is merely a technology to be used when the benefits are clear and the costs are not prohibitive to the developer or to the user.

Not like other GUI books

Books on user interfaces tend to be rather broad and general. This can be good, but only gets you so far when you are asked by the marketing department to "add a little 3D" to the new product with the beta release only weeks away. The text on computer graphics by Foley, van Dam, et al. is a bit closer to the mark. It includes a discussion of user interfaces in the specific context of computer graphics, but it lacks specifics about how to design a 3D user interface for a real application.

This book takes a specific approach to designing and implementing user interfaces for a specific but important class of interactive problems: direct 3D manipulation. The concrete examples and software framework offered by this book should make easier the job of incorporating, or at least prototyping, 3D in visually oriented applications, even for designers who are relatively new to 3D.

What is not in this book

To give the reader a clearer sense of where this book is coming from, here are a few words about what was intentionally omitted from the book.

This book does not consider the unique aspects of developing 3D applications for a ten-year-old 286 PC running Windows 3.1 or a high-end SGI Onyx in a virtual reality (VR) game palace. Instead, it focuses on the current generation of POCS—Plain Old Computer System—characterized outwardly by a 2D display, a mouse, a keyboard, and maybe sound output. In terms of performance, however, the POCS is not quite as ordinary as its name states or its humble countenance might lead you to believe. The generation of POCS that is now emerging is sporting greatly accelerated graphics and clock speeds surpassing 500 MHz. Such computers are starting to find their way into offices and homes today, and should become ubiquitous in the next few years (perhaps even being reborn in the form of computer appliances).

This book does not plead the case for using 3D. If you think 3D makes sense for your problem, then this book provides ideas and some of the means to help make solutions happen. For 3D to be successful in applications, it needs to fade into the application woodwork, becoming just as unnoticed but essential as the mouse. As applications grow in sophistication, 3D can offer a more natural and intuitive user interface. The whole issue of whether or not 3D is "worth it" will become moot.

This book does not directly address the large fields of data visualization and games. Instead, it offers techniques and software examples that could be applied to such applications. The visualization techniques that are provided in the book play a specific supporting role to the central theme of 3D user interfaces. They are not meant to serve as the core of a visualization package. Similarly, this book will not pretend to be about the ever-popular field of game development. It does, however, share with games the common goal of providing intuitive and easy-to-navigate user interfaces, so there should be plenty of opportunities for cross-pollination.

Finally and perhaps most controversially, this book does not try to define what is a "good" UI. Such a determination is highly subjective and 3D user-interface design is still too young for such absolutes. (In fact, some might claim that such absolutes are ill-advised even for 2D user interfaces.) Instead, this book suggests techniques, describes their advantages, and leaves it to the developer to decide what is best for his or her targeted audience in terms of UI usability and intuitiveness. As such, the book takes a rather utilitarian approach in its examples, providing enough of a UI to demonstrate a technique. It is left to you and to the future of 3D to determine the definition of 3D UI perfection.

How to use this book

This book can be used as a reference. It provides a hierarchical structure for classifying 3D user interface problems, designing solutions, and implementing them in a Java 3D framework. The classification and layering of the problem and solution spaces can be used as 3D design patterns, but in a much broader and less formal sense than the popular patterns used for object-oriented software design.

This book can be used as a toolkit. It provides an introduction to Java 3D programming and a cross-reference between the 3D techniques and those aspects of Java 3D that support them. It includes application utilities, a framework of Java 3D classes, and examples of how to glue them together into a useful interface. You can "wire up" your own widgets, extend the provided object classes, and borrow and modify the source code to try out your own ideas.

This book can be used as a tutorial. Its practical introduction to Java 3D programming should prove valuable to readers familiar with Java and 3D, but who want a jump start on using Java 3D in real applications. The framework makes it easy to experiment with Java 3D and the source code provides plenty of examples of how to move beyond the basics and into the realm of practical use. References throughout the book lead the user between conceptual 3D techniques and their concrete UI implementation.

Contents of this book

Parts 1 and 2 are conceptual. They assume that the reader is familiar with 3D concepts, but they do not discuss programming issues and are not specific as to implementation of any particular language, platform, or 3D API. Parts 3 and 4 are concrete. They include an introduction to Java 3D with emphasis on development of 3D user interfaces and some of the more practical aspects of interactive application development. It uses Java and Java 3D as the basis for a framework of classes that demonstrate the concepts introduced in the conceptual portion of the book.

Part 1: 3D, the next generation.   Part 1 (chapters 1 through 3) establishes the book's view on the future of 3D applications and discusses the essential role that the user interface plays. Applications are the top level of design abstraction presented in the book. Here, applications are classified by purpose and functionality, and patterns are noted in their use of user interface techniques. To establish a proper frame of reference for discussion, common 3D terminology and concepts are defined and discussed.

Part 2: 3D user interface techniques.   Part 2 (chapters 4 through 9) describes patterns and techniques for developing 3D user interfaces. Techniques are the middle level of design abstraction presented in the book. Concepts, methods, rules of thumb, controls, and widgets that address common user interface needs in 3D applications are classified and discussed. References are made to software examples that demonstrate particular techniques in part 4 of the book.

Part 3: Java 3D user interface essentials.   Part 3 (chapters 10 through 14) introduces the Java 3D application program interface (API). It describes those features useful for developing 3D user interfaces and, more generally, 3D applications. It identifies the Java 3D classes that support the various user interface coordinate spaces, provides guidance on the proper care and feeding of scene graphs, and discusses the foundation that Java 3D provides for the user interface framework in part 4.

Part 4: Java 3D framework and examples.   Part 4 (chapters 15 through 24) describes a lightweight Java/Java 3D framework that demonstrates many of the 3D user interface techniques described in part 2. The software framework is the bottom level of design abstraction presented in the book. Its architecture and examples parallel the organization of techniques in part 2. Code samples and diagrams describe how the framework and UI pieces fit together, and examples give you an opportunity to "kick the tires."

Source code downloads

Source code for all of the examples presented in this book is available from the publisher's website. Please go to www.manning.com/barrilleaux.

Conventions used in this book

The following typographical conventions are used throughout the book:

- Code examples and code references, such as class names, are set in `Courier`, which is a fixed-width font.
- Sections of code that are of special significance are set in **`Courier bold`**.

- Comments in code are set off with a double forward slash (//) at the beginning of each comment line.
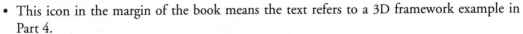
- This icon in the margin of the book means the text refers to a 3D framework example in Part 4.
- UML-like class diagrams appear in the latter part of the book. In these diagrams, hollow arrowheads indicate class inheritance, diamonds indicate aggregation and composition, and finally, the solid arrowheads indicate a navigable relationship.

Author Online

Purchase of *3D User Interfaces with Java 3D* includes free access to a private Internet forum where you can go to make comments about the book, ask technical questions, and receive help from the author and other Java users.

To access the Author Online forum, point your browser to www.manning.com/barrilleaux.

There you will be able to subscribe to the forum. This site also provides information on how to access the forum once you are registered, what kind of help is available, and the rules of conduct on the forum.

acknowledgments

I want to thank the people at TechniCon Corporation for giving me the opportunity to explore next-generation 3D applications for the web, with special thanks to Tony Mirante, for providing the impetus to combine 3D and e-commerce, and to Jake Roberts and Elijah Saxon, who conceived and prototyped many of the early UI techniques.

Thanks to 3D Designs for permission to use one of their models; and to TechniCon Corporation and GB Multimedia for permission to reproduce figures used in the text.

I also want to thank Manning Publications for the opportunity to write the book, and for all of their help, guidance, and support in getting it completed, especially publisher Marjan Bace, review editor Ted Kennedy as well as Ben Kovitz, Syd Brown, and Tony Roberts for their assistance in getting the many graphics in the book just right. Many thanks also go to the following reviewers who offered great feedback and kept the writing honest: Arish Ali, Steven Bellenot, Dennis J. Bouvier, Tony Burrows, Stephen Chan, Randall Chesnut, Ed Falis, Carl Ferreira, Jack Gundrum, Kevin L. Hamilton, Brad Hein, Stefan Hendrickx, Rikard Herlitz, Gregory Hopkins, Alan Hudson, Shui Hung Kwok, Peter Kovach, Kyle Lussier, Mario Maccarini, Dion Picco, Robert W. Schmieder, Jennifer Stewart, Bob Sutherland, Dan Todor, Doug Twilleager, Paco Venegas, Leo Wang, and Mark Young.

And, most important, I want to thank my wife, Michelle, for having the patience and strength to contend with the simultaneous gestation and birth of this book and our son, Francois.

about the cover illustration

The cover illustration of this book is from the 1805 edition of Sylvain Maréchal's four-volume compendium of regional dress customs. This book was first published in Paris in 1788, one year before the French Revolution. Its title alone required no fewer than 30 words.

> *Costumes Civils actuels de tous les peuples connus dessinés d'après nature gravés et coloriés, accompagnés d'une notice historique sur leurs coutumes, moeurs, religions, etc., etc., redigés par M. Sylvain Maréchal*

The four volumes include an annotation on the illustrations: "gravé à manière noire par Mixelle d'après Desrais et colorié." Clearly, the engraver and illustrator deserved no more than to be listed by their last names—after all they were mere technicians. The workers who colored each illustration by hand remain nameless.

The colorful variety of this collection reminds us vividly of how culturally apart the world's towns and regions were just 200 years ago. Dress codes have changed everywhere and the diversity by region, so rich at the time, has faded away. It is now hard to tell the inhabitant of one continent from another. Perhaps we have traded cultural diversity for a more varied personal life—certainly a more varied and exciting technological environment. At a time when it is hard to tell one computer book from another, Manning celebrates the inventiveness and initiative of the computer business with book covers based on the rich diversity of regional life of two centuries ago, brought back to life by Maréchal's pictures. Just think, Maréchal's was a world so different from ours people would take the time to read a book title 30 words long!

PART 1

3D: the next generation

This book is about developing 3D user interfaces for next-generation applications. Before beginning, let's establish a frame of reference for the concepts discussed in the book, including the meaning of the term "next generation."

Chapter 1 starts by defining everyday terms such as "application," "user interface," and "computer system." Most people use these terms without much regard for their specific meaning, and they can mean different things to different people. Beside providing an important conceptual foundation, these discussions will set forth some of the motivation for writing this book and express my hopes and desires for 3D to play a significant role in next generation applications. The chapter's definition of the user interface provides the central organization for the techniques discussed in the next part of the book. Also, its definition of the target computer system narrows the focus of those techniques to applications intended for the common user.

Chapter 2 focuses on the application level. It offers a system for classifying 3D applications that highlights the general patterns of user interface. It also provides insight into how to shape and constrain 3D applications to make the user's job easier. Chapter 3 finishes by defining more terminology, but this time with more deliberate emphasis on 3D user interfaces. Here the "display," "view," and "world" spaces are defined, which are home to different aspects of the user-interface solution. Although technical in nature, this discussion pulls important information together into one place.

C H A P T E R   1

What's in a name?

Evolutions in technology have provided us with a wealth of new opportunities for exploring and interacting with 3D worlds, both real and virtual. Head-mounted displays (HMD) and data gloves enable immersion and interaction in a virtual 3D environment. Such devices have been popularized in the entertainment media and are recognized by the public as the symbols of virtual reality (VR). On the horizon is an offshoot of VR called Augmented Reality (AR) that strives to blend the virtual world with the real one. Such devices as wearable computers, virtual retinal displays (VRD), head-mounted gyro trackers, and haptic devices promise to overlay virtual sights, sounds, and feelings onto our senses of the real world, thereby augmenting our natural experiences.

It is against this backdrop of paradigm shifts and promises of virtual fantasy worlds that this book approaches to say that the near future of 3D lies not in cyberpunk-enabling technologies, but in the lowly personal computer. This contention comes from my belief that the forces propelling 3D user interfaces into this new century will come from the gray-suited world of e-commerce and the jeans-style comfort of home on the web. This is not to say that VR and AR will have to wait their turn, only that the vast majority of users at the start of this new century will likely experience 3D in their everyday lives through their humble PCs rather than through their cyberspace body suit.

1.1 THE APPLICATION

In the grand scheme of this book the application is defined as the top level of design abstraction. Stated simply, applications are built from conceptually based techniques; and techniques are built from software building blocks. Applications are at the top layer, techniques represent the middle layer, and the software lies at the bottom layer of abstraction. Looking at this as application designers, we can say that an application defines what we want to do; and the techniques and building blocks define how we want to do it.

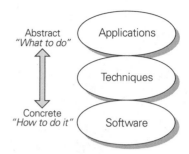

Figure 1.1 Layers of abstraction in application development

Speaking broadly, an *application* is a set of software and data that accomplishes a given task. The definition of what constitutes an application has evolved greatly in recent times. At one time an application was a specific piece of software that the user purchased, took home in a box, installed on his/her computer, and then spent hours learning to operate. Nowadays an application might be downloaded and installed via the web, or it would be accessed directly and used without installation. Neither training seminars nor manuals are (usually) necessary for learning to use such software. A different paradigm is at work. Instead of a user buying an application and mastering it over time, it is borrowed for a brief period and is immediately usable.

1.1.1 The familiar

In its most basic form, an application consists of a user interface, a model, and data (or at least some way to access the data, such as through a network). The user interface allows the user to talk to the application and the application to talk to the user. The model listens to the user and modifies the data accordingly, and it listens to the data and notifies the user interface if data changes occur. This process, shown in figure 1.2, is the classic model-view-control (MVC) pattern applied in a user-interface-centric way to the application as a whole. MVC is a concept that dates back to the late 1970s. It is an important milestone in object-oriented design because it separated out the major user interface and non-user interface elements.

1.1.2 The dream

The web is redefining our notion of what an application is. Some changes are architectural in nature, with pieces of the application flung to the four corners of the world. The client is in one location; the server is in another location; the database is elsewhere; and the whole apparatus is connected by the global Internet and squeezed through the browser on your desk or in your TV. Other changes, which some say are revolutionary, are sociological in nature, with the whole way we interact with others and do business at a distance being redefined. In the future, imagine selecting your

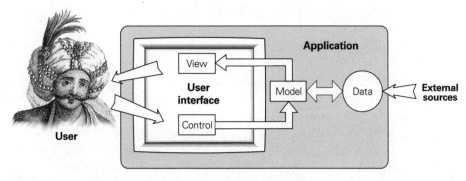

Figure 1.2   Application based on the model-view-control pattern

dream car online, entering your credit card information and address, and having your new sportster teleported to your driveway.

Although the VR dream that books like *Neuromancer* proffered is still science fiction, the intuitiveness of VR's user interface and its ability to make the abstract tangible is not lost on people. To this end, 3D is not an all-or-nothing proposition but just one of the many technologies that come together in next-generation applications to offer the user a richer, more intuitive user interface experience, perhaps one that is greater than the sum of its parts.

1.1.3   The reality

E-commerce is currently riding the crest of the Internet wave. As an industry it has high visibility because it is promising to fundamentally change the way we do business. Reinforcing this wave is the shift occurring in manufacturing. Massive application of computers to manufacturing and business systems in general is transforming the old concept of mass consumerism into the new and improved concept of mass customization. Consumers will soon be able to get exactly what they want, when they want it.

In such a world, the applications that everyday users utilize must be innately intuitive. 3D offers one of the ways for applications to achieve this—after all, we were born into a three-dimensional world. 3D user-interface techniques are bound to find their way into mainstream applications of all sorts. Which applications will use 3D? The ones that need it. 3D must stand on its own alongside other user interface techniques and multimedia technologies.

1.1.4   The rebirth

If e-commerce and the web in general are teaching us anything, it is that the days of expecting people to take the time to read a user's manual or attend a training class are coming to an end. Users and consumers now expect to be able to sit down in front of their computers and get something done, quickly and easily. This means that web applications have to be smaller, nimbler, and more task-specific than older applications.

In fact, many of the forces driving traditional business and technology applications to grow ever larger (as a means of differentiating themselves from the next product) are evaporating. Web-based data and software distribution are cheap and becoming easier by the day. If you don't like a particular application, there are (or will soon be) a dozen more like it waiting to be used.

Here are some examples. You need to know what time it is in Calcutta: go to a web site with a world time clock. You need to buy flowers for a special occasion: go to a web site, pick your flowers, and send them. You want to buy clothes fit to your increasingly unique body style: go to a web site, enter your measurements, and start dressing a likeness of yourself with your selections. You want to share your latest theory of neutrino oscillations with your colleagues: go to a web site, enter the data, and you all can see, discuss, and interact with the data together, online. These applications are simple and focused; each does one thing well. They also have to abide by the "learn-as-you-go" philosophy of user interface design, which is prevalent on the web.

1.2 THE USER INTERFACE

What is a computer user interface? The user interface is everything having to do with the computer that the user can touch, see, and hear (and someday taste and smell). Although this is a true statement, it probably isn't very meaningful. Delving into the matter a bit more deeply, the user-computer dialogue conducted through the user interface can be described from three different views.

1.2.1 The primal

This aspect concerns how the user interacts with the computer at an almost subconscious level, interpreting stimuli and responding accordingly. For example, in a game when you see a "bad guy," you hit the keyboard space bar to fire a "gun." This is the "twitch" factor that makes games exciting. You don't have time to think. You see, hear, and react.

This level of the user interface deals with matters such as hand-eye coordination, stimulus-response, and reflexes. The dialogue between the user and the computer is almost primal. Short of a direct connection between the computer and the user's brain, the user must rely on using eyes, ears, and limbs to interact with the computer. The user sees and hears what the computer has to say through its display screen and speakers, and in response the user talks to the computer through the mouse and keyboard. At this most fundamental level, the dialogue is important, but it is by its nature limited in content.

1.2.2 The virtual

This aspect of a user interface allows the user and an application running on the computer more time for each to reflect on what the other is doing. The application tells the user what the state of its "virtual" world is, and the user tells the application how he would like to change that state. The virtual world is built from data provided by

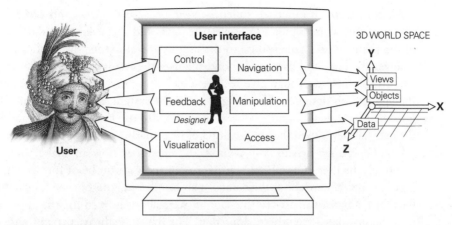

Figure 1.3 Functional components in an application user interface

the application or created within the application by the user. From application to application, there is no predicting what the data might be. It could be as disparate as clothing draped on life-like mannequins in a sales application, or modular office furniture in a facilities management application.

In this view of the user interface, the application and computer—the system— are working hard to maintain the illusion that the data is real and the user can really change it. The system generates an aesthetically pleasing presentation of the data on the display screen. For example, in sales-oriented applications, the presentation often strives to accurately reflect the products that the vendor is trying to sell the user. While generating the presentation, the system is attentively listening to what the user has to say about the data and presentation through its input devices such as the mouse and keyboard. In other words, while the application is showing the user what is available, the user is selecting what he/she wants and arranging it in a manner that best suits his/ her needs.

1.2.3 The analytical

Sandwiched between the other two views of the user interface is where the work gets done—getting the application and its interface to do something useful. This aspect deals with the specific details of how the dialogue is conducted between the user and the application; and this is where the focus of the book lies. Here the user talks to the application through something called *control*, and sees the system's response through something called *visualization*. Taking a closer look at these inner workings, you would also notice a second dialogue going on between the application and the user, called *feedback*.

In the main dialogue the user can direct the application to change the data or its view. Using the examples above, the user can ask to see the mannequin from the side, or to move the desk next to the window. The user performs these and other necessary operations through functions called *navigation*, *manipulation*, and *access*. Navigation moves the view; manipulation moves the data; and access gets the data into and out of the virtual world. In response to the user's control inputs, the application dutifully changes the view and data, and shows the user the result through visualization.

In the second dialogue we see the user talking not so much to the system as to the application designer. The designer is in the system, not in body but in spirit, to give the user guidance and feedback about how to use the application and its data. If the user has never used the application before or perhaps has not used it recently, there is a good chance he/she won't know or remember how to make things happen. Although the user knows he/she wants to replace a wardrobe or furnish an office, the user may not be sure about the details of accomplishing this or even how to get started.

One way for the user to find out answers about how to use the application is to read the manual—been there, done that! The first time the user tried to use the application, he/she spent four hours reading about orthographic projections and world-to-display space transformations, and still couldn't manage to buy clothes or order a desk for the office. The other way to get answers is to listen to the designer, not literally, but in the form of hints and messages embedded in the user interface.

Some forms of feedback are as subtle as a well-chosen color scheme, so the control objects stand out from the data objects in the display. Some are more obvious, like highlighting movable objects such as desks and chairs when the mouse passes over them, or changing the cursor shape to indicate whether or not the user can put the desk in front of a door. Others are even more obvious, like announcing to the user in an audio message that the desk is too long for the space between the door and window, and then automatically moving the desk to a better location. Such feedback offers help to the user when the person is actually in front of the computer trying to do something. This is the essence of the learn-as-you-go philosophy that is prevalent in many web applications.

1.3   THE COMPUTER SYSTEM

"POTS" is an acronym in the telecommunications industry that stands for Plain Old Telephone System. It refers to the capabilities of the analog telephone system that was established in the early twentieth century and hadn't appreciably changed in function or capability until the end of the century. With the advent of new functionality and digital services, there was a need to identify the old unadorned system that most of the world still used, which is POTS. With the development of new types of applications we find ourselves in a similar situation; we need to differentiate the typical computer system from the atypical.

1.3.1   The Plain Old Computer System

Previously I discussed what I meant by an application and its user interface. To complete the picture, we need to pin down what is meant by a "computer system." In order to do that, we have to decide what kind of user we want to support. In keeping with the spirit of the next-generation, easy-to-use application and the egalitarian nature of the Internet, I have chosen the common layperson as the designated application user. The type of computer system these people use is that which they use every day in their offices and homes. Such a computer is in marked contrast to high-end 3D systems used in research and entertainment production, which use specialized graphics hardware such as multiple graphics pipelines, and virtual reality peripherals such as head-mounted displays, data gloves, and 3D mice. To differentiate these kinds of computer systems from those that I am targeting in this book, I've coined the term *POCS*, which means Plain Old Computer System.

A POCS is characterized outwardly by a 2D display, a mouse, a keyboard, and sound-generation capability. In terms of performance, the POCS is not quite as ordinary as it may seem. The generation of POCS that is now emerging is sporting greatly accelerated graphics and processor speeds in excess of 500 MHz. Such computers are becoming commonplace in offices and homes today, and should become ubiquitous in the next few years.

1.3.2   The mouse

In a POCS, the mouse is the user's primary means of spatial control. It is a 2D-locator (i.e. pointing) device with buttons. More formally, it can be used as a 2D relative, indirect, continuous locator device. This means it can be picked up and repositioned, it is moved on the desk and not on the screen directly, and the output values from the mouse are proportional to its movement. Movement of the mouse corresponds to 2D movement of the mouse cursor in the plane of the display screen. This simple 2D motion can be interpreted for the purposes of 3D view navigation and object manipulation in a number of clever ways, as we shall see in the coming chapters.

A typical mouse can have anywhere from one to three buttons (very early mice had more, which seems to be coming back into vogue.) Button actions combined with mouse motion, or lack of motion, consitute gestures, called drags and clicks. A few basic conventions for mouse buttons have been widely established: clicking the primary button (the left button on a right hand mouse) selects an object; dragging with the primary button manipulates the underlying object; and clicking the secondary button (the right button) causes a popup menu to appear at the mouse position. There are many more button interpretations that are useful but not as well established, and therefore should be used for non-critical or alternative control functions.

1.3.3   The keyboard

The *keyboard* is the user's primary means for manual data entry, which is a fancy way to say typing. Although these keys can also be used for control input, such as typing "F" to make a game go faster and "S" to make it go slower, the keyboard provides keys that are dedicated to control input. Most keyboards have a dozen or so non-specific function keys, typically labeled "F1," "F2," and so on. There are few conventions for using them, so it is usually best not to use them as a primary means of control.

Instead, they are often used to provide "power users" with short cuts to often-used or user-defined functions.

Arrow and modifier keys are another story. The arrow keys on the keyboard offer the user a secondary means of spatial control. As a set, they can be used as a 2D relative, indirect, *discrete* locator device. It is a discrete device because hitting an arrow key produces a single valueless event, not a continuously changing value. Some keyboards have four arrow keys, one for each cardinal direction, and others have eight, for finer directional control.

As with other keyboard keys, holding down an arrow key causes its output to repeat, which we can put to good use in certain situations. With a bit of processing, the arrow keys can act as a continuous locator. Interpreting key presses as incrementing and decrementing a 2D position value allows the arrow keys to be used like a mouse. If we use this value to move the mouse cursor itself, then the arrow keys could be used in place of the mouse, or in addition to the mouse, such as for precision object movement.

The most common modifier keys available in a POCS are *Shift*, *Ctrl*, and *Alt*. They are typically used to modify the effect of other control actions, such as while dragging the mouse or pressing an arrow key. The modifier keys can be used alone or in combination (called *chording*) to achieve a range of modifications. As with the keyboard function keys, there are few conventions for using modifier keys, so they should be used sparingly and only for non-essential functions.

1.4   SUMMARY

Before getting into the thick of things it was important to establish where this book is coming from with respect to terms such as application, user interface, and computer system. Understanding this book's definitions for these terms is important to understanding its choice of user interface techniques and software building blocks. It is also helpful in broadly understanding the categorization of user interface techniques in terms of *control*, *feedback*, and *visualization*, and more specifically in terms of *navigation*, *manipulation*, and *access*.

In this book's vision of an application and its use of 3D in the user interface, it looks to the future and to the past. It recognizes the past evolutionary contributions of the desktop metaphor, the migration of drag-and-drop into 2D and 3D, and the migration of 3D applications from the workplace to the home. It also recognizes the future revolutionary trends brought on by the confluence of mass customization and e-commerce on the Internet. With customers physically separated from the products and services they are buying, there is greater need for the kinds of remote visualization yet intuitive interaction that 3D techniques can provide.

Mass customization is redefining how we as a society think about products, consumerism, and commerce: Salespeople are starting to use applications to better inform consumers about more and more complex products. Consumers are beginning to embrace applications that help them to design customized product solutions for their specific needs. Configurator-engine technology is providing the basic intelligence these applications need to manage the myriad product options and to help guide the user. An intuitive user interface and the ability to present the product as realistically as possible are essential to the success of mass customization.

The Internet is redefining the role and substance of what an application is, whether for commerce, science, or entertainment. On the web, applications are perceived as small, nimble appliances that do one thing well. Users are encouraged to explore and learn. The ability to "back up" and "go home" and the philosophy of learn-as-you-go are pervasive. These seemingly innocuous user interface concepts are defining a fundamental paradigm shift in how easy an application should be for people to use.

It would seem that 3D, a paradigm intimately familiar and intuitive to everyone, at least in the real world, is a natural choice in this renaissance of the application. It can be, but not until a corresponding paradigm shift occurs in our perception of 3D technology. Traditionally, most designers have viewed 3D as a technology that an application can be built around. The premise of this book is that, to achieve its true potential as a major player in the next generation of easy-to-use applications, 3D will have to be perceived as one of many weapons that the designer wields in the quest for an intuitive user interface.

CHAPTER 2

Patterns and constraints

The application and its requirements are the starting point on any road to user interface development, 3D or otherwise. To help chart the way to the next generation of 3D-enabled applications, it might be helpful to take a look at current patterns of 3D usage and the areas of the user interface they emphasize. When dealing with non-visual 1D applications, and even most 2D applications, the question of what is real and what is not does not often arise when discussing requirements. In 3D, the answer to this question can be crucial to developing an intuitive and efficient user interface.

2.1 APPLICATION PATTERNS

3D applications, or rather applications that might benefit from 3D, can be summarized in a few broad categories: *design*, *simulation*, *analysis*, and *control*. What distinguishes one category from the next is a combination of what the user needs to accomplish, the nature of the underlying application data, and the manner in which that data is presented to and manipulated by the user. The following classification helps to tie the top level of design abstraction, applications, to the middle level, techniques.

Each of the following tables defines an application class, describes its major variations (subclasses), identifies patterns of what techniques can be used and how, and lists familiar application examples. As with software patterns, outlining the categories helps with the identification, combination, and communication of the underlying concepts and patterns of usage. These lists are meant to be encompassing but not exhaustive. They are representative of some of the application types that have and will continue to benefit from well-integrated 3D techniques for a more intuitive user interface.

As with any classification scheme, there is an unavoidable degree of arbitrariness and artificiality. Real applications, unlike the stylized application categories described here, have to satisfy real user needs in a real world. Applications and their designers will do whatever is necessary to meet these needs. It is not unusual for applications to have qualities that span more than one category, just as it is not unusual for a 3D application to contain significant amounts of 2D visualization and simple 1D user interface elements such as menus and toolbars. In other words, these application categories are not intended as a system for completely describing a given application. Instead, they are intended to help identify and illustrate common patterns for 3D user interface usage.

2.1.1 Design applications

A *design application* lets the user design objects, systems, or environments for such purposes as engineering, architecture, or product sales. This includes traditional computer aided design (CAD) as well as chic product selection and configuration applications.

Table 2.1 Design applications

Attributes	• The user adds, removes, groups, connects, and configures objects to form new objects, systems, selections, or environments. • The data utilized is often "concrete" in nature with a direct representation of physical objects and systems such as furniture, automobiles, communications networks, and chemical plants.
Variations	• Design applications have two major forms: geometrical and topological. • In geometrical design, object layout, connection, and containment are geometric in nature with a direct physical interpretation. Pulling on one object would also pull any objects connected to or contained within it. • In topological design, object layout, connection, and containment are topological in nature with a relational interpretation, perhaps indicated explicitly by lines or other symbology. Pulling on one object may not pull objects connected to or contained within it. • Design applications can serve as visual "front-ends" for configuration engines and electronic catalogs integral to product mass customization for sales automation and e-commerce.
Patterns	• Design applications most often utilize data access, navigation, and especially manipulation techniques. • Visualization techniques are less often needed since design applications generally involve concrete data with physical representations instead of abstract data.

Table 2.1 Design applications (continued)

Examples	• Geometric: Online- and kiosk-based visualization, information, and selling for automobiles and other "big-ticket" items with numerous options and opportunities for upselling.
	• Geometric: Interior space planning and selling including space modeling, floor planning, modular furniture layout and configuration, and architectural fixture selection.
	• Geometric: Design, visualization, and selling for interior designers and homeowners for paint, carpet, draperies, furniture, kitchen cabinets, appliances, and so forth.
	• Topological: Design and sales for data networks spanning multiple contextual levels of detail and including data circuit design and loading, equipment selection and configuration, wiring layout.
	• Geometric/topological: Utility distribution (water, gas, electric) design spanning multiple technical and contextual levels of detail.

2.1.2   Simulation applications

A *simulation application* allows the user to experience a particular situation or environment—fantastical, hypothetical, or real. This includes the ever-popular field of gaming and its more staid relative training.

Table 2.2 Simulation applications

Attributes	• The user performs operations in and navigates about the simulated environment or virtual "world" in a manner often constrained to mimic that in the real world.
	• The data utilized is often "concrete" in nature with a direct representation of physical objects and surroundings such as battlefields, building sites, or operating rooms.
Variations	• Simulation applications have four major forms: *training*, *prototyping*, *demonstration*, and *gaming*.
	• In training simulation, the emphasis is on teaching the user how to do something new or to handle unusual circumstances, generally in a qualitative manner. The user is provided with an experience that mimics a hypothetical or real one. User movement and interaction are constrained by the physics of the simulated situation.
	• In prototyping simulation, the emphasis is on verifying the viability or improving the effectiveness of the simulated system, generally in a quantitative manner. As such, the user may be allowed to alter the simulation in rather arbitrary ways to best suit a task. Quantitative performance and spatial measurements are significant.
	• In demonstration simulation, the emphasis is on providing the user with a proposed or replicated experience, generally in a qualitative manner. As such, user movement through the world is often scripted and interaction with the world is generally not allowed or severely limited. This variation would include many educational and tutorial applications with limited interaction.
	• In gaming simulation, the emphasis is on providing the user with an interactive and entertaining experience, often in fantasy worlds. As such, this variation is open to most anything and everything.

Table 2.2   Simulation applications (continued)

Patterns	• Simulation applications most often utilize navigation techniques, with some manipulation. • Data management and visualization techniques are much less often needed since the emphasis is on experiencing a predefined realistic world.
Examples	• Training: Military, police, fire, and disaster service training. • Prototyping: Personal, commercial, and public transportation vehicle and system evaluation and improvement. • Prototyping: Development of living spaces, hand tools, and repair procedures for the space station. • Demonstration: Court room crime and accident re-creations. • Demonstration: Architectural proposals in boardrooms, city hall, and for the community.

2.1.3   Analysis applications

An *analysis application* provides the user with the means to perceive patterns, detect anomalies, and to draw conclusions about the circumstances that the presented data represents. This includes scientific visualization as well as more intuitive applications such as financial prognostication.

Table 2.3   Analysis applications

Attributes	• The user adjusts the data presentation, measures the data, and draws quantitative and qualitative conclusions about the process, system, or situation under study. • The data utilized is often abstract in nature with an indirect representation of higher-dimensional data, such as that from business, economic, social, scientific, and engineering processes and systems.
Variations	• Analysis applications have two major forms: *quantitative* and *qualitative*. • In quantitative analysis, the exact values of the data are significant, often having a direct physical interpretation. Often there is significant geometric or spatial structure to the data. The application must carefully preserve and present these quantities so as not to affect the user's interpretation. • In qualitative analysis, general relationships in the data are significant, such as trends, proximity, or coincidence. There may be no tangible physical interpretation or spatial structure in the data, such as stock prices or airline on-time arrival statistics. It is left to the user to decide how best to arrange the data for interpretation.
Patterns	• Analysis applications most often utilize visualization and navigation techniques. • Manipulation and data management techniques are less often needed since the emphasis in analysis applications is on interpretation of the available data, not the creation of new data.

Table 2.3 Analysis applications (continued)

Examples	• Quantitative: Medical imaging and diagnostics. • Quantitative: Seismic imaging and geophysical research. • Quantitative/Qualitative: Product failure analysis. • Qualitative: Financial, organizational, manufacturing, and such, performance analysis.

2.1.4 Control applications

A *control application* lets the user remotely control a process, system, or vehicle. This includes traditional command and control applications as well as those involving remotely piloted vehicles. The distinction between an analysis application and a control application can seem subtle, especially since a control application will often include an analysis component. The main distinction between the two categories is that an analysis application is geared toward collecting information, while the intent of a control application is to act upon the information.

Table 2.4 Control applications

Attributes	• The user navigates location and level of detail in a visualization of the controlled system's state or the vehicle's surroundings, and activates virtual switches, knobs, valves, and so forth, to accomplish the remote operation. • The data utilized can be abstract or concrete with indirect representations of business, engineering, military situation data, and direct representation of a remote vehicle's locale.
Variations	• Control applications have three major forms: *abstract*, *geometrical*, and *topological*. • In abstract control, the state space and controls have no inherent spatial or relational properties, but represent arbitrary information dimensions or nodes of control. • In geometrical control, there is a direct geometric relationship between control movement and the resulting system state. Moving a control has an analogous effect on the physical state of the system, such as a telerobotic manipulator. • In topographical control, the system state and its controls can be represented stylistically, without the need for a direct spatial correspondence. The topology of the system state is critical, not the precise geometry, such as in a subway routing or utility distribution system.
Patterns	• Control applications most often utilize navigation and manipulation techniques. • Data management techniques are less often needed since the emphasis in control applications is on management of system state, not the creation of new data. • Control and analysis applications are often combined so that the user can better assess a situation before taking actions to control it. In this context, visualization techniques can be used to help interpret the system state before taking action to change it.

Table 2.4   Control applications   (continued)

Examples	• Abstract: Sales, accounting, manufacturing, shipping business systems tracking and control. • Abstract/Topological: Industrial and manufacturing process control. • Geometrical: Remotely piloted vehicles in remote, hostile, or hazardous areas. • Topological: Transportation tracking and management, such as for freeways, buses, subways, trucking, rail, and so forth. • Topological: Electric, gas, and water utility distribution monitoring and control. • Geometrical: Military command and control system with situation displays.

2.2   APPLICATION CONSTRAINTS

In the real world, the laws of physics infallibly regulate what we do and how we do it. We can no more walk through a brick wall than we can fly by flapping our arms. In a computer-generated world, though, the tables are completely turned. Unlike the real world, there is no inherent notion of substance, force, or physical interaction. Polygons are free to pass through one another like ghosts and the mouse cursor can no more influence their destiny than the entreaties of the ancient Greeks to their gods could influence their own destiny.

In a virtual world, if objects are to interact and if the mouse cursor is to have an effect, we as 3D application developers must design and program it to happen. This also means that we as programmers, given sufficient time and resources, could bring to life the most fantastical world imaginable. Unlike mechanical and civil engineers, we are not bound by the laws of nature. Cartoon laws of physics can be made to work just as easily as real ones, with solid objects bending, bullets going around corners, and even time itself running backward. There are literally no restrictions on what we could provide the user, and this is where we must pause and reflect upon our responsibilities as 3D application developers.

2.2.1   Goldilocks and the three dees

Giving users unlimited freedom to do anything they want may seem like the most beneficent act of engineering possible, but it's not. Often, such freedom in the hands of neophytes is tantamount to giving them enough rope to hang themselves. It gives them the freedom to become irretrievably lost or to create objects bearing no resemblance to an actual product that can be purchased, such as a 10-meter-high desk. This is the problem with trying to use CAD applications as a basis for next-generation 3D applications. They give users the freedom to build anything they want and to see it from wherever they want.

Going to the other extreme can be equally frustrating to the user. Imagine strictly imposing real-world constraints in a furniture layout application. To move a virtual desk from one floor of a virtual office building to another, the user would be forced to drag it down the virtual hall and up the building's virtual stairs. When it comes to freedom and constraints in a 3D application, the Goldilocks principle applies: just the right amount of reality is needed. Building a useful 3D application is based around knowing what rules to apply, and when to apply them. Even within a single application, it may be useful for some constraints to be valid only some of the time according to the user's ability and situation.

With a deep understanding of the application domain and a judicious application of constraints, the application designer can make the application much easier to use. By introducing constraints you can make the user's life easier by eliminating unnecessary options and degrees of freedom. Ideally, mouse controls can be constrained such that even a casual user can master interactions in a 3D world. This helps to shift the user's attention from mastering the mechanics of the user interface to performing some real work, in 3D.

2.2.2   Let gravity pull

Because we grow up in a world where constraints are the norm, natural laws subconsciously affect everything that we do, whether real or imagined. It helps us to make sense of other things. A common reference point—like the ground—aids the brain in subconsciously putting other things into perspective. We don't jump off cliffs because we know that gravity will take over and make a mess of us at the bottom when we hit a solid object that we can't pass through. When rearranging the furniture in your office, you only have to contend with a 2D layout problem, not a 3D one, because the furniture stays stuck to the floor.

When we develop an application, these real-world models are what the user subconsciously compares to the virtual world. People naturally understand it. Because of this understanding, applications for the casual user work best if the constraints model the real world. For example, the user's viewpoint should not go below the floor because it can be disorienting. When walking on virtual stairs, the user should move forward as well as up to the next floor. When the user moves furniture about a room, the furniture should stick to the floor and not pass through the wall. Such constraints and intuitive action can seem almost trivial in the context of the real world, but to achieve them in a virtual world often requires complex programming.

A complicating factor in all of this is that there are no hard and fast rules. Users are quick to suspend reality if it suits the situation or their needs. Suspension of reality occurs every time we read a book or watch a movie. It comes naturally to us, almost as naturally as the reality we are suspending. What may seem intuitive to one person may seem inconvenient to another. Having to use the virtual stairs may be appropriate and intuitive in an adventure game but, as we saw previously, it would be annoying in a furniture layout application. The golden rule of "know your audience" is still very much alive and well in the third dimension.

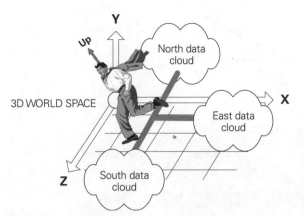

Figure 2.1
Even in abstract 3D data worlds, artificial directions such as north and up can help orient the user.

2.2.3 Creating your own reality

When an application involves concrete data such as desks and stairs, the choice of imposing reality or suspending it can be a difficult decision, but the choice is at least obvious: make it real or not. In many applications, the data is abstract in nature without a tangible presence, such as an investment's rate of return or the multidimensional clustering of similar documents. In these situations there is no such thing as a ground. There is no "up" to define which way gravity will pull "down." Data are, in a sense, floating about in the ether.

In order to keep the user from getting completely disoriented in such a *Twilight Zone* world, even cartoon physics can be a welcome addition. For example, imposing an artificial "up" in this abstract data world can keep data labels and symbology conveniently oriented. Organizing the data in regular spatial locations can provide a sense of "north" and "south," which allows users to take advantage of their innate spatial mapping abilities. Deviating further from the familiar, lines connecting data clusters could serve as pathways constraining the user's movement. It might even be advantageous for the user to rotate about the path, in which case "up" is defined by the user's head and "down" is defined by his feet on the path line.

Such constraints on the user's worldview may not model the real world but they do become part of the illusion of reality that the application is trying to maintain for the user. Part of building this new reality is making it believable within the context of the world that you are presenting and to the audience that is experiencing it.

2.2.4 Flavors of constraint

Two application areas that best highlight the needs and benefits of constraints are user navigation through and object manipulation in the 3D virtual world. Navigation defines how the user is allowed to move about the scene. Is the user allowed to walk up a set of stairs, or is the user constrained to moving between a limited set of predefined viewpoints? Manipulation defines how the user can move or change objects in the scene, such as sliding, stretching, and coloring them. Can objects slide through

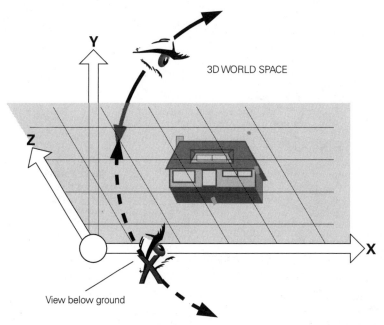

Figure 2.2   By not constraining the viewpoint to remain above the ground, the user can become disoriented when looking up at the world.

other objects or will they collide? Can an object be stretched and colored arbitrarily or is it constrained by the properties of the real object it represents?

Navigation constraints

Probably the easiest way to maintain the illusion of reality is by making sure that the user never gets disoriented or lost. Can the subject of the user's work always be kept in view or, if not, can the user be provided with enough visual aids to easily become unlost? Providing the virtual world with an artificial ground and sky is a simple example. So long as the user can see both, he/she has a fairly good idea of which way is up. If the user looks directly at the floor, he/she knows that by simply rotating the view a bit he/she will see the sky and then better know how to right him/herself. But what if the user falls through the floor? In this case, the real direction of up is toward the floor, not away from it. Suddenly the illusion of reality is broken because the user must do something out of the ordinary—travelling toward the floor to get back to seeing the sky. Thus, one form of navigation constraint might be to not let the user's viewpoint move below the floor—easy to say but not quite so easy to do. Imposing such a constraint requires knowledge of where the user and floor are because one, the other, or both may move through the virtual world.

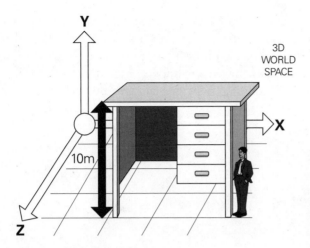

3D
WORLD
SPACE

Y

X

10m

Z

Figure 2.3
By not constraining data objects to their true dimensions, users would be able to create objects that can not be ordered from a manufacturer.

Manipulation constraints

We've already seen how constraints on in-scene object movement can affect usability, with having to use the stairs perhaps being a plus in a simulation application but a minus in a design application. A different area of manipulation that is becoming important for next-generation applications is direct manipulation of an object's attributes. Consider the furniture layout application. A CAD-like user interface might allow the user to apply any color to any object surface and to stretch any object to any size. Although these might be desirable features if the user is creating new furniture, they can be very undesirable features if the user needs to order the furniture for delivery by end of the week. Chances are a manufacturer can not be found on short order that can make shocking pink wooden bookshelves or 10-meter-high desks. For such applications where the user is supposed to be configuring objects representing real products, attribute and even geometric manipulation constraints are a must.

2.3   SUMMARY

To create an effective application, you as the 3D application developer must understand your users, their problem domain, and how their needs might be satisfied. Part of this is identifying the type of application that is needed and the sorts of user interaction that are involved. The tables provided early in this chapter offer a starting point in this process. As the application designer, a small bit of laziness on your part may mean the difference between an average application and an outstanding one. If you don't write the code to do something or to prevent something, then the user won't get to do it or will have to do it too much—Goldilocks rules when it comes to user interfaces.

General purpose application programming interfaces (APIs) like Open Inventor, Virtual Reality Modeling Language (VRML), and Java 3D won't give you everything you want or need for building effective 3D applications. It would be surprising if they did since the variety of problems and the kinds of realities required are innumerable.

This book tries to highlight common user interface themes and techniques in dealing with next-generation 3D applications, and provides examples of how they can be implemented. All of this can be a great help but it is still up to the 3D developer to make the tough decisions about how best to impose constraints, assemble the building blocks, and to construct the most appropriate reality for the user.

C H A P T E R   3

Spaces and relations

There are many ways to define the coordinate spaces used in a 3D application. There are a few standards but a lot of variability in how the matter is formulated and described. As might be expected, this book takes a UI-centric view in describing 3D problems and their solutions. The concepts and terms described in this chapter are fundamental to the coming discussions about 3D techniques and the building blocks to implement them. They concern the conceptual and geometric coordinate spaces associated with viewing and manipulating objects in 3D.

3.1 SPACE, THE INITIAL FRONTIER

In an application, objects can live in various places or spaces. In each of these spaces the same object requires a different data representation and can take on a different visual appearance. Consider an application containing an object representing your personal jumbo jet. The jet object can live in a database, abstractly, as an N-dimensional set of information describing how far the jet has flown, how much you pay for maintenance each month, and the date of the last tune-up. It can also live in an electronic catalog, iconically, as a little 2D picture of your jet on a page titled "Toys of the Rich and Famous." And, the object can live in the 3D virtual world, graphically, as a texture-mapped polygonal representation of your jet.

   Most of the UI techniques described in this book concern the 3D graphical form of objects and the spaces they live in. The following sections define these spaces and

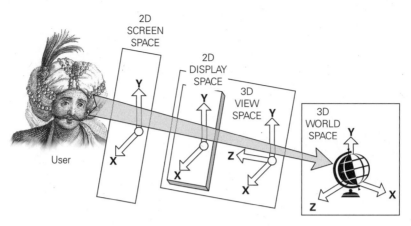

Figure 3.1 UI-centric coordinate spaces, their dimensionality, and their relationships

their use in detail. Because 3D applications come in many forms and involve more than just 3D objects, it can also be helpful to consider the non-3D forms of objects. For example, the chapters on manipulation and access techniques will discuss an object's transition between its 2D iconic and 3D graphical form during a 3D drag-and-drop operation.

3.1.1 The world

The *world* is a 3D frame of reference where objects can live. For the user to see 3D objects, these objects must be living in the 3D world. A 3D Cartesian coordinate system defines the *world space;* and objects in the world space are characterized as having a 3D position and orientation. (I'll save the coordinate system details for all the spaces for a separate section later.) Objects living in the world space must be in their 3D graphical model form.

An application can have more than one world, although typically there is only one and, as such, the world is usually referred to in the singular. Each world has a separate world space with its own coordinate system. Objects from different worlds can not interact with one another or be seen in the same display. For example, you can have one world defined by a virtual airport showing your jumbo jet parked at your private gate burning through your inheritance, and another world defined by a virtual showroom containing your jumbo jet that you are trying to unload. The same 3D model of the jet is used in each world; but the models can not interact (e.g., collide) and the worlds must be viewed in separate display spaces.

3.1.2 The view

The *view* defines how the user sees the world. The focus on POCS applications simplifies the notion of a view. The view is the user's virtual "eyeball" on the world showing the contents of the 3D world as projected upon a 2D display plane. This is

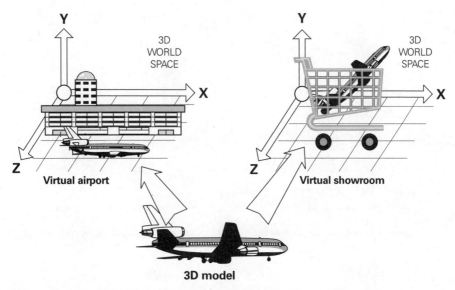

Figure 3.2   Two different virtual world spaces showing the same 3D model

analogous to a real eyeball where an image of the world is projected onto the retina. The view's geometry describes where the view is located in the world, which direction it is looking, and the particulars of how it projects the 3D world onto its 2D display. Such planar projections come in two forms, parallel (e.g., orthographic, isometric) and perspective.

Sometimes it is convenient to consider the view as possessing its own 3D *view space*. The view space is not a separate space from the world; it is just a different frame of reference for positioning and orienting objects in the world but relative to the view. In other words, objects living in the view space still live in the world, but they move with the view. This has the effect of making objects in the view space appear stationary in the view's display while the view is moving.

Typically we think of a view as something that is actively displaying the world to us from a particular vantage point. However, another way to think of a view is as just another object that can be positioned and oriented in the 3D world. Consistent with this notion of a view, we can have more than one "view object" living in a world. Furthermore, the views don't all have to be actively displaying their view of the world to the user. But what good is a view that isn't displaying something?

As a view object, a view can serve as a placeholder. We can define several views in the world and then switch to a particular one so the user can see the world from that particular vantage point. In this context the view objects can be thought of as cameras. If permitted by the application, the user can reach out and manipulate one of these cameras before using it to display a picture of the world. We'll see more about views as objects in chapters 4 and 7.

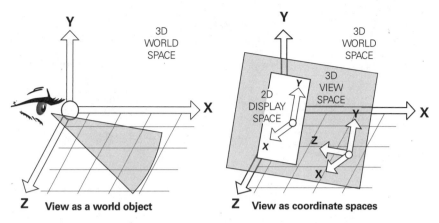

Y

3D
WORLD
SPACE

X

Z   **View as a world object**

Y

3D
WORLD
SPACE

3D
VIEW
SPACE

2D
DISPLAY
SPACE

X

Z   **View as coordinate spaces**

Figure 3.3   A view can be treated as an object in the world space, as well as a set of view-relative coordinate spaces.

3.1.3   The display

The *display* presents a 2D representation of the virtual world from the vantage point of its host view. In this context, the display can be thought of as living in the world at the position of the view and facing in the direction of the view. When the display is active, the user sees the view's presentation of the world in a window on the computer's 2D display screen. An application can have more than one display on the screen at a time, which can be of the same world or of different worlds.

Similar to the view, it can be useful to think of the display as possessing its own 2D *display space*. Objects living in the display space must be in their 2D graphical model form. Such 2D objects can be placed in the display space directly, such as a game's "dashboard" decorations. Or, they can originate as the 2D projections of 3D models living in the world space. Analogous to 3D world space, objects in 2D display space are characterized as having a 2D position and orientation. Even though a display is closely associated with a view, the 2D display space is separate from the 3D world space. Objects in the display space cannot mix with those in the world space because the 2D display space and the objects in it lack depth: The display space and everything in it is flat. If you want a flat object to appear between 3D objects, you can't use the display space to do it. Instead, the flat object must be placed in the world or view space so that its depth position can be specified to position it between other world objects.

Although the display space and the 2D objects in it lack depth, they can overlap one another. This is commonly seen in 2D graphics applications where some objects will always appear in front of or behind others. It is also seen in the GUI desktop itself, where the desktop is always in back, the mouse cursor is always in front, and application windows can overlap one another in between. Overlap order can be described in terms of overlapping "Z-planes" or overlap priority. In a GUI desktop, the mouse cursor has the highest priority—appearing frontmost—and the desktop has the lowest priority—appearing backmost.

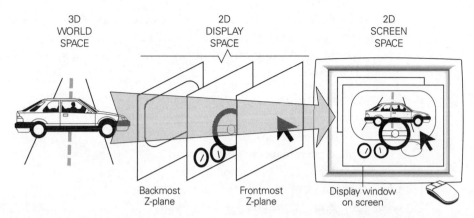

Figure 3.4 The display space can contain a set of overlapping *Z*-planes that combine with the world view to form a composite image in the display window.

Even though display and world objects cannot intermingle, display objects can appear to be always in front of or in back of the projected world objects. Display objects that always appear in front of world objects are said to be in display overlay; and objects that always appear in back are said to be in display underlay. In chapter 6, we'll see more about overlay and underlay, and how objects can be positioned in the world but overlaid in the display.

3.1.4 The screen

The *screen* belongs to the computer system and, unlike the other spaces, is very much in the real world. In a POCS, the screen is a single contiguous 2D entity. It is the 2D container holding the view displays that appear in GUI windows. The size and location of a display image on the screen is determined manually by the user through dragging and resizing its display window or perhaps automatically by the application, such as in a multi-view presentation.

A screen has a definite physical size and its associated *screen space* is measured in physical units. Although the other spaces can be treated as being unitless, the physical dimensions of the real screen are important for situations where displayed objects need to be optimally sized for presentation to the user's equally real eyeballs. As discussed in the chapters 5 and 6, informational UI objects such as in-scene callouts and manipulation handles need to be physically large enough to be read and used but not so large that they interfere with seeing the rest of the 3D scene.

3.2 SPATIAL COORDINATES

Summarizing what has been discussed so far about spaces, the view specifies where in the world we are looking, the view's display shows us what in the world we are looking at, and the screen brings it into the real world. Although these general spatial relationships will go far in supporting the discussions in the rest of the book, they lack precision about how to position and orient objects in the various spaces. Because there is no one standard regarding spatial coordinate systems, the following sections define the coordinate systems used in this book. Figure 3.1 above introduced the spaces and their coordinate axes.

3.2.1 Right-handed system

Right-hand Cartesian coordinate systems are used for all the geometric spaces in the book. The right-handed coordinate system is the standard system used in mathematics; and it is used in a number of popular graphics platforms such as Open Inventor, OpenGL, VRML, and Java 3D. As the name implies, you use your right hand to figure out the axes and angles in a coordinate space.

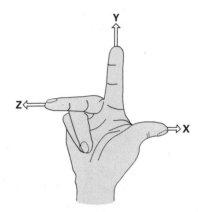

Hold out your right hand with your thumb pointing right, your index finger up, and your middle finger pointing straight at you. The X axis points to the right along your thumb; the Y axis points up along your index finger; and the Z axis points toward you along your middle fin-

Figure 3.5   Right-handed coordinate system

ger. This defines the axes in the 3D world and view spaces. The axes for the 2D display and screen space are similar, with X to the right and Y up, only there is no Z (you can leave your middle finger tucked in). This is illustrated in figure 3.5.

3.2.2 Position

For positioning objects, coordinates increase in the direction their axes are pointing. For example, to move an object in front of us in the view space to the right (along your thumb), you increase its X-axis coordinate value. To move the object closer to you (along your middle finger), you increase its Z-axis coordinate value. The same goes for the display space, only there is no Z coordinate, only X and Y. Unless noted otherwise, the view and display space origin are at the center of the display window.

For world coordinates, you can't say "right" or "closer" because these terms are relative to your particular view of the world. Instead, general world directions are used, with terms such as *up* (increasing world Y value), *north* (decreasing world Z value), and *east* (increasing world X value). Object positioning is illustrated in figure 3.6.

3.2.3 Rotation

Object rotation is just as consistent as position, but a little harder to describe. Again we use our right hand to help us out. Grasping a coordinate axis with your thumb pointing in the same direction as the axis, your fingers will wrap around the axis in

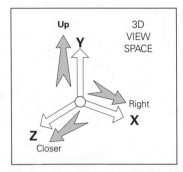 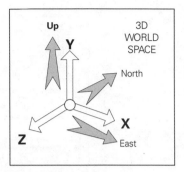

Figure 3.6   View and world relative directions

the direction of the increasing angle. This is illustrated in figure 3.7. This works for all three axes in 3D, but only for the Z axis (if there were a Z axis) in 2D.

As we rotate an object in front of us in the view space so we can see more of its top, essentially tipping the object toward us, we increase its X-axis angle value. To turn an object in the world so its north side now faces east, we decrease its Y-axis angle value by 90 degrees. To turn a 2D object in the display space so its right side is up, we increase its rotation angle value by 90 degrees.

There is more than one way to express rotation. The system just described is called *Euler angles*, with angles defined about the principal axes. Other systems that are popular include *axis-angle*, where an arbitrary axis is defined in 3D space and rotation occurs about that axis; and *quaternion*, where rotation is defined in a coherent algebraic structure based on the 4D unit sphere. The quaternion system is particularly useful for doing smooth (but unconstrained) interpolation between two orientations.

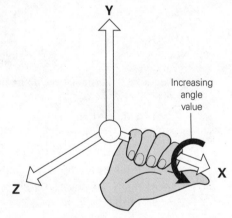

Figure 3.7   Right-handed direction of rotation

3.2.4   Mouse coordinates

One note before we leave coordinate systems. In some computer systems and graphics platforms, mouse position is defined in terms of matrix coordinates, as row and column, but the coordinates are named X and Y, as in a Cartesian coordinate system. In matrix coordinates, as in a matrix, the origin (0,0) is in the upper left corner of the display; the row coordinate increases going down; and the column coordinate increases to the right. Simply labeling the column coordinate X and the row coordinate Y is inconsistent with a right-hand coordinate system, and even a left-hand

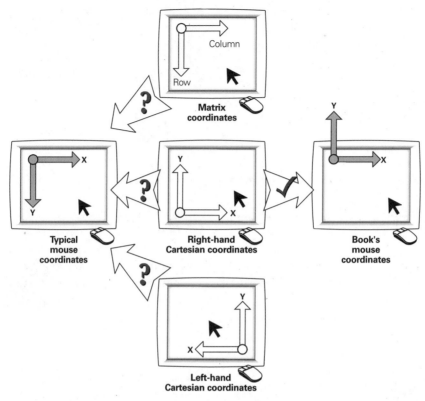

Figure 3.8   This book uses a true right-hand coordinate system for the mouse.

coordinate system. This is because the coordinate system is neither; it is a matrix coordinate system.

This has been a long-standing source of confusion for developers going back to the earliest generations of graphics and imaging systems. Many a programmer has spent many an hour struggling to figure out why objects are moving up instead of down in the display.

In a small attempt to rectify this issue, this book and the code accompanying it, uses a standard right-hand Cartesian coordinate system—the same as in all the other 2D and 3D spaces—to describe the mouse position. For practical reasons of efficiency and logistics, the origin of this *mouse space* (as distinct from the display space that it parallels) is in the upper left corner of the display window, the same as in a matrix coordinate system, although matrix coordinates are not used. With this placement of the origin, when the mouse is within the bounds of its host display window, its X coordinate is zero or positive but its Y coordinate is zero or negative.

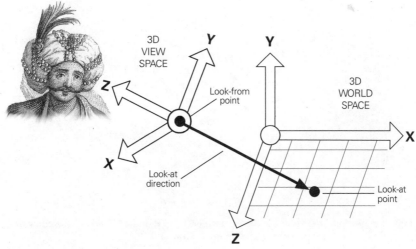

Figure 3.9   An overview of external view geometry

3.3   SPATIAL RELATIONSHIPS

User interface techniques are particularly interested in the geometry of the view space. For example, navigation techniques are concerned with controlling the *external* geometry of the view. As the term implies, a view's external geometry involves geometric relationships outside the view space itself, specifically the position and orientation of the view space as it exists in the world space. Other techniques, such as for feedback and visualization, sometimes need to track the view's *internal* geometry. A view's internal geometry concerns the geometric relationships within the view space itself, such as the size of the display window and the degree of perspective projection used to generate the display image.

The following sections define the more common geometric terms and spatial relationships that you will encounter in this book and in the related source code. As with coordinate systems, there is more than one way to describe a given geometric relationship. The terms and definitions here are chosen to best serve the needs of this book for discussing 3D user interface techniques.

3.3.1   External view geometry

One way to define a view's external geometry is in terms of its look-from point (LFP) and look-at direction (LAD). Another and sometimes more useful way to define it is relative to a point in the world, the look-at point (LAP). In this case, the position of the LFP is defined relative to the LAP in terms of a look-from offset (LFO). The two approaches are somewhat interchangeable. Which one to use depends on the situation that is being described or modeled.

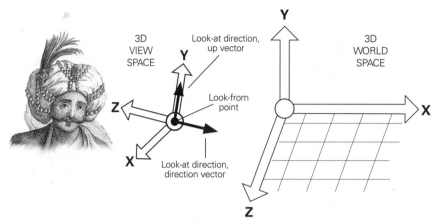

Figure 3.10 External view geometry defined by LFP and LAD, with LAD consisting of a direction vector and an up vector

LFP and LAD

The LFP (look-from point) is the point in the world from which the view is looking. It is the view's 3D position in the world. The LAD (look-at direction) is the direction and attitude of the view in the world. One way to define LAD is simply as a 3D rotation, which can be specified using any of the rotation coordinate systems described in the previous section (Euler angles, axis-angle, quaternion). Sometimes, however, it is convenient to define LAD in terms of vector directions.

Two vectors are needed to uniquely define LAD. The LAD direction vector (LAD-DV) specifies the direction in the world that the view is facing, which corresponds to the view space's negative Z axis—a vector normal to the view's display plane. The LAD up vector (LAD-UV) specifies the direction in the world representing *up* in the view's display plane, which corresponds to the view and display space Y axis as shown in figure 3.10.

LAP and LFO

The LAP (look-at point) is the point in the world at which the view is looking. The LFO (look-from offset) is the offset of the LFP from the LAP relative to the view space. The LFO is defined such that the Z offset is normal to the view display plane and the X-Y offset is parallel to it.

To better see the relationship of the LAP with the view and its display, let's start with the LFO *X-Y* offset set to zero. Thinking of the LAD-DV as a ray shooting off into the world from the LFP, the ray will intersect the LAP; the distance from the LAP to the LFP will be the LFO *Z* offset (LFOz). Putting this in human terms, you see a ball (the LAP) in a field and fix your gaze on it (LAD-DV). As you walk straight past the ball, your LFP and LFOz are changing, with LFOz decreasing as you approach the ball

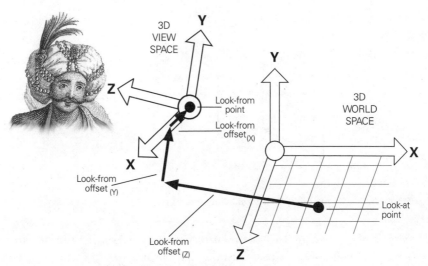

Figure 3.11 The LFP as defined by the LAP and LFO, with LFO consisting of X, Y, and Z components

and increasing after you pass it. If instead you walk around the ball in a circle, your LFP is changing as it moves in a circle, but your LFO_Z stays constant.

The LFO X-Y offset is parallel to the view display plane. As LFO_Y (the LFO Y off-set) increases, the LFP moves up in the plane of the display relative to the position of the projected LAP. Because the display space is defined relative to the LFP and not the LAP, to the user the LAP will appear to move down in the display. In terms of the viewer's avatar (virtual presence), LFO_Z would be the distance from the LAP to the avatar's feet; LFO_Y would be the height of its eyes above its feet; and, if a POCS had a stereo display, $\pm LFO_X$ (LFO X offset) would be the offset of the avatar's right and left eye relative to its center line. This is illustrated in figure 3.11.

Note that LAP and LFO alone are insufficient for defining the complete view orientation. Although we don't need the LAD direction vector we still need its up vector. In other words, a complete specification of the view external geometry requires LAP, LFO, and LAD-UV.

3.3.2 Internal view geometry

The internal geometry of the view is a little more complicated than its external geometry. Here we must deal with the projection of the view space onto the display plane as well as the geometry of the display space itself—the display window. Since objects can be placed directly in the world, view, and display spaces, it is best not to think of the world-to-display space transformation as a monolithic process. Instead it can be divided into a *view side* and a *display side*.

The view side of the world-to-display space transformation projects the contents of the world/view space onto the display plane to form an intermediate *view image*.

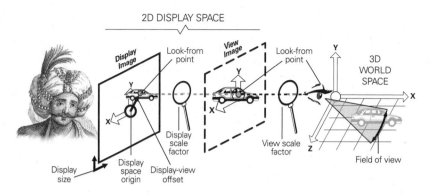

Figure 3.12 An overview of internal view geometry

The display side completes the transformation by converting the view image and the contents of the display space into the final display window image. The view side is defined in terms of field of view (FOV) and view scale factor (VSF). Display size (DS) and display scale factor (DSF) describe the display side. The display-view offset (DVO) connects the view and display sides of the transformation.

LFP, LAP, and DVO

DVO (display-view offset) describes the relative offset of the view space from the display space relative to the display space. The view reference point is defined by the LFP, which corresponds to the view space center axis and, accordingly, the projection of the LAP onto the display. The display reference point is the display origin, which by definition is the center of the display window. The DVO is the 2D offset of the view origin from the display origin in the plane of the display. As the DVO Y offset (DVO$_Y$) increases, the LFP and correspondingly the projection of the LAP will appear to move up in the display, as shown in figure 3.13. DVO is often used in games to position the action, which is centered on the LAP, in the upper portion of the display area while providing room in the lower portion for status displays, controls, and the user's avatar.

DS and FOV

The DS (display size) is simply the size of the display image, or window, as it appears on the computer display screen. The FOV (field of view) is the angle that defines the degree of perspective projection. A large FOV is comparable to a wide-angle camera lens; and a small FOV produces an effect like a telephoto lens. As with camera lenses, the wider the FOV, the more exaggerated the perspective effects will appear. The narrower the FOV, the flatter the view will appear. As the FOV approaches an angle of zero, the display effect approaches that of a parallel projection. For parallel projections, the FOV angle is considered to be zero (some might say it is undefined).

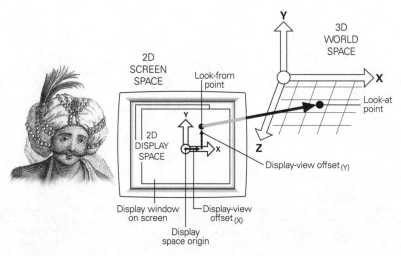

Figure 3.13 Relationship between LFP and DVO in defining the internal view geometry

For the purposes of this book, the FOV is defined to be equal in the horizontal and vertical directions, and independent of DS. For example, leaving VSF and DSF aside for now, if the user stretches the display window to increase its horizontal size, the view of the world does not stretch with it. Instead, the degree of perspective projection will stay the same horizontally and vertically, and the user will see more of the world horizontally in the display window. As an interesting aside, because the LFP defines the view space center axis in the display, as the FOV increases or decreases, the LAP will always appear at the same relative position in the display window.

VSF and DSF

VSF is the scale factor applied to the projection of the view space contents onto the display plane. It describes how much the view image is stretched relative to the display space. DSF is the scale factor applied to the contents of the display space as well as to the view image to form the display image on the display screen. In other words, DSF is applied to everything in the display space, whether from view-projected world objects or from objects placed directly in the display space. For a POCS, the VSF and DSF can be defined as scalars that apply equally to the horizontal and vertical directions.

VSF and DSF are independent of FOV and DS. Increasing the VSF does not affect the perspective projection in the display; and increasing the DSF does not affect the size of the display window. Instead, increasing VSF means that we see less of the world, but what we do see is in greater detail. Increasing VSF is like blowing up the view's projection of the world and cropping it to fit the display window. The same goes for DSF, except that the view image together with any display space objects are blown up and cropped to the display window.

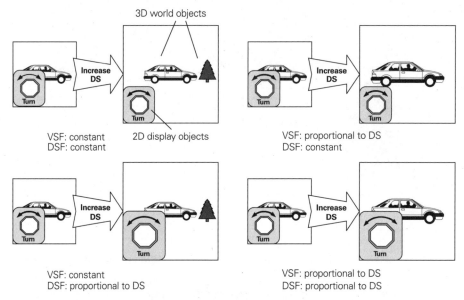

Figure 3.14 The effect of different VSF and DSF policies with changing display size (DS)

Setting DSF to 1 means that the display image is 1:1 with the display objects and the view image. Setting VSF and DSF to 1 means that the display image is 1:1 with the display objects, and the perspective projection of the view objects is 1:1 with the view image. If we also set the FOV to zero, meaning a parallel projection, then the display image will be 1:1 with the display and view objects. In other words, a cube in the world measuring 1 meter on the side will appear 1 meter wide and high when viewed head-on in the display. Because most displays aren't 1 meter wide, VSF is typically adjusted to make world objects fit into the display, and DSF is adjusted to make the display as a whole a comfortable size.

VSF, DSF, and DS

Earlier when we discussed resizing the display window we ignored VSF and DSF. Let's revisit display resizing, but this time we'll consider VSF and DSF. Ignoring FOV, if the user changes the DS to make the display window uniformly bigger in both dimensions, what do we see in the display? One approach is to leave VSF and DSF alone (we are already leaving FOV alone). In this case we will simply see more of the display and view space with no scaling. Another approach is to adjust the DSF such that we see the same amount of the display and view space, only magnified to fill the larger display area. Variations on this theme are to adjust VSF and not DSF so the view content appears larger but we see more of the display space. Or, we can adjust DSF and keep VSF constant so the display space appears larger but we see more of the view space at its original size.

CHAPTER 3 SPACES AND RELATIONS

What happens if the user stretches only one dimension of the display window? Because the scale factors are defined equally in both dimensions, non-uniform stretching is not allowed. Even so we have some decisions to make. As before, we can leave VSF and DSF alone, in which case more of the view and display spaces will be seen along the stretched dimension. If we are trying to fill the display window with the contents of the view and display, then typically the shorter display dimension guides the scaling with the shorter dimension being filled and the longer one showing more of the display and view space.

3.4   SUMMARY

3D can play a fundamental role in next-generation applications, specifically applications for the web, but the term "3D" can cut a wide swath. The discussion here established the portion of the 3D user interface space that this book tries to cover, which is that of the plain old computer system rather than that of the latex cybersuit. Even from this rather narrow perspective, user interfaces can be approached at several levels. The analytical approach—where the UI is described in terms of control, feedback, visualization, navigation, and access—provides a system for organizing the techniques and software presented in the rest of the book. To provide context for this endeavor, 3D applications can be grouped into common patterns of UI usage, which include design, simulation, analysis, and control. To help with the detailed discussions to come, an application's spatial geometry can be described in a UI-centric manner, in terms of world, view, display, and screen spaces.

PART 2

3D user interface techniques

The 3D user interface techniques presented in this book are organized according to the functional schema introduced in section 1.2.3, in the analytical view of a user interface. The first three components—*control*, *feedback*, and *visualization*—deal with the more fundamental issues regarding the dialogue between the user and the application. Control interprets user inputs as meaningful actions in an application; feedback tells the user what to do and how to do it; and visualization allows the user to see the application's data and the results of his/her interactions with it. The last three components—*navigation*, *manipulation*, and *access*—build on the earlier ones. Navigation enables the user to move about the application's 3D world; manipulation permits the user to change the data content of that world; and access allows the user to get the data into and out of the world.

Within each of these functional components or areas, a number of *3D UI* techniques will be presented. There are no right or wrong answers in choosing one technique or variation over another. What to choose and why can be answered only by the designer with a good understanding of the application's problem domain and user community. Application design must be based on an understanding of what the user needs to accomplish, both within a given task and in the context of the application as a whole. The goal of the designer is to allow the user to achieve his goal as quickly and as easily as possible. Intuitive control and enlightening feedback can play significant roles in accomplishing this. In next-generation 3D applications, users will expect things to be almost as easy as in the real world, and to be told what the control idioms are and how they work in the course of using the application. Users want to learn as they go and do not want to rely on reading the manual.

Many techniques presented here will be seen again in later parts of the book. Part 3 will highlight how Java 3D supports these techniques, and part 4 will provide a framework and examples that demonstrate them.

C H A P T E R   4

Control

Control is interpreting user inputs as meaningful actions in an application. In the context of a 3D application implemented on a POCS, a significant portion of this interpretation is devoted to converting 2D mouse inputs into 3D changes to the application's data and its presentation. In terms of the user interface as a whole, control addresses one direction of the interaction dialogue that occurs between the user and the application. As previously described, conceptually there are two dialogues going on between the user and the application. For the user's part, he/she has only an application's controls with which to talk to the application. The application, on the other hand, talks to the user through data visualization and instructional feedback.

This chapter starts by describing the source of all user inputs in an application, which are the raw inputs generated by the physical input devices—the mouse and keyboard. The rest of the chapter is devoted to the important problem of how to interpret these primitive inputs as meaningful actions in a 3D virtual world. Interpretation is what gives a control its overall personality. It allows a single physical device such as a 2D mouse to masquerade as many different controls, even controls that can be used in a 3D world. The interpretation process is described here in terms of a control chain and the techniques employed by it to overcome the problems of getting a 2D mouse to control 3D objects, regardless of the direction from which the view is looking at them. Solving such problems is key to providing users with intuitive controls that

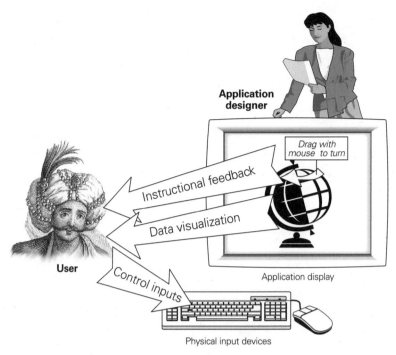

**Figure 4.1   Control as part of the visualization and feedback dialogues
between the user and the application**

allow them to work more as they do in the real world. For example, the technique called *world-relative mapping* interprets the 2D mouse position as a 3D position relative to objects in the virtual world. It allows the user to directly drag an object across the floor of a room, out the door, and down a hallway with one continuous mouse drag.

4.1   PHYSICAL INPUT DEVICES

As user interface designers we have a very limited choice of physical input devices in a POCS: a mouse and a keyboard. There are, however, quite a number of ways in which these mere "stone knives and bear skins" can be used. For example, the normal action of dragging the mouse on an object in the display might be to slide the object. If in the middle of a slide the user wants to rotate the object, he/she stops the drag and starts a new drag using a rotation handle on the object. Realizing how inconvenient this can be, especially if it is common to mix object sliding and rotating, the designer might offer the user an alternative. If the user holds down the Shift key during a drag, the object stops sliding and starts rotating. This is considerably more convenient than starting a new drag with the rotation handle; but often convenience and intuitiveness do not equate.

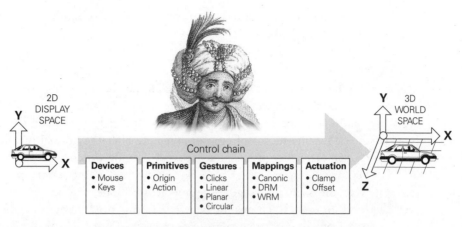

Figure 4.2   Forms of input interpretation along the control chain

In terms of intuitiveness, there is an important distinction between using the mouse and using the keyboard keys as control devices. The mouse, with its display cursor and spatial presence, lends itself to direct interaction with objects in the scene—the user can see where the mouse is in the scene, and the application can offer feedback as to what it is doing near where it is doing it. The keyboard, on the other hand, has no direct presence in the scene and, as such, it is difficult for the designer to provide the user with feedback for how to use it.

 Raw outputs from the mouse and keyboard are demonstrated in the InputSensors example in part 4, section 17.1.7.

4.1.1   The keyboard

It is difficult to provide the user with direct feedback as to what a keyboard key does. There is no keyboard equivalent of a mouseover that pops up a message when the user's finger passes over a key to say what the key will do if it is pressed. In the example above, the user can see that an object has separate handles on it for sliding and turning, but the Shift key has no such feedback to tell the user what it does. To learn that the Shift key can be used to switch a drag operation from a slide to a turn, the user has to either read the manual, or guess that the designer may have done something clever with the Shift key and try it.

Another drawback to using keyboard keys is that there are few conventions for how to use the keyboard keys. The designer can't just assume that users will know what to do with them. In general, keyboard keys, and especially the function keys, should be used as an alternative means for accessing non-essential control functions, perhaps as a more convenient way to perform a common action, or as a shortcut for power users. There are situations, however, where modifier and arrow keys offer control actions that are unique. For example, being able to nudge an object in the scene with the arrow keys is hard to duplicate with the mouse. In these cases you have to weigh the advantages of providing such controls against the disadvantages of limited user feedback and conventions.

Modifier keys

Modifier keys by their very nature are supposed to be used in conjunction with other controls, such as holding down the Shift key while dragging the mouse. During a drag, the mouse and the user's hand on it are completely occupied. The keyboard provides the only other means of control usage. To alter the normal function of the mouse drag, you can either provide the user with a mode switch or let the user press a modifier key. As seen in the earlier example, having to stop one action, like a drag, to start a new action, such as changing the interaction mode, can be inconvenient and even awkward. In these situations the benefits of using modifier keys can be compelling. Chapter 5 will discuss ways to mitigate the lack of feedback when modifier keys are used.

Here are a few examples of how modifier keys can be used to select alternative control action or to modify some characteristic of a control, such as sensitivity (the ratio of control to target movement). You as the designer have to decide, based on the user's tasks and the user's skills, whether offering such control functionality makes the user interface seem easier to use or just more complicated.

- The normal action of a click gesture might be to select the target object and to deselect any previous object that was selected. Holding down the Control key instead causes the new object to be selected in addition to any previously selected objects.

- The default action for drag-and-drop may be to move the target object. Holding down the Control key instead causes a copy of the target object to be dragged and dropped.

- For arrow key nudging, the modifier keys might control the step size, with no modifiers for the smallest steps, Shift for medium steps, and Control for the largest steps.

- In some VRML browsers, dragging in the display causes the view to move forward and to steer from side to side. Using different modifier keys causes the rate of movement and the navigation mode to change on the fly.

Arrow keys

Although arrow keys can serve as a continuous locator (pointing device), the mouse is far superior in this role. What the arrow keys do offer, because of their discrete nature, is the unique ability to precisely control the magnitude and direction of target object movement. For example, hitting an arrow key can have the effect of nudging the target object by a fixed amount in the direction indicated by its arrow. This is in contrast to the mouse, which is difficult to use for precise placement of a dragged object.

Being able to nudge objects is especially attractive when you look at the alternatives. A common technique used in drawing applications is to allow the user to numerically enter exact position and orientation specifications in a dialogue box, numerically. The cycle of entering a number, hitting the apply button, and seeing if the object moved to the correct position can be tedious. Arrow key nudging can be a good alternative, sort of midway between the precision of direct entry and the intuitiveness of direct manipulation.

As with modifier keys, the designer must decide if the use of arrow keys will help or hinder the quest for an intuitive user interface.

Escape key

One more key on the keyboard that can be put to good use is the Escape key. Although technically not a modifier key in that it can not be used in combination with modifier keys, it nevertheless serves as a modifier key in that it is typically used while another control is in use.

A somewhat well established convention for the Escape key is to tell the application to stop whatever operation is in progress, such as a mouse drag. Not only does the operation stop but the application rolls back its state to that which existed just prior to the start of the operation, such as in a drag-and-drop operation.

4.1.2   The mouse

In a POCS, the mouse is king. It is the user's primary means for controlling the placement and orientation of objects. It is also the device of choice for performing nonspatial tasks such as pressing toolbar buttons and selecting menu entries. It is the heart and soul of any graphical user interface.

Besides being inexpensive and readily available, it is reliable, takes up little desk space, and simply works well as a pointing device. It also conveniently combines two types of control devices into one: a locator and a choice device. This combination of pointer and mouse buttons is what gives the mouse its popular point-and-click ability. Later, in section 4.3.2, you'll see different ways to combine mouse position with button actions to form click and drag gestures that are integral to most virtual controls.

In our quest for the intuitive user interface, a device with good mechanical and data input characteristics such as a mouse may be necessary, but it is certainly not sufficient. A previous example illustrated how the Shift key could be used as a control device to make the user's job easier, but it probably wouldn't make the user interface any more intuitive. With a mouse, the designer can employ dynamic feedback that is location sensitive, such as mouseover feedback, to tell the user that something is a control before actually using it.

Everyone knows what a mouse does. Why all this fuss about feedback? In the quest for an intuitive UI, the feedback opportunities offered by a mouse are just as important as its ability to function as a control device. Shifting the design emphasis from mouse control to mouse control with feedback represents the kind of consideration that will be needed for next-generation applications. Mouse and other forms of feedback will be addressed separately in chapter 7.

Throughout this book, the term "mouse" is used. This is meant to include all pointing devices, which for a POCS is the mouse and, if so configured, the arrow keys.

4.2   INPUT INTERPRETATION

If I told you "five to the left" you would probably ask me to repeat myself. Although you may pick up on the fact that this is a request and that it means changing the location of something, there is no way for you to comply because I have not told you what to move or assigned any units to the spatial quantity "five." We have a similar problem with physical device inputs. In response to user actions, the physical devices dutifully generate raw input values such as *X-Y* position, button up-down status, and the time at which each value was generated. When the application receives a raw input value it would like to ask the device, "What are you controlling?" and "What are the units of measure?" In most systems, however, the raw input values are all that the application designer has at his/her disposal.

Input interpretation involves asking the right questions for a given control situation, and answering those questions such that raw inputs are translated into directed and quantifiable control results. Often, for a given situation there can be many equally valid answers as to what the raw inputs mean. How the interpretation questions are answered determines the personality of the control, and often its intuitive feel for a given task. Is moving the mouse to the right interpreted as a first-person movement of the user's view of the scene, or as a second-person movement of an object in the scene? You'll see answers to these and many other interpretation questions throughout this chapter.

4.2.1   Asking the right questions

As is the case with most problems, the better you understand the situation the better the solution is likely to be. To understand the situation you have to ask questions, especially the right questions. For example, in a given application, under different circumstances, mouse movement can be interpreted in different ways. In one instance, it could be interpreted as sliding a bookshelf "up over here;" and in another it could be interpreted as rotating the view of the bookshelf "a little to the right." In the first instance, when the user moves the mouse "up," does that mean for the application to slide the bookshelf away from the user across the floor, or to lift the bookshelf up off of the floor into the air? In the second instance, when the user moves the mouse "right," does that mean to turn the *object* to the right so its left side is exposed, or to move the *view* to the right so the right side of the object is seen? And to think, we haven't even begun to ask questions about what units of measure to use!

These examples illustrate two of the central issues concerning control interpretation in the discussions to follow. One issue is that the input devices and the targets being controlled have more than one dimension. The mouse position in the display has two dimensions, and an object's position in the world has three. This means there is more than one way to connect or map a particular input coordinate to a particular target coordinate. We must decide if the mouse X value should control the target's X value, Y value, or Z value. And, once that is decided, we still have to ask what the mouse Y value should control.

The other issue is that a POCS user has only 2D devices with which to work, yet many user tasks occur in 3D space. This is an underspecified problem, meaning there is insufficient information available from a 2D input device alone to unambiguously control a 3D target. Who or what controls the extra dimension? Without getting too far ahead of the discussion, this dilemma can be resolved by making intelligent assumptions about the value of the extra dimension, or by getting more information from the user about what to do with the extra dimension. This subject will be discussed at length in section 4.4 on coordinate mapping.

4.2.2   Other interpretations

Up to this point, only interpretations that directly control an object in space have been mentioned, such as positioning and orienting a target object in the 3D world. Equally important are indirect and non-spatial interpretations. In an indirect interpretation, the inputs control a process that in turn controls an object. For example, mouse movement could be interpreted as a change in the rate of position movement rather than a simple position change: Moving the mouse up would make the target object move faster.

Input devices can also be used for non-spatial control. For example, the mouse could control a color value, with left-right position controlling the color's hue, and up-down position controlling its intensity. The discussions here and in other chapters emphasize spatial interpretations because 3D user interfaces are by definition spatial. Nevertheless, non-spatial interpretations such as color or temperature can be no less important to the overall success of a 3D application.

4.2.3   Control personae

From a much higher conceptual level, interpretation involves the relationships and roles played by the user, the virtual control, and the target of the control action. A convenient way to classify controls is according to which player in the "control chain" the user is directly manipulating. This classification scheme lends itself to the notion of control *personae*, which mirror those used for participants in everyday speech: first person, second person, and third person. Being a relatively high-level concept, control personae will be covered in detail in chapter 8, which covers manipulation. For now, a few examples should give you a qualitative feel for them.

A first-person control is one where the user directly manipulates his view of the world. The view is a proxy for the user—his virtual presence in the 3D world. This form of control is popular in adventure games and VRML players: When the user drags the mouse to the right in the display, the user and his view of the world turn to the right. When he drags the mouse up, the view begins to slide forward in the world.

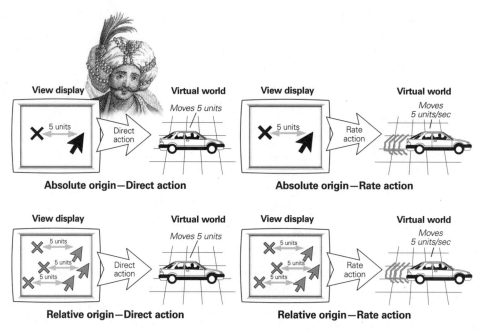

Figure 4.3   Examples of primitive control interpretation combinations

With a second-person control, the user is allowed to drag and manipulate objects directly in the scene. This is often referred to as "direct manipulation," and can be a very intuitive form of control. It is the epitome of WYSIWYG—What You See Is What You Get—only here we have to do it in 3D. To help the user figure out which objects can be manipulated and how, they can be decorated using mouseover feedback, such as highlighting and control handles.

In a third-person control, the user manipulates a virtual control such as a button, knob, or slider in a control panel. In response, the target object in the scene moves, stretches, changes color, blows up, and so forth. Third-person control is also called "indirect manipulation." Although not as chic as direct WYSIWYG manipulation, it definitely has its place in a 3D UI.

4.3   CONTROL BASICS

As seen from the brief discussion so far, mouse position can be interpreted in many different ways, and there are many more to come. Even the most basic forms of input interpretation can have a significant impact on a control's personality and therefore are covered here in some detail. Because they are not specific to 3D, however, readers who are already familiar with them may want only to skim the following sections or even skip ahead and go straight to the more 3D specific aspects of control, beginning in section 4.4 on coordinate mapping.

4.3.1   Control primitives

The most primitive level of control interpretation involves the translation of a raw mouse input position into something more useful for the application. These primitive translation techniques and their combinations are summarized in table 4.1. As with most control techniques, interpretations can be used alone or in combination.

    Many of the control primitives are demonstrated in the InputFilters example in part 4, section 17.3.2. Use it to observe the techniques and experience their relative merits.

Table 4.1   Primitive control interpretations and their combinations

	Direct Action	Rate Action
Absolute origin	• The control origin is predefined in the control. • Target movement is proportional to control distance from the origin.	• The control origin is predefined in the control. • The rate of target movement is proportional to control distance from origin.
Relative origin	• The control origin is established on-the-fly (i.e., the mouse down position). • Target movement is proportional to control distance from the origin.	• The control origin is established on-the-fly (i.e., the mouse down position). • The rate of target movement is proportional to control distance from origin.

Absolute origin

When interpreting raw mouse input, the user must ask to what it is relative. Do you just assume the origin of the control is the same as that of the mouse space and pass on the mouse position as the control output? What if the control were not centered at the mouse space origin but was someplace else in the display? In this case positioning the mouse on the control would not produce an output of zero; instead, the value of the control output would reflect the distance that the control is offset from the mouse space origin. This is seen in the InputSensors example in part 4, section 17.1.7. To rectify this situation, a separate control origin can be defined in the mouse space.

In an *absolute origin* control, the control origin is predefined in the mouse space at some location obvious to the user, such as the center of a virtual knob control. The origin should be an integral part of the control; if the control were relocated, so too should its control origin. If the internal view geometry is not fixed, however, this can be a non-trivial problem. For example, if the user resizes the display window, then the control will likely change its absolute position in the display space; and thus the control origin should be updated accordingly. This problem is seen in the InputFilters example, which does not update the control origin when the window is resized.

The big advantage of absolute origin is that the reference point is always in the same place for the user, and clicking on the control can generate a specific single output value. Disadvantages are that the display screen defines the bounds on the output value. When the mouse reaches the edge of the screen, the control value cannot increase any farther. And, in order to start a drag with a zero output value, the user must start the mouse exactly on the control's origin.

Relative origin

The disadvantages of an absolute origin control can be ameliorated with a *relative origin* control. In this type input interpretation, the control origin is established on the fly, such as when a mouse button or modifier key is pressed. Once the origin is established, the mouse input position is interpreted relative to this origin, just as it is for an absolute origin control. A relative style of interpretation, such as relative physical devices, allows the user in effect to pick up the control and reposition it.

For example, when the mouse button is pressed, a tic mark appears at that position in the display and the control values are interpreted in the display plane relative to that origin. In some cases the whole display is the active control area: The user is allowed to start dragging anywhere in the display. This style control has been used in some VRML browsers where the user can drag the mouse anywhere in the display to slide and turn the display view. The farther the user drags from the initial drag point, the more the view slides forward or turns to the side. In most cases, however, the active area is confined to a visible representation of a virtual control, such as a knob or slider. The user can start a drag only within this active control area.

The advantages of a relative origin are that the user can choose any starting point. Disadvantages are that a given output value can be attained only by starting from the origin and moving the mouse until the desired value is reached. Except for zero, a single specific value can not be generated. This is because the starting point is by definition the origin, which represents an output of zero.

Direct action

So far, the controls that have been discussed all move the target directly. If you move the mouse five units, the target object moves five units. If you stop moving the mouse, the target stops moving. This type of control interpretation is called *direct action*. Because of its direct nature, this control technique is often considered the most intuitive type action. For this reason, and because it is easy to implement, it is also the most common control action technique.

The major disadvantage of direct action is that when the mouse reaches the edge of the screen, the target stops moving. This is a different way of looking at the same problem seen with absolute origin controls; but here the discussion focuses on target movement instead of the control output value.

Rate action

Suppose you have a videotape player and you want to control the movement of the tape so you can examine what is on it. Using a direct action control, you'd have to have a slider that is as long as the tape so you can move from one end of the tape to the other. This is not very practical. Perhaps you can increase the control sensitivity so that moving the slider a little moves the tape a lot. This is a bit better but you need a steady hand or the good scenes on the tape will go whizzing by. How do you get around this dilemma? The same way that real videotape players do it. They use a shuttle knob that controls the tape's velocity instead of its position.

This type of control interpretation is called *rate action*. Move the mouse a little and the target object starts moving slowly. Move the mouse farther and the target moves more quickly. Stop moving the mouse and the target continues moving, at a rate proportional to the distance from the mouse to the control origin. This is what makes rate controls so useful. This is also what gets users into so much trouble. Intuitively you think that if you stop moving the control then the object should stop moving also. Instead, the object keeps zipping along and before you realize your mistake, the object is out of sight. This seems both unintuitive and undesirable.

In some applications, however, rate controls can be quite intuitive, such as in a flight simulator, where absolute rate controls can mimic real flight controls. In other applications, rate controls can be downright practical, as when they allow the user to quickly zip from one place to another in the world without having to repeatedly click and drag the mouse in little steps as with a relative-direct style of control. A common example of this is a GUI technique called bump scrolling. Say you are trying to drag an item that is at the beginning of a long list to the end of the list. Suppose the list is too long to fit in the widget window. With bump scrolling you can start dragging the target item and when the cursor gets near the bottom of the window the list starts to automatically scroll down. The farther the mouse is dragged past the end of the window, the quicker the list scrolls.

An important aspect of a rate control that is often overlooked or dismissed is how the target position is updated according to the rate. One way to time position updates is to rely on the CPU speed, which is easy to implement, is still in common use, but can be quite unsatisfactory. Users may do fine walking around their virtual world on last year's 100 MHz computer; but the walk will turn into a mad dash on next year's 1 GHz screamer. To avoid this problem, rate position updates should be made using a real timer that measures the actual passage of time.

4.3.2 Mouse gestures

A *gesture* involves interpreting the mouse position and mouse button state together over time, with the button state indicating the start and end of the gesture. As an alternative to mouse buttons, a modifier key could be used to indicate gesture start and end, although this is not very common and therefore wouldn't be very intuitive for most users. Gestures are closely allied with origin and action interpretation, but are considered a higher level of control interpretation. Primitive and gesture techniques form the basis for most virtual controls.

Table 4.2 summarizes the gesture control interpretations, which come in two forms: clicks and drags. A click is a quick press then release of a mouse button, with no significant mouse movement. A drag begins when a mouse button is pressed and held. The hold continues while the mouse is moved, and terminates when the mouse button is released.

Mouse gestures are so useful that most applications use more than one type of gesture to control a given object. For example, clicking on an object may select it; but dragging the object may move it. In these situations it is particularly important to distinguish between a click and a drag. Because slight movement often occurs when the mouse is clicked, a position threshold or "dead band" should be incorporated into basic gesture interpretations.

Table 4.2   Gesture control interpretations and their characteristics

Clicks	• Occurs at a single position. • Time-sensitive sequence of one or more mouse button clicks. • Called a "single-click" if one click, and a "double-click" if two clicks. • Greater than two clicks is a "multi-click."
Planar	• Interprets a drag as a 2D position or as two 1D positions. • Called a "stroke" if time is a factor. • Called "drag-and-drop" if object drag and over-detection are involved.
Linear	• Detects the length and direction of a straight-line drag. • Called a "flick" if time is a factor. • Example: A VRML CylinderSensor can interpret linear motion perpendicular to a 3D object's axis of rotation as a rotation.
Circular	• Detects the angular position and radial distance of a control drag. • Example: A VRML CylinderSensor can interpret circular motion around a 3D object's axis of rotation as a rotation.

Clicks

Clicking the mouse is the simplest form of gesture. The mouse can be clicked one or more times at the same position to produce various click gestures. The most common ones are the *single-click* and the *double-click*. More than two clicks, or multi-clicking, is possible, although there are few conventions for interpreting such a gesture. One possibility is to use the number of clicks to select one of several choices, making the mouse a virtual choice device.

Interpretation of a click gesture often depends on the current state of the target object, the view, or the application. The following examples illustrate some of the possibilities.

• Single-clicking an object might select it as the target for some subsequent action, such as copying or deleting it, or adding it to a group. If the object were already selected, then single-clicking it would deselect the object.

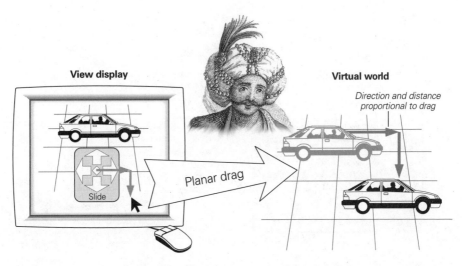

Figure 4.4   An example of planar drag with a virtual control widget

- Double-clicking an object might navigate the user's view "into" that object, as in drilling down into the next level of detail within the target object. For example, double-clicking a network node would switch the view to reveal the next level of network detail within the node.
- Multi-clicking an object might change the object's appearance, scope of selection, or manner of manipulation. For example, the first click on an object might reveal manipulation handles for sliding the object; the second click would expose a rotation handle; and the third click would give the user a handle for lifting the object.

Planar drags

A *planar drag* in its simplest interpretation is not much of a gesture; and some might deem it unworthy of the title. In a planar drag control, mouse motion can be interpreted simply as a 2D value changing over time, or as two 1D control sliders oriented along the display axes and coupled together. Moving the mouse in a circle moves each slider back and forth in an out-of-phase fashion. In a POCS, with only a mouse and keyboard, all drag gestures are derivations of a planar drag.

Higher-level information provided by a planar drag control is starting and ending position, with a stream of position samples generated while going from start to finish. If time information is also captured for each position sample in the stream, then the gesture is called a "stroke." A stroke can be used for very high-level interpretation such as handwriting recognition, where the speed of the stroke segments may be significant. More typically, the distance and only the overall duration of the drag is used to compute a drag rate.

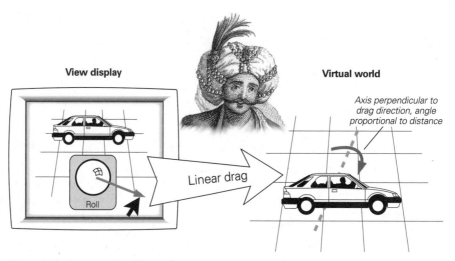

View display

Roll

Linear drag

Virtual world

Axis perpendicular to drag direction, angle proportional to distance

Figure 4.5 An example of linear drag with a virtual trackball widget

An important form of planar drag gesture is drag-and-drop (DnD). DnD is a second-person control technique used extensively in 2D GUIs. In a DnD operation the object on which the drag starts, the objects that it passes over, and the object on which it ends are often significant, and the user needs a fair amount of feedback to know what is happening. DnD touches on a number of UI concepts, and presents some interesting challenges when used in a 3D environment. As such, the discussion on 3D DnD will be deferred to Chapter 9, which discusses data access.

Linear drags

In a *linear drag* gesture, mouse motion is interpreted as movement in a particular vector direction. Detecting linear gestures along an axis is easy: Simply ignore the unwanted coordinate value and the mouse becomes a 1D slider. For the general case, however, the direction of the drag is unknown and must be determined. In this case you can compute the direction vector from the drag start and end positions.

Because it is difficult to draw a straight line with a mouse, the drag end points may not be indicative of the overall direction of the drag. A more robust approach would be to fit the drag position samples to a line segment to provide the direction and magnitude of the linear gesture. If speed information is also included, then the gesture is called a "flick" or "jerk."

A simple example of linear gesture is interpreting general left-right movement of the mouse as a pan of the view from side to side, with up-down motion being ignored. A more dignified example, specifically a flick, is provided in some VRML browsers. In "examine" (WorldView) or "rotate" (CosmoPlayer) mode, flicking the mouse— quickly dragging then releasing it—will spin the target object about an axis perpendicular to the flick direction and at a rate proportional to the flick speed.

CHAPTER 4 CONTROL

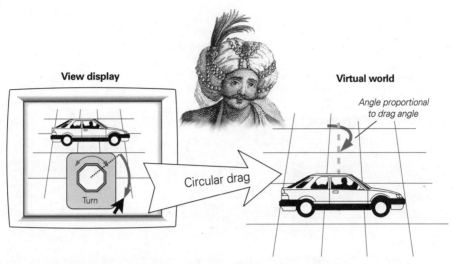

Figure 4.6   An example of circular drag with a virtual control widget

Circular drags

In a *circular drag* gesture, mouse motion is interpreted as turning a control "knob." The angle of rotation is determined by the angular position of the mouse relative to the control origin and reference axis, such as the X axis. Moving the mouse in a circle around the origin turns the control. Other than angle, the gesture can also output the radial distance of the drag from the control origin. The InputFilters example includes the use of a circular drag gesture.

The VRML CylinderSensor provides a good example of both circular and linear gestures. If a drag is started near the axis of the sensor, then the drag is interpreted as a circular gesture—e.g., turning a disk. If the drag is started elsewhere on the sensor, away from the axis, then the drag is interpreted as a linear gesture—e.g., rolling a barrel. In general, the decision to use a linear or a circular control gesture to rotate an object is often dictated by the angle at which the object is viewed. If the object's rotation axis is viewed end-on, then turning the object like a knob using a circular gesture might be more intuitive. If the object is viewed from the side, then rolling the object side-to-side using a linear gesture might be more practical.

4.3.3   Target actuation

Looking farther down the control chain, toward the target end, is a whole new set of interpretation questions that need to be answered. Questions arising here concern how to connect the input coordinates to those of the target, the manner in which the target's state is updated, and whether or not the target's state is preserved between drags. Questions concerning coordinates are covered in section 4.4, which looks at coordinate mapping. The remaining questions fall under an area of control interpretation called target *actuation*.

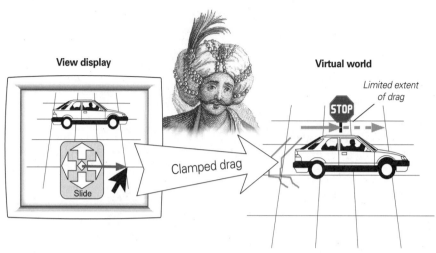

View display

Slide

Clamped drag

Virtual world

*Limited extent
of drag*

STOP

**Figure 4.7   Clamping constrains the range over which the state of the control
target can change.**

An actuator makes the final connection between a still rather generic control action, such as a circle gesture, and the effect of that action on the target, such as a rotation. Actuators are often specific to the effect they have on the target. For example, an actuator that rotates a 3D object must change the state of the object's geometric transformation, and will need to know the object's axis of rotation. An actuator that changes the color of an object must change the state of the object's appearance, and will need to know the type of color space in which it is working: RGB, CMYK, YIQ, HSV, and so on.

Although basic in concept, actuation becomes a rather involved subject in terms of implementation. Part of this is from dealing with 3D-specific issues. Actuation, actuators, and actuator grouping are covered in the Actuators and ActuatorGroups examples in part 4, sections 18.2.6 and 18.3.5.

Clamping

A simple but important aspect of actuation is limiting or *clamping* the range of the target state change. Range limits are among the simplest form of constraints, and can go far in making life easier for the user. For example, if the target of a rotation operation is the vertical tilt of the user's view, the user is less likely to become disoriented if the tilt is limited to between straight up and straight down. An even better choice, if the application allows it, would be to limit the tilt to between a little less than straight up and horizontal.

Although conceptually clamping is associated with target actuation, for practical reasons it is often applied at other stages of the control chain, from raw mouse input through coordinate mapping.

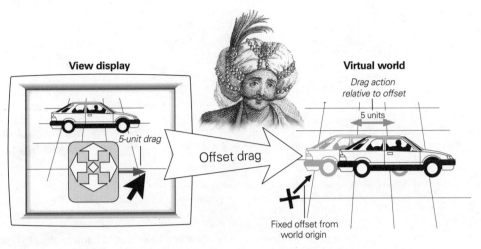

Figure 4.8   A fixed offset allows a target object to be offset from the target space origin.

Offset

When a drag starts, the target is in a given state, such as a rotation angle of 90 degrees. When the drag stops, the target is usually in a different state, such as a rotation angle of 180 degrees. What happens to the target state the next time a drag starts? Will the target start at 90 degrees or 180 degrees? This is referred to as target state *offset*, and there are two types: fixed and cumulative.

With fixed offset the target state always starts at the same absolute offset position. Fixed offset is often used in conjunction with absolute origin so that a click on a virtual control produces a single specific value, which in turn is manifested in the target as a single absolute state. For example, clicking on the horizontal tic mark in a view tilt control would orient the view horizontally—guaranteed, without any guesswork.

Cumulative offset effectively preserves the state of the target between drags. For first- and second-person controls, this is often the most intuitive form of state offset. With a first-person control and cumulative offset, the user can drag up in the display to tilt his head up a bit, and then drag again to tilt his head up a bit more. Tracking and updating the target state between and during drags can be performed in a number of ways, but this is left to part 4 as implementation details.

4.4   COORDINATE MAPPING

In getting from the input device end of the control interpretation chain to the target actuation end, input values have to be translated from 2D mouse space into the coordinates of the target space, typically the 3D world space in a 3D application. This middle link in the control chain is where a significant portion of the 3D user interface challenge lies.

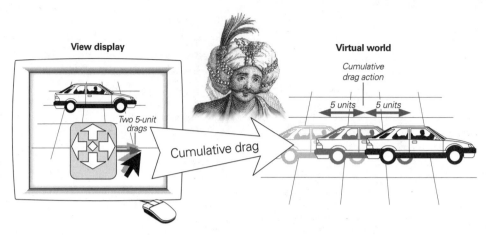

Figure 4.9   A cumulative offset adds the effect of a new control input to the previous one.

Coordinate mapping is a form of control interpretation that answers two questions at the heart of 3D object control: Which dimension of the input value is connected or mapped to which dimension of the target value? And, where does the information for controlling the target object's extra dimension come from? This last question arises from the mismatch that occurs when a 2D control such as a mouse tries to position or rotate a 3D object.

Coordinate mapping is a concern when dealing with any multi-dimensional control device or target space, not just a 3D space. With just a 2D mouse and a 2D display space, there are situations where it may be desirable to cross-connect the mouse's X dimension to the object's Y dimension, or to not connect one of the mouse's dimensions at all. There are other situations where nonspatial control values are involved, such as in color space. Although non-3D and nonspatial coordinate mapping are important, even in 3D applications, the discussion here will focus on 3D spatial coordinate mapping.

Many input interpretation questions arise at this point. Does increasing the mouse Y value (moving the mouse cursor up in the display) decrease the target object's Z position (moving the target bookshelf away from the user)? Or does it increase the target's Y dimension (lifting the bookshelf up in the world)? Does pressing the right arrow key increment the X position of all the objects in the world (moving what the user sees in the display to the right)? Or does it increment the X position of the user's eyeball in the world (moving what the user sees in the display to the left)? A few terms need to be clarified before answering these questions.

4.4.1   Movement, objects, and views

The discussions to follow will refer to the target object, which is the object whose state is being controlled by the user's inputs. It is the object at the end of the control chain. Given the focus on 3D spatial control, user actions will generally involve

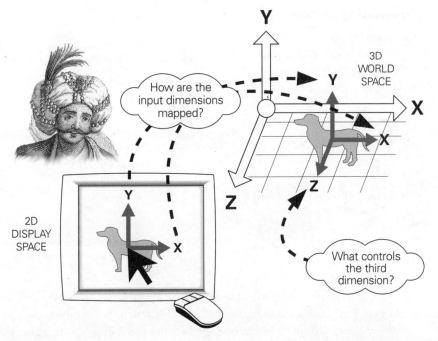

Figure 4.10   The two control interpretation questions answered by coordinate mapping

moving the target object. Movement here refers to positioning and rotating the target. As you'll see below, controlling position and controlling rotation are similar, but each requires its own special considerations. The nature of the target object has a bearing on these discussions.

In the context of 3D spatial control, the target object can be some data object, such as a piece of furniture or your personal jumbo jet, or it can be the user's view of the world, as a view object. For brevity, data objects will be referred to as *objects*, and view objects will be referred to as *views*. In terms of the earlier discussion on the nature of a user interface, manipulation is control action that moves—positions and rotates—data objects in the world; and, navigation is like manipulation, only the target is a view object rather than a data object. Although coordinate mapping deals with both, techniques specifically for navigation and manipulation are discussed at length in later chapters.

4.4.2   Direct mapping

The simplest form of coordinate mapping is *direct mapping*. Direct mapping connects a given input-value dimension to one or more output-value dimensions (or even none) without any fancy mathematics. It is a simple case of wiring, with perhaps a bit of value scaling and sign reversal thrown in as a convenience. Direct mapping is included as part of the Actuators examples in part 4, section 18.2.6.

Positioning an object

Suppose you want to move an object in the world using the mouse. An obvious mapping from a 2D device to 3D world coordinates is to let the mouse's *X* and *Y* position values specify the object's *X* and *Y* position in the world. This is the canonical mapping for object positioning. In this case, the mapping is relative to the world. To address the question raised earlier about what to do with the target's extra dimension, assume the

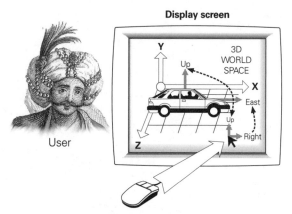

Figure 4.11 Canonical coordinate mapping for object positioning; view looking north

object's *Z* position is fixed at zero. Looking northward along the world's −*Z* axis toward the target object, as shown in figure 4.11, you see that as the mouse moves, so too does the object appear to move in the display. Moving the mouse up (increasing mouse *Y*) moves the object up (increasing world *Y*), and moving the mouse right (increasing mouse *X*) moves the object right in the display (east in the world, increasing world *X*). Just as a reminder, this book uses a mouse space that conforms to a right-hand coordinate space with mouse *Y* increasing up, not down, as in many 2D and 3D APIs.

What if instead you change your view to look at the object from behind, along the world's +*Z* axis, toward the South? In this case moving the mouse up moves the object up just as before, but moving the mouse right moves the object left in the display (east in the world) instead of right, as shown in figure 4.12. No problem, this can easily be fixed by mapping mouse *X* to object −*X* instead of +*X*. Now,

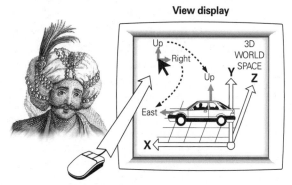

Figure 4.12 Canonical coordinate mapping for object positioning; view looking south

when the mouse moves right, the object also appears to move right.

Continuing a little further with this example, what if you now change the view to look down on the target object from above, along the world's −*Y* axis, as shown in figure 4.13? To make the object's movement match that of the mouse you'd have to map mouse *X* to object *X*, and map mouse *Y* to object −*Z*.

Maintaining an intuitive feel between the user's control actions and

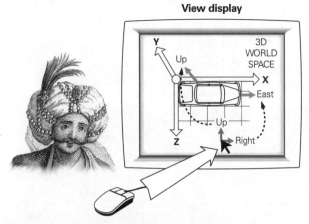

Figure 4.13   Canonical coordinate mapping for object positioning; view looking down

the object's movement in the display is a worthwhile goal, but making this happen seems rather complicated. Every time you change your view of the target object in the world, you have to adjust the mouse-to-world coordinate mapping. Thankfully, 3D graphics systems can perform this kind of 3D coordinate transformation efficiently, but the control interpretation still has to figure out what to tell the system to do. This helps to illustrate a point made earlier, that the computer and designer will have to work harder to make next-generation applications seem easier.

Positioning the view

The previous example showed some of the issues involved in moving an object in the world. Now let's take a look at some of the specifics involved in moving the view in the world. Starting as before, looking along the world's −*Z* axis at an object, this time let's map mouse *X* to the view's *X* position in the world, and mouse *Y* to the view's *Y* position. This is the canonical mapping for positioning the view relative to the world.

When the user moves the mouse up (increasing mouse *Y*) the view moves up (increasing world *Y*), and the target object appears to move down in the display. When the user moves the mouse right (increasing mouse *X*), the view moves right (east in the world, increasing world *X*), and the object appears to move left in the display. This is shown in figure 4.14.

Some designers would say this is intuitive—move the mouse right and the view moves right. When you observe users trying to use this configuration for the first time, however, many will move the mouse right and expect the object in the view to move right, as in the first example in the previous section. Doing it the opposite way, as would seem to be the case in this example, seems unintuitive.

Expectations govern how we perceive the world. The designer *knows* that the mouse moves the view so his/her expectation is that when the view moves, what is seen in the display will appear to move in the opposite direction. First-time users, not being

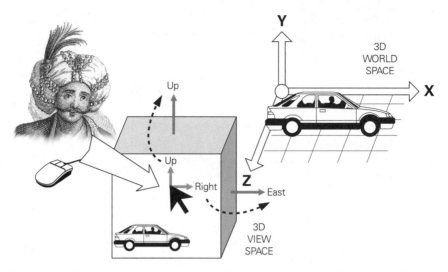

Figure 4.14 Canonical coordinate mapping for view positioning; view looking North

privy to this information, or not having read the manual, will more than likely rely on their instincts of how things work in the real world. There, people think about moving an object to the right, not about moving their head to the left to make the object appear to move to the right.

But, what if you wanted to design a simple spaceship simulator where the view moves forward through space at a fixed rate while the user moves the mouse to fire thrusters that slide the ship, and the user's view from it, up and down and side to side? You would use the same mapping as before, with mouse X to view X, and mouse Y to view Y. This will feel fairly intuitive to most users because their expectation (formally called the user interface metaphor) is that of being in a vehicle. Moving the mouse right moves the vehicle—the view—right, which is consistent with what the user sees on the display: The space station in the foreground and the stars in the background all move to the left. Decorating the display as a view port in the front of the spaceship would help to reinforce the notion that the user is in a spaceship.

Beside control coordinate mapping, the simple lessons to be learned here are that intuitiveness is in the eye of the beholder, literally and figuratively, and that the beholder is the user and not the designer. Thus far the examples have shown how the choice of coordinate mapping is used to move an object in the world. Moving our view of that object can have a significant effect on the intuitive feel of the user interface. What kind of trouble will we run into when we try to rotate an object or the view?

Rotating an object

Controlling position involves sliding the target along spatial axes, whereas controlling orientation involves rotating the target about these axes. Unlike movement, the simple mapping of mouse X to world X, and mouse Y to world Y, is not very intuitive for orienting an object. For example, with such a mapping, moving the mouse right (increasing mouse X) would rotate the object about the world X axis (increasing

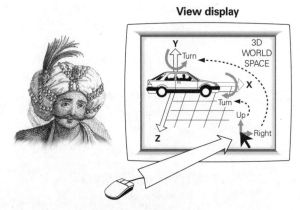

View display

Figure 4.15 Canonical coordinate mapping for object rotation; view looking north

world X angle). In the display, the target object would appear to turn head over heels, not side to side as you might hope.

To get the object to turn side to side and up and down when the mouse moves in a like fashion, you have to map mouse X to target rotation about the world Y axis, and mouse Y to rotation of the target about the world $-X$ axis. This is the canonical mapping for object rotation relative to the world. To handle that nagging question about what to do with the "third" dimension, assume for now that rotation about the Z axis is fixed at zero. Thus, looking northward along the world's $-Z$ axis toward the target object, as shown in figure 4.15, when you move the mouse right the object turns right, exposing its left side in the display; and when you move the mouse up, the object rotates up, exposing its bottom side.

Rotating the view

Continuing with the spaceship example from before, suppose you want to do something more fun and natural than just sliding the view up and down and from side to side. How about actually steering the spaceship, with the mouse controlling the orientation of the vehicle—the view—instead of its lateral position?

To steer the spaceship in an intuitive manner you want it (and your view) to turn toward the right when you move the mouse to the right, and to angle upward when you move the mouse up. (Some might contend that it would be more intuitive to angle the spaceship down when the mouse moves up, like in an airplane; but that is an airplane and this is a spaceship—actions must be consistent with the established user interface metaphor.) This requires mapping mouse X to the view's $-Y$ world axis, and mouse Y to the view's X world axis. This is the canonical mapping for view rotation relative to the world. Now, if the user moves the mouse right to steer right, the vehicle—the view—turns toward the right; and if the mouse moves up to steer up, the view turns upward. This seems to work OK. Or does it?

As long as you steer only left and right all seems fine. If instead you steer up, rotating the view up, and then try to steer left, rotating the view to the left, you notice something odd. The view turns left but not quite the way you would expect it to if you were really steering a vehicle. This is because the rotations were defined about the world axes, which remain fixed regardless of what the view does. As you saw with position control, you would have to adjust the coordinate mapping each time the view changes so that the user inputs remain consistent and therefore intuitive. The next section describes a general approach for adjusting the coordinate mapping to match the view.

4.5   INTUITIVE MAPPING

So far you've seen how you must change the coordinate mapping each time the view changes so that the action of the mouse on an object continues to feel intuitive. This addresses the first question posed at the beginning of this discussion on coordinate mapping—how to connect the input and output dimensions. The second question—what to do with the "extra" dimension—has pretty much been ignored. The target's Z-axis position and angle have just been set to zero.

This section addresses both coordinate re-mapping and the target's complete 3D geometry. Although the discussion here is still about coordinate mapping, the focus is on *intuitive* coordinate mapping, which goes far beyond the simple wiring problem introduced in the previous section. Unlike direct mapping, the implementation details of intuitive mapping tend to be complex and are left to be addressed in parts 3 and 4.

4.5.1   Source and target space

The key to meeting the challenge of developing intuitive coordinate mappings lies in establishing the proper frames of reference from which to work, for both the user and the developer. For the user it's fairly straightforward. The two spaces that count are the display and the world. Movement of objects and the view can occur relative to the display—left-right, up-down—or relative to the world—north-south, east-west, up-down. The situation for the developer is a bit more complicated (which is consistent with the notion that the developer and computer have to work harder for the benefit of the user).

When the user moves the mouse right, meaning to move the object it controls to the right, the developer must first know how all the players involved in the control action are situated. He/she must translate the local movement in the display into an absolute direction in the world, no matter how the view display is situated. And, he/she must translate this absolute world direction into one that is relative to the local space of the target object, no matter how the target is situated. A more complicated situation involves letting the user move objects relative to other objects in the world, such as sliding the desk on the floor toward the window, regardless of where the desk and window are in the display. All of this will become clearer as it is explained in detail later.

The point here is that to perform intuitive coordinate mapping, the control input must be interpreted relative to a *source* space and the control actuation must be interpreted relative to a *target* space. The source space might be defined by the display plane itself, or by some object in the world, such as the floor. The target space might be defined by the world space itself, as in the case of navigation, or by some nested object in the world space, like the handle on a drawer in a desk, as in the case of manipulation.

4.5.2 Display-relative mapping

For certain situations, it is desirable for user inputs to map to a coordinate system that is relative to the view display. One such case was described previously in the spaceship simulator example. The user's expectation was that of being in a moving vehicle; controlling the display view instead of the objects seen in the display seemed intuitive. In a vehicle, steering inputs are relative to the vehicle's frame of reference and not the world's. In other words, you turn the steering wheel right to turn the vehicle to the right.

Generalizing this concept for objects as well as views results in a technique called *display-relative mapping* (DRM). In DRM, mouse inputs are interpreted relative to the position and orientation of the view's 2D display in the 3D world; the display plane defines the coordinate mapping source space. DRM also provides a convenient solution for handling all three dimensions of the target's geometry. DRM is demonstrated in the DrmMapping example in part 4, section 19.3.2.

Positioning with DRM

Imagine you are sitting at a large square table with three friends. You are all trying to talk to one another but a flower arrangement in the middle of the table makes it difficult to see across the table. You reach out and move the flowers to the right. Now you can see your friend across the table. What if the friend to your right decided to move the flowers first? He/she might reach out and move the flowers to his/her right also. In both cases the viewer moved the flowers to the right relative to themselves; and in both cases the object remained at about the same distance from the viewer, at arm's length.

This example suggests a way to re-map the coordinate system to accommodate view changes while handling the target's full geometry specification: Move the target relative to the view space instead of the world space (as when each person moves the flowers to his/her respective right). While performing the move, keep the distance between the display plane and the target object constant (such as moving the flowers at arm's length). As with the flowers, the position of the target object in front of the view along the view's $-Z$ axis can be fixed at its present value. Assuming canonical coordinate mapping for view-relative object positioning, when the mouse moves right,

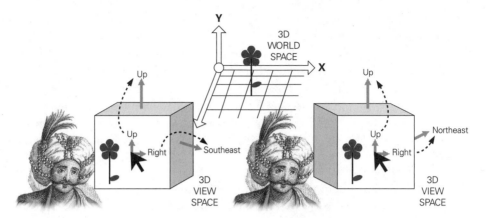

Figure 4.16   DRM with canonical coordinate mapping for view positioning

the target object will always appear to move right in the display regardless of how the view is positioned and oriented in the world.

What if the control target is the view itself? You can use the same setup as previously described for moving a target object, only fix the display-to-target distance at zero (since the target is the display). Moving the mouse right moves the view right, with any world objects in the display appearing to move left. As before, the control action remains intuitive because to the user it appears to be independent of the view's position or orientation. This is shown in figure 4.16.

Rotating with DRM

An analogous approach can be used for DRM rotation, but using angles instead of position: You rotate the target relative to the view's space, but fix the target's display-relative Z angle, called "twist," to its present value. In the flower example above, this is comparable to each viewer reaching out and spinning the flowers on the table (about its Y axis), or tilting the flowers toward or away from themselves (about its view-relative X axis), but not tipping the flowers side to side (zero twist).

As with DRM positioning, the DRM rotation technique works for both target objects and views. Assuming canonical coordinate mapping for object rotation relative to the view, when the mouse moves right, the target object will always appear to turn to the right regardless of how the view is situated in the world. An added benefit is that this display-relative rotation is independent of the sequence of up-down and left-right mouse movements, which wasn't the case when direct coordinate mapping was used.

4.5.3   World-relative mapping

With DRM the user can consistently and intuitively manipulate objects and navigate the view; and, for us as 3D user interface designers, it makes for a more general, and in the long run, easier solution than using direct mapping alone. You might even be tempted to think that DRM is the most intuitive and general technique possible for coordinate mapping and full target geometry specification. DRM is good, but there are situations where it does not help us at all, such as when we need world-relative constraints instead of display-relative movement. For example, what if we wanted to position and orient furniture in a room while always keeping the furniture on the floor and oriented upright, regardless of how the view is situated? DRM can't handle this.

Keeping the furniture flat on the floor is good, but to really convince the user that the furniture and room are real, he should be able to reach into the room and slide the desk along the floor toward a particular wall, such as the north wall. First consider how the view and room are situated. "Right" in the display meaning "north" in the room just won't do. In terms of coordinate mapping, the control interpretation must account for how the view is situated while imposing world-relative constraints to keep the furniture flat.

DRM isn't up to this job. It was intentionally designed to take the world space out of the equation and to effectively consider only the target as living in the view space. It knows nothing about world-relative matters. What is needed is a technique that has the view independence of DRM but which can move objects in a world-relative manner. Generalizing this concept for views as well as objects results in a technique called *world-relative mapping* (WRM). The WrmMapping example in section 19.4.4, demonstrates several flavors of WRM.

Positioning with WRM

Imagine that you are on a dock fishing with a friend, and you are both getting bored. You look down at the still surface of the lake and see a large leaf floating there. You both reel in your lines and hold your fishing poles at arm's length, pointing down into the water. Standing apart on the dock you both sight the leaf along the length of the pole, and you both start nudging the leaf around with your poles. Being especially observant, both you

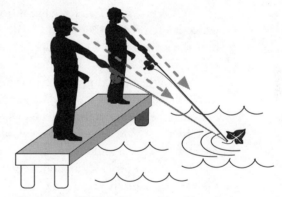

Figure 4.17   Fishing for a real-world analogy of WRM

and your friend notice that no matter where the two of you push the leaf, you are both always looking down the length of your poles towards the leaf. Also, the whole leaf can't be seen because your hand, holding the pole, is partially blocking your views of it. This suggests—you guessed it—a solution for how to move objects in world space regardless of how your view is situated.

In WRM, the 2D mouse position, indicated by the mouse cursor in the display (like your hand holding the fishing pole in front of you), is projected into the 3D world

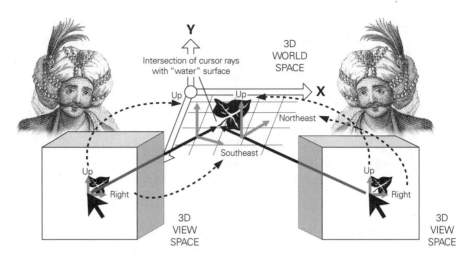

Figure 4.18 WRM with canonical coordinate mapping for object positioning

space in the direction of the view (e.g., sticking your pole into the water in the direction you are looking). The intersection of this ray with some surface in the world (like the pole intersecting the surface of the water) results in a world-relative 3D position (the leaf on the water) that appears to lie under the mouse cursor (like the leaf being partially hidden by your hand). This is shown in figure 4.18.

WRM provides a direct solution for fully specifying the target object's position, which is the precise 3D position of the intersection point; and it works regardless of how the view is situated (as it does for both you and your friend). It also handles the notion of moving the desk "north" in the furniture example: The user simply drags the desk in that direction as seen in the display, and the intersection point on the floor under the mouse cursor will follow accordingly, toward the north. It is interesting to note that the surface of intersection, which defines the mapping source space, does not have to be flat. The technique also works with non-flat surfaces, such as rolling terrain or the walls, floor, and ceiling in a room.

WRM also provides a good solution, but not an exact one, for fully controlling the view position. If you want to move the view relative to some surface in the world instead of an object, the simplest solution is to fix the distance between the view and the intersection point. From the earlier DRM discussion you already know how to maintain such a view-relative distance. With this hybrid technique—using DRM inside of WRM—as the view moves it will appear to slide along the surface in the world but at a fixed distance from the surface. If the surface of intersection is rolling terrain the resulting effect is a form of "terrain following."

Rotating with WRM

For view and object rotation you have to make an assumption about how to fully specify the target orientation. The simplest solution for both of these cases is to make the target's axis of rotation perpendicular to the surface of intersection. Applying this to the furniture example, to rotate the desk we can use a canonical coordinate mapping for object rotation, but leave the mouse Y coordinate disconnected. Thus the furniture only rotates about a vertical axis in the world space. Moving the mouse left-right spins the furniture left-right. Moving the mouse up-down has no effect, otherwise the furniture wouldn't remain flat on the floor as does real furniture.

To rotate your view you can use a fixed distance between the view and a target point on the surface of intersection, and use canonical coordinate mapping for view rotation. Thus, moving the mouse left-right makes the view orbit about the point in a circle of fixed radius parallel to the surface of intersection. Moving the mouse up-down makes the view tilt up and down about the point, in a circle of fixed radius perpendicular to the surface.

4.5.4   Object picking

In many of the examples presented so far you may have found it suspicious that the system always seems to know which object the user is dragging with the mouse. When the user drags the desk towards the north wall, how does the system know that the drag is referring to the desk and not the lamp on the desk, or the drawers attached to the desk? The answer to this question was actually revealed in the previous discussion on WRM, but in a rather primitive form.

A fundamental aspect of WRM is being able to determine a 3D position in the world that underlies the mouse cursor. This requires casting a ray into the scene from the user's virtual eye through the mouse position in the view's display plane. If the ray hits an object, such as the floor in the example, the 3D hit point can provide the fully specified 3D position of the object being dragged, such as the desk on the floor. Generalizing this concept results in a technique called *object picking*. Object picking, unlike WRM, is interested not so much in determining a hit point but in determining the object that the hit point belongs to. The implementation details are left to parts 3 and 4 of the book, and the technique is demonstrated in the OverEnabling example in section 19.1.4.

As in a 2D UI, the ability to pick an object in a 3D UI is invaluable. Picking not only tells the system which object the user is pointing to and wanting to drag, it is also the basis of mouseover feedback, which is a cornerstone of intuitive user feedback. With mouseover feedback, the designer can tell the user that an object is special, by highlighting it when the mouse is over it, and what to do with the object, such as revealing its drag handles.

You might be asking at this point what does object picking have to do with intuitive coordinate mapping? Well, it is certainly intuitive and useful in a control situation; it involves mapping 2D coordinates into 3D objects, and you might even say that it offers object-relative coordinate mapping. In other words, it is closely associated with the control interpretation chain, but it is not actually a link in it, such as DRM and WRM. Instead, picking is typically used as a traffic cop to tell the chain where to direct the control input—the desk, the lamp, or the drawers.

With DRM, WRM, and picking in your UI arsenal, you now have all the weapons you need to free the user from the bonds of present-day unintuitive 3D controls, whether in a display, world, or object-relative situation.

4.6 MIXED USAGE

It is common for different control interpretations, coordinate mappings, and personae to be used in combination. Combinations are usually specific to a given application or task and may only be intuitive in that limited context. Although you've seen several examples of mixed controls already, mixed usage was not highlighted as an issue. Here are a few specific examples of mixing control techniques.

- In some VRML browsers, such as Cosmo Player, a lot of use is made of first-person controls with mixed styles and coordinate mappings. For instance, in walk mode, mouse up-down controls the rate of forward *linear* motion relative to the *display*, but mouse left-right controls the rate of *angular* motion relative to the *world* vertical axis. Other navigation modes use *direct* controls for position and angle. The user can switch navigation modes on-the-fly using modifier keys, or with third-person virtual buttons in a dashboard placed in display space.
- In a flight simulator game that only approximates the physics of flight, the user might operate first-person controls to steer the direction of flight, with mouse up-down controlling *direct* vehicle pitch, and mouse left-right controlling the *rate* of vehicle turn. A third-person slider in display space controls the speed of flight.
- In a furniture layout application, third-person controls might orbit the view around the room, with *circular* gesture knobs for direction and tilt, and a *linear* gesture slider for zoom. The user selects furniture in the office with a *single-click* gesture; and moves furniture with a planar drag gesture using WRM to keep the furniture on the floor and movement relative to the world.

4.7 SUMMARY

Controls allow the user to talk to the system. The basis of control is input interpretation, which answers specific questions about what the control is controlling and how. At the highest level, controls can be categorized by persona: first, second, or third person. At a lower level, control interpretation can be thought of as a chain, starting with input devices and ending with target objects. Along the way the control action goes through a series of interpretations. The first stage involves primitives dealing with control origin, action, and gestures. The next stage involves coordinate mapping, which determines how to get a 2D input device to control a 3D target. The final stage, actuation, makes the connection from abstract input value to concrete target state. It deals with such matters as target state update, offset, and range clamping.

In terms of control, coordinate mapping and object picking are the crux of an intuitive user interface. Users want to think of problems in familiar frames of reference: themselves, represented by the view display itself, and the world, with WYSIWYG-like manipulation of objects. DRM and WRM are the techniques that offer intuitive coordinate mapping, independent of view position and orientation. Picking is the technique that gives the user intuitive object selection and dragging.

C H A P T E R   5

Feedback

Feedback is the designer's opportunity to guide the user through using an application. Feedback can also tell the user what the system is doing and provide the user with information about the data objects in the application. Feedback is one of two interactive dialogues between the application and the user. Conceptually, it occurs between the designer and the user, allowing the designer to inform and guide the user. The other dialogue involves visualization, which is covered in chapter 6.

In the real world, people rely on their natural ability to see spatial relationships to help them figure out new situations. If observation alone does not work, they experiment through physical manipulation of objects. When presented with a situation involving pegs and holes, a person can quickly surmise that a square peg will not fit into a round hole, and that square pegs must be rotated to fit into square holes. In a software application, however, the laws of physics rarely apply; direct physical manipulation is impossible, and it may not even be obvious to the user that anything could or should be done with the pegs and holes. To help compensate for these differences between the real and virtual world, user feedback in an application is essential. It tells the user that the pegs can be dragged, that some pegs can be rotated, that the holes are receptacles for the pegs, and perhaps even that some pegs do not fit into some holes.

The variety of feedback form and purpose is striking. Some forms, such as instruction manuals, are textual, are often provided in hard copy, and can convey a

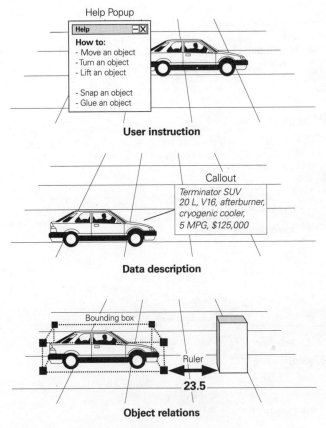

Help Popup

Help ─X

How to:
- Move an object
- Turn an object
- Lift an object

- Snap an object
- Glue an object

User instruction

Callout

Terminator SUV
20 L, V16, afterburner,
cryogenic cooler,
5 MPG, $125,000

Data description

Bounding box

Ruler

23.5

Object relations

Figure 5.1   Examples of information feedback

long and detailed message. Other forms, such as mouseover highlighting, are visual, can only be provided in soft copy, can convey only the briefest of messages, and tend to be idiomatic in nature. This chapter discusses a wide range of feedback techniques and concepts that can help make 3D user interfaces more intuitive. It presents feedback from several different and often complementary viewpoints: roles, elements, attributes, dynamics, and state. Although many are not specific to 3D, these basic techniques are just as vital to the success of a 3D UI as they are to a 2D interface, if not more so. A 3D UI introduces significant visual and operational complexity in comparison to a 2D UI, which requires more and better feedback to assist the user. As such, this discussion will maintain a strong 3D "perspective" in its treatment of feedback.

5.1   FEEDBACK ROLES

Anyone who sits down in front of a new application brings to the situation his/her own set of personal experiences, whether from real life or from other software applications, and perhaps even other 3D applications. If it were possible for the designer to

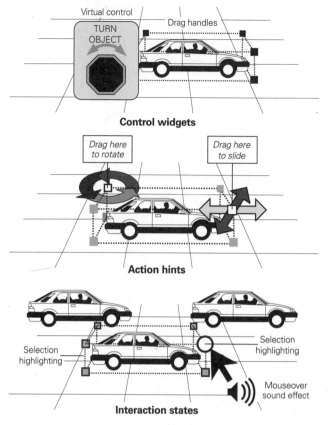

Figure 5.2 Examples of control feedback

anticipate the user's experiences, then he/she could design the perfect intuitive user interface. Except for special cases, it is impossible for the designer to anticipate what the user knows and what he/she will do in a given situation. This makes feedback from the designer to the user—whether observed, read, or heard—a necessity.

Feedback can be divided into two broad categories: information and control. *Information* feedback is passive in nature. It provides the user with information such as how to use the application, a control, or what a particular data object is named. By contrast, *control* feedback plays a more active role. It provides the user with the means to manipulate the data in an application, or to modify the configuration of the application itself. For example, in-scene (second-person) control handles might allow the user to slide and rotate an object within a scene; out-of-scene (third-person) controls might allow the user to open and arrange multiple display windows within the application.

The following sections classify information and control feedback according to the roles they play in an application, which are summarized in table 5.1. This "big picture" treatment of feedback is intended as a broad backdrop against which 3D applications have and must continue to play. Those categories that are most applicable to next generation UIs will be revisited in greater detail later in this chapter and in subsequent chapters.

Table 5.1 Classification of feedback roles in an application

Information feedback	• Passive in nature • Indirectly assists in using the application and data
User instruction	• Instructions on how to use the application and its controls • Example: User manuals, help systems, tutorials, wizards
Data description	• Information about data objects • Example: Product information, part number, size, and cost
Object relations	• Relationship of objects and surroundings • Example: Rulers, dimensioning, bounding boxes, connection points, and alignment marks
Control feedback	• Active in nature • Directly aids in controlling the application and data
Control widgets	• Visible manifestations of controls • Example: Color schemes, menus, buttons, knobs, and drag handles
Action hints	• Hints about how to use a control and what they do • Example: Tooltips, arrows, symbology, and animation
Interaction state	• Status and usability of an object or control • Example: Mouse-over, selection highlighting, disabled lowlighting, and sound effects

5.1.1 Information feedback

User instruction

One of the most venerable forms of feedback is the user's manual. It provides the user with instructions, usually detailed, about how to use an application. Such *instructional* feedback ranges from the traditional user's manual to fancy wizards. Often, instructional feedback exists apart from the application, such as in a separate help and tutorial system. Links between the user interface elements and the help system can provide context-sensitive help to the user. This same approach can be useful in an in-scene situation, with the user pointing to an object or its handle, hitting the F1 key, and information about the item popping up near the item in the scene.

Instructional feedback allows the designer to go into great detail about the design, appearance, and use of the application controls. It can describe at great length how the user can perform common and not-so-common tasks with the application. Typical forms of instructional feedback are user manuals, online help, multimedia tutorials, and various kinds of wizards. Tutorials are useful for quickly leading the user on a visual and audio tour of the user interface. Wizards can come in various forms, ranging from a list of steps with direct links to application controls, to a sequence of automatic operations with Next and Previous buttons.

Out-of-scene instructional feedback has played a leading role in traditional applications. In next-generation web-like and web-based applications, most users will not have the time to use instructional information such as manuals and online help. Instead, applications and their user interfaces will have to rely on their own intuitiveness and adopt more of a learn-as-you-go style. To this end, brief online tutorials, show-me-how wizards, and in-scene instructions will be crucial.

Data description

Another role of information feedback is to tell the user about the data objects that appear in the application. This is *descriptive* feedback. Descriptive feedback can be general in nature, such as why a product is better than that of a competitor, or specific, such as the name, part number, and cost of the selected data object. Typical forms of descriptive feedback range from the simple, such as a callout with the object's name, to the elaborate, such as a hyperlink on the object that leads to a multimedia presentation about it. Because of the relationship between a given class or instance of a data object and collateral information about the object, descriptive feedback is often supported by relational database concepts and technology.

Traditional forms of descriptive feedback may have put information about an object in a dialogue or highlighted the information in an entry in a table. Next-generation applications will benefit the most from in-scene forms of descriptive information such as callouts, which put timely information about an object in the scene right next to the object where the user is looking. Using such in-scene descriptive feedback should help to simplify the user interface by reducing the need for separate windows. Such feedback also minimizes confusion as to which object the information belongs, since there is a direct visual association between the callout information and the target object.

Object relations

Because of the visual ambiguity that exists when 3D objects are viewed on a 2D display, it is often helpful to enhance the spatial relationships that exist among objects in the scene. This can be done through information feedback that is often highly visual in nature. Such information, called *relational* feedback, can provide information about an object in relation to its surroundings, such as where a desk is in relation to the walls in a room. It can also provide information about how two or more objects are situated with respect to one another, such as whether two objects are connected together or just flush against one another.

A traditional way to provide such information to the user is to pop up a dialog box listing the distances between the target object and the walls, or listing which pairs of objects are connected. A more direct and visual way to provide this information is to indicate it in the scene on the objects themselves. Object distances might be shown as little rulers between the objects involved. Object connections might be shown with snap points at the connected vertices, and with a bounding box around the whole connected group. As with descriptive feedback, next-generation applications will benefit the most from such in-scene forms of relational feedback which puts the information in the scene exactly where and when it is needed.

Here are a few examples to better illustrate the significance of relational feedback. For relational feedback about an object and its surroundings, a bounding box might indicate the extent of the object, tic marks might indicate surrounding spatial alignment, projecting lines and planes might indicate vertical and horizontal proximity, and rulers might indicate numerically the object's relative position or angle. For relational feedback between objects, a bounding box might indicate object grouping, highlighting a common face might indicate when two objects are flush, snap points might indicate where objects are connected together, and a sound effect might play when two objects are aligned.

5.1.2   Control feedback

Control widgets

Controls do not have to have a visible form. In older applications that attempted in-scene manipulation, this was all too often the case. At best they would provide mouseover highlighting as a vague hint that the object could be dragged, with the user left to guess as to whether the dragging will cause the object to slide, rotate, stretch, or change color. *Control widgets* are the visible manifestation of application controls. This form of feedback gives the user the tangible means to control the application itself and the objects in the application. Traditional GUIs stick to control widgets such as menus and toolbars. More visually oriented 2D, and more recently 3D, applications attach control elements to the objects in the scene for direct manipulation of the objects. Often these control handles are shaped and colored to indicate the operation they perform.

At the lowest level of semantics, control widgets help the user to recognize what in the user interface is a control. A simple way to indicate this is by its appearance, such as a distinctive color scheme or shape. At a higher level of semantics, the shape of a control widget and its mouse cursor could give some indication of how the control should be used. For example, a handle for rotating an object might be in the shape of a circular arrow, and the cursor, when over a knob, might change into a stylized circular gesture. If used consistently and repeatedly throughout the UI the distinctive appearance becomes an idiom for a control, and the specific shapes become idioms for specific actions.

Action hints

The presence of artificial controls in a supposedly real virtual world can be a bit confusing to the user. The designer can help by emphasizing to the user what can be manipulated, how the manipulation is performed, and what will happen or is happening as a result of the manipulation. *Action hints* are brief messages to the user providing such clues about controls. An out-of-scene form of control hint common in many older applications showed a textual message in the status bar at the bottom of the application window, which provided hints about the control to which the mouse was pointing. A more recent in-scene version is the tooltip, which puts a textual hint right next to the control in question in the form of a callout. Hints, as with all the control feedback forms, are often tightly interwoven with the control itself. For the purposes of this discussion, the exact point where one stops and the other starts is not important.

Control feedback is intended as an integral part of the user interface. It also has the advantage of being able to tell the user what is happening with a control, right now and in the scene, which is something that traditional instructional feedback can't do. With action hints being part of the user interface, the visual forms of control feedback tend to be small and compact, like a callout, so as not to obscure its neighbors; and its audio forms tend to be terse, like a sound effect, so as not to be annoying when often repeated. Control hints can occur in-scene in the 3D world, such as a callout saying "turn object" or animated arrows circling the knob indicating that a circular gesture—not a linear one—is required. Control hints can also occur out-of-scene, in the 2D portion of the user interface, such as on toolbars, in data object drag-and-drop palettes, or as support for third-person controls in a control panel.

The use of dynamic control feedback, where elements appear or change their appearance in time, can give the user interface an almost tactile quality, with visual and audio effects helping to substitute for the feel of real controls. Because of their importance in next-generation applications, dynamic and especially tactile-like feedback will be discussed later.

Interaction state

A cross between control widgets and action hints, but yet distinctive enough to be given its own category, is *interaction state* feedback. State feedback indicates the status and usability of a control, an object, or specifically the controls on an object. A change of color and brightness makes a good state indicator, such as disabled controls appearing dim or lowlighted, and selected controls that are ready for action appearing bright or highlighted. Shape and color can be combined to provide controls with a more dramatic and suggestive appearance, such as the 3D chiseled look of buttons indicating whether or not the button is pressed.

There are many uses for state feedback, and it is often inseparably intertwined with the other control feedback forms. For example, pausing over an object—a change of interaction state—might trigger the appearance of a tooltip showing the name of the object—descriptive feedback. Sometimes it may not be obvious to the user where the "hot spot" is on a control. At other times it may not be easy for the user to position the mouse on the control, especially if the control appears small in the scene. Mouse-over state feedback can tell the user when he is on a control and in the hot spot. Such state changes can be manifested through the object's appearance, the cursor's appearance, the control's appearance, the playing of a sound effect, or all of the above. If used consistently and judiciously, an appearance or sound can serve as a familiar and reassuring control idiom for the user.

One of the more sophisticated applications of all the control feedback forms is seen in drag-and-drop. Control handles might appear on a drag source object when it is selected, and action hint "no-drop" and "drop" icons, driven by the mouseover state, may appear on potential drop targets. Mouseover highlighting of the control handles aids the user in locating them, and the state change from "over" to "drag" might cause the handles to disappear so they don't obscure the work area in the scene. As an action hint, the cursor shape could indicate the nature of the operation, such as a normal cursor for a move, an added plus sign for a copy, and an added arrow for a link.

5.2   BASIC ELEMENTS

Feedback roles are rather abstract in nature, focusing on how the feedback benefits the user. To make feedback tangible, something more concrete is required. That something is a feedback *element*. Feedback elements are textual, graphical, and audio components used by the designer to fulfill the roles of feedback in an application. There is no one-to-one mapping between elements and roles: A given feedback element can be used in a number of roles. For example, a simple textual label could provide user instruction, data description, or action hint feedback depending on what it says and where it is said.

The elements described here are the more basic ones. These elements, which are summarized in table 5.2, can be used as-is; or more complicated and application-specific ones can be built from them and their concepts. Many of the elements are demonstrated in the TargetDecorating example in section 20.3.4. Some might ask why go into such detail over such basic elements? Although a lot of the discussion focuses on 3D and especially in-scene feedback, which should be of direct benefit, more importantly it addresses the question of why one form of feedback might be better than another in a given situation. Such basic concepts are durable, and can be applied to the more sophisticated forms of feedback to come.

One of the more important jobs for feedback in a 3D UI is to help give the user a sense of feel during direct manipulation. In the real world we have tactile feedback, we can pick up and examine objects, and we can walk around objects and through their surroundings. These capabilities are important for judging how objects are situated with one another and their surroundings. In a POCS these are denied to us.

Instead, artificial means are needed to explicitly show the user the relationships of the objects in 3D space. Chapter 8, which looks at manipulation, will discuss more sophisticated forms of feedback, specifically 3D relational and pseudo-tactile feedback (PTF), which together can provide users with a feel for their virtual world.

Table 5.2 Basic feedback elements and their distinguishing characteristics

Identifiers	• Identify and decorate controls; proxies for data objects • Labels and icons; static appearance; integral part of the control or proxy
Callouts	• Like a label or icon but detached from its host; can decorate data objects • Dynamic placement; can live in display space
Tooltips	• Like a callout • Dynamic visibility; controlled manually or by interaction state
Indicators	• Like a callout; shaped graphics for action hints and drag handles • Dynamic appearance; controlled by interaction state
Handles	• Idiom for control and selection; widget for direct manipulation • Dynamic appearance; controlled by interaction state
Cursor	• Small indicator; tracks the mouse position on the display screen • Dynamic shape, automatic placement, useful in many feedback roles, overused
Audio	• Does not compete with visual feedback; amenable to long messages • Not reliable—sound can be turned off or too low
Sound Effects	• Audio that is brief and idiomatic • Action confirmation, differentiation, and quantification

5.2.1 Identifiers

The simplest feedback elements are labels and icons, which are collectively called *identifiers*. As their name suggests, they identify entities in the UI, such as controls and data objects. For example, labels could name controls in a control panel, and icons could distinguish buttons in a toolbar. Identifiers can be proxies for data objects, such as names in a list widget or labeled icons in a drag-and-drop palette.

In their most basic form, identifiers are an integral part of the host control or object to which they belong. They are static, always present, and live in the same space as the host. If the host is in the world space, then the host and its identifiers can be covered up by other objects—any objects—in the world space. Also, legibility of the host's identifiers would be a function of the host's position and orientation relative to the view display. The host object's identifier, such as a part number, may become illegible long before the user is unable to manipulate the object itself, such as a desk. It is often desirable for data objects to be clearly identified even when subjected to such geometric distortions encountered during in-scene manipulation. For example, the user may need to see the part numbers on the furniture in an office layout application, no matter where the pieces are located in the room or how the view is oriented.

Another problem with ordinary labels and icons is that such static elements tend to be wasteful of precious screen real estate. In a toolbar it is desirable to have both an icon and a label on the buttons, but often there is barely enough room for just the icon. Also, it may be difficult to fit the identifier into a host object, such as a part number on a small desk lamp. The next feedback element offers a less static and more ubiquitous solution for such situations.

5.2.2   Callouts

The *callout* is a special form of identifier that is particularly suited for in-scene use. A callout consists of text or graphics usually in a small box that is positioned near a host object or control. The callout can be connected to the host with a line pointing to a particular spot on the host. This helps to clearly associate the two but it can also add to the visual clutter in the scene.

Being detached from its host gives the callout an advantage over its integral and static cousin, the identifier. In more sophisticated variations, the placement of a callout relative to its host and the style of the line connecting it could be selected automatically according to the local situation. For example, if the host object is near the edge of the display, then the callout could be positioned away from the edge so that it can be seen in whole. Or, if the host is near other objects with callouts, then the callouts could be mutually arranged to prevent their overlap.

Unlike an ordinary label or icon, the callout doesn't have to be an integral part of its host. Instead it can be positioned near the host—off to the side and out of the way—instead of on the control or object. More importantly, the callout and its host can live in different spaces. For in-scene use, the host object could live in world space, and the callout could live in display space. Such an arrangement permits the callout to appear overlaid in the display, in front of any world objects, at a constant size, and with a fixed orientation. This makes the callout visible and readable even though its host object may be obscured, far away, or turned around in the view. These matters, which concern visualization, will be addressed further in chapter 6.

Callouts are good at providing in-scene descriptive feedback, such as abstract information about a concrete data object. For example, in a control application, a numerical callout attached to a pipe valve might indicate the flow rate through the valve. To warn the operator of special situations, such as overflow or underflow conditions, an iconic callout such as a big red exclamation point could be added next to the numerical one. For situations requiring more extensive descriptive information, callouts provide a convenient way to attach hyperlinks to the host object, with the callout itself being the hyperlink. Clicking on the callout might open a separate window or browser describing the host object in greater detail, such as in a product ad or a detailed engineering drawing.

5.2.3   Tooltips

A drawback of the callout is that it is always visible, which can obscure areas around the host object and which can add to the clutter in the display. An important and popular variation of the callout that addresses these problems is the *tooltip*. The tooltip is like a callout but it remains hidden until needed or requested. In recent years the tooltip has become ubiquitous in GUI design to name user interface controls without cluttering up the presentation as would static labels. Figure 5.3 shows a tooltip on a drag handle that instructs the user how to use the handle.

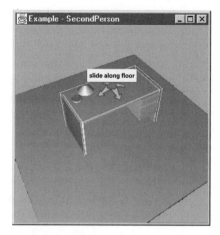

Figure 5.3   Tooltip on a drag handle instructs the user what to do.

The most common way to control a tooltip's visibility is through interaction state: Show it when the mouse cursor pauses over the host object, and hide it when the cursor starts to move again. This form of the tooltip is also called a *flyover*. Tooltip visibility could also be controlled manually, with the user specifying the type of information to be shown or the type of host object to be described, and the corresponding tooltips appearing. Tooltips could also appear automatically as a result of the application mode, such as showing them in a design application when in "design" mode but hiding them when in "demo" mode.

The previous chapter on controls discussed how modifier keys are at a disadvantage in comparison to the mouse as an input device because the mouse permits mouse-over feedback to tell the user that the item the mouse is over is controllable. In a POCS there is no keyover feedback equivalent. The tooltip offers a way to help make up for this deficiency. In situations where a control or object can be manipulated using arrow keys, or where its manipulation can be influenced using modifier keys, a tooltip message or idiomatic icon could appear as an action hint to the user.

5.2.4   Indicators

Callouts are good at conveying narrative, quantitative, or iconic feedback. Sometimes, however, it is useful for the feedback element to have some shape other than a box or a compact graphic. For example, controls are action oriented. They often demand action hint feedback that is directional in nature, such as large arrows, to tell the user how to manipulate the control, or how the target object will be or is being affected by the control. *Indicators* are feedback elements that have many of the characteristics of callouts but are specially shaped to guide the user or to indicate some action. Like callouts, they can appear separate from the host control or object and are often overlaid in the display so they are less likely to be obscured.

By far the most common form of indicator is the directional arrow with its many variations, such as straight arrows, curved arrows, multi-directional arrows, and single- and double-headed arrows. Arrows are good at showing the kind of gesture required to manipulate a control or the type of constraint imposed on the target object's motion. For example, a circular arrow might appear next to a knob control directing the user to turn it instead of sliding it; and a set of four-way arrows over an object might serve as handles for sliding the object in specific directions. Figure 5.4 shows such an indicator over an object, which tells the user that manipulation causes the object to slide horizontally.

Figure 5.4 The four-way arrow indicator tells the user that the object can slide horizontally.

Indicators can also be symbolic in nature, indicating the system's consent, prohibition, or preference for user interaction. For example, a check mark might indicate preferred selections, "Xs" might indicate disallowed selections, and an exclamation point might indicate selections that are in conflict with some data configuration constraint. In an earlier example, drop and no-drop indicators were used to indicate which objects were valid drop targets during a drag-and-drop operation. Indicators can also be used for relational feedback, showing spatial and conceptual relationships between objects. For example, the topological associations among nodes in a data network might be indicated with interconnecting shaped or patterned lines; and anticipated associations might be indicated with specially decorated arrows, such as a lightning bolt pointing to the closest snap point during a drag.

Another variation on the indicator theme is to vary the arrow size or length to convey quantitative information, such as a small arrow for fine control adjustments, and a big one for gross adjustments. An indicator's size and length can show the magnitude and direction of abstract data, such as flow rate and direction through a pipe valve. Because indicators are used where action is involved, animation is a natural. For example, a static arrow might indicate potential action whereas an animated arrow might indicate that an action is in progress, such as a drag. The general benefits of animation in a UI for drawing user attention and for indicating transitions of action or state have long been recognized.

The distinction between an icon and an indicator might seem subtle because that distinction is based more on function than form. Although not critical to the discussion, an icon tends to play a passive role by acting as a graphical substitute for an object's name, by acting as a surrogate for a real object in a palette, or by acting as a placeholder for a hyperlink in a scene. Indicators, on the other hand, play a more active role. They often tell the user to do something, to go in a particular direction, or not to do something, and why.

5.2.5 Handles

If the main goal of an application is to show the user a view of the virtual world, then the fewer non-world items that an application adds to the scene, the better. There is a large class of applications, however, that involve direct manipulation. Direct manipulation—second person—controls allow the user to directly manipulate objects in the scene by dragging the object itself. Without some form of feedback (for example, artificial, non-world items), the user is left to guess whether or not an object can be manipulated and how. We might use labels and callouts to tell the user that an object can be slid or rotated, but after using the application for a minute or two, such wordy messages might seem superfluous and perhaps even annoying because they obscure the surrounding scene. Another issue is that in the real world you can reach out and simultaneously slide and rotate objects with a single movement of your hand. In a POCS we are limited to manipulating only two of many possible degrees of freedom (three translation, three rotation, three scale, and so on.) at a time. So, how can we show the user that direct manipulation is available, while providing convenient translation and rotation of objects in the scene?

From the previous section you should already know that in-scene control widget feedback is able to fill this role. The specific elements for such feedback are called *handles*. Handles are compact but distinctive control widgets attached to objects that the user can directly manipulate. They serve as both an idiom for direct manipulation and as the controls for performing the manipulation. More than one type of handle can be attached to an object at a time. Each handle provides a different type of control action, such as sliding, turning, and stretching. To minimize clutter in the scene, the number and type of handle elements are usually limited. More importantly, the handles are usually visible only

Figure 5.5 The circular indicator over the target object also serves as a drag handle.

when the host object is ready to be directly manipulated. Because only one object in the scene is ready for manipulation at any given time, many applications make control handles serve double feedback duty as idioms for object selection as well as for direct manipulation. Such mouseover and selection status characteristics are handled by interaction state feedback. As with callouts, usability is enhanced if the active control handles are always visible, sized, and oriented for optimal use. Figure 5.5 shows a circular indicator over an object that also serves as a handle for rotating the object.

5.2.6   Cursor

A cursor is a special form of indicator that is tightly coupled with the physical implementation of a POCS. It is automatically positioned on the computer screen by the mouse, and it appears as a small graphics entity such as an icon that is overlaid on the display in front of everything else, even other display space objects—it has the highest overlap priority. A change in its shape often indicates mouseover status, such as when the mouse is over an active control, a selectable object, or a candidate drop target in a drag-and-drop operation.

Designers often use the cursor as the primary and sometimes the only means for providing user control feedback. There are a number of reasons for this: The cursor is a consistent feature in all POCS; its shape can be easily changed; it is always at the focus of the user's attention; and its feedback can be easily added to application data and controls at the last minute. These are good (and not so good) reasons to use the cursor as a feedback element, but over-reliance on a single element drastically limits the feedback message to the user. It is like playing a single-finger version of a symphony's melody on a piano. The listener might be able to recognize the piece but the experience can't even begin to compare with that from a full orchestra. Such lack of communication from designer to user can leave the user guessing as to what to do or what is going on, which detracts from the intuitiveness of the user interface. Using even a few of the many feedback elements and techniques described in this chapter can only but improve the quality of the message.

A common and somewhat consistent use of the cursor is for modifier and arrow key action hinting, such as when a key can influence an object's manipulation, or when a key is pressed and actively doing something. For the cursor, and action hinting in general, to be effective in this capacity the feedback must be immediate. When the key is pressed or released and the modification action has correspondingly changed, the cursor shape should change to reflect this. This is often not the case in traditional applications. Without such immediate feedback, when the cursor eventually does change, the user won't know if the change was due to the modifier key change or due to a change in some other condition. Immediate feedback imposes the control interpretation requirement on modifier keys that they can be pressed or released any time before or during a drag operation. Although this is often the exception in traditional applications, it is generally the rule in system-supported drag-and-drop operations. For example, in many systems, pressing a particular modifier key before or during a drag-and-drop operation immediately changes the operation from a move to a copy, with a plus sign (+) appearing in the cursor graphic. Releasing the key during the drag changes the operation back to a move.

In general, the designer should keep the cursor message as simple and focused as possible, and he/she should rely on other feedback techniques to provide the rest of the feedback message to the user.

5.2.7 Audio

Unlike visual elements, audio information never competes for precious screen real estate, and it never obscures the contents of the display. Also, because we experience audio inputs on a separate sensory "channel" than visual ones, users can choose to ignore the audio while continuing to use the application. In other words, audio messages can be more detailed than visual ones, and the user doesn't have to wait for them to complete before continuing on with the job at hand. For example, in a design application, visual cues might indicate when and where objects can be connected, and visual warnings may warn against connecting two objects together. If the user tries to connect them anyway, a verbal message might explain why the connection is not allowed. In this way, the audio supplements the visual information to provide a much more detailed message. At any time during the message, however, the user can continue on with the work and not wait for the message to finish.

Audio has some drawbacks. The most obvious one is that, unlike visual feedback, audio feedback can not be readily or precisely localized (even if spatialized sound were used). Because of this, when a sound occurs it has to be associated with the control or object that the user is actively manipulating; otherwise, the user won't know to what the sound corresponds. On a more practical level, sound is not a reliable form of feedback. The user may have the sound turned down or disabled completely, and ambient noise can mask sound effects and interfere with verbal message comprehension. As such, sound should be a secondary means of feedback, supplementing visual feedback.

Another drawback of audio is the perception that users don't like sound. In his book *About Face*, Alan Cooper makes a compelling argument for using lots of audio feedback in applications, but not just any kind of audio feedback. He suggests using a steady stream of gentle sound effects to let the user know that actions are proceeding along as expected. The emphasis here is on gentle *positive* feedback, which is quite different from the obnoxious *negative* feedback that is traditionally employed in user interfaces—seemingly as punishment for wrong actions. To this end, many of the examples in part 4 use gentle action hint and interaction state sound effects.

The foregoing guidelines on sound use are augmented here to accommodate verbal messages, which are great at providing detailed information without visual interference. Verbal messages should be used sparingly. If they are too common they will be ignored, like background conversations in a restaurant. Even worse, if the audio is jarring or repetitive it might become annoying—like the proverbial broken record—and the user may disable the sound completely. In general, verbal messages should explain the abnormal, not the normal; and, they should be loud and distinct enough to be understood, but not annoying. In contrast, sound effects should be gentle and constant, providing an undertone of reassurance to the user that user interaction is proceeding normally.

5.2.8   Sound effects

Verbal elements are useful but sometimes something much shorter and more idiomatic is needed, such as a *sound effect*. Sound effects are useful for action hint and interaction state feedback, especially as reinforcement for visual feedback effects. Like visual effects, they can be triggered by interaction states. For example, when the mouse moves over a handle that slides the target object, the handle highlights and a sound effect might play. When the mouse moves over an adjacent handle that rotates the object, that handle highlights and a different sound effect might play. Thus, the user is told in multiple ways that the control is ready for action, and that one control is for sliding and the other is for rotating—two very common operations in a 3D user interface. Such multi-source reinforcement of feedback is especially important in situations where the visual presentation is crowded and the user finds it hard to distinguish the precise handle over which the cursor is positioned. Sound effects are used in the TargetDecorating example in section 20.3.4 to indicate mouseover and start of drag.

   Sound effects can also be useful in situations where the user's attention is divided between two places in the display. For example, in a third-person control, the user might be turning a knob with the mouse while observing the object it controls spinning in the scene. A sound effect can play when a control limit is reached to warn the user that further target movement should not be expected. In another example, the user may be sliding an object until it is aligned with some other object, perhaps in another part of the scene. As relational feedback, a tic mark might appear next to the objects when alignment is achieved, but a sound effect might be a better way to indicate alignment because the user may not know where to look for the tic mark or may overlook it in the scene clutter. Even better, the sound might rise and fall in tone to provide feedback as to how close the objects are to alignment. Such multi-source feedback is used in some electronic stud finders. As the device approaches a stud, a tone rises and more of its indicator lights illuminate. Sound effects are also important in pseudo-tactile feedback, where sight and sound cues help substitute for touch. In this capacity, sound effects help reinforce the suggestion of physical sensation, the same way that the thud of a bullet or the crunch of a fist does in a movie or game.

5.3   *VISUAL ATTRIBUTES*

Feedback elements are artificial. They are not meant to be part of the application's "real" world. Instead, they stand apart from the application's data, telling the user what to do through information feedback and providing the user with the means for doing it in the role of control feedback. It is important that the user recognize this distinction between the artificial and the real to avoid any possibility of confusing what in the scene is part of a real data object and what was artificially added by the designer to make the user's job easier. Looking at this another way, feedback elements need to call attention to themselves so that the user can readily find them in the scene and use them. For similar reasons, feedback elements need to be easily distinguished from one another, such as two drag handles on the same object that perform similar but different functions such as horizontal sliding and vertical lifting.

For in-scene use, it is often desirable for feedback elements to stand up to the visual distortions introduced by in-scene manipulation. They need to remain usable no matter where they are in the scene or how they are oriented relative to the view. Having them remain visible even if other objects in the world are in the way can also be useful, such as always being able to get to the selected object's drag handles. If feedback elements don't stand out or remain legible under normal use, then the user has to waste time on non-productive actions—playing hide-and-seek with the control elements, or jockeying the view and data objects so they are legible.

The visual attributes of feedback elements and their collective presentation in the scene are key to an effective 3D UI. Issues include element distinctiveness, size, orientation, visibility, and density. To avoid getting ahead of things, these and other issues surrounding the visual aspects of feedback will be covered in chapter 6, which is devoted to concepts and techniques concerning visualization. Techniques for handling the visualization problems of in-scene manipulation are also addressed. As with feedback roles and elements, visual attributes offer the designer yet another perspective on the same problem, that of incorporating effective feedback into next-generation applications.

5.4   SIMPLE DYNAMICS

Clutter can be a real problem if feedback elements are static and always visible. The elements make the scene appear busy, can obscure the subject and the surrounding work area, and can distract the user's attention from the focus of the immediate task. This is much more of an issue in 3D user interfaces than in traditional ones because feedback, although spread throughout the 3D scene, can appear rather dense when projected onto the 2D display. Perspective foreshortening in 3D scenes also contributes to feedback clutter and other usability difficulties.

Static elements are able to send only a limited repertoire of messages to the user. They can tell the user what something is and what to do with it, but they can't tell the user when something is happening, such as when the mouse is over a drag handle, when a control is active, or when an object is selected or disabled. Adding simple dynamics to feedback elements can address this problem and that of clutter. Showing elements only when they are needed or requested helps to reduce clutter. Changing the appearance of elements as a function of the interaction state helps to tell the user what is going on. Feedback dynamics offers yet another dimension to consider in the problem space of designing effective 3D UI feedback.

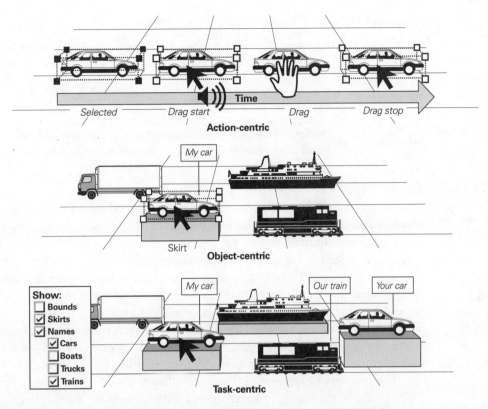

Figure 5.6   Examples of transient feedback, which involves simple dynamics

In the previous sections, reference has been made to feedback dynamics. For example, a tooltip was described as a special form of callout that shows itself when the mouse pauses over its host object. This section delves a bit deeper into such transient forms of feedback. *Transient feedback* is a collective term for the simpler forms of dynamic feedback, as distinct from its more sophisticated PTF relatives. Transient feedback appears and disappears upon user request or when the application determines that it may be needed. The common thread here is that the feedback element says what it has to say, and goes away or is sent away when its job is done. It doesn't hang around the scene cluttering things up; and the very fact that it appears or disappears can alert the user to pay attention. The classes of transient feedback are summarized in table 5.3. The easy part of transient feedback is showing and hiding an element; the hard part is figuring out when to do it.

Table 5.3 Classes and characteristics of transient feedback

Action-centric	• Triggered by user interaction with target objects—in-scene or out-of-scene • Combines mouse location and action, and target selection and status
Object-centric	• Reduces clutter; puts only feedback at the center of the action • Local; hard to see the big picture; feedback is often after-the-fact
Task-centric	• Shows all feedback matching a set of criteria; manual or automatic • Global; increases clutter; easily combined with other transient forms

5.4.1 Action-centric feedback

Detecting when the mouse is paused over an object to show a feedback element is a simple and effective form of transient feedback. It is so effective that tooltips have become quite ubiquitous in user interfaces of all sorts. We all have seen tooltips in action, but understanding why they are so effective can be helpful in adding dynamics to other feedback elements. In a tooltip, the element is shown where the user is most likely to need it, which is near the mouse. It's also shown when the user is most likely to need it, which is when the mouse pauses while the user tries to decide what to do. The user can easily control when the feedback disappears by moving the cursor somewhere else or by starting to use the control. Also the user can control when the feedback reappears by moving the cursor away from and then back over the host object.

The concept of triggering feedback according to mouse-object interaction can be generalized beyond just mouseover. Mouse actions such as "start of drag," "end of drag," and the "drop" in a drag-and-drop operation can also trigger transient feedback. For example, when a drag operation commences, the tooltips and control handles on the host object might disappear, and relational feedback such as rulers and bounding boxes might appear. This provides the user with only what is needed when it is needed thereby minimizing clutter. Looking beyond simple mouse actions and toward the semantics of those actions, object and control selection can also serve as a trigger for transient feedback. Other than directly clicking on the target object, selection might be performed manually through a third-person control, such as selecting the name of the target object in a list, or programmatically, such as the result of a search for a particular object.

5.4.2 Object-centric feedback

So far, dynamic feedback has been discussed only as affecting a single object. For example, the tooltip and the bounding box might appear at different times during the user's interaction, but they appear only on the one target object affected by the interaction. This notion of *object-centric* dynamic feedback can be good, as was noted in the analysis of why the tooltip is so popular. But it has drawbacks.

One problem with object-centric dynamics is that only a few of the feedback elements can be seen at one time. Recall that an advantage of action-centric feedback is that feedback elements could be made to appear only on the active target object, as a means for reducing in-scene clutter. Such an approach, however, does not permit the user to size up the overall situation in a scene through its feedback elements. For example, it might be useful for the user to see all the data objects with their bounding boxes at the same time to get a feel for how objects are situated with respect to one another. Of course, this is at odds with the notion that clutter is bad—no one said 3D UI design was going to be easy.

Another problem is that the user is aware of the feedback only after the fact—after the target object becomes active. If the user doesn't suspect that some target object in the world or display might harbor a tooltip or a particular handle, then he/she might not stop there to see it. Some useful information about the object or the fact that it can be manipulated in a certain way might be completely missed. Who hasn't played "bumblebee" with the mouse, flitting around the GUI trying to read all the tooltips to find a particular toolbar function (in spite of the intuitive icons), or poking around the data objects looking for the wanted but well-hidden control handle?

5.4.3 Task-centric feedback

An alternative to object-centric transient feedback is to show all the feedback elements that match some set of selection criteria. This way all the feedback elements that might be helpful in a given situation can be seen at the same time. The target group of such *task-centric* dynamic feedback can be specified by the host object type, such as all the feedback associated with desk objects; or by the feedback information type, such as all the part number callouts. More than one type of criterion can be used at a time, such as all the part number callouts but only on the desks.

Such global, task-oriented selection can occur automatically according to application state, such as hiding all feedback when in demonstration mode, or manually by the user. For example, when the user chooses a rotation tool from a tool palette in place of a slide tool, the application might show the rotation handles on all the objects and hide all the slide handles. Going full circle away from global, task-oriented feedback and back toward local, object-centric feedback, the two can work together. For example, in a sort of reverse tooltip, the user might request that the part numbers of all the data objects be shown in the scene. When the mouse is over a data object, however, its and its neighbors' part numbers disappear so that the part number callouts do not interfere with the user's manipulation and placement of the target object. The combinations and permutations on the themes of action versus object versus task-based selection and presentation criteria are almost endless.

5.5 INTERACTION STATES

Interaction states seem to keep coming up. They should. Interaction is what user interfaces are all about—or at least should be. *Interaction states* are the low-level dynamic and functional states associated with data objects and feedback elements in an application. Interaction states and the events that trigger them can be grouped into the categories of mouse action, drag-and-drop action, object selection, and object status or condition. Interaction states from more than one of these categories can apply to a given feedback element at the same time, such as the mouse being over a selected object. Also, interaction event detection can be local to a specific object, such as when the mouse is over a particular drag handle; or it can be global, such as when selecting an object causes all other objects in the scene to be deselected. Of the many different windows onto the world of feedback, interaction states offer an almost primal view, focusing on the action-reaction aspect of the user-interface definition in chapter 1.

The following discussions on interaction states and how they are manifested in feedback appearance may seem familiar. Many are commonplace in traditional GUI applications. Often, however, this simple form of dynamic feedback is minimal or completely absent from the in-scene portion of 3D applications. This is unfortunate because the 3D user needs more help, not less, than the traditional GUI user. With the ability to detect so many interaction states the question arises, how can all these states be manifested in a feedback element? A technique for managing the many state-driven appearances of a feedback element is included as part of this discussion on interaction states. Since both the states and the technique for manifesting them are such an important aspect of 3D user interfaces, they are covered here in detail as well as in part 4, starting with the MultiShaping example in section 20.1.6.

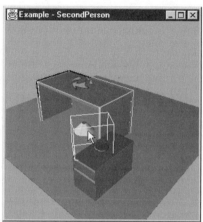

Figure 5.7   Interaction state feedback shows the desk selected and the mouse over the lamp.

Here is a recap of some of the many possibilities for state-driven feedback appearance. Mouse and selection states can drive the showing and hiding of transient feedback elements, such as callouts and control handles; and color, intensity, and brightness attributes make good visual indicators of action, selection, and status. For example, with a virtual control such as a slider or knob, when the mouse enters over the control you can highlight it by brightening its colors and increasing the contrast of its color scheme. During a drag you can change the control's color hues and brightness as an idiom to reassure the user that the control is active. While the control is disabled, you can lowlight it by darkening its colors and reducing the contrast of its color scheme. For more complex actions, such as during the phases of a drag-and-drop operation, shape in addition to color might be used. For example, target objects would highlight when the mouse is over them and the mouse cursor shape would change to indicate that a drag is active, with the specific shape indicating the type of drag—move, copy, or link.

Although interaction states are hard to show in a static image, figure 5.7 shows a desk selected, with its manipulation indicator and a medium intensity bounding box showing, while the high intensity bounding box around the lamp indicates mouse-over. You can try it for yourself in the SecondPerson example in section 22.2.2

5.5.1 State definitions

The following classification is but one of many possible ways to identify interaction states. These have been useful in developing design applications that are heavy on in-scene manipulation. There are, however, other ways to organize and define them. Also, don't be overwhelmed by the number of states described here. In most situations, feedback elements will need to respond only to a very small number of them.

Raw mouse action states

Raw mouse states are defined simply by the interplay of the mouse position relative to a given target object. The status of the mouse buttons is not a factor. Raw states are more important for implementation, such as in a mouse motion "sensor," but are included here for completeness.

- *Normal.* The normal state is true when the *over* state is false.
- *Over.* The *over* state is true while the mouse is actually over the target, regardless of the mouse button status.
- *Pause.* The *pause* state goes true when the raw *over* state is true and the mouse stops moving for a predefined duration. It goes false when the mouse moves.

Mouse action states

Mouse states are defined by the interplay of the button status and the mouse position relative to a given target object. Note that the drag state defined here is a bit different from the drag state that will be defined later for drag-and-drop. Here, drag is intended as a simple indication that the user is dragging the mouse, and not as some higher-level semantic such as an object being dragged so it can be dropped elsewhere.

- *Normal.* The *normal* state is true when the *over* state is false.
- *Over.* The *over* state goes true when the mouse enters over the target while no buttons are down; and, it stays true as long as the mouse remains over the target or while the *drag* state remains true for the target (e.g., a drag is in progress).
- *Pause.* The *pause* state goes true when the *over* state is true, no buttons are down, *pause* has not previously occurred since *over* went true, and the mouse stops moving for a predefined duration; and, it goes false when the mouse moves, or the button or keyboard status changes.
- *Down.* The *down* state goes true when the *over* state is true and a button goes down; and it stays true as long as that button stays down (e.g., the mouse remains captured).

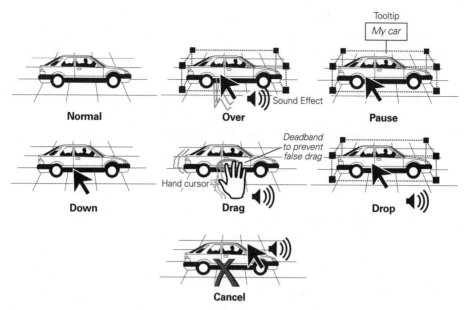

Figure 5.8   Examples of object manipulation feedback based on mouse action states

- *Drag.*   The *drag* state goes true when *down* is true for a duration longer than a click or the mouse moves beyond a predefined deadband around the down position. It stays true until the *down* state goes false. Note that incorporating a time factor and deadband into the drag operations is important for preventing false drags.
- *Drop.*   The *drop* state goes true when drag goes false. It stays true until the mouse moves, or the button or keyboard status changes.
- *Cancel.*   The *cancel* state goes true when a drag is canceled, such as when the Escape key is pressed while *drag* is true; and it stays true until the mouse moves, or the button or keyboard status changes.

Drag-and-drop action states

The following phases occur during a typical drag-and-drop (DnD) operation:

- *Over-no-drag.*   The *over-no-drag* state is true while the mouse is over a target that is not a potential drag (source) target and DnD *drag* is false.
- *Over-drag.*   The *over-drag* state is true while the mouse is over a potential drag (source) target and DnD *drag* is false.
- *Drag.*   The *drag* state goes true when the mouse *drag* goes true and *over-drag* is true; and it stays true until mouse *drag* goes false or the DnD operation is canceled, such as when the Escape key is pressed.
- *Over-no-drop.*   The *over-no-drop* state is true while the mouse is over a target that is not a potential drop target and DnD *drag* is true.

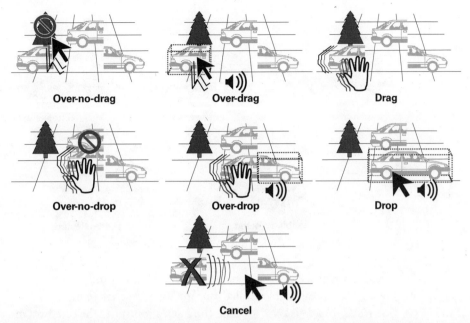

Figure 5.9 Examples of object manipulation feedback based on drag-and-drop action states

- *Over-drop.* The *over-drop* state is true while the mouse is over a potential drop target and DnD *drag* is true.
- *Drop.* The *drop* state goes true when the mouse *drag* goes false and *over-drop* is true; and it stays true until the mouse moves, or the button or keyboard status changes.
- *Cancel.* The *cancel* state goes true when a drag-and-drop operation is canceled, such as when the Escape key is pressed while *drag* is true; and it stays true until the mouse moves, or the button or keyboard status changes.

Target selection states

Functional selection states are more difficult to generalize than mouse states. Some possibilities are to differentiate between manual and automatic selection, and between single and double mouse-click selection. Other situations require multiple selection states that are generic, such as for a multiple-state push button, or that are application specific, such as for cycle-selecting target object scope (e.g., object part, object, object's group) or object control handles (e.g., slide, rotate, lift). The selection states here are rather generic, but suggestions for alternative or semantic designations are provided in parentheses.

- *Selection0 (Normal).* The first selection state. (Not selected.)
- *Selection1 (Auto-selected).* The second selection state. (Automatically selected by the application, such as the default selection. The distinction between auto

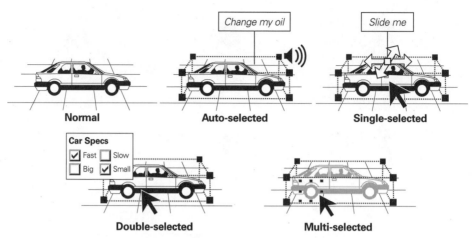

Figure 5.10   Examples of feedback based on target selection states

versus manual selection can be an important idiom indicating that the designer has selected a reasonable choice, but the user can change it.)

- *Selection2 (Single-selected).*   The third selection state. (Selected by the user with a mouse single-click. Single-selection is generally associated with the most common and often-used target manipulations, such as copy, move, and delete.)

- *Selection3 (Double-selected).*   The fourth selection state. (Selected by the user with a mouse double-click. Double-selection is often reserved for less common interactions with the target, such as modification of its internal properties. It can also be used for other alternative actions, such as automatically zooming in on the target object.)

- *SelectionN (N-1-selected).*   The N+1'th selection state. (Selected by the user with a mouse N-1 click. Considering that some beginners have trouble with double-clicking, multi-clicking should be reserved for non-essential target manipulation modes, such as selecting nested group levels within a multiple-grouped assembly.)

Target status states

As with selection states, functional condition or status states are also difficult to generalize. For both objects and controls, some possibilities are to differentiate between unusable and usable, and between discommended and recommended, with recommendation being a factor in configurator-mediated manipulation. As with the selection states, generic status states are defined, with suggested semantic designations shown in parentheses.

- *Status0 (Normal).*   The first status state. (Target is usable.)
- *Status1 (Disabled).*   The second status state. (Target is not usable.)

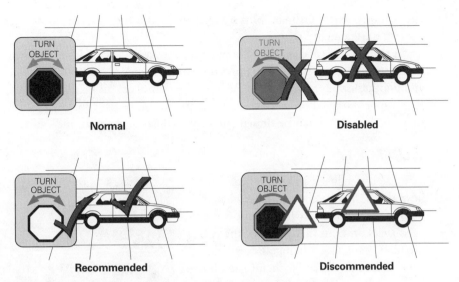

Figure 5.11 Examples of feedback based on target status states

- *Status2 (Recommended).*   The third status state. (Target is usable and its use is recommended.)
- *Status3 (Discommended).*   The fourth status state. (Target is usable but its use is not recommended.)
- *StatusN.*   The N+1'th status state.

5.5.2 Multi-shape

Trying to develop feedback elements that programmatically respond in color and shape to all the likely interaction states can be a daunting task, especially if this book's recommendation to use copious amounts of feedback is practiced. A much easier and simpler alternative is to develop a separate shape and image for each state of each feedback element, with the image being texture-mapped onto the shape. This technique, called *multi-shape*, supports multiple appearances of the same basic feedback element as separate entities or "shapes."

If a feedback element responds to more than one type of state, such as mouse action and target selection, then an image is needed for each combination of state values. Although this sounds like a lot of work, in the long run it can pay off handsomely in terms of quality and reduced programming time: A graphic artist instead of a software programmer can develop the feedback element shapes and colors. Also, revisions to the visual appearance of the feedback elements can and should happen often during the UI development cycle, and therefore should be easy to do. Using multi-shapes, most of the changes can be done with a paint package, which is easier than having to reprogram and debug "smart" shapes each time. Letting artists do what they are good at when it comes to control and feedback design is employed in most games and web applications, where ordinary buttons and knobs and their various feedback states can take on quite fanciful shapes.

Figure 5.12 is a screenshot showing three objects, each with a different manipulation state selected. Each object uses one multi-shape for the manipulation indicator and another one for the tooltip. Because the shapes are all texture mapped, any text that can be rendered on the screen and captured can be used for the tooltips, and any shape of arrow that can be drawn and captured can serve as an indicator.

5.6 SUMMARY

The use of feedback in an application is how the designer tells the user what to do, how to do it, and what is happening. Feedback comes in many forms, the two broadest categories being information and control feedback, with information being passive and controls being active in nature. Information feedback can be classified as instructional, which tells the user how to use the application; descriptive, which tells the user about the data in the application; and relational, which tells the user how objects in the scene are associated. Control feedback categories are control widgets, which are the visible manifestations of a control; action hints, which provide the user with idiomatic cues for using the controls; and interaction states, which classify the status and usability of an object or control.

Figure 5.12 Using multi-shapes for target decorations facilitates using texture mapping for feedback elements, which makes it easy to use any style of tooltip text or indicator arrow.

Feedback is manifested in an application in terms of visual and audio elements. Basic visual feedback elements include labels and icons, callouts and tooltips, indicators, handles, and cursors. Basic elements for audio feedback include verbal messages and sound effects. More sophisticated forms of feedback that are specialized for 3D manipulation can be built from these simpler forms. Feedback elements, being artificial, need to stand out from the ordinary data objects in the scene. To maximize the effectiveness of feedback elements, issues such as element size, orientation, and visibility must be addressed.

A different aspect of feedback involves dynamics. Unlike static feedback, dynamic feedback is often better at conveying what is currently happening in the application. Dynamic feedback can be applied to data objects in the scene, in an action, object, or task-oriented manner. Allied with dynamics are user interaction states, which include those for mouse actions and for target selection and status. Multi-shaping is a convenient technique for managing the many feedback elements associated with the interaction states as a single element. Multi-shaping also promotes the use of texture mapping in forming sophisticated feedback elements made from simple geometric shapes. Such an approach allows artists instead of programmers to design dynamic feedback elements.

CHAPTER 6

Visualization

Visualization is the process by which an application presents its data to the user. Visualization is what comes to mind for most people when they think about the human-computer dialogue in a GUI application. The user operates the controls, and the system changes the visual presentation of—or visualizes—the data accordingly. In control applications, the user is allowed to interact with the system in which data state is being presented, such as turning a virtual valve in a remotely controlled chemical plant. In a design application, the user is often allowed to directly manipulate the data in the presentation, such as a 3D model of a proposed kitchen remodel. As discussed in chapter 5, feedback is the other user-system dialogue in a GUI application, which is the designer's opportunity to help the user.

The subject of visualization, specifically data visualization, far exceeds the scope of this book. As a topic, visualization is centuries old, mapmaking being the classic example of how to create a 2D presentation of 3D data. One of the more noted examples of data visualization is the map created by Charles Joseph Minard in 1869 (figure 6.1), which portrayed the losses suffered by Napoleon's army in its Russian campaign of 1812. Using color, line width, spatial relations, and line graphs in the context of a map, Minard plotted six variables to tell the grim story of a 442,000-man army being whittled down to 10,000 after its march on and retreat from Moscow in the bitter cold. Figure 6.1 is not the actual map created by Michaud, only an illustration of it.

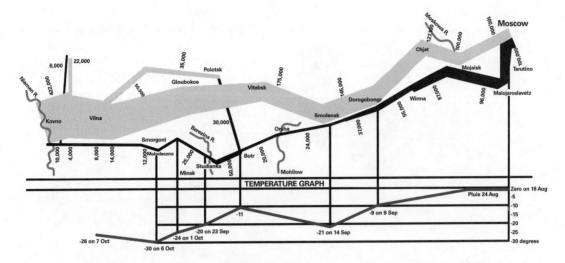

Figure 6.1   **This often-cited example of data visualization plots six dimensions of data about Napoleon's Russian campaign.**

Not wishing to repeat Napoleon's mistake by attacking the vast subject of visualization, this chapter will execute a surgical strike on some of the more practical issues surrounding the visual presentation of data objects and their feedback elements in a 3D application, especially those concerning in-scene manipulation.

6.1 DATA VISUALIZATION

3D applications generally deal with one of two types of environments: those modeling something that could conceptually exist within the real world, and those representing abstract spaces that have no tangible equivalent. Techniques for visualizing these models abound. Many of them are very problem- and domain-specific. For example, users of analysis applications tend to be specialists. They have a preferred way of investigating problems and studying the data. 3D visualization aids the process rather than radically transforming it. Visual data forms occupy a wide range, from photorealism to iconic and textual. The best form for an application depends on the nature of its data and its users. Often, multiple forms can be effectively used in a given application.

Models of real-world situations often involve data corresponding to real-world objects, such as reactors and pumps in a chemical plant. They can also involve less material data, such as temperature and pressure, which cannot be represented by real objects (unless, perhaps, someone decides to make a game out of it). In terms of next-generation applications, the distinction between *concrete* data, representing real-world objects, and *abstract* data, representing quantities, relationships, and abstract information, is an important one. In the previous chapters, you already have seen how concrete data,

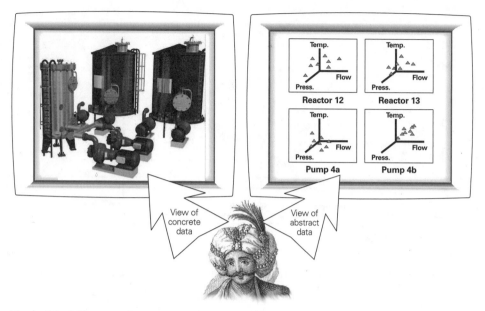

Figure 6.2 Different views of the same chemical plant model, one showing concrete data and the other abstract data

representing orderable products, are vital to e-commerce applications; and abstract data, in the form of callouts, rulers, and handles, are key to application feedback.

In a concrete world

The visual representation of concrete data—data that represents real touchable objects—is meant to approximate that of the real objects in the real world, or at least a world that is reasonably plausible or which does not compromise the veracity of the object. As in the furniture example, the user may select a desk from an e-catalog and see the desk presented in 3D against a dark background, one that does not detract from the realness of the desk. The user can examine the desk from various angles and study its features. It is unlikely the user would draw the conclusion that, since the desk appears to be floating in space, it might be the size of Jupiter. Instead, users are likely to conclude it is a normal desk suitable for use by normal people.

Free-floating desks will only get the user so far. Concrete data often needs to be put into a plausible and useful context, which would be a concrete one. For example, after deciding that the desk is of the right style and color, the user would probably want to make sure that it fits into his/her own office and allows proper clearance. The application could accommodate this by placing the selected desk in a model of a room that the user could arrange like a real office—sizing the walls, dragging and dropping doors and windows, and including pre-existing furniture.

In an abstract world

Since abstract data does not represent real objects, it can be represented in any number of forms and contexts. Its visual representation is not meant to approximate a real view of the world even though the information may describe the real world. The previous example, in which a maplike presentation was used to present the destruction of Napoleon's army in terms of space, time, falling temperature, and increasing body count, is a good one. This example also helps to highlight the distinction between abstract data and the often-real objects and circumstances that created such data. In general, abstract data, like the gas pressure in a pipeline or the rate of productivity on the factory floor, does not have a real-world visual analogue. We have to create one.

When abstract data are involved, the emphasis of the visual presentation is to maximize the user's understanding of what the data represents and its relationships, making it easy to extract information from the data. As such, abstract data is usually the subject of analysis applications; and, abstract data visualization is often the visualization of relationships. From this viewpoint, abstract data and its presentation can be considered in terms of their dimensionality. In a control application, such as that for a chemical plant, the visual dimension of color might represent the data dimension of pipe content. The visual geometric placement and interconnection of the pipes and valves would convey the staging and mixing of the pipe content. The visual pipe diameter could represent the data dimension of flow rate through the pipe. And, decorations such as indicators and callouts might provide flow direction, quantitative pressure measurements, and alarm conditions.

6.2   FEEDBACK VISUAL ATTRIBUTES

This section picks up on the subject of feedback visual attributes where section 5.3 left off. Here, the focus is on issues that are important in the visual design of feedback elements themselves, as well as their overall presentation in the 3D scene. For example, feedback elements should be big enough to be seen and manipulated, but not so big that they interfere with their neighbors—an obvious statement, but not always easy to achieve.

The concern for feedback elements is that, being abstract in nature, they need to be easily distinguished from their neighboring concrete data elements. If handles and callouts were shaped and colored the same as the data objects, not only would it be difficult to see them if they were overlapping the objects, but the user would have a hard time figuring out what is what in the scene. Even in applications where the subject is abstract data, the feedback elements are in some sense more abstract than the application data, and, as such, must remain distinct.

Beside achieving a separation of function, visual attributes allow feedback elements to call attention to themselves so the user can easily find them. Another challenge for feedback element design is that they remain usable in spite of in-scene manipulation of their host object. This raises questions about size, orientation, and visibility. Table 6.1 summarizes some of the factors to consider in the visual design of feedback elements and their overall presentation in the 3D scene.

In the course of this discussion, a number of visual techniques are mentioned for enhancing the visibility and usability of feedback elements. Most involve the automatic control of an element's geometric properties. The techniques, as functional building blocks, are described in detail later in this chapter, and are demonstrated in part 4 of the book, starting with the DisplayFacing example in section 21.2.2.

Table 6.1   Visual attributes for the design of feedback elements and their presentation

Distinction	• Consistent shape and color schemes; idiomatic; distinct by function. • Use borders and saturated colors; shape for function, color for state.
Size	• Elements unusable if too big or small; absolute physical size is key. • Use auto-sizing based on internal, external, and physical display attributes.
Orientation	• Elements unusable or distorted if not facing display; full or partial constraint. • Use auto-orienting based on facing the display; different from billboarding.
Visibility	• Elements unusable if hidden by other objects. • Use overlay, but confusing; use X-ray overlay, but limited.
Density	• Minimize element size; reduces clutter; enhances distinction. • Good size and placement require careful design; can use proxy elements.

6.2.1   Distinction

Shape, color, brightness, and contrast are key factors in making feedback elements stand out in the virtual world, distinct from one another. An approach that seems to work well is to use shape to distinguish functionality, such as linear arrows for sliding an object and curved arrows for rotating it, and to use color and brightness to distinguish interaction states, such as for mouseover, selection, and usability status.

A distinctive and consistent color scheme for feedback elements can go far in helping the user to recognize what is supposed to be real in the scene and what has been artificially added for feedback purposes. Using separate color schemes for information and control feedback can further help the user by distinguishing what is an information aid and what is a control. Applying these color schemes consistently throughout the application, not only to in-scene 3D elements but also to out-of-scene GUI elements, further reinforces the visual idioms that tell the user what is a control, what is information, and what is data.

It is not always possible to choose feedback colors distinct from those in the scene, especially since the apparent color of objects can change dramatically depending on lighting and viewing angle. A simple way to make feedback elements stand out in a scene regardless of their color and that of their surroundings is to use a thin contrasting border around them. Studies have shown that adding such a border can also help in shape recognition. Typically, element colors are bright and saturated so they can be readily identified by the user even when the element is small, which means that the border should be dark. Figure 6.3 shows a drag handle outlined with a thin, dark border. Notice how the handle shape

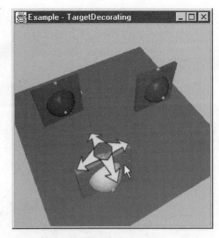

Figure 6.3 A thin contrasting border around feedback elements allows them to stand out regardless of the surrounding colors in the scene.

can still be easily seen even though it is the same color as the underlying object ball. (Including such outlines is easy if texture mapping is used, which is simplified through the use of multishaping.) Before picking the border color, however, let's look at an unexpected ramification of having added a border to feedback elements.

For small elements, the border can be a significant portion of the element's display area. If the user is accustomed to seeing the border around a small element and the border suddenly seems to disappear, such as when the element is in front of a like-colored background, the user may think that this apparent change in element shape is significant. Putting a border around the border is a bit much. A judicious choice of border color is a more practical approach. For example, dark backgrounds are often used in product sales applications to make the product stand out. In such cases, medium gray might be a better choice of border color than black or dark gray.

6.2.2 Size

Size does matter, at least for feedback elements. It becomes important when the user needs to operate control widgets and read informational elements. If feedback elements were simply incorporated into the world space like any other object, the feedback elements might become too big or too small to be usable. As the view and object move closer together and farther apart, the apparent size of the feedback elements will grow and shrink. Even under normal circumstances, control widgets such as drag handles could become quite large, filling the display and obscuring the work area. They can also become so small that it may be difficult to see when the mouse is actually over them before trying to start a drag. A similar problem applies to informational elements such as callouts; they can become too large or too small to be

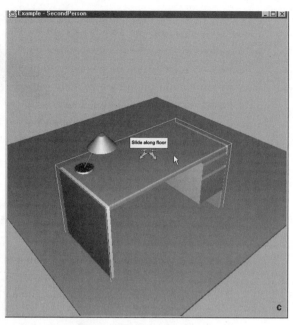

Figure 6.4   In spite of varying display sizes (a, b, c) and object positions (b, d), the object decorations remain the same absolute size on the display screen.

readable. In any case, the usability of feedback elements implemented as simple world objects, the same as the data objects, is limited.

What if we put the feedback elements in the display space instead of the world space? This would allow them to remain constant in size, but this would also fix their position in the display, which is not a good idea if the control is supposed to be attached to an object in the scene. The control widget wouldn't be able to track its host object as the host appears to move in the display. What is needed are elements that can be positioned as if they were in world space, but sized as if in display space. But this is not the complete answer. What happens if the user makes the size of the display window bigger or smaller? What if the display's field of view changes? Or, what if some users have big screens and others have small screens? The absolute perceived size of an element as it appears on the display screen—not just the size of the element relative to its display window—is also a factor.

These questions can be addressed through an auto-sizing technique called *constant size*. It accounts for all the available view parameters except for one, which must be addressed with a bit of hand waving. Although the physical size and resolution of the screen can be accounted for in most systems, in a POCS there is no way to determine the distance from the user's eyeballs to the display screen. Hence, there is no way to absolutely assure that the size of an element on the screen will allow the user to comfortably see it. Designers can reasonably assume, however, that users will position themselves at a comfortable and effective distance from their computer screens. Thus, element size can simply be adjusted for optimal viewing when the user is sitting at a nominal distance from the screen. If the size of all the elements is consistently off, then the user will, presumably, move a bit closer or farther from the screen.

In figure 6.4, views *a*, *b*, and *c* show the same scene and object decorations but at different display window sizes. Note how the tooltip and slide indicator always stay the same absolute physical size. Views *b* and *d* show the objects near and far in the scene, respectively. Again, note how the absolute size of the decorations remains the same.

6.2.3   Orientation

As with size, the orientation of feedback elements can be important for easy comprehension and use. If the feedback elements are put in the world space, just as are their host data objects, then as the view or host object moved, the elements might appear to turn upside down, making them useless. We can try putting the feedback elements in the display space, where they are always parallel to the display and right-side up, but they would not track the host object as it appears to move in the display. The solution is similar to the one used for constant size. A technique is needed that allows elements to be positioned in world space, but oriented as if in display space. Such a technique is called *display facing*, which is like billboarding but with an

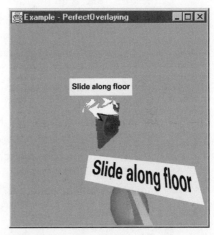

Figure 6.5   Orientation of the upper tooltip uses *display facing*, which keeps it parallel to the display, but the lower tooltip uses *billboarding*, which causes it to appear distorted.

important difference. Instead of facing the user's eye as in a billboard, display facing keeps the object facing the display plane. The difference in appearance between the two is shown in figure 6.5.

Most information feedback can benefit from use of the display facing technique, whether through a numerical value in a ruler or a hint on a control to "turn the knob." A variation of this technique selectively limits the automatic orientation to a particular object-relative axis. For example, an arrow-shaped handle pointing up in the world might be used as a lift handle. Selective display-facing about the world vertical axis allows the arrow to always point up in the world space while still facing the display.

6.2.4   Visibility

You can make a feedback element auto-sizing and auto-orienting, but what good is it if the user can't actually see the element? What if the element is hidden behind another object or by its own host object, such as a snap point or drag handle on the far side of a desk? Forcing the user to navigate to the other side of the object so the element can be seen is inconvenient for the user.

One approach is to make the data objects semi-transparent. Although this would allow the user to see informational feedback through the objects, there can still be a problem for control widgets. Although the widgets can be seen through objects, they are still behind those objects. If an application only allows its data objects to be manipulated using drag handles, then there is no problem. Dragging on the handle seen through an object is interpreted as dragging on the handle. For the general and often more desirable case, however, where dragging can occur on the object as well as its handles, the drag is ambiguous. Is the user dragging the object or the handle behind the object? Making the data objects semi-transparent can also lead to confusion about what is in front of what, since the objects in the scene all look like ghosts.

Another simple approach that can work in certain situations is to relocate the feedback elements, such as placing drag handles on the top of their host object. As before, this can lead to other difficulties, such as the user always having to see the upper part of the target object in order to manipulate it. This can be a serious drawback if there is a mix of short and tall objects in the scene that both require manipulation, such as low desks and tall bookcases.

A more general approach to the problem of visibility is to position feedback elements in world space but to overlay them in the display space, in front of all the world objects. In display space, the information feedback is always visible, and the control widgets are always usable. The technique that does this is called *world overlay*. An example with a drag handle in world overlay is shown in figure 6.6. Making the feedback elements semi-transparent can mitigate the fact that overlaid elements will obstruct their host object and the work area. Using semi-transparency on the feedback elements doesn't have the same problems as it would if used for the data objects. Feedback elements are clearly artificial, they are usually much smaller than the data objects, and if the feedback is object-centric, then they are also less populous than the data objects.

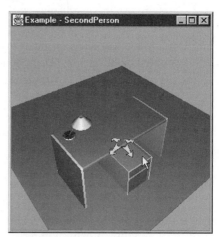

Figure 6.6 World overlay allows the drag handle to always appear on the host object but in front of any surrounding world objects.

Although overlay works well for some elements, like callouts, it has a major drawback with most others: overlaid elements can seem to float in space, with the user unable to tell if an element is supposed to be in front of or behind its host object in the scene. Like semi-transparent data objects, this can be disorienting. Callouts do not have a problem because they are completely artificial, with minimal ties to the world space. Their depth position in the scene is not important, and users quickly get used to the idea that they are always in front. For elements that need to have a more substantial presence in the world space, such as bounding boxes, tic marks, and snap points, simple overlay can be a real problem. A good example is a wireframe bounding box. If the bounding box is overlaid, the user will have difficulty figuring out which portion of the outline is in front of the object and which portion is behind it. All the user sees is a Necker cube optical illusion floating in front of the object. For situations such as this, where overlay is desirable but the loss of depth perception is unacceptable, a variation of world overlay, called *X-ray overlay*, might do. With X-ray overlay, the feedback element is still overlaid, but it has a different appearance depending on whether or not it is "hidden."

6.2.5 Density

Although not as critical to readability and usability as size and orientation, the density and spacing of feedback elements is important and can have a large impact on aesthetics. In general, feedback elements should appear in the display as small as possible. Making them small reduces clutter in the display and minimizes their obscuration of the work area. It also has the benefit of increasing the separation between feedback elements in the display, which helps with visual distinction. A key to making feedback elements small is to make them simple. A visually complex element will quickly become hard to distinguish as its size is reduced.

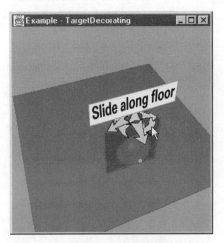

Figure 6.7 Failing to minimize the number, size, and overlap of feedback elements can hamper usability.

Separation is important for minimizing element overlap and avoiding ambiguous selection and use of control elements. Making them small is one way to increase separation. The other way is through careful design and layout of the feedback element decorations on a data object. For example, if possible, snap points should not be placed so close together on the object as to be almost on top of one another. Sometimes, however, the data strictly dictates where the snap points should go. In such cases, a callout could be used as a proxy for a snap point. The callout is used as a snap point, but the actual attachment point is on the host object where the callout is pointing. Such proxy callouts can be used as a way out of other tight situations. For example, proxy callouts could be used for control handles and object part (vertex, edge, face) selection when separation is a problem.

6.3 DISPLAY SPACE TECHNIQUES

As previously defined, the display space is a 2D space separate from the 3D world space. According to this definition, objects placed in the display space must be in their 2D graphical form, such as the 2D projections of 3D world objects. The display objects can overlap one another, and they can overlay and underlay the world objects. This view of the display space and its inhabitants is a conceptual one, and ideally 3D systems would support it. In practical terms, however, a present-day POCS might have the 3D platform (software and hardware) to support a primitive separation of display space from the world space, but it won't have a general overlap capability (e.g., overlay and underlay planes). And, it definitely won't have the ability to handle 3D object projections as 2D objects, or to selectively place them in overlay and underlay.

Assuming for now that the problem of generalized display overlay of world objects can be solved for a POCS, there are some interesting questions about how to size and place objects in the display. For example, if you wanted to place a virtual control panel in the lower right corner of the display space, what happens to it when the user or application resizes the display window? Does the absolute size of the panel stay the same or does it grow and shrink with the display window? Does the panel remain fixed in absolute display space or does its lower right corner track the lower right corner of the display window? Let's start getting some answers.

6.3.1 Display layout

The questions raised about how to size and position display objects are not new. They may seem new because they are expressed in the context of 3D applications, but these questions have been asked since when GUIs were still thought to be new. The fact that the control panel is overlaid on a 3D scene introduces a few new twists to the problem, but the techniques for 2D layout—object sizing and placement—remain the same.

The simplest approach is to treat the display layout space as being absolute or relative. In an absolute space, its scale is independent of the display window size. In terms of the part 1 spatial definitions, the display scale factor (DSF) is always 1:1. An absolute display space is useful if the size of a display object should remain constant. For example, a virtual control knob only has to be so large in order for it to be used. Making it larger would only block out more of the underlying 3D scene, and making it smaller may render it unusable.

In a relative layout space, the scale of the space, the DSF, is proportional to the display window size. As the window size increases so too does the size of all the objects in it, but the relative position of everything stays the same. For example, if the control panel is flush with the lower right corner of the display window, then it will remain so regardless of the display window size.

You may have figured out by now that neither of these simplistic approaches makes a very general solution. What is often needed is a combination of the two, with objects being sized absolutely but positioned relatively, or something even more

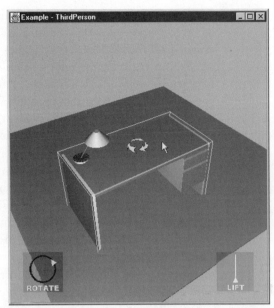

Figure 6.8 The two controls in display overlay are sized absolutely in screen space but are positioned relative to the display window.

elaborate, such as aligning objects to be flush or centered, or even defining algorithms to lay out groups of objects. Algorithmic layout is employed in HTML such as in table layouts, and in Java in the form of layout managers.

Figure 6.8 shows how controls in display overlay can be sized absolutely but positioned relative to the display window. Note how the lower corners of the controls remain at their same relative positions in the display window as the window size changes.

6.3.2   Overlay, underlay, and overlap

It is sometimes advantageous for objects to always appear in front of other objects. A good example of this is the tooltip. No matter what object it is attached to, whether out-of-scene on a toolbar button or in-scene as a part number on a desk, it is generally desirable and even expected for tooltips to appear in front of their less privileged neighbors. The way to make this happen is not to place the tooltip in the world space where it must jockey for position with its neighbors, but to place it in the display space where it will appear in front of everything else in the world space. This is referred to as placing the object into *overlay*. What if, however, there are other feedback elements in overlay, such as drag handles, other tooltips, and a dashboard? What if they are trying to occupy the same spot in the display?

One approach is to put all display space objects on an equal footing and simply blend them together. This might work in limited situations, but in the general case it would make a lot of the feedback elements unusable and, more importantly, appear confusing. A more general approach is to allow the objects in display space to overlap one another. This approach requires thinking of the display space as more than a single simple plane that moves and rotates with the view. Instead, the display space is made up of one or more planes into which display objects are placed, which are called over-lay or *Z planes*. Although the display space has no depth per se, the Z planes are assigned an overlap priority or Z order. Objects in planes with a higher priority, or Z value (Z order having the same sense as the Z dimension in the view space), will appear in front. Figure 6.9 shows the use of Z planes to keep the arrow, circle, and semi-transparent background in the lower control properly overlapped.

Even though overlay planes give you a reasonable chance of keeping objects separated, this still begs the question of what to do if two objects in the same plane want to be at the same place at the same time. You can always fall back on blending, but what is often done is to assign each object in the display space to its own personal Z plane. This, by the way, is what most 2D drawing packages do, which brings up an important side issue. Often, in the rush and struggle to build 3D platforms or to pump 3D into applications, many hard-won lessons from the 2D world are cast aside or considered of lesser importance. Matters such as providing for a separate 2D display space, much less dealing with 2D layout and overlap in

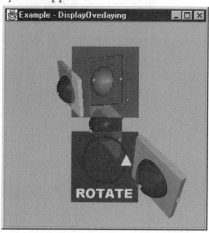

Figure 6.9 Each object in display overlay is in its own Z-plane to achieve the correct overlap.

that space, seem to be often forgotten or trivialized. With next-generation applications, we can't afford to ignore good capabilities and solutions, even 2D ones.

Before leaving this subject, there is one more matter to be addressed. *Underlay* is similar in concept to overlay, only in reverse. Instead of an object always appearing in front of its worldly neighbors, the object always appears behind them, such as stars or mountains off in the distance. Underlay and overlay use the same display Z planes, except that underlay is behind the world space. This might seem to contradict the notion that the display space is 2D. After all, how can overlay and underlay objects be in the display space yet have the whole 3D world space sandwiched between them? The answer requires an adjustment in how we think about the world space. Taking a display-space-centric view of the matter, the projection of the world space onto the display plane can be considered as occupying a single Z plane lying between the display overlay and underlay Z planes. At a more sophisticated level of conceptualization, the projection of each 3D object onto the 2D display plane can be considered as a 2D object in display space, with normal world objects occupying the middle Z planes and those in world overlay occupying the frontmost Z planes.

6.3.3 Pseudo-display overlay

As previously mentioned, support for a separate display space, much less overlay and underlay Z planes, is practically non-existent in a POCS graphics platform. If it exists at all, it tends to be rather platform-dependent and of a limited and inconvenient nature. The bottom line—at least for the foreseeable future—is that the POCS designer cannot assume native support of Z planes for display overlay, underlay, and overlap. Fortunately, there are a couple of 3D-only alternatives that do a reasonable job of creating synthetic display spaces. One technique, called *world overlay*, is capable of addressing the whole display space problem, including display and world overlay and underlay. It is also much more demanding on the underlying 3D platform, and some are not up to the task.

The second technique, called *pseudo-display overlay* (PDO), is much less demanding on the platform but is also much less generic. It is generally only used for overlay, and only that of static display objects—not dynamic world-based objects. PDO, as a display-only technique, is addressed here. World overlay, which can be used on world space objects, will be discussed later, in section 6.4, as a world space technique.

In PDO there is no real display space and, as such, there are no real display objects. Instead, all objects live in the world space. Once you accept this, PDO is a simple technique to understand: to make a "display object" appear overlaid move it really close to the user's eye, while at the same time shrinking it just the right amount. This has the desired effect of moving the object in front of other objects while keeping its apparent size in the display constant. If the display objects are relatively flat, then moving an object with a higher overlap priority closer to the eye than those with lower priority effectively creates pseudo-Z planes.

Of course, the devil is in the details. How much to shrink the object depends on the view FOV and DSF. Since the display objects really live in the world space, you also have to account for the VSF and DVO. Also, you have to be careful to keep the world objects that are supposed to stay in the world space from bumping into the pseudo display objects, such as when the user's eye navigates close to and through world objects. Additional complications arise if you want to do display space layout relative to the display window. If the position of an object is to remain fixed in the display space relative to some location other than the origin (the center of the display), then the object must be shrunk about that reference point and not the origin.

The statement that PDO does not handle world overlay is not completely true. If PDO is used on a world object—one that is not flat—then it will appear as an overlaid world object that is in the view space. It would appear as 3D and overlaid, but it would remain stationary as the view moved. An example can be seen in the upper part of figure 6.9, where a 3D object appears in front of its semi-transparent background, both of which are in PDO. A rather general implementation of PDO that addresses

 many of the issues raised in this section is provided in the DisplayOverlaying example in section 21.3.2.

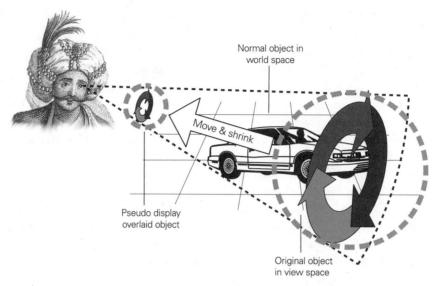

Normal object in
world space

Move & shrink

Pseudo display
overlaid object

Original object
in view space

Figure 6.10 **Objects in pseudo-display overlay (PDO) live in the view space, and are moved close to the eye while being reduced in size to maintain a constant apparent size.**

6.4 WORLD SPACE TECHNIQUES

The following visual techniques address many of the issues raised in the earlier discussion concerning the usability of feedback elements when subjected to in-scene manipulation. Problems that arise concern the orientation, size, and visibility of display elements as their host object is rotated, moved away from the user's eye, and obscured by other world objects. Many of the techniques discussed here were shown in previous figures, and are demonstrated in part 4, starting with the DisplayFacing example in section 21.2.2.

These techniques are intended for use with objects residing in the world space. The techniques are also intended to be used in combination to satisfy specific feedback needs, such as a feedback element that should always appear facing the display and overlaid, but whose apparent size should be allowed to vary as would that of a normal object. These techniques generally require knowledge about where the view is relative to the object—the object and view's external geometry. Many also require knowledge about the view's internal geometry, such as the degree of perspective, expressed as FOV, and the scaling factor used in forming the display image of the scene, expressed routinely as VSF.

6.4.1 Display facing

Display facing is a technique that keeps an object always facing toward the display plane and upright. It does this by simply orienting the target world object in the same manner as the view observing it; as the view twists and turns, so too does the displayfacing object. If the target object were a small flat rectangle such as a tooltip, it would always appear parallel to the display plane without distortion. An important variation of display facing allows an axis of rotation to be defined relative to some frame of reference, such as the world space. As before, the target object's orientation tries to match that of the view but is constrained by the rotation axis. This is useful where an element must rotate to face the display but must remain pointing in a given direction, such as up for a lift handle.

You might wonder if display facing is the same as billboarding, which is offered by many 3D platforms. The two techniques are similar, but with an important difference. With billboarding, the target object faces toward the view position—the LFP. Objects that are close to the display in the 3D world space but which do not appear near the center of the display will appear turned toward the display center. If the view uses a perspective projection, the objects will also appear distorted, which is called *keystoning*. The degree of distortion increases as the object moves farther from the view center, or closer to the display, or as the perspective's FOV increases. With display facing, the target object always faces parallel to the display plane, head-on, no matter where it is located in the display window or what value the FOV has. One drawback of display facing that is not apparent in billboarding is that the object must be relatively flat, or a different form of distortion in the object will appear. For feedback elements, this limitation is usually not a problem.

6.4.2   Constant size

The *constant size* technique keeps the target object the same size no matter how close or far it is from the viewer's eye. It does this by carefully adjusting the target object's geometric scaling factor according to the distance of the object from the view display plane as well as the view's internal geometry, including the screen geometry. The net effect is that the target object will appear at the same apparent size on the display screen no matter where the object is in the scene or how the display window is stretched and sized. The object's size also remains constant no matter what the degree of perspective is, and even if a parallel projection is used. The purpose of making the object size constant in real-world space is so that feedback elements can be set to their optimal size—big enough for comfortable use while minimizing interference with neighboring elements and the scene as a whole.

Note that if the distance from the eye were used instead of the distance to the view display plane, the object size will seem to vary according to where it appeared in the display window. For example, a target object that is moving in the world parallel to the display plane and toward the view center axis would appear to shrink as it approached the center of the display. This is because the eye-to-object distance would be decreasing as the object approached the view center axis.

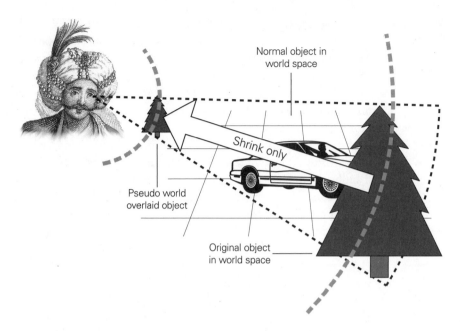

Figure 6.11 Objects in pseudo-world overlay (PWO) live in the world space, and are scaled about the view position, which moves them close to and aligned with the eye while maintaining a constant apparent size.

6.4.3 World overlay

PDO was described as a display space technique suitable only for overlay of static display objects; it could not handle dynamic world objects. *World overlay* is a much more general technique that is capable of handling all of the advanced aspects of the display space in a consistent manner, including display and world overlay and underlay. In practice, true world overlay is difficult to achieve, so *pseudo-world overlay* (PWO) is used. Like PDO, PWO does not rely on any special system software or hardware to achieve overlay; it is a geometry-only 3D solution. Due to its nature, however, the technique will quickly expose common flaws in many 3D platforms.

PWO and PDO are similar in that all objects live in the world space, and the target object is repositioned and its scaling factor carefully adjusted so that the apparent size of the object remains the same. The difference between the techniques is in how the repositioning is performed. In PDO, the target object is moved toward the display and then scaled down relative to some reference point in the display Z plane, such as the center of the display. World overlay uses a nifty trick where the target object is scaled relative to the view position, the LFP. A scaling factor less than one produces overlay, and a factor greater than one produces underlay. Scaling the target object about the LFP has the effect of simultaneously moving the object closer (overlay) or farther (underlay) from the user's eye, while scaling it just the right amount to keep its apparent size constant. For a given scale factor, the overlap of world-overlaid objects is the same as if the objects were not in overlay—the closer object will appear in front. With PWO, the target object is allowed to move anywhere in the world space, and the scaling factor can remain constant.

Unlike PDO, which assumes target objects are statically positioned in view space, PWO requires knowledge of the view's position. Also, the scaling factor must be quite large or small in order to move the target objects clear of any normal world objects. These two factors, combined, are where world overlay puts a 3D platform to the test. If the view position is not precisely known at the same time that the target object is being updated, then any error will be grossly exaggerated, causing the overlaid object to lag or jitter. Errors can arise from round-off error in the view position, but more likely from the view position reporting and scale factor updating being out of synch; most 3D platforms do a poor job of this. As of this writing, tests indicate that Cosmo is the only popular VRML player that performs the update timing correctly, and that Java 3D 1.1.2 does not.

Figure 6.12 In pseudo-world overlay, the overlay effect can be lost if the scaling factor is not small enough or world objects are allowed to get too close to the view.

The result of not making the scale factor small enough for overlay, or letting the world objects get too close to the view is shown in figure 6.12. Notice that the tooltip and indicator appear to intersect the near object instead of overlaying it.

6.4.4 Perfect overlay

The basic visual techniques of display facing, constant size, and world overlay are rarely used alone. In order to maximize the usability of feedback elements they are generally used in combination, often all three together. In recognition of this common usage and in deference to efficiency consideration during implementation, the basic visual techniques can be packaged as a single composite visual technique called *perfect overlay* (overlay being the dominant attribute of the group). For convenience, the capability to selectively enable individual techniques could be provided so that perfect overlay can be tuned to a specific visual need. For example, world overlay and constant size could be used on a rotation handle, but not display facing, so the handle will appear to rotate as the user turns it.

6.4.5 Revealment

World overlay is a technique that addresses the issue of visibility as it primarily concerns feedback elements. It works well in this capacity because feedback is artificial and is meant to appear that way; but at times even feedback elements can have problems with world overlay. Depth cues are lost and objects can seem to free-float in space, such as bounding boxes appearing as visually ambiguous Necker cubes; you can't tell which corner is in front and which is in back of the object it outlines. And, when data objects are involved, using world overlay to handle visibility problems is seldom a good choice. Unlike feedback elements, which beg to stand out and be the center of attention, data objects have to remain in the context of their virtual world environment. For example, in a furniture layout application the user's eyeball may wander outside of the room, in which case all the user would see is the backside of the near wall. If the desk and other furniture were placed in world overlay then the user could always see them, but the scene would become surrealistic, to say the least.

The general problem of making the invisible visible is called *revealment*. World overlay is one such technique, but it is fairly heavy-handed for use with data objects and even for some feedback elements. Semitransparency has already been mentioned as a way to reveal hidden objects. If applied to the scene globally the result can be confusing since all the objects appear ghostly and it can be difficult to judge what is in front of what without close inspection. Semitransparency also cuts down on the clarity with which hidden objects can be seen. Limiting the application of the transparency, such as to the selected object, can help considerably, but it requires manual intervention on the part of the user to reveal a hidden object. Such approaches are often inconvenient since objects generally become hidden while the user is in the middle of doing something else, such as arranging objects in the scene or navigating through it. What is needed are techniques that work automatically and in a limited way.

X-ray overlay

A simple technique used in pencil and paper days for revealing hidden detail is to indicate hidden lines with dashes. And, for solid objects, the hidden detail might appear ghosted behind the overlying structure. A simple variation of world overlay that can automatically handle visibility using such dual appearances is a technique called *X-ray overlay*.

With X-ray overlay the target object has two different but overlapping shapes. One shape, the "visible" one, is a normal world object that appears when the target is visible, such as a normal bounding box outline around a desk. The other shape, the "hidden" one, is in world overlay so that it appears all the time, even when it would normally be hidden, such as a dashed version of the bounding box outline. If the color of the visible and hidden shapes is the same, then the composite outline will appear solid when the outline is normally visible; when a world object covers the outline, only the dashed version—in world overlay—would be seen wherever it was covered. To reveal a solid object, such as a desk, its visible version would be the normal desk and its hidden version would be a semitransparent version. Thus, when the desk is hidden, such as behind a wall, the ghosted version of the desk would be seen instead of the normal solid version.

Although X-ray overlay can be quite effective, it is also limited. It only works if the visible and hidden shapes can appear simultaneously and indistinguishably, such as same-colored dashed and solid lines, and semitransparent and solid polygons. Given this restriction, a good choice other than line characteristics and transparency is relative size. For example, a large version of a snap point could be used for its visible shape, and a smaller version, suggesting distance, could be used for its hidden appearance. Conventions such as dashed lines, ghosting, and

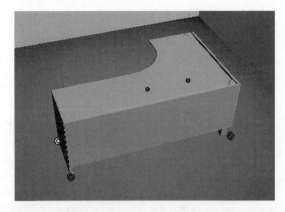

Figure 6.13 By using X-ray overlay snap points, the hidden ones (middle of the desk) appear smaller than the visible ones (corners of the desk), even though they all use constant size. (Courtesy of TechniCon Corporation)

size and brightness-based depth cues are familiar to the general public and should be used where possible for these and other visibility situations.

Snap points constructed using X-ray overlay are shown in figure 6.13, and appear as small balls. Although the snap points use constant size, notice how the hidden ones in the middle of the desk appear smaller than visible ones at the lower corners as a result of the X-ray overlay.

Cutaway

A more general form of X-ray overlay is the *cutaway*. In a cutaway the overlying portion of an object is made invisible or semitransparent to reveal the object's inner detail. The simplest form of cutaway is the cutting plane, where everything belonging to an object on the cutting side of the plane is eliminated. The effect is like slicing through the object and brushing away the part closest to the user. More sophisticated forms of cutaway might selectively eliminate obstructing components, or even portions of components. For example, a jagged hole could be cut into the side of a submarine to reveal its nuclear missiles, or a corner of a car could be cut away to reveal the features of its superior suspension system. Such techniques are often found in print media where real artists are making the tough decisions about what to remove and how. Aside from letting the user interactively apply cutting shapes to an object, such as planes and holes, more sophisticated forms of cutaway are difficult to perform automatically in a generalized manner.

Single-sidedness

A very simple technique that works with polygons and that comes for free with most 3D platforms is *single-sidedness*. As its name implies, a polygon that is single-sided has only one side. In other words, if seen from one side the polygon appears solid, but from the other side it appears invisible. Single-sidedness is a good choice for enclosed spaces that the user needs to move or orbit about, such as a room full of furniture. By making the walls, floor and ceiling single-sided, with the visible side facing inward, the room will appear normal from the inside but, if the user's eye wanders outside of the room, the surfaces facing the user are invisible allowing the room and its contents to still be seen. The effect for room-like settings is quite pleasing and readily accepted in spite of the fact that there is no analogue in the real world. Perhaps the reason for this acceptance is due to a similar effect used in television and films,

Figure 6.14 A portion of this heat exchanger's container has been cut away to reveal its inner details. (Courtesy of GB Multimedia Productions)

where one or two walls and the ceiling are often left off of a room so that the camera can move about unhindered.

Line-of-sight

For situations where objects must have thickness and therefore cannot be single-sided, or where suitable visible and hidden forms cannot be derived, then another technique can be used which relies on more sophisticated programmatic means. With a *line-of-sight* (LOS) technique the application actively determines if any objects are in the LOS from the user's eyeball to designated target objects in the scene. Any objects that block the LOS are made invisible. For instance, in the room example, the furniture would be designated as LOS targets. Then, as the user's eye roamed about inside and outside the room, internal and external walls, doors, the floor and the ceiling, and so on. would disappear as needed to keep the furniture clearly in sight. An example is shown in figure 6.15, which is two different views of the same scene.

LOS targets can also be selected automatically and on-the-fly, such as designating the currently selected manipulation target also as an LOS target. Using this approach, any objects that are blocking the LOS to the target while it is being manipulated or while the view is being orbited about it would conveniently be made invisible.

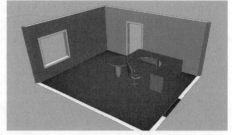

Figure 6.15   Line-of-sight revealment causes the near walls to disappear as the view changes. (Courtesy of TechniCon Corporation)

Although a rather general and effective technique for revealment, in practical terms it can be quite expensive since visibility must be computed across the LOS targets and throughout the scene.

6.5   MULTIPLE VIEWS

Using multiple 2D views to visualize problems with three or more dimensions is quite common in science, engineering, and architecture. Three and even four views of the same subject are not uncommon. Any good CAD system offers multiple views and many options about how to set, arrange and adjust the views. Although multiple views can be a wonderful visualization tool, having to arrange the display windows and manage their view content can be a daunting challenge to the casual user. Often such users are willing to give up flexibility to gain ease of use. For next-generation applications, multiple views as well as single views must be easy to use, requiring little or no user input. This section addresses some of the general issues, techniques, and problems that arise with multiple views. The next chapter, on navigation, will address the problem of how to simplify the user's job of controlling what appears in a view, whether for single or multiple views.

View layout

One of the advantages of HTML is that it is not a page layout language. With HTML, you tell the rendering engine what font and paragraph styles you want, and the renderer takes whatever page size and shape it is given and fits the textflow to it. Generally, the user is freed from having to horizontally size and scroll the browser window. Such activities add little value to the end result, especially for the casual user. They are merely a means to an end. The HTML approach of getting the data up on the screen with minimum bother to the user is consistent with the whole web approach to applications; less is often more.

There are numerous ways to arrange 3D displays in an application. The best ones are specific to the application's problem domain and the user's needs for specific tasks. Rather than getting into particular display arrangements, the point here is that the displays should be self-arranging; they should take care of themselves instead of the user having to do it. As the user resizes the application window, the internal display areas should size and adjust automatically according to the available space in the containing application window and the viewed data's spatial extent and level of detail. In the ideal application the most the user should have to do is select the general type of presentation, such as overview versus orthographic, and the application does the rest— arranging, sizing, and scaling the display areas and their contents accordingly.

Orthographic views

Orthographic views are the traditional starting point for any discussion of multiple views. The specific number and content of the views can vary depending on how much screen real estate is available and the user's actions and preferences. For design applications involving planar layout, such as of an office or manufacturing floor, many CAD-trained users prefer a 2D planar view for direct manipulation. If screen space is minimal, then an application for such users might only include two views: a 2D plan view for manipulation and a 3D perspective view for reassurance. If more screen space is available and the user is up to the task, then a full complement of orthographic displays could be presented: 2D plan, elevation, side views, and a 3D perspective view.

Regardless of how many and what kinds of views are offered to the user, next-generation applications demand that all the views be simultaneously updated in real time. Gone are the days of playing around in one view and then having to push a button to update the other views, especially the 3D view. Also, for next-generation applications, this book maintains that CAD and its orthographic views do not provide a very appealing model. Instead, direct manipulation in a 3D perspective view is the key, especially for casual users who do not have training on CAD systems. Even so, having more than one perspective of the 3D world can be beneficial as long as the user is not burdened with maintaining multiple views.

6.5.1   Overviews

After orthographic views, the next most popular multiview technique is probably the overview. With overview, one view shows a limited portion of the subject area but in great detail, and the other view shows a larger portion of the subject area but in less detail. Typically, the overview shows the entire subject area and requires no interaction on the part of the user. The area of the subject that the detail view presents is shown outlined or highlighted in the overview. Overview is helpful in the same way that "You Are Here" signs help at the local shopping mall. You might get lost in the mall because of your limited view, all the visual clutter, and the repetitiveness of the architecture, but with a few visual landmarks and the map overview in the sign, you can usually find your way around.

With only a single view, a typical scenario might require the user to zoom in on the subject to manipulate it with precision, and then to zoom out from it to assess the overall effect of the manipulation. With overview, the user has immediate access to separate views specialized for these two competing requirements. Overview also goes far in keeping the user from getting lost or severely disoriented as might happen if only a single detailed view were available. Another advantage of overview is that it can simplify navigation, with the user moving and orienting the detail view outline in the overview from a bird's-eye perspective. The goal of overview is to give users the presentations they are most likely to need while performing their job. They don't have to select menu items and OK dialogues in order to locate where they are or to change their view. With overview, their location is already presented on the screen and the detail view can be easily maneuvered from a big-picture perspective—literally.

View problems

With multiple views come a few interesting problems, both philosophically and practically. If an object in the scene is a target for display facing or billboarding, one might wonder which display it will face if there is more than one display? Since the object is living in the world, if it turns to face one display then it can be seen in other displays doing so, which defeats the whole purpose of these techniques. The object is always supposed to face the display, which means any and all displays. Similar problems occur with the pseudo-overlay techniques of PDO and PWO. Which display will the target objects be moved toward and away from? Also, since the target objects are world objects, then it is possible to see them in other displays—shrunken or bloated as needed to make them appear overlaid in the one privileged view.

Unfortunately, the news is not good. The current generation of popular 3D platforms, Java 3D 1.1.2 included, cannot easily handle these multiple-view problems. The designer must designate a primary view and that is the one that receives the benefits of any built-in display-dependent visual techniques. Needless to say, this presents difficulties for visual feedback. In practical terms, however, the picture may not be quite so bleak. Since most pseudo-overlay is truly overlay, not underlay, the target objects are moved close to the view and shrunk to an extremely small size. From the perspective of another view, the overlaid objects may appear as dust specks clustered about a point in the distance—the LFP of another view. Accepting this minor imperfection, you could multiply/clone a given target object and assign a clone to each of the views in use, with the host view controlling the target clone's visual geometry.

Of course, the ideal situation would be a 3D platform capable of true overlay of world and display objects, which may be a few years out for a POCS. Short of that, a simpler software-only solution might allow the designer to designate in which display a given object will appear. An object so designated, such as a display facing tooltip, would be invisible in all but its host display. This capability, combined with the object-cloning described above, would provide a reasonable solution for the multiview problems discussed.

6.6 SUMMARY

Data visualization is a subject area that is alive and well and has been thriving for centuries. Rather than attacking this broad subject head-on, this chapter demonstrated valor through discretion and beat a hasty retreat to more familiar ground, specifically the concerns of next-generation 3D user interfaces.

Data visualization can be described in terms of concrete versus abstract data modeling and presentation, with concrete data presentation being a faithful rendering of a real object, such as a pipe valve, and abstract presentation making the invisible visible, such as a graph of temperature versus time. Regarding 3D user interfaces, visual attributes such as size and orientation are an important aspect of feedback element design. Many of these visual attributes are satisfied through the use of world and display space techniques which can maintain proper size, orientation, and overlay of feedback elements under varying viewing conditions. A popular class of visualization techniques is based on the use of multiple views to present the same data from different perspectives, which also introduces some interesting problems.

With this chapter on visualization and the two previous chapters on control and feedback, you have the foundation upon which all the other user-interface techniques can rest. With the functionality covered in these chapters, the user can interact with the virtual world and see the results of that interaction. The remaining chapters in part 2 are important and contain more specialized variations on these basic themes.

C H A P T E R 7

Navigation

An important aspect of living in the real world is investigating it. Moving through the world and examining its objects is how we gain direct knowledge of it. Navigating ourselves through the world is just as natural as manipulating objects within our reach. If an object is too big to move, we crane our necks over it and walk around it. Changing our viewpoint and examining objects within our view are how we build up a mental map of our world and develop a better understanding of the objects in it. The two operations of navigation and manipulation are so intertwined that it may be difficult to tell when we are doing one and not the other. In the real world, our sense of sight, sound, touch, and motion combine to make navigation and manipulation inseparable experiences. In a POCS, the user experience is closer to being in a virtual sensory deprivation tank than to being in a virtual world.

In a computer application, especially one on a POCS without the benefits of VR data gloves and head-mounted displays, the distinction between navigation and manipulation can be painfully obvious. In navigation, the user or system moves a view object, making a new portion of the virtual world visible. In manipulation, the user or system moves a data object, modifying the contents of the world that the user sees. The simplest approach for the designer is to hook up two sets of controls, one set to the views and another set to the objects. Although easy for the designer, such a configuration can seem quite unnatural, awkward, and confusing to the user. To many, the rigid distinction between navigation and manipulation will seem an artificial and unnecessary annoyance. The challenge in next-generation applications is to minimize this distinction and to get the user back to a more familiar setting, with navigation being a more integral part of the overall user experience.

7.1 FORMS OF NAVIGATION

Many users have been subjected to guided tours and data wizards that pass for navigation in many applications. Although such approaches have their place, they generally fail to address the user's urges to wander off the predefined path or to go straight to where they know they must go. Such approaches are easy to design, but they show the user only what the designer felt was necessary and in the sequence that the designer thought was best. Although they involve movement through the spatial and conceptual data worlds, and perhaps the user is given a modicum of control over whether to go forward and back, most would agree that such approaches fulfill only the narrowest definition of navigation.

In its most general form, navigation is a broad concept that involves the user moving through a world of data to seek information. Spatial navigation techniques are most immediately familiar. Spatial navigation is what you do every morning when you climb out of bed and make your way to the kitchen for your first cup of coffee. Spatial navigation is typically linear in nature, with a small movement changing your view a little bit, and a large movement changing your view a lot. The data can be abstract, such as orbiting about a data cluster representing this year's gross national product, or concrete, such as orbiting about an office desk.

A different form of navigation is nongeometric in nature. Rather than moving the user through space, it allows the user to change data contexts. Contextual navigation is generally nonlinear and conceptual in nature, but the data itself can be abstract or concrete. Navigation of this form is more closely associated with hierarchical and topological representations of the application data in the virtual world. A common form of contextual navigation is a change in level of detail, such as double clicking on a city in an aerial photo to change the view to a more detailed and alternative presentation of the selected city as a street map. Another example is shown in figure 7.1, where selecting a piece of equipment zooms in on it and reveals its inner detail.

7.1.1 Spatial navigation

The traditional definition of navigation involves movement through geometric space, which involves positioning and directing the user's eyes in the 3D virtual world. Often the analogy of a camera is used where the system or user manipulates the view of the virtual world as an object—a camera. Cameras can be imbued with control interpretations and constraints that approximate familiar actions, such as walking, driving, and flying. Unlike the simple versions of navigation in common use today, where users point themselves in a particular direction and go in a straight line, next-generation applications will have to be smarter about how people really move through their world.

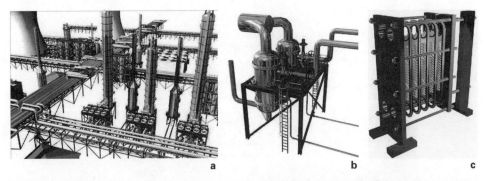

a   b   c

Figure 7.1 **The transition from a to b represents spatial navigation, with a change of camera position. The transition from b to c represents contextual navigation, with the inner detail of an object being revealed—a view that cannot be obtained through simple camera movement. (Courtesy of GB Multimedia Productions)**

When you walk to the bus stop or hop in a car to get to work you focus on the goal—getting to work. Often you mentally switch to automatic pilot, leaving your mind and body to deal subconsciously with many of the details, such as waiting for traffic lights, turning down familiar streets, and avoiding the provocation of road rage. In many virtual worlds you are hard-pressed to get from point A to point B without incident, much less perform information gathering along the way. Users, especially new ones, are often overwhelmed with the mechanics of navigating through the world. They run over and through objects, get stuck in dead ends, can't get through doors, or find themselves inexplicably teleported to some unknown location.

To approximate what goes on in our heads when we switch to automatic pilot would require high-level artificial intelligence (AI). However, given the current state of affairs, even the simplest goal-directed route planning strategies might go far in making the user's experience in the virtual world seem more natural. To work up to that point, let's first start with the basics. A familiar way to categorize navigation is according to personae, similar to that done for application controls in chapter 4. Although navigation is simply control of the user's view object—the camera—the personae used for navigation are focused more on the user experience than on the technical details of what the controls are doing. As such, it is helpful to consider navigation personae separate from those of the controls that are manipulating the view.

First person

In first-person navigation, the user is the view and is controlling it from that perspective. Dragging the mouse to the left in the display or pressing the left arrow key will cause the view to slide, turn, or bank to the left depending on whether the user is walking, driving, or flying. An important point here is that, as with data manipulation, it is important for the system to maintain the illusion of a virtual world or reality. In the case of first-person navigation, the illusion is that of moving through the world using a

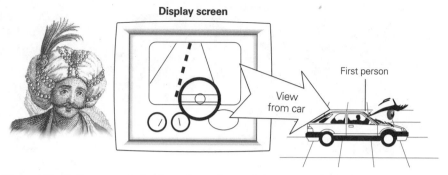

Figure 7.2   First-person navigation where the user's vantage point is from a car in the scene that he is driving

particular mode of transportation. Maintaining the illusion makes the user experience more familiar and predictable, and therefore more intuitive.

Although the navigation mode is first-person—the user is the view—the means for controlling it may involve third-person controls, such as a virtual steering wheel and throttle control in a display dashboard. The difference between this and third-person navigation, covered a little later, is that the controls are part of your vehicle's metaphor. They are an integral part of your first-person experience, the same as would be a real steering wheel in a real car.

Second person

In second-person navigation the user is once removed from the focus of the action, which is in the scene. As with second-person controls, second-person navigation requires interaction with objects and controls that appear in the scene. You might think that second-person navigation would seem unnatural to the user. After all, most of our navigation experiences in the real world are first-person. As it turns out, if done well, people will quickly accept second- and even third-person navigation modes.

A simple example of second-person navigation involves object-centric view orbiting, where the user clicks on an object to establish the view LAP, and then uses controls to rotate about the object in order to examine it *in situ*. This can be thought of as an inverse examine mode, where instead of turning and tilting an object to examine it, you walk around and fly over the object to examine it and its neighbors. A different form of in-scene navigation involves goal-directed movement, such as clicking on an object or distant landmark in the scene and then having the system drive your view there. Yet another form of second-person navigation involves tagging along after some other object moving in the scene, such as flying in formation behind the Red Baron in an aerial combat game.

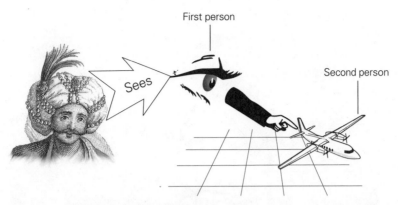

Figure 7.3 Second-person navigation where the user's view is tagging along behind another object in the scene

Third person

As you might suspect from its name, third-person navigation involves a third party in the navigation equation. As in third-person controls, the third entity is a separate control that lives outside of the user's first-person identity and outside of the scene's second-person realm. A good example of third-person navigation is moving a cursor on a map, which correspondingly moves the user's view through the virtual world. As you may recall from the previous chapter, this is a feature of the multi-view technique of overview, which allows the user to adjust the placement of the detail view from a bird's-eye overview of the problem space. A single-view example of third-person navigation might allow the user to arbitrarily slide the view and to rotate and tilt it about the LAP using third-person rotate and tilt knobs in a control panel.

You might be wondering what the difference is between second-person orbiting and the third-person version mentioned here. In second-person navigation, the motion is relative to some object or landmark in the scene, representing the second person. In third-person navigation, rather than being defined by an object, the LAP may be fixed at some impersonal position such as the origin of the world space; or it may be arbitrarily controlled through other third person controls, such as scrollbars around the display window. Third-person navigation is generally used in CAD packages. Fancier versions might allow the user to click in one view to set the LAP, with the other views centering themselves about the point in their respective views. What makes this third-person navigation is that the application is making no attempt to interpret the click position in the context of the scene's content—the point is simply an arbitrary coordinate in the virtual world space. The burden is on the user to adjust the point so that something useful is displayed in the view.

7.1.2 Contextual navigation

Unlike spatial navigation, contextual navigation moves the user through a nonlinear conceptual space from one data representation or level of detail to another. Contextual

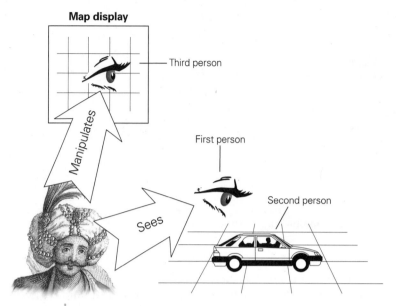

Figure 7.4 **Third-person navigation where the user moves his view using an icon in an overview map display**

navigation may seem abstract and remote until you realize that web surfing is just a form of contextual navigation. You start at one page about a given subject; find some interesting links related to that subject; click on one of the links; and you arrive at a new context or point of view about the subject, or at an alternative or more detailed presentation of its data. You can even travel back and forth along the context stream using the forward and back buttons. Contextual navigation techniques allow the user to go conveniently to alternative representations of the same or related data according to personal interests and the demands of the task at hand.

The following discussion categorizes contextual navigation into several basic forms according to how the data context is changing. An application can mix and match these contextual forms and even throw in a bit of spatial navigation for good measure. Also keep in mind that although the concept of contextual navigation is abstract, the data that it deals with can be just as concrete or abstract as that found in spatial navigation.

Selection

Navigation involving selection is probably the least navigation-like form. It entails selecting among alternative views of the same basic data. A simple example is choosing between a photorealistic rendering of your kitchen remodel plans and a 3D schematic view of its plumbing and wiring. Both presentations are of the same subject— your kitchen—but the kinds of information they present, although interrelated, are quite distinct. You might be thinking that this matter has more to do with data visualization than with navigation. How the data is presented certainly involves data visualization, but the fact that the user has a particular choice of presentations and how those presentations are selected brings the matter into the domain of navigation. It is navigation in the sense of button pushing instead of scrollbar dragging. As in any good UI design, the user's most frequent choices should be the easiest ones to get to, perhaps being offered as buttons on a toolbar. Choices that are less frequently used should be kept out of the way so the UI remains uncluttered. The secondary choices may require an extra level of UI navigation to be reached, such as selecting a presentation choice from a dropdown menu.

A different aspect of contextual navigation for selection is in the form of data filtering. For example, in an office layout application it may be useful at times for the user to see the furniture and the architecture together, perhaps to check clearances and to see if the layout feels right. At other times it may be useful to selectively turn off data in the scene, such as hiding all the walls to make layout easier, or to only show the cubicle partitions and not the furniture to make their alignment and connection easier. In this form of contextual navigation, the view is of the same data set and representational form, but different members of the data set are made visible at different times according to the user's problem-specific needs. An example of combining this form of selection and the previous one would be an astronomical analysis application where the user can select among X-ray, visible, and infrared views of a given galaxy—presentation selection—and in that view only show stars that are smaller than our sun—data filtering.

Traversal

Data traversal is closer to what people normally think of as navigation. In this form of contextual navigation, the user changes context by actually going somewhere. Traversal navigation generally involves topological representations of the application data, such as communication, utility, and information networks. Hypertext and web browsing—information networks—are the forms of data traversal with which most people are now familiar.

Contextual forms of navigation are generally nonlinear, and traversal highlights this fact. In geographic space, clicking on a web link may bring you to a site hosted on a server in the next office, or in a country on the other side of the world. In information space, one link may bring you to an article about varieties of tea, and another may land you in the middle of a treatise on the price of tea in China. In other words, traversal and its nonlinearities can appear along many different dimensions of the data, not just the three dimensions available through spatial navigation. For example, in a control application that allows the user to manage a chemical plant, clicking in the display on a pipe leading out of one production unit may switch the view to show the unit at the other end of that pipe. Double-clicking the pipe might instead pop up a control panel showing the history of the flow rate through the pipe. Simply selecting the pipe might allow access to a whole host of secondary information, such as the last time the pipe was inspected or a log of who repaired the pipe.

The types of data involved in traversal navigation are limited only by the application's problem domain. The mechanisms for traversing that data are limited only by the designer's imagination, tempered by the user's familiarity with domain-specific control metaphors. Using an adventure-like game as a model for navigating a chemical plant might be novel, but it may not be appreciated in an emergency situation.

Detail

Navigation through levels of detail is a powerful tool in helping the user to use effectively large volumes of data that span a wide range of detail. It can be similar in nature to geometric zoom, but often it involves a true context shift, with different kinds of data being hidden and exposed at different levels. This context change is useful because the user's tasks generally change with the change in detail. For example, in a communication network application used for design and control, the problem space may be as large as the world, with network nodes in major cities across the globe. Double-clicking a city node may expand the presentation to show the business campuses within that city connected to the network, with the bandwidth bottlenecks highlighted. Double-clicking a campus may reveal the buildings in the campus and the available space in underground conduits for increasing capacity. Double-clicking a building would reveal its ceiling cableways and wiring closets, and double clicking on a closet might show the equipment in the closet, and so on down to the rack, device, and card level, which may be needed for troubleshooting and maintenance dispatching.

The utility of combining detail navigation with selection and traversal navigation is easy to see. The user could choose between hardware, software, and data views in the communications network example. In switching from a hardware to a data view, the user would see data circuits, node addresses, and data protocols instead of hubs, routers, and cableways. And, clicking on links of the data circuit would allow the user to traverse the network through a building or to another continent. Detail navigation is also useful in analysis applications by allowing the researcher to quickly winnow down a mountain of data into something more manageable. For example, information may have been gathered about stars in a number of galaxies. Rather than having to sort through it all, the researcher may double-click on a galaxy and then on a particular star in that galaxy in order to see its detailed data.

7.2　CAMERA TECHNIQUES

The previous section made a number of suggestions for how to perform contextual navigation. Because of its abstract nature and the discrete nature of its control inputs, it is hard to classify techniques for contextual navigation other than the obvious—second-person click gestures, and third-person toolbar buttons and menu selections.

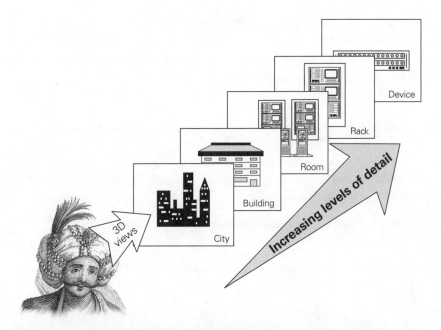

Figure 7.5 Contextual navigation with increasing levels of internal detail

Many have suggested more fanciful approaches, such as in-scene 3D menus, buttons, and wormholes, but there seem to be few conventions and the advantages are contested. As such, the rest of this chapter is devoted to the more workable subject of spatial navigation, specifically techniques for manual and automatic camera manipulation.

In simple terms, the camera has a position and orientation in the 3D world space—its external geometry—and it can be controlled by the user, by the system, or through a combination of the two. Getting into second-order effects, the camera's internal geometry may be controllable, such as its various scaling factors and the FOV, but this is rare. Usually the designer picks the internal geometry to help the user perform a particular job and it remains fixed. With only six degrees of freedom in the problem—three for position and three for orientation—camera control should be rather straightforward. Wrong! As you will soon see, there is quite a variety of ways for the user and system to push these six variables around. Only a representative sampling is provided here.

7.2.1 Manual control

Manually controlled cameras are ones that are under the user's direct control. The system has no say in the matter. Manual control is the easiest form to implement and therefore it is the form most commonly found in applications, old and new. With a bit of instructional feedback and some well-placed action hints from the designer, most users can figure out the basics of how manual controls work. Proficiency in using the controls, however, is another matter entirely. Take, for instance, the controls provided in most VRML players. Since the players are meant to be used in a wide variety of situations they are general in nature and are for the most part manual—the designers have tried to make as few assumptions as possible. Although a good strategy for the player vendors, it is often not a very good one for the common user. Users who play games and like flight simulators can generally get by, but for the general public, proficiency may be a long time in coming.

In order for manual controls to work for the common user, a good dose of constraints is needed. To impose constraints, the problem domain must be known and understood by the designer. The following techniques, which are summarized in table 7.1, are examples of first-, second-, and third-person manual camera techniques that exercise constraint for the sake of the user.

Table 7.1 Examples of manually controlled camera techniques

Orbit camera	• First-person navigation. • Fixed LAP; requires small limited world space. • First- or third-person rotate, tilt, and zoom controls.
Puck camera	• Second-person navigation. • Drag puck widget such as an in-scene object. • Second-person control of LAP and orbit, third person control of zoom.
Pinocchio camera	• Third-person navigation. • Drag Pinocchio widget to control position and orientation. • Third-person overview control of LAP and direction, third-person control of zoom, tilt, and LAP height.

Orbit camera

A major problem with techniques that allow the user to walk or fly through the virtual world is that it is easy for the user to get lost. If the controls use rate action, as most do when large expanses must be covered, then the user can get completely disoriented. If the application does not require the user to freely roam about the world, then don't let him. Even if situations arise where a little roaming might be useful, resist the temptation. If you can structure the problem such that the user is confined to work in a limited space or on a single object or assembly at a time, then a good candidate for navigation is the *orbit camera*.

In a first-person orbit camera, the range and motion of the camera is severely restricted. The LAP is fixed at some well-known spot, such as the center of the scene. This leaves only the camera LFP and orientation to worry about. As its name implies, an orbit camera ties together the LFP and orientation so that the user is restricted to orbiting about the LAP while always looking at the LAP. Most applications can assume an up direction, which further reduces the degrees of freedom. In its most basic form an orbit camera has one degree of freedom, which is horizontal rotation about the LAP.

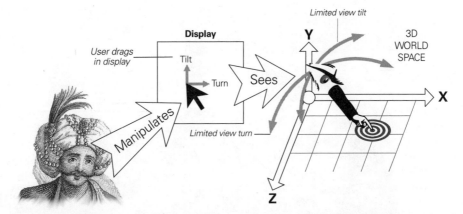

Figure 7.6 **First-person navigation using an orbit camera with fixed look-at-point, and limited turn and tilt range**

More sophisticated versions allow tilt as well as rotation, so the top and bottom of the subject can be seen. And, if absolutely necessary, you can also let the user zoom in and out from the LAP, which makes for, at most, three degrees of freedom. These can easily fit on a small control panel and it is unlikely that the user will get lost using them.

Let's be clear. You are conceding that navigation and manipulation in a virtual 3D space is a lot less intuitive and a lot more difficult than in the real one, especially when using a POCS. By restructuring the problem and constraining the user's actions, you as designer are playing an active role in trying to maximize the user's chances of success. If the user never gets lost, you are halfway there. If the user has just the right amount of freedom to get the job done quickly, then both you and the user have won.

An example of an application where the orbit camera would be a good choice is one involving single-room layout for home or office. The size of the space is fairly limited and often compact in shape. Fixing the LAP in the center of the room and a bit off the floor allows the user to see the entire room while orbiting around and tilting up and down. The limitation of not being able to move the LAP is mitigated by the fact that the view is never very far from any point in the room. Limiting tilt to keep the view above the floor avoids disorientation. In the same application, but for a different task, a second view might show the currently selected piece of furniture free-floating. The user would be allowed to select surfaces and apply valid materials and finishes, or to select options and see them appear on the furniture. Using an orbit camera, the user could examine the piece and its features in detail with minimal fuss.

An orbit camera with first-person controls—drag in the display to rotate and tilt the view—is used throughout part 4 of this book, starting with the FancyApp example in section 23.1.2.

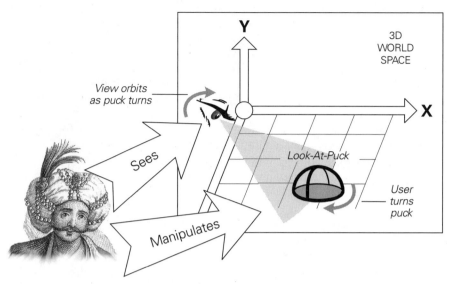

Figure 7.7 Second-person navigation using a Look-At-Puck widget

Puck camera

For the daring designer, a second-person version of an orbit control could be offered in the form of a *puck camera*. The name comes from the puck-like view control widget that appears in the scene at the location of the view LAP—a look-at-puck. Instead of putting rotate and tilt controls in a control panel, the user chooses drag handles on the puck itself to manipulate the view. As with other objects in the scene that can be directly manipulated, the user can move the puck with slide handles, which has the effect of also moving the view LAP. Rotation is a little different than rotating a data object in that dragging the puck's rotation handle causes the view to rotate—not the puck. This is shown in figure 7.7. In other words, the user manipulates the view puck a lot like he or she would any other object in the scene, but instead of simply moving the object, the view also tags along.

The puck camera should only be considered if the application requires the user to move the LAP. Unlike third-person controls, the puck camera places the controls directly in the scene in a single convenient control widget in the middle of the action, which makes it easy to switch between manipulation and navigation. Although it takes a little getting used to, if the user knows how to slide, lift, and rotate an object in the scene, then he/she knows how to operate the view puck. Placing the puck in perfect overlay allows it to be accessed at all times yet remain a constant size no matter how far the view is zoomed in or out. Because the view puck is always in the scene, it provides a reassuring visual landmark for the user. This, however, can also be a drawback since the puck is always stuck there in the middle of the scene.

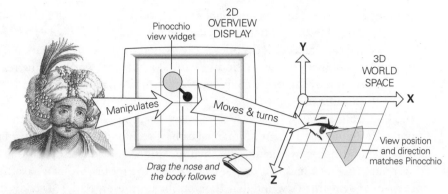

Figure 7.8   Third-person navigation using a Pinocchio widget

Pinocchio camera

A third-person camera that offers puck-like navigation control is the *Pinocchio camera*. The user controls the camera by dragging a control widget in a separate third-person control area. What gives it its name is that the view widget has a body and a small stick—the nose. Dragging the body slides the view, with the nose indicating the view direction, which is illustrated in figure 7.8. When you drag the nose, however, the body trails along after it. This simple action gives the user the wonderful and rather intuitive ability to simultaneously position and orient the view with a single continuous mouse gesture. It offers the all-in-one advantage of the puck camera with the intuitiveness of an overview technique, and the conventionality of a third-person control.

Unlike the puck camera, the vertical angle of the view and the height of the LAP cannot be readily controlled. Perhaps the application will allow the view to be set horizontally at eye level; or, the vertical parameters could be controlled using separate third-person controls. If your users are really savvy, you could even provide additional pinocchio drag areas, for front and side overviews. If the application has more than one 3D view of the scene then you could show the pinocchios of the other views as entities in the views. Dragging a pinocchio/puck in the scene would correspondingly change its parent view, which is a cross between second- and third-person navigation.

7.2.2   Assisted control

For many situations, offering strictly manual control of the camera may be a bit much for many users to handle. For example, in terrain-following, the user wants to fly over a landscape or structure that varies in height while seeing the subject from a comfortable distance. Having to constantly adjust the height to maintain a sufficiently close view can be tedious and problematic, such as when the user flies into a hill or building and becomes disoriented because the sky and ground are no longer visible. Another situation is formation flying, where the user wants to tag along after some entity moving in the scene, such as another player in a game or a student in a training simulation. Instead of concentrating on the action, the user will have to devote appreciable attention to jockeying the navigation controls.

Assisted camera techniques offer a way to merge the acts of navigation and manipulation, a combination that we find so natural in the real world. In the real world, if you wanted to move an office chair you would simply walk over to it and start rolling it. While pushing it, you would turn you head to look at where the chair needs to go and figure out ahead of time how to maneuver it around the furniture and into position in front of your desk. With manual camera techniques, especially in a POCS with only a single mouse, navigation and manipulation are separate operations that must occur at different times. To drag a chair across the room you may have to alternate between moving the view and dragging the chair, or resort to the 3D equivalent of cut and paste. Neither of these approaches is very intuitive or natural, but at least the latter one is convenient, as long as the user knows it is available and how to use it.

In the following selection of camera techniques, which are summarized in table 7.2, the focus is on trying to blend the actions of navigation and manipulation. Unlike the manual techniques, the assisted ones here exhibit an awareness of the objects in the scene and the user's actions on them. In response, the techniques try to automatically adjust the view to help the user perform his task.

Table 7.2   Examples of assisted camera techniques that blend navigation and manipulation

Home View	• The view goes to a standard vantage point and adjusts to fill the display with the scene contents. • The 3D equivalent of a web site home button or a "you are here" sign.
Bump Scroll	• The view adjusts during a drag to keep the target object in view. • The 3D equivalent of bump scrolling during a drag operation.
Selection Scroll	• The view adjusts to center the currently selected data object. • The 3D equivalent of synchronized list, choice, and document view widgets.
Walk Around	• The navigation path alters to avoid objects. • The 3D equivalent of goal oriented route planning.

Home view

A great way to keep the user from getting lost is to show him the virtual equivalent of a "You Are Here" sign. One approach for doing this is to use the overview visual technique where the application presents the user with an overview and detail view of the world. This is a fine technique, but many applications don't have the luxury of being able to afford room for two displays. Also, seeing two displays, much less having to use them both, can give casual users the impression that the UI is complicated. A single-display technique that offers many of the advantages of overview is the *home view* technique.

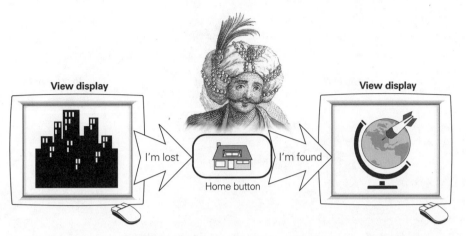

Figure 7.9 The home view button can bring the user back to a known view overlooking the scene with his previous position marked.

When the user pushes the Home button, the view gracefully flies up to a standard vantage point, such as looking down from the southwest, while pulling back to reveal the entire contents of the virtual world. Moving the view to a standard position and direction provides the 3D equivalent of a web site's home button. If the user is ever lost or wants to get back to a well-known 3D starting position, salvation is only a button push away with the home view technique.

The animation is an important aspect of the technique because it helps to give the user a sense of continuity and context. It shows him where he was and provides confirmation that he is really going home. The previous position of the user can be marked in the home view for further reassurance. By making the operation aware of its virtual world, the view automatically adjusts so that the user can see everything in the world at the closest possible distance. For some applications, such as those using the orbit camera, this might be an acceptable view for manipulating objects and performing useful work—a simple example of assisting navigation for the sake of manipulation.

A simple variation on home view is to use a toggle for the home button; the first press sends the user home and the second press returns him/her to the starting place. A more sophisticated version might use a multistate button, with the first press causing the view to zoom out until the world contents fill the display; the second press sending the view home, and the third press returning it to the start point.

Bump scroll

A handy form of navigation common in most GUIs (although not very well implemented in some) is a technique called bump scroll. In a drawing program, for example, you may need to drag a small figure that you made from one side of the virtual page to the other. As is often the case in such circumstances, you are probably zoomed in on the figure, and the whole page cannot be seen in the display. As you start

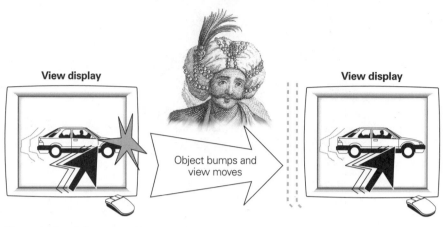

Figure 7.10   3D bump scroll moves the view to keep the target object in the scene during a drag.

dragging the figure, you will quickly come to the edge of the view but not the edge of the page, which is where you want to drop it. Any decent GUI would start scrolling the page for you automatically as your dragging bumped up against the display edge, hence the name bump scrolling.

Stealing a play from the 2D playbook, the *bump scroll* technique described here is simply a 3D equivalent of 2D bump scrolling. If the user is in the middle of dragging a data object in the scene, the view will start to scroll in the appropriate direction so the user can continue the drag uninterrupted. In 3D, the synergy between navigation and manipulation seems a bit more natural than it did in 2D. It feels a bit like turning your head while dragging a real object—or is it like stepping sideways? In 3D, it's difficult to take anything for granted because there are so many more degrees of freedom with which to contend. One possibility for scrolling the view is to simply slide the view along with the object, but this doesn't provide the user with much in the way of a look-ahead for avoiding obstacles and planning how best to drop the object. If instead of sliding the view you turn it, so it tracks the drag, the user gets a chance to see ahead of the object as it is dragged past the view. Although turning the view keeps the target object in the view, the object will start to rapidly shrink as the user continues to drag it away from the view position. A solution for this is to have the view turn as the drag goes by and, when the object gets too far away, the view will start to follow along behind it. This, by the way, is much like the second-person puck camera, except here it is more intuitive.

Another issue to contend with in 3D is deciding in which direction the user is intending to drag the object. In 2D, the drag direction is clear and unambiguous. In 3D, if the user is dragging the object right in the display and the view turns, does that mean the user will continue to drag the object right as seen in the display, or will the object continue to move in a straight line in the virtual world? This question gives a

Figure 7.11 Selection scroll moves the view to focus on the selected object.

new twist to the notions of display- and world-relative control mapping—DRM and WRM. Taking a DRM interpretation, continuing to drag the object right would in essence drag the object in a circle around the view's current position, and no view tag-along action would be needed. If, however, a more WRM interpretation were used, the object would always move in the direction that the user was dragging it in the world. To keep the object moving in a straight line the user would have to adjust the direction of the drag as the view turns. For example, at the start of the drag, north is down and to the right in the display; but as the user drags in that direction and the view swings to track it, north shifts to being straight up. This is not an ideal situation if straight-line drags are important, but it can seem intuitive to a user as long as there are adequate visual details in the scene to orient him/her in the world as the view turns.

Selection scroll

Often, when a user selects a target object, he/she intends to manipulate it. In order to do so, the user needs to see the object and the area around it, assuming that direct manipulation is being used. For this reason, in certain situations some 2D GUIs tie selection to scrolling. For example, a document-viewing application may show an overview of the document on the left and a detail view of it on the right (e.g., a variation of the display overview technique). Clicking on a section title or page thumbnail in the overview causes the detail view to scroll to that portion of the document. This technique, called *selection scroll*, can be generalized for use in 3D.

With 3D selection scroll, when the user selects a data object the view scrolls to show the object in the view. As with a bump scroll, several questions arise about the details. Does the view turn, tilt, slide, or a little of everything? How close does the view zoom in on the selected object and, correspondingly, how much of the neighborhood does it show? Unlike the bump scroll, the answers to these questions are not quite as clear. What must happen has a lot to do with the application problem space and the user's needs, but here are a few things to consider.

Object selection can occur when the user clicks directly on an object in the scene, or when he/she clicks on the name or icon of an object in an out-of-scene widget, such as a data object list or tree. The combination of out-of-scene selection with selection scroll is an effective way to find lost objects in the scene. Having the view move every time an object is selected, however, might become annoying to users. If the target object is already in the view, relatively close and reasonably visible, then it might be best to leave the view where it is, especially if the selection is occurring in-scene. On the other hand, user expectation for the view to change every time an object is selected out-of-scene has already been established in the 2D version of the technique, and seems to be more readily accepted than for in-scene selection.

Walk around

To get from point A to point B in the real world, such as from your cubicle to your buddy's across the office, you would look over toward where you need to go, start walking in that direction, and along the way you would walk around obstacles and update your course accordingly. In other words, when we move through the world we generally have a destination in mind. While moving toward that goal, we are sizing up the situation so we don't bang into things or make unnecessary side trips. Most of this happens subconsciously while we are on mental automatic pilot; we think of the goal and go for it. With strictly manual navigation through a virtual world on a POCS, getting from point A to point B is a very conscious and often tedious procedure. In many ways, users welcome being able to walk through walls just so they are not burdened with having to meticulously plan and execute every step of the way around them. Unfortunately, being able to walk through objects destroys any sense of reality, and users can become disoriented when they burst through walls or find themselves inside of enclosed objects.

With a bit of goal-directed route planning, the *walk around* technique allows the user to pick a goal and to just start walking toward it. While the user keeps moving forward, the view automatically follows an unobstructed path to the goal. Along the way, the view would turn to keep the goal in site, similar to what you would probably do in the real world. In essence, the system's automatic route planning and obstacle avoidance substitute for the user's subconscious autopilot. Keeping the goal in sight helps reassure the user as to the progress of the operation. The overall effect is to unburden the user from the detailed mechanics of the navigation process, while maintaining a strong sense of reality by having him/her move around objects instead of through them. If the user is allowed some freedom over turning the view during the operation then, while getting somewhere useful, he/she can also look around to check out this virtual neighborhood.

At this point, you should have two big questions: how does the user pick the goal, and where do you get a goal-directed route planner? The simplest way for the

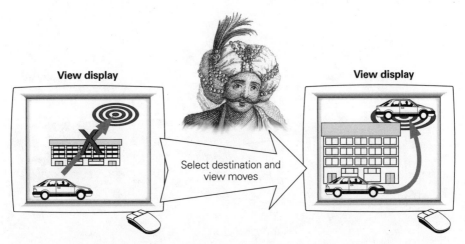

Figure 7.12 Walk around moves the view from "here" to "there" while avoiding objects in between.

user to pick the goal is to select it, either by clicking on it in the scene or in a list. It may be useful to introduce landmarks in the scene, artificial or real ones. The designer could place artificial ones at or over strategic spots in the scene, or the user could be allowed to designate them. Prominent or common features such as windows or doors in a room could be made selectable as navigational landmarks, with the user being able to move through a building by going from door to door using walk around. The answer to the second question—where to get goal directed route planning—is a bit more complicated.

Route planning involves developing candidate routes from start to end point, and assigning costs to various key aspects about the routes. For example, a longer route might have a higher cost than a shorter one, turns might have a higher cost than straight segments, and objects that block the user's view of the goal might have a higher cost than other objects along the route. The route with the lowest overall cost is chosen as the optimal route for the user to follow. In various forms, route planning has been used in robotics, military planning and war game simulation, and network routing. In recent years, it has emerged as part of intelligent agents and in mapping software on the web to tell you how to drive from one place to another.

7.2.3 Scripted control

In spite of all the goodness and wisdom of giving the user the freedom to explore his/ her virtual world at will, there are situations where such freedom may not be appropriate. Many simulation applications, such as for demonstration and training, need to move the user through the scene in a scripted manner. For example, your kitchen designer may want to take you on a tour of your planned kitchen. Rather than subjecting you to all the mechanics and missteps of doing it live, the designer might prefer to plan the tour ahead of time, stopping along the way to show you key features.

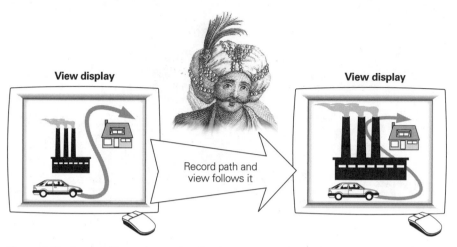

View display   **View display**

Record path and
view follows it

Figure 7.13 **A recording captures the view's movement through the scene.**

At the stops, he/she may even let you take the controls and look around a bit. Trading navigational freedom and flexibility for showmanship and dependability can also be effective in sales pitches to customers and presentations to audiences, such as at a conference or to your boss and his flunkies.

The following navigational techniques, which are summarized in table 7.3, allow the user to pre-plan camera movements through the virtual world, which is not unlike scripting a movie. Taking this analogy a bit further, scripting can also be extended to object manipulation. For example, combining scripted navigation and manipulation, during the kitchen fly-through your designer may want to stop in front of the refrigerator and stove, and have their doors swing open to show clearance with the center island. Also, scripting can perform contextual navigation, such as switching to a different form of data presentation or level of detail, as well as in-scene spatial navigation.

Table 7.3 **Summary of scripted navigation techniques**

Recording	• The user navigates through the scene. • The system records the motion for later playback.
Waypoints	• The user designates key camera positions and orientations. • The system interpolates the path between the key views.
Behaviors	• The user specifies criteria for triggering scripted object manipulation and sounds. • During scripted navigation playback, the system triggers the behaviors.

Recording

In many respects, the simplest way to perform scripted navigation is for the user to perform the navigation while the system records it. When done, the user can play it

Figure 7.14 Waypoints let the system worry about moving the view from one point to the next.

back, pause it, and even fast-forward or reverse it like a digital VCR. If no user interaction were allowed during the playback then the effect would be the same as a "screen cam," which effectively records the video on the screen. The power of using the *recording* technique in a live 3D application is that it offers the ability for improvisation during a presentation; the playback can be stopped and the user can interact with the scene. A presenter could even stop and hand over controls to a client, such as in the kitchen tour example.

Typical embellishments are to allow multiple recordings and editing. The user may want to record several passes of the same tour or several different tours. The best version of the tour can then be selected, or the user may want to splice the best pieces together from a given tour or from different tours, which is a lot like editing a movie. Unlike a movie, however, pauses can be put into the tour for *ad libs* and possible audience participation.

Waypoints

The same reasons used to describe manual navigation as being tedious and difficult can be applied to scripted recording. Again looking to Hollywood, *key framing* is a technique used in animated cartoons where the best artists draw key frames of the movie and less experienced artists draw all the in-between frames. The *waypoint* navigation technique is similar in concept, except that the user navigates to and saves a series of view positions and orientations, called waypoints. Then, during playback, the system smoothly interpolates the view position and orientation between the waypoints over time similar to the way that junior artists filled in the action between the key frames. A variation would be to allow a pause at the waypoints, with the view's motion decelerating as it approaches a waypoint, and accelerating as it leaves.

The same embellishments discussed for recording also apply here, such as multiple tours and editing. One interesting variation is to allow the user to specify the waypoints by placing and manipulating in-scene camera objects. During tour development the camera widgets would be visible and available for second-person adjustment, but during playback they would be hidden. This brings up another point, that during playback for any of the scripted techniques it is a good idea to turn off all in-scene feedback, unless it is part of the presentation such as callouts labeling key items in the scene.

Behaviors

Scripting other objects and actions, such as sounds, as part of an overall presentation is collectively called *behavior* techniques. They are included here because they are usually triggered during navigation—manual, assisted, or scripted. Triggering can occur when the view reaches a particular volume of space or the scripted object becomes visible in the view. For scripted navigation, triggering can occur when the playback starts or stops, or when it reaches a particular waypoint or time mark. There are really no limits on what form the scripting can take. In the kitchen tour example, it can be as simple as making the French doors swing open as the tour makes its grand entrance into the new kitchen, or as complex as showing a customer how the refrigerator shelves and dishwasher racks can be adjusted.

A question that arrises concerning the interaction of navigation and behaviors is: What happens after the view passes or the scripted object becomes hidden? For a one-time, one-direction tour, nothing needs to be reset to its starting position or state. For situations involving non-scripted navigation, or navigation with a bit of freedom, then some thought must be given to whether or not things need to be reset, when, and how. For example, if a tree falls in a forest it should probably stay down, until, of course, the script is restarted. For the kitchen doors, you may want them to close behind you as the view enters or, for effect and lighting, you may want them to stay open until you leave the kitchen.

7.3   SUMMARY

Navigation comes in two flavors: spatial and contextual. Spatial navigation is the one that has been traditionally dealt with in 3D applications, and can be described in terms of persona—first, second, and third. Navigation personae are somewhat distinct from control personae. For example, a first-person orbit camera might be controlled through third-person knobs in a control panel. Although less glamorous, contextual navigation is an extremely important aspect of many applications, especially those involving multiple versions of the same data, such as in an analysis application, or data with a wide range of detail, such as in a control application.

Within spatial navigation there are many categories of techniques for helping the user to explore virtual worlds. A key consideration in all of these is that, due to the difficulty of getting around in a virtual world on a POCS in comparison to navigating the real one, you are often doing users a favor by imposing constraints and severely limiting their freedom. If needed, you can try to restructure and partition the problem to make the application more constrainable. After all, if the user is lost, the user cannot function. Likewise, the user is seriously handicapped if he/she is spending most of the time on negotiating the problem space instead of building or exploring it.

Spatial navigation, or camera techniques can be manual, assisted, or scripted. Manual techniques are the easiest to implement, but the hardest for casual users to employ effectively. Assisted techniques are, perhaps, the most interesting ones since they attempt to combine navigation and manipulation, and to introduce a bit of intelligence to the problem of navigation. As you might imagine, they are also the most difficult ones to implement effectively. Scripted techniques are a special class used primarily for demonstration, which is usually associated with simulation types of applications. Often, however, design applications require a simulation/demonstration mode so that the user can show off what he/she has done.

C H A P T E R   8

Manipulation

In real life, people rely on sight and touch to help them manipulate objects. Before we move an object, sight allows us to size up the situation and to plan a strategy for performing the action. In addition, touch can help guide our hands and fingers to grasp tools, to move controls, and to feel when objects are flush. During the operation, sight provides us with a continuously updated overview of how the matter is progressing. By contrast, touch offers a more visceral and sometimes more detailed sense for what is happening than sight, such as whether the target object is moving smoothly, has bumped into something, is locked firmly into place, or is flush with another object. A big advantage of touch over sight is that you can get a good sense for what is happening, regardless of your vantage point or how cluttered the environment is; you do not have to see something in order to feel what is going on. All of this points to the fact that manipulation is a lot more intuitive in the real world than it ever will be on a POCS, which has no mechanism for providing the user with tactile feedback. The outlook for effective 3D manipulation on a POCS seems pretty bleak. Or is it?

With only a computer screen and a mouse, what can we as 3D user interface designers do? We cheat! We introduce artificial devices and decorations, judiciously bend the rules of physics, offer the user X-ray vision, and create a make-believe form of tactile feedback. Some of these cheats were already introduced in previous chapters.

In chapter 4, Control, you saw how DRM and WRM could make manipulation a lot more intuitive for the 3D user. (Meager, but it's a start.) Next, in chapter 5, you learned how feedback could help guide the user to the controls and indicate when his hand—the mouse—is in the right position to use them. (Things are starting to look up.) Chapter 6 discussed how to let the user see through clutter with overlay and X-ray vision, and chapter 7 described ways to let the user easily move around for a better view of the work. (Maybe there is hope for 3D manipulation.)

Manipulation is how users interact with the data in the application scene. It provides them with the means to move and arrange objects, connect and group them together, and to internally configure them. Manipulation requires the close cooperation of control, feedback, and visualization. This chapter builds upon these basic concepts to provide manipulation techniques that are effective and compelling in a 3D setting.

8.1 CONTROL PERSONAE

A convenient way to classify user manipulation is according to which entity in the control chain the user seems to be manipulating directly. The relation of that entity to the user, which names the *persona* of the manipulation control, can be described in terms of participants in everyday speech: first person, second person, and third person.

The elements in the control chain that are pertinent to defining control personae are the user, the control, and the target of the control action, which are shown in figure 8.1. The user's role is to work the controls and to see the results of that action in the display. The view, as a cameralike object, serves as a proxy for the user in the virtual world. In this context, moving the view is comparable to moving the user in the world. The next entity in the control chain is the control itself. When the user operates the control, the target object reacts in a manner prescribed by the control's input interpretation. The final entity in the control chain is the target object. In response to control inputs, the target object may slide or rotate, grow or shrink, change color, or react in any number of other ways.

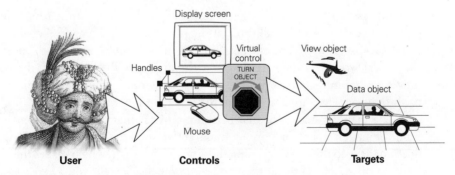

Figure 8.1   Control chain elements involved in defining control personae

As you may recall from the previous chapter, view navigation is also described in terms of personae (section 7.1.1). Although often related in terms of implementation, conceptually the two forms are distinct, with navigation personae describing the user's relationship with the moving view, and control personae describing different ways the user can control the movement of the view. Table 8.1 summarizes the control personae covered in this section.

Table 8.1   Control personae used for manipulation

First person	• The user controls himself, the first person. Example: Drag right in the display to turn the view—the user—to the right. • Pros: Manipulation occurs in the same frame of reference that the user sees in the view. Intuitive form of navigation that is similar to walking through the world. • Cons: Can be unintuitive in situations where the view is not represented as a vehicle. The target—the view—cannot be seen in the context of its surroundings.
Second person	• The user controls the target object, the second person. Example: Drag on an object to slide it across the floor. • Pros: Direct WYSIWYG manipulation of objects. Intuitive form of manipulation that is similar to reaching out and moving an object in the world. Can see the target in context of its surroundings. • Cons: Difficult to directly manipulate objects in 3D using a 2D mouse and display.
Third person	• The user controls a widget, the third person, which remotely controls the target object. Example: Virtual knob in a control panel that rotates a target object. • Pros: Controls are obvious—sliders, knobs, and buttons—and are always available. Familiar form of control—HUD or dashboard control panel. • Cons: Difficult to convey to the user what target object a control manipulates and how.

8.1.1   First person

In a first-person control, the user is essentially controlling himself/herself, the first person. The user performs all three of the player roles in the control chain: The control is the display itself; and the target object of the control action is the user's view in the virtual world. As the user drags on the display with the mouse, the user's view moves around in the virtual world, which is shown in figure 8.2. First-person control of an orbit camera is used in most of the examples in part 4.

The main advantage of first-person control is that user interactions occur in a frame of reference that does not require translation to that of another object. The user does not have to think, "I'm sliding this knob to the right, which makes the desk move north in the room." Instead, what you see in the display tells you where you are in the world and where you will go. In other words, you see that you are some distance away

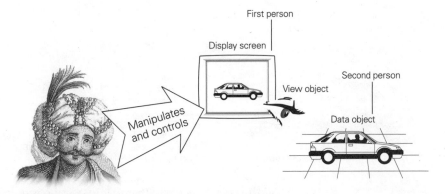

Figure 8.2   Manipulation through first-person control

from the north wall of a room. You know that if you move yourself forward, you will be moving in a northerly direction closer to the wall.

For some tasks, such as navigation, first-person control seems intuitive and works well. First-person navigation is popular because it approximates what happens when we walk through our everyday real world. We will ourselves to move forward and we do so. For this reason, VRML browsers use first-person control extensively for navigation, with the user dragging on the display (as opposed to some object or control widget) to move forward, steer left and right, and to tilt up and down. For other tasks, like manipulation, where the user's view is attached to the target object, first-person control can sometimes seem odd. For example, trying to convince the user that he/she is a bookshelf that needs to scoot forward and stand against the wall is a bit of a reach. In other situations, however, it can seem quite natural, such as when the user feels he is in a moving vehicle, and dragging on the screen makes the vehicle turn in the direction of the drag.

8.1.2   Second person

In a second-person control, the user has the feeling of directly manipulating an object in the scene, the second person. The control and target objects move as one, in unison. Typically, the control appears as drag handles attached to the target object, which is shown in figure 8.3. This form of control is often referred to as direct or WYSIWYG manipulation. It is probably the most intuitive form of interaction between a user and an object because it approximates what we all do in our everyday lives: reach out and move objects.

An interesting form of second-person control is when the target of the control action is the view itself. The target object, the view, is represented by a widget in the scene, called the look-at puck. The user manipulates the puck in the scene the same as he would a data object, but in this case the view tags along for the ride. This is the puck camera navigation technique described in chapter 7.

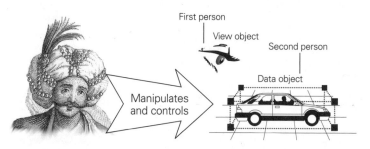

First person

View object

Second person

Data object

Manipulates and controls

Figure 8.3   Manipulation through second-person control

The advantages of second-person control are that the interaction is quite familiar to users—reach out and move an object—and that the target can be seen in the context of its surroundings, something that is missing in first-person control. A big disadvantage is that it is difficult to position and orient an object in three dimensions on a 2D display. One issue is the difficulty in using a 2D device like a mouse to control an object in three dimensions. The use of DRM and WRM coordinate mapping can help, which can constrain motion to a 2D frame of reference such as, in the case of WRM, a floor plane. Another issue with 3D manipulation is the ambiguity of viewing an object in three dimensions on a two-dimensional display. For example, looking at a box in a room from a bird's-eye view you might wonder whether the box is small, above the floor, and near you; or whether it is large, on the floor, and far from you. This is illustrated in figures 8.4 and 8.5. Such visual ambiguity is unavoidable, especially if the user is not familiar with the inherent size of the objects in the world, or if similar looking objects come in various sizes, such as desks and bookshelves. Section 8.2 will describe how adding relational feedback to objects can help mitigate this problem. Second-person object manipulation with feedback is demonstrated in the SecondPerson example in section 22.2.2.

8.1.3   Third person

In a third-person control, the user manipulates a control widget, the third person in the user's relationship, which in turn remotely controls the target object. Typically, the control itself is a virtual control device that approximates a physical control such as a slider, knob, or button. The virtual control can be in a separate GUI panel or overlaid onto the user's view of the world e.g., a heads-up display (HUD) or a vehicle dashboard. The target of the control action can be a data object or the view object, as shown in figure 8.6.

When compared to second-person direct manipulation, this type of control may not seem very intuitive because the link between the control and its target is not direct: the user is required to make a mental transposition of actions. But practical experience does not support this conclusion. We are all accustomed to using third-person controls whether they are the set of buttons in an elevator or scrollbars in a GUI application. The user understands that manipulating a control in one place—pressing a floor

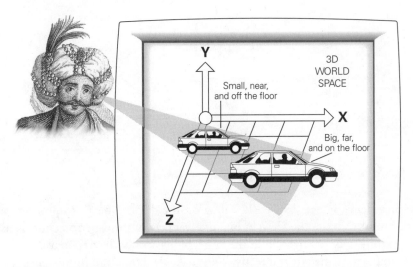

Figure 8.4   Illustration of the size-position ambiguity in 3D

button in the elevator—leads to some desired action somewhere else, the elevator moving up and down in the building.

The advantages of third-person control are that the controls are obvious because they look like real controls—sliders, knobs, and buttons—and so too are the actions required to manipulate them—slide a slider, turn a knob, press a button. Unlike in-scene controls, the position, size, and visibility of out-of-scene controls are certain: The user doesn't have to guess where the controls are, select an object to make them appear, or fiddle with the view so that the controls can be seen. Third-person controls also avoid the ambiguity that can occur with first- and second-person controls fighting

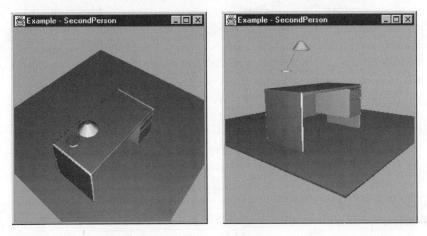

Figure 8.5   Two views of the same scene demonstrating the visual ambiguity that the user must contend with in a POCS

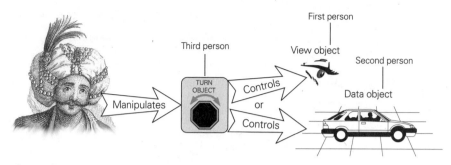

First person
Third person
View object
Second person

Data object

Manipulates

TURN
OBJECT

Controls
or
Controls

Figure 8.6   Manipulation through third-person control

for precedence in the display: Is a drag on the display meant to position an object, rotate it, or navigate the view? A big disadvantage of third-person controls is that the user is truly once removed from the target of his actions, having to use a proxy instead of manipulating the target directly. This makes it difficult to intuitively convey to the user what the target of the control action is and what the result of the control action will be. Third-person object manipulation with feedback and display overlaid controls is demonstrated in the ThirdPerson example in section 22.2.3.

8.2   FEEDBACK ELEMENTS

Of the basic feedback elements, described in section 5.2, those that are especially useful in manipulation are indicators, handles, verbal messages, and sound effects. Here the focus is on elements that are suited for relational feedback, in particular ones formulated to provide the user with a visual feel for how objects are situated during direct manipulation in a 3D scene.

One way to categorize relational feedback elements is by how they indicate object and environmental relationships. For example, one type projects—sticks out—into the surrounding space from the host object. Another type encloses the host object to indicate its spatial extent. And yet another type, the tic mark, is a small line or symbol that assists with alignment or that indicates when alignment is achieved. A different way to distinguish relational feedback elements is by whether they participate by showing relations actively or passively. Passive elements, such as outlines and projections, are decorations that require no active processing. Instead, they do their job strictly by their visual appearance and the manner in which they occlude or reveal surrounding objects. Active elements, on the other hand, require explicit geometric processing to determine when specific spatial relationships occur, such as when two edges align and a tic mark appears.

Because of their use for in-scene manipulation, many of these elements benefit from revealment techniques discussed as part of feedback and visibility. For example, snap elements on objects are used to snap and attach objects together—two critical functions in manipulation. It is convenient, if not vital, for the user to see and access the snap elements even if surrounding objects hide them. Use of the X-ray overlay technique is one way to satisfy this need. Many of the visual attributes for feedback elements discussed earlier in section 6.2, such as distinction, size, and orientation, are also applicable to snap elements and the other feedback elements described here.

Table 8.2 Relational feedback elements for manipulation

Feelers	• Visual aids showing the relation of an object to its neighbors and surroundings • Passive feelers are visual only • Active feelers require real-time geometric processing
Projections	• A feeler that projects from an object into the scene • Line, plane, or complex shape indicating proximity, alignment, or affinity
Skirts	• A projection appearing as a translucent box underneath or beside an object • Idiom for a lifted object • Intersects with surrounding objects to show proximity
Shadows	• A feeler that appears on neighboring objects • Silhouette or icon indicating proximity or alignment
Outlines	• Encloses or delineates an object, object part (vertex, edge, face), or object group • As a feeler, shows spatial extent • As control feedback, indicates selection and mouseover • As a control widget, serves as a drag handle
Tic marks	• A small line or symbol marking a spatial position, graduating a spatial range, or indicating alignment • As a feeler, indicates proximity or alignment • As control feedback, indicates graduations over a range of motion
Rulers	• Provides quantitative measurement of size, distance, angle, and so on • As a feeler, indicates distance between or position of objects in the scene • As descriptive feedback, indicates size, angle, curvature, and so on of an object • As a tool, an active or passive measuring tool manipulated by the user
Snaps	• Hybrid of relational and control feedback indicating where and how attachment can occur • Can have a type to enforce selective matching • Can have an orientation to enforce geometric alignment

8.2.1   Feelers

When the user views a 3D world on a 2D display, there can be confusion as to how far away objects are from the user or from other objects. This was described earlier by the example of looking at an object in the scene and not being able to tell whether it is small, above the floor, and near; or whether it is large, on the floor, and far. It is generally useful and sometimes even necessary to provide visual aids showing where an object is in the world in relation to its neighbors and surroundings. Elements used to provide this type of relational feedback are called *feelers*.

Relational feedback elements can serve in many feedback and control capacities, feelers being a major one. The term feeler refers to both a class of elements as well as a role in which other elements can serve. Most of the elements described below are either a specific type of feeler element, or can serve in the capacity of a feeler.

8.2.2 Projections

Projecting feelers, or *projections*, can take the form of lines, planes, boxes, outlines, and even lightning bolts. Some show proximity and alignment, and others show affinity. For example, a plane might project from an edge of the host object parallel to a face of the object. As the user moves the object, so too moves the plane projecting into space. By moving the target object, the user can get a sense for where the object is in relation to neighboring objects by the way the plane intersects them, and whether or not the target face is aligned with some other object. A special form of planar projection feeler is the skirt, which is described and shown in section 8.2.3.

An example of a projecting feeler with affinity might be a lightning bolt that appears between snap points on nearby objects. A snap point indicates where, on an object, other objects can be connected. The lightning bolt's appearance is an idiom telling the user that the points will be snapped together if the user lets go of the mouse button. An example is shown in figure 8.7.

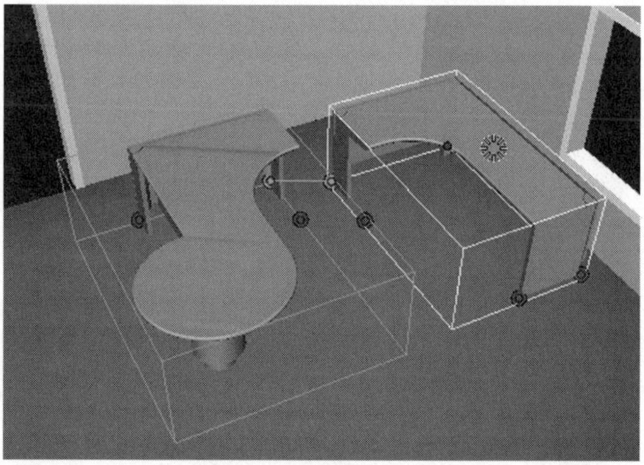

As with any feedback

Figure 8.7 When opposing snap points are close enough to snap, they highlight and a feeler (line between highlighted snap points) indicates what will be snapped. (Courtesy of TechniCon Corporation)

technique, it is important for projecting feelers to minimize their interference with the user's view of the surroundings; otherwise, the solution might be worse than the problem. In general, feelers should be visible only when the host object is selected or being manipulated; and they should be as small as possible while still getting the job done. If a line will do, then use it instead of a plane because the line will be less intrusive. The position of the feeler on the target can also help. For example, lines projecting at floor level from the target object would help indicate proximity to and alignment with other objects on the floor with minimal interference to viewing the contents of the room. If the feeler must be a plane, then consider making the plane semitransparent so surrounding objects can be seen through it. This also helps the user with depth perception because near objects will appear clearly, and far objects will appear hazy through the feeler plane. Limiting the extent of the feeler, rather than letting it stretch to infinity, can also help to minimize presentation clutter. For example, the extent can be limited to the nearest intersecting object or to a particular surrounding entity, such as the floor or walls in a room. This, however, makes the projection an active feeler—the length must be computed—instead of a passive one.

8.2.3 Skirts

Design applications for e-commerce, which involve arranging, assembling, and configuring data objects, will be a prevalent form of next-generation application. Such applications generally involve concrete real world data, such as architecture, furniture, and industrial parts. As such, there is a strong sense of "up" and often some notion of a ground plane like a floor. As long as all the data objects remain on the floor and the user knows this to be true, visual ambiguity is not much of a problem. If, however, some objects are inherently off the floor, like lighting fixtures, or can be lifted off of the floor by the user, like stackable bookshelves, then visual ambiguity becomes a significant problem. A *skirt* is a type of projecting feeler that is specially suited to address this problem.

A skirt is a set of semitransparent surfaces projecting down from the outer edges of the host object to the floor. For a rectangular-shaped profile, the skirt will appear as a translucent box underneath the object, sort of like a Plexiglas pedestal. This is shown in figure 8.8, and demonstrated in part 4 starting with the PassiveFeeling example in section 22.1.3. The skirt simultaneously provides the user with several types of feedback. It serves as an idiom telling the user to pay special attention to the object's apparent position because the object is not on the floor. In terms of relational feedback, it indicates how far the object is off the floor, where the footprint of the object is on the floor, whether the object is over or in front of any other objects, and whether an edge of the object is aligned with a neighboring object.

An important question remains: When should the skirt be visible? Showing the skirt only on the target object while it is actively being dragged minimizes presentation clutter and is adequate for providing most relational feedback. This approach, however, leaves the user wondering about all the nontarget objects in the scene, whose vertical position can be resolved only one object at a time by selecting an object and observing its skirt or lack thereof. One possible compromise is to show the skirt as part of the mouseover feedback for all the objects in the scene. Another possibility is to show all nontarget skirts all the time but dimly, with a high transparency factor, to minimize clutter.

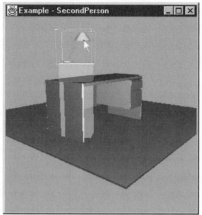

Figure 8.8   Adding a skirt to the lamp, which appears during mouseover, clearly shows the user that the lamp is not on the desk.

8.2.4   Shadows

Shadow feelers, or shadows, typically take the form of a dark solid silhouette projected onto neigboring objects, such as the floor or ground beneath the host object. Variations might use 3D, 2D or iconic representations of the host object as the shadow instead of a true silhouette. As the host object moves so too moves its shadow (or shadows). The shadow size can vary to indicate proximity, with the size increasing as the object approaches its neighbor. Shadows are useful in situations where projecting feelers may present too much visual clutter. Depending on the application, they may also appear more natural and intuitive, such as in a situation display for air or sea vehicles, where shadows might almost be expected underneath the objects.

8.2.5   Outlines

A rather simple but versatile element is the *outline*. Visually an outline encloses or delineates its host object or object group. The most common forms of outlines are the wireframe and the semitransparent bounding box. Nonbox shapes such as spheres, cylinders, and polyhedrons can also be used; and patterns of dots or lines can be used for the faces instead of semitransparent polygons. As a means of feedback, an outline's talents are many and somewhat specialized. Wireframe object outlines are demonstrated in part 4 of the book starting with the PassiveFeeling example in section 22.1.3, and several examples are shown in figure 8.9.

As a feeler, an outline can show the spatial extent of the host. As control feedback, its presence around a host object can indicate that the host is selected or highlighted in some manner. As relational feedback, an outline can enclose a group of objects thereby serving as an idiom for grouping. As a control widget, the outline can serve as a control handle allowing the user to drag the host object by dragging on the outline. For both efficiency and clutter reduction, an outline can serve as a proxy for the host object, with only the outline being seen and not its host object. In terms of efficiency, the outline is often quicker to render than the object itself, especially during user interaction if the object is large or complex. In terms of clutter, the outline obscures a lot less of the surrounding scene than the object itself.

Outlines can also enclose or highlight parts within an object, such as faces, edges, and vertices. For example, the user might select an edge or face in an object to serve as the reference for an alignment operation. As the object is dragged, an outline around the reference part might highlight when the part aligns with a neighboring object. A part outline can take a number of forms. For example, a 2D polyline or semitransparent polygon might be used to delineate an object face, a fat 1D line might delineate an edge, and a small 2D circle might outline a vertex.

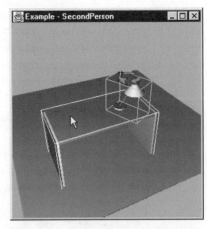

Figure 8.9   Object outlines can indicate interaction states and the spatial extent of their host objects.

8.2.6   Tic marks

A *tic mark* is some small line or symbol that marks a particular spatial position, graduates a range of spatial positions, or assists with alignment, like a feeler. A common form of tic mark is a small line next to a vertex or collinear with an edge on the target object that appears to show alignment with surrounding objects. An example is shown in figure 8.10. Unlike projecting feelers, tic marks are less obtrusive and can make the display appear less cluttered. The flip side is that they don't provide as much feedback information as a projecting feeler. A tic mark simply marks a single position or angle instead of extending to surrounding objects to indicate proximity as well as alignment. Tic marks can be passive, being visible whenever the host object is selected or being dragged; or, more typically they can be active and dynamic, appearing or highlighting when the host object aligns with a part—vertex, edge, face—in another object.

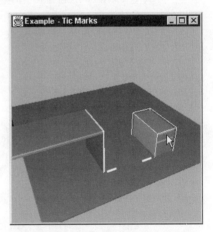

Figure 8.10   An example of a tic mark indicating when a target object edge is aligned with that of a neighboring object

A common use of tic marks is to indicate graduations for sliding or rotating a target object, similar to the tic marks on a ruler or protractor. For example, sometimes it's desirable for rotations to be delimited at certain increments, such as 15 degrees, in which case radial tic marks might indicate these positions and tell the user that such delimitations will be imposed. For a linear position, tic marks might indicate graduations in physical units such as inches, feet, or meters. A special form of tic mark is the "grid," where the marks themselves are taken to the extreme and are shown as complete intersecting lines. Grids are useful for aligning and snapping objects at regular but predefined positions, and are often used in 2D drawing applications. In 3D applications, grids and tic marks aren't limited to the ground plane. They can be applied to the walls, ceiling, floor, and even to an empty volume of space.

8.2.7 Rulers

A *ruler* provides quantitative spatial measurement, such as a graduated scale or a numerical readout. The most common form of ruler is a linear dimension such as in a mechanical drawing, with end marks and arrows showing the extent of the measurement, and a numerical callout showing the value. Other variations include dimensioning for angle, area, and radius of curvature. Rulers can measure the host object itself, such as the dimensions of its bounding box; or they can measure the spatial relationship between the host object and its surrounding objects, as a quantitative feeler. For example, while an object is being dragged, the distance between the host object and its neighboring objects might appear, as shown in figure 8.11.

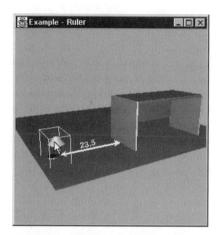

Figure 8.11 An example of a ruler showing the distance between the target object and the nearest neighboring object

Rulers can also be used as tools without a predefined host object. The user selects a particular tool from a toolbox depending on the kind of measurement needed, and snaps the ends of it to the objects to be measured. A familiar metaphor is a tape measure, where the user snaps one end to an object and moves the other end around in the world to measure distance. A similar scheme can be used for tools that measure angle, area, and volume.

Often rulers are dynamic, stretching as the host object is manipulated, and with the numerical callout updating continuously. They can also be passive, like a traditional ruler with tic marks. For example, static rulers might be placed alongside the edges of the floor in the office layout example to assist the user in placing furniture.

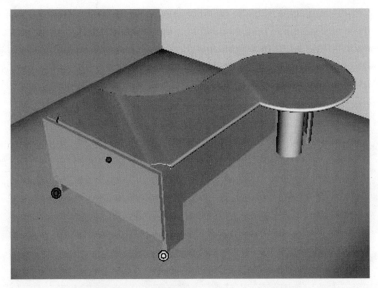

Figure 8.12 Snap points indicate points on an object where object snapping and attachment can occur. (Courtesy of TechniCon Corporation)

Doing the real ruler one better, live tic marks on the ruler might indicate the position and extent of the currently selected target object.

8.2.8 Snaps

In design applications some assembly is often required, but arbitrary attachment of objects is often not allowed. In these cases, feedback is needed on an object to tell the user that other objects can be attached to it, and to indicate where and how the attachment can be made. Feedback elements that provide this hybrid of relational and control feedback are called *snaps*. The most common form of snap element is the snap point, which is a point position on or near the host object that is often represented by a small graphic symbol, such as a dot or ball. Figure 8.12 shows a desk with several snap points. Notice that the "hidden" one in the middle appears smaller than the other two because of X-ray overlay. Snaps can also be associated with higher dimensional geometric elements, such as 1D snap edges and 2D snap faces.

Different forms of attachment require different forms of snap feedback. Typed attachments are selective about with whom they will partner, and oriented snaps impose a particular geometry on the connected objects. Each requires a different representation in the form of visual and audio snap elements so the user can easily tell them apart and get a sense for what will happen as a result of the attachment. For example, typed snaps may take male and female forms to indicate which attachments go together, and oriented snaps may use indicators to show the orientation that the attachment will impose.

Two important concepts in manipulation, attachment and snapping, were touched on here. These will be discussed at greater length and from other perspectives in later sections. Because of its common use in other 2D and 3D applications, the term "snaps" was chosen to name this form of feedback element although it is needed for all forms of attachment, not just snapping.

Table 8.3   Summary of PTF drags and grips

Marked drag	• Sight and sound feedback only; no change in control dynamics. • Weak tactile effect; relational feedback indicates proximity or alignment.
Sticky drag	• During drag, object stutters to indicate proximity and to help alignment. • Strong tactile effect; object stays where left; can require forced cursor movement; can interfere with precise adjustments.
Snap drag	• At drag end, object jumps into alignment. • Weak tactile effect; unexpected object jump; can interfere with precise adjustments.
Solid drag	• Dragged objects are solid. • Prevents confusion of objects intersecting; can interfere with object layout.
Strong grip	• During drag, no slippage or twisting of object upon collision. • No real-world dynamics.
Weak grip	• During drag, object is allowed to slip and twist upon collision. • Effect can be unexpected and unappreciated.

8.3   PSEUDO-TACTILE FEEDBACK

PTF is the combination of sight, sound, and control movement effects that serve as a substitute for the sense of touch. This is useful in manipulating real-world objects. The simplest form of substitution is to use sight for touch. For example, a tic mark might appear or an object face might highlight when the user drags the target object into some desired position. This is simply relational feedback, which was already discussed above. A more sophisticated approach, which gets to the heart of PTF, tightly couples control dynamics with sight and sound cues to impart a stronger suggestion of natural feel. For instance, in the furniture layout example, a user might drag a desk that is in some arbitrary orientation toward a wall. When the desk hits the wall, the desk highlights and a soft "collision" sound effect plays. As the user continues to drag the mouse toward the wall, the desk begins to turn, as would a real desk if dragged in a similar fashion, while an undertone of "scraping" is heard. If the user persists with the drag, the desk will eventually turn flush with the wall and stop, at which point the desk highlight flashes once, returns to normal, and a gentle sound effect of finality plays. The intent of these effects is to evoke in the user impressions that the objects and their interactions are real—or at least as real as they might seem if

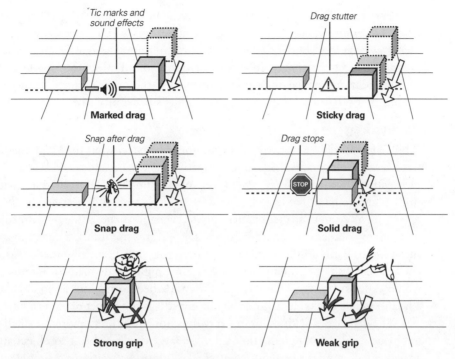

Figure 8.13   Examples of PTF drags and grips

used in a movie—with visual and audio feedback providing idioms that reinforce a sense of feel.

This section covers these and other variations on PTF techniques, which are summarized in table 8.3, and illustrated in figure 8.13. Some emphasize visual and sound effects; others emphasize object and control dynamics. As with many of the other techniques presented throughout this part of the book, you can mix and match the PTF variations as you see fit.

8.3.1   Marked drag

Starting with the simplest form of PTF, *marked drag* relies on sight and sound effects only, with no change in control dynamics. While the user is dragging an object, relational feedback such as tic marks might appear alongside the target object and its neighbors as alignment of various sorts occurs. Variations might use outline feedback to highlight the matching objects and object parts (vertex, edge, and face). Information feedback, like callouts, might appear to provide further detail about the type and location of the relationship achieved. In addition to its normal supporting role, sound might help to differentiate the type of relationship achieved, with variations on the basic "alignment achieved" sound effect indicating different types of alignments, such as edge, face, or midpoint.

Variations on marked drag might also include feedback regarding spatial proximity. For example, skirts and rulers might appear on the target object when near other objects, which serve both as a forewarning of collision and as assistance in performing precision object placement. In these situations, sound effects can reinforce warnings of imminent and actual collision. Additionally, the pitch of a mild tone or the frequency of a soft click could indicate the target's proximity to alignment or collision.

8.3.2   Sticky drag

People are naturally sensitive to discontinuities between what the hand does and what the eye sees. Taking advantage of this sensitivity is what really sets PTF apart from simple relational feedback. *Sticky drag* is one of the simpler PTF techniques that benefits from such eye-hand control effects. With sticky drag, while the user is dragging an object, it will seem to stutter or stick slightly when it reaches some predefined position, or aligns or collides with another object. The effect is not unlike a detent in a multiposition knob. For example, to help the user during layout, an alignment grid might be defined for position, and angular graduations might be defined for rotation. Objects would slide and rotate smoothly until they reached a grid line or an angular detent. The movement sticks there until the user overdrags the object or starts a new drag.

The degree of stickiness might vary depending on the situation. A small overdrag might be needed for a graduation detent, a large one for object-to-object alignment, and a new drag might be required after a collision. A variation on simple overdrag is to use a more pronounced gesture, such as a flick or jerk, to resume object movement. As with marked drag, sound effects can reinforce the tactile sensation and provide a feeling of proximity. Outline feedback can highlight the aligned or colliding objects and object parts.

The tactile effect of sticky drag is more pronounced than that of marked drag because marked drag relies solely on sight and sound whereas sticky drag also affects eye-hand coordination. This can be good, but it can also be bad. Techniques that affect the drag dynamics can seem unexpected to users if they are not familiar with the effect. Like any good idiom, this one can be quickly learned by the user. Another drawback of sticky drag is that the mouse cursor must be forcibly moved by the system to affect the stutter. Some designers reject such forced cursor movement on principle.

A more serious problem is that sticky drag can interfere with precise object placement when the object is near a sticky point. One possible remedy is to introduce hysteresis into the stickiness so that the drag doesn't immediately stick to the same point. A simpler but more direct way around this problem is to allow the user to momentarily disable the stickiness, such as by pressing a modifier key during a drag. Another possibility is to let the user perform fine adjustments with the arrow keys, which are not subject to the sticky effect. Although such keyboard-based alternatives sound good and can be effective, trying to let the user know they exist and how to use them is another matter, which is often the problem when keyboard controls are used.

8.3.3   Snap drag

If the idea of programmatically moving the mouse cursor is distasteful, even for a little stutter, then *snap drag* is a possible alternative to sticky drag. In snap drag, when the dragged object is released, it jumps or snaps to the nearest valid position, such as a mutual alignment with a neighboring object, a predefined graduation detent, or a snap point on another object. In other words, we've traded cursor jumping for object jumping. In both cases what is important to PTF is the discontinuity, which is what hopefully conveys a tactile feeling to the user. As with the other PTF drags, sound effects can significantly reinforce the tactile effect.

A drawback of snap drag is that its tactile effect is weaker than in sticky drag because there is no feedback during the operation, only after the drag is done. Another problem is that the dynamic discontinuity can be startling and at times unappreciated, perhaps even more so than with sticky drag. In sticky drag, the stutter occurs while the drag is underway. Once the user releases the mouse button, however, the object stays where the user left it. In snap drag, the snap occurs when the drag is done, just when the user thinks everything is positioned just right. An idea that might come to mind is to perform the snap during the drag rather than after it. This solution is probably worse than the problem because the target object tends to jump and squirm around while the user is trying to drag it into position.

As with sticky drag, the user can have problems performing fine adjustments near a snap position. These problems can be mitigated by using a modifier key to block the snap or through subsequent adjustment with the arrow keys.

8.3.4   Solid drag

One aspect of drags that must be resolved is what to do when two objects collide. One extreme is for the objects to act like ghosts and simply pass through one another. The other extreme is for the target object to stop dead in its tracks, as would an object in the real world. This latter approach, where the objects involved act like solids, is called *solid drag*. In some sense, a solid drag is like a sticky drag with infinite stick when a collision occurs. Overlapping objects can confuse users because they are inconsistent with real-world experiences, so solid drag should be highly desirable. Unfortunately, it has some undesirable side effects.

Solid drag prevents objects from passing through one another. This means that to move an object from one place to another in the scene, the user must maneuver it around any obstructions. For example, in an office layout application, to move a desk from one office to an adjacent one, the user may have to walk the desk down the hall, around the corner, and up a parallel hallway. What if the door opening is too narrow to slide the desk through? Does this mean the user has to tip the desk on its side and remove the legs, as might have to be done in the real world? Obviously the need for intuitive simulated reality has to be balanced with the need for user effectiveness. User-interface metaphors can give you enough rope to hang yourself, which is why some designers eschew their use. As with the other drags, modifier and arrow keys can be used as a means to escape from such predicaments.

8.3.5 Strong grip

Drag grip describes the kind of dynamics that occur during a drag when the target object encounters another object or an alignment point. A *strong grip* is analogous to the user having a firm grasp on the target object. As in the real world, if the object is firmly held, it is prevented from changing its orientation when slid and another object is bumped. It is also prevented from changing its center of rotation when turned and a corner catches on another object. This may sound a lot like solid drag, but here the focus is only on that aspect of the operation that keeps the target from wiggling around under the cursor. Strong grip is by far the most common form of drag grip because it requires that the programmer do nothing. In the virtual world, objects have to be programmed in order for them to react to one another.

8.3.6 Weak grip

Unlike a strong grip, a *weak grip* gives the target object a bit of freedom to slide around under the drag point or to rotate about it if the target encounters another object or an alignment point. As the name implies, this is analogous to the user having a weak grip on the object as the user drags it around in the scene. For example, if while sliding a desk in a room and a corner hits a wall, the desk might start to rotate. If the user continues to drag the object, it might eventually rotate so it becomes flush with the wall. Similarly, if while rotating a desk a corner hits a wall, then the desk might start to slide away from the wall to allow the desk to turn.

Whenever multi-object dynamics are involved, questions arise as to which objects remain stationary and which objects react, especially if chain reactions can potentially occur. A full-blown distributed dynamics simulation is probably overkill. Usually, letting only the dragged object move is a good idea because it is already moving and any additional movement of it as a result of a weak grip effect would not be unexpected to the user.

8.4 SNAPPING

A big part of manipulation is assembling objects together to form a larger whole, and a big part of assembly is getting objects together at the right place in the correct orientation. Doing this manually requires orienting the objects and then sliding them together so they are flush and evenly aligned. A better approach is to build some smarts into the system so objects "know" where to go and how to orient themselves. This aspect of manipulation is called *snapping*. Snapping often also implies attachment, which will be covered in a section 8.5. Essentially, snapping gets the objects together, and, if needed, attachment makes them stay together.

8.4.1 Explicit versus implicit

Explicit snapping requires that objects be marked with snap elements so that the user clearly sees where and how objects can be connected together. For example, snap elements might correspond to actual mechanical attachment points on the real objects represented by the virtual ones. Alternatively, the system could automatically place snap elements at strategic positions on objects, such as their bounding-box corners, whether or not they correspond to mechanically accurate attachment points.

Implicit snapping involves the system automatically determining spatial relationships that are deemed significant to the user, and causing the objects to align accordingly. For example, objects might snap so their faces are evenly aligned or flush against one another. For implicit snapping to be effective, good heuristics consistent with the user's task are needed, which require that the designer have a good understanding of the user tasks and data objects involved. Explicit snapping, on the other hand, better lends itself to generalization.

8.4.2 Snap operations

An explicit snap operation involves two or more objects, each with a selected snap element. When the snap occurs, the objects jump together and position themselves so that the selected snap points are touching. Such snap operations are not immediately obvious or intuitive to the user because snapping is an artificial activity not often found in the real world. However, if the user is provided with adequate feedback, as with any good idiom, he should get the hang of it rather quickly. A snap operation seems straightforward, but is it? How are the snap elements selected? When the snap occurs, which objects move and which ones stay in place?

Snap movement

Starting with the question of object movement, one approach is to let all the objects move at once. This, however, can result in a 3D version of anarchy. For example, the user may have a partial assembly nicely arranged and positioned in the world. Trying to snap a new piece to it can result in the assembly coming apart if its pieces are not firmly attached; or, if its pieces are attached, the whole assembly can end up moving toward the single piece. In any case, this approach can seem counterintuitive and even counterproductive to the user. A more useful approach is to designate one object in the operation as the target object and the others as source objects. Then, when the snap occurs, the source objects jump over to the target object and position themselves. This works well as long as it's clear to the user which object is the target and which are the sources. But how are the source and target objects chosen?

Snap operations can occur directly as a result of dragging an object, or indirectly as a result of commanding the snap to occur, such as with a third-person control button or menu item. Both forms are shown in figure 8.14. In the case of dragging, because the user has already decided to move an object, the most intuitive approach is to designate it as the snap source object. You saw this in the case of PTF snap drag:

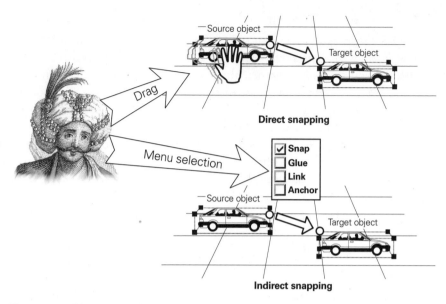

Figure 8.14   Direct snapping via mouse dragging, and indirect snapping via menu selection

When the drag ends, the dragged object—the snap source—jumps into place. In the case of an indirect snap operation, the choices for designating objects are not so obvious. Order of selection can be a good criterion, with the first selected object designated as the snap target, and all subsequently selected objects designated as snap sources. Other possibilities include using menu selection or tool modes to designate the selected object as being a source or a target, but these approaches are less desirable because setting up the snap operation may seem like more trouble than it is worth to the user.

Snap selection

A snap operation requires selection of a snap element on each source and target object. A good way to classify snap element selection is by the degree of manual selection involved, which is shown in figure 8.15.

The first approach is "no selection," where the system performs all snap element selections automatically. Typically, proximity is used as the selection criterion with the closest snap elements between two objects being selected. For example, during a drag, the system would determine the snap element on the source object—the one being dragged—that is closest to a snap element on a neighboring object. The system would autoselect these snap elements and designate the neighboring object as the target of the snap operation. Something similar can be done for indirect snapping, but with the currently selected object designated as the snap source. The no-selection approach is very easy to use because all the user does is select or drag an object: All snap element

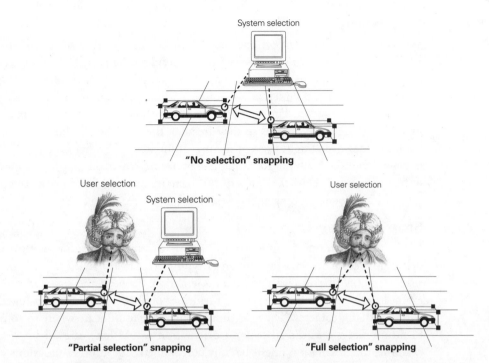

Figure 8.15 Different approaches to snap point selection, which involve varying degrees of manual selection

and target object selection is automatic. Unfortunately, it lacks a degree of control that many assembly tasks require.

The next possibility is "partial selection," where the user selects a snap element on an object and then drags either that object or another nearby object. As before, the dragged object is the snap source object and distance is the criterion for snap element selection. The closest snap element to the manually selected one, whether on the dragged object or a neighboring one, is autoselected as the mate. Indirect snapping would work the same, but the host object of the manually selected snap element would be designated as the source object. The partial selection approach is a little harder for the user to perform because it requires a selection and then a drag, but it can often provide a satisfactory level of control over the snapping.

The final approach, which offers the most control, is "full selection." In this approach, the user selects a snap element on both the source and target snap objects. In this case, indirect snapping may seem like the only alternative, with the user commanding the snap to happen: A drag may seem superfluous, but it is not. Dragging one object or the other after selecting the snap elements could be a simple way to designate which one is the snap source. Also, as you'll see in later sections, snapping and attachment do not have to affect the complete geometry of the participants, in which case a drag could still influence the final outcome geometry of the snap operation.

8.4.3   Snap typing

Typically, a snap element on one object can be connected to any snap element on another object. Sometimes, however, it is helpful to the user if the designer imposes constraints on how objects can be snapped together. With *snap typing*, a snap type is assigned to the snaps, which allows only snaps of matching or complementary types to be snapped together. For example, top surface snaps on furniture might assist the user in aligning work surfaces so they are all at the same height, bookshelf snaps on a bookcase, however, might prevent the user from attaching a light fixture where only a movable bookshelf should go. Complementary male-female snaps on opposite sides of furniture might constrain rows of furniture items to all face in one direction. The possibilities for snap typing are endless.

8.4.4   Snap geometry

In many applications, snapping implies only a jump in position, with orientation being unaffected. A variation on snap typing is snap orientation, with the mating snap elements imposing a particular orientation between the snapped objects. For example, when assembling modular furniture, often the pieces can go together only with a certain geometry. The user should only have to indicate where to connect two furniture pieces and the snap point orientation would take care of the rest. In this example, the orientation might be fully constrained, but in other situations you want the snap orientation to be partially constrained. For example, snapping two snap edges together might force the edges to be colinear, but the relative orientation of the host objects about the colinear edges would remain the same. Limiting the snap's effect on the resulting geometry configuration can also apply to position. For example, snapping two faces together might assure that they are coplanar, thereby making them flush or at least even, but it wouldn't necessarily cause the faces to overlap.

8.5   ATTACHMENT

When assembling objects in the real world to form a more complex whole there must be some means for holding the objects together. Real world *attachments* can be whimsical (bailing wire and chewing gum), utilitarian (nails, glue, welds), ingenious (snaps, zippers, Velcro), and specialized (magnetic, tongue-in-groove, ball-and-socket). The quality of attachment can be permanent (welds), temporary (Velcro), and even non-rigid (ball-and-socket). In a virtual world, as in the real one, connecting objects together and specifying the nature of that connection can be important. This is especially so in 3D design applications, where object assembly is often a major goal.

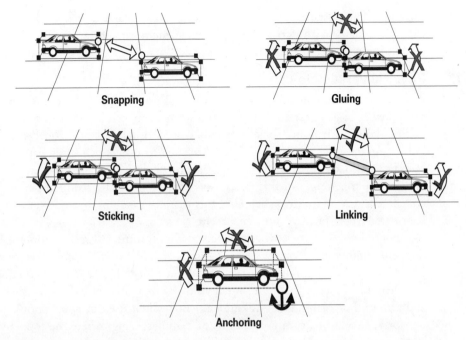

Figure 8.16 Examples of object attachment

Table 8.4 summarizes the specific forms of attachment covered in this section, and figure 8.16 illustrates them.

Table 8.4 Attachment types and characteristics

Snapping	• Not real attachment; touching or not touching • Objects jump into position without permanence
Gluing	• Rigid physical attachment; touching
Sticking	• Non-rigid physical attachment; touching • Objects can slide and twist according to attachment type
Linking	• Logical attachment; non-touching • Topology of attachments maintained when objects are pulled
Anchoring	• Fixes object geometry in world space • Generally needed if sticky attachments are involved

The distinction between attachment and grouping can be murky. For this discussion, attachment is confined to a one-to-one relationship between two connected snap elements, whereas grouping implies a possibly diffuse relationship among two or more objects that are probably not touching and may only be for convenient reference.

Although some aspects of grouping involve manipulation, many others are more closely associated with data access and management; therefore, grouping will be covered in the next chapter.

8.5.1 Physical versus logical

Physical attachment is analogous to real-world attachment, where objects maintain some spatial or geometric relationship between them, which can be rigid like a weld or flexible like a ball-and-socket. This has both visual and functional implications. Pulling on an object that is physically attached to others can often cause the other objects to also move. Also, physical attachment typically requires that the objects involved be touching. For this reason, snapping is generally required before physical attachment can occur. Two snap elements that are touching but not yet attached are considered to be "primed" for attachment.

Logical attachment is where objects maintain some abstract or topological relationship. Pulling on an object that is logically attached to other objects does not necessarily move the other objects. Also, logically attached objects generally do not touch, and their attachments are often shown visibly with relational indicators, such as lines and arrows. For example, logical attachment is often used in applications involving networks, such as for communications or manufacturing, where the topology of the layout, not its literal geometry, is significant. In such cases, nodes in the network do not touch and could be dragged around in the scene, with their connections stretching and bending accordingly.

8.5.2 Attachment versus snapping

Snapping and attachment are usually separate operations. For example, you might perform a "dry fit" to assemble objects the way you think they should go, using snapping. When you are satisfied with their fit, you would apply the attachment "glue" to hold them all together. Because of the difficulty of getting objects together in the right geometry so they can be physically attached (their snap elements must be touching, or primed), snapping of some sort is generally necessary before physical forms of attachment can occur. Persistent forms of physical attachment such as "sticking" and "gluing" will often be combined with snapping such that snapping and attachment are performed as a single operation. Thus, objects that are snapped together are also immediately and persistently attached together.

8.5.3 Attachment operations

Whereas a snap has an implied direction, with the source object jumping to the target object, a physical attachment has none. Snap elements participating in such an attachment are equals because no movement is involved and the relationship is bilateral. This makes creating a physical attachment a lot simpler than performing a snap because there is no need to differentiate source and target objects and snap elements.

As with snapping, the user can perform physical attachment operations directly through dragging or indirectly through commands. Direct physical attachment is simply a snap and attachment combined into a single drag operation. Indirect physical attachment involves the user selecting one or more primed snap elements and commanding them to be attached. A variation is for the user to select one or more objects and to command that all of their primed snap elements be attached. Yet another variation is to use an attachment tool or mode that creates an attachment upon selecting the primed snap elements, directly with the mouse or indirectly in a list. Most of these approaches could be used in the earlier dry fit scenario, where attachments are added to an assembly after snapping all of its objects together.

Logical attachment operations must be handled a bit differently. Because the snap elements do not have to touch, the user must explicitly designate the two snap elements to attach. Such an operation is more akin to snapping than to physical attachment, although no object movement is involved. As in snapping, the user can designate source and target snap elements if the logical attachment is directional, and proximity during drag can drive snap element autoselection. Selecting the objects to be attached instead of their snap elements can work, but problems might arise if the objects contain multiple snap elements.

8.5.4 Detachment operations

Unlike snapping, where no persistence is involved, attachments generally need to be broken. One approach is suggested by PTF sticky drag, where overdragging or jerking an attached object can break it free from its attachments. This is analogous to breaking certain kinds of temporary attachments in the real world, such as those made with Velcro. As is often the case with gesture-based actions, if the user is unsuspecting or lacking in skill, he or she might end up with an unexpected result, such as dragging only a single object when the intent was to drag the whole assembly. An alternative approach that avoids this problem and which parallels one we saw for attachment operations is to select the attachments and then to indirectly command their detachment. A variation is to select one or more objects and command that any attachments on them be broken. Another variation would be to use a detachment tool or mode to break individual attachments when they are selected, on an object or in a list.

8.5.5 Gluing

The most common form of physical attachment and the easiest to implement and control is where the participating objects are held rigidly together. This form of attachment is called *gluing*. When attachments are glued, pulling on one object would also pull any other objects attached to it, and any objects attached to those objects, and so on. In other words, tugging on any part of a glued assembly of objects results in the whole assembly moving without deformation.

8.5.6   Sticking

Less common and more difficult to implement and manage are physical attachments that are flexible or non-rigid. In this form of attachment, which is called *sticking*, the geometry of the attachment is not fully constrained. The simplest form of sticking involves two snap points where the position of the attachment is constrained but not its rotation. The result is like a ball-and-socket joint. Using different forms of snap elements intuitively suggests different forms of sticking attachment. For example, sticking two snap edges together forces the object edges to be colinear but the user can still rotate the objects about the colinear edges like an axis. Similarly, sticking two faces together assures that the two are flush but the user can still slide and possibly rotate the objects along their coplanar faces.

Philosophical problems can arise when we consider what happens when objects that are only stuck together are pulled. In general, the objects involved would behave as in a physical simulation of a dynamic system, with flexing, sliding, and rotation occurring at the joints according to distributed forces and simulated friction. This is overkill for most applications. An easy and effective alternative is to allow only the dragged object to move, and only if its attachments would mutually allow such a movement. For example, given a door in a doorframe connected with two hinge attachments, dragging on the door would swing the door open while the doorframe remains stationary. If, however, a third hinge were added to the door opposite the first two hinges, then the door would be prevented from swinging. Does this now mean that tugging on the door moves the house to which the doorframe is glued? This problem will be discussed a later.

8.5.7   Linking

Many aspects of logical attachment, or *linking*, have already been discussed. The big difference between physical and logical attachment is that in logical attachment the snap elements do not have to touch, so the participating objects can stay where they are. If the user tugs on a linked object, then the object moves and the links stretch accordingly. More sophisticated linking schemes might allow the nodes to automatically rearrange themselves to minimize connection crossings or to improve the layout.

Linking is useful in design and control applications where connections must be established or modified between objects representing nodes in a network, such as for telecommunications, transportation, and utilities. Often in such networks only the topology is important, not the actual spatial geometry. For example, in a telecommunications application, the nodes might represent company offices or, at a lower level of abstraction, computer equipment. The links might represent physical communication connections or logical data circuits, or both. Snap point typing by protocol or physical medium could constrain how nodes are connected. The links themselves could be "dumb" lines or arrows that form straight-line connections, or they could be "smart" ones that bend around intervening objects automatically or with some manual intervention.

8.5.8 Anchoring

In the real world you don't have to worry about moving the whole house if you try to open a locked door. In the virtual world, where the laws of physics do not naturally apply, such matters are not as clear-cut. Maybe the house should move and maybe it shouldn't. One simple way to address this problem is with *anchoring*, which is a special form of attachment between an object and the world. When an object is anchored, it is held rigidly in place relative to the world. In the door example, it would be wise to anchor the house, or at least some foundation component of the house, such as its floor. That way the floor and all the rest of house's components glued to it remain firmly in place, no matter how the user manipulates the house's sticky attachments, such as the door. Anchoring can also be useful when logical attachments are involved, such as in the case where linked nodes rearrange automatically to minimize crossings. In this case, anchoring allows key nodes to remain fixed in place.

The simplest way to perform anchoring is to select one or more objects to be anchored and to command them to be anchored. Anchoring may sound like overkill, and often it is. If an application allows only gluing, then anchoring might be needed only as a convenience, to keep a layout from being accidentally altered. If sticking is allowed, then anchoring can become a serious issue, unless you don't mind the house moving when you try to open its door.

8.6 *SPECIFICATION*

So far the discussion has addressed only forms of manipulation that involve the relationship of data objects with other data objects, such as attachments, or with their surroundings, such as feelers. In a sense, these interactions were external to the data objects themselves. A different form of manipulation involves changes within individual data objects, such as changes to a data object's makeup, state, or attributes. These internal forms of object manipulation are called *specification*.

Specification is an important aspect of many design applications, especially those involving product selection. With the advent of computerized manufacturing, customers have more choices and greater flexibility in specifying standard products. Depending on how a manufacturer organizes product options and how the application exposes those options to a customer, the user might select a different kind of product from a catalog of available product models, or the user might specify individual parameter values and option choices for the product.

Closely related to specification is the concept of *configuration*, where the designer constrains the specification of an object to allowable values, perhaps through the use of rules. Configuration for the purpose of specification and other forms of manipulation is discussed in section 8.7.

8.6.1 Dumb shapes

The simplest form of specification is to choose a different object of the same general class. For example, the user may like the placement of a desk in an office layout but not the type of the desk. Perhaps the desk should have the drawers on the left instead of the right, or it should have a computer keyboard tray. The user chooses a different desk and it is immediately instantiated in the scene replacing the old one. A new 3D model changes the appearance of the desk and has new descriptive feedback changing its identity, such as a model number callout. This is called *dumb shape* specification because the individual data objects are static and immutable. With dumb shapes the user can't change just a part of an object; instead, the whole object must be changed, with the new data object replacing an existing one in the scene.

Although rather simple for the designer to implement and easy for the user to comprehend, dumb shape specification has significant drawbacks. It does not lend itself to direct in-scene manipulation, which is often more intuitive than indirect methods; and the need to represent every combination of options with a separate object can be impractical. For example, if a product has 10 options and each option has five mutually exclusive choices, then the data catalog would have to contain 50 versions of the same basic object. If, instead, the choices are inclusive, then permutations must be considered and catalog size can become a serious problem.

8.6.2 Smart shapes

An alternative approach to dumb shape specification is to make the objects dynamically adjustable. As the user specifies option choices and parameter values, the data object reshapes itself accordingly. This is called *smart shape* specification because the data objects are dynamic and changeable. Smart shapes lend themselves to direct manipulation and avoid the combinatorial explosion problem of dumb shapes. Smart shapes are most readily supported by 3D platforms that provide for "parametric modeling," where the model geometry can be constructed to directly parallel the product specification parameters. You may be wondering what is the difference between a smart shape and a constrained assembly of objects. As with a dumb shape, a smart shape refers to a single data object, or logical entity, which may be modeled as an assembly of individual components or objects, or as a single parameterized object model. In other words, shape here refers to the entity whose parameters are being specified, not necessarily to the manner in which it is constructed.

As with other forms of manipulation, smart shape specification can occur directly or indirectly. Direct smart shape manipulation can offer a more intuitive feel than indirect manipulation. For example, to move a desk's drawers from the right side of the desk to the left side, the user might simply drag them to the desired position. Similarly, if a larger desk is needed, the user might drag a corner to resize it. For direct shape manipulation to work well, the objects must be intelligent enough to keep the arrangement of their internal components consistent and valid. For example, when the drawers are slid from one side to the other, they should snap into place on the right

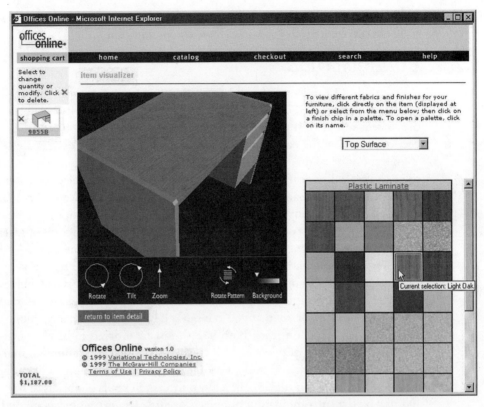

Figure 8.17 In this 3D configurator, the user can select a surface, apply a valid finish, and see the result on the 3D desk model. (Courtesy of TechniCon Corporation)

or the left and not be allowed to remain in some intermediate position; and, while the desk is being stretched, the drawers should be kept flush against the side of the desk even though that side might be the one being adjusted.

Other forms of direct shape manipulation can be nongeometric in nature, dealing with visual or even non-visual attributes of the object. For example, to change the color or finish of a desk, the user might select a desk surface and choose a new finish from a palette of finish swatches. The new finish would appear immediately on the selected surface. Nonvisual options such as connecting braces and electrical cableways might be selected automatically when the user connects two desks together or attaches a lighting fixture, but this is getting into configuration, a separate subject. Figure 8.17 shows an example of a 3D configurator in an e-commerce application.

Indirect forms of smart shape manipulation might be desirable in certain situations. If the specification requires precision, such as the exact dimensions of a desk, then a dialog box with entry fields or radio buttons might be preferable to direct in-scene resizing. If the specification is somewhat complicated, then a more aggressive technique such as a wizard might be useful. For industrial-strength applications, configuration techniques might be used to handle guided selection, to constrain the available choices, and to validate the overall specification.

8.7   CONFIGURATION

A major advance realized with the introduction of the graphical user interface was that the designer could easily guide the user to a set of action choices appropriate for the current situation. If the user is not allowed to connect two objects, then the Connect command in the edit menu appears dimmed when those objects are selected. If an object can be colored only red or green but not blue, then only the red and green color choices will appear in a color palette when that object is selected. Extending this notion on a larger, broader, and more industrial scale is the concept of *configuration*.

Configuration constrains the user to an allowed set of operations that can be performed on a set of data objects or within a given data object, as a form of specification, according to the current situation. The situation might be defined completely within the application, such as the arrangement of data objects in the scene, or by external circumstances, such as product availability or even the day of the week. These are often expressed as rules. Simple rules might be to restrict a given parameter to a range. More convoluted ones might say that you can buy a desk or chair with any color, but if you want the special discount then both items must be ordered in black and it must be Thursday. The results of rules can be exclusive—in which you cannot do something— or inclusive—in which you must do something. For example, in connecting objects together, configuration rules might allow only certain kinds of objects to be connected and, if a particular combination of objects occurs, then extra objects might be added automatically. In the office furniture example, connecting brackets might be separate orderable items. When a modular desk is attached to a panel, no bracket is needed; but when two desks are attached, brackets are required and will be added to the order to assure a correct and complete product assembly.

This chapter has already mentioned a number of areas where configuration may be useful in 3D manipulation. In terms of external manipulation, configuration can constrain which objects can be snapped, attached, grouped together, and how. In terms of internal manipulation, configuration can play a major role in guiding the user's specification of an object. Incorporating configuration concepts into the user interface is not an all-or-nothing proposition. There is a wide range of possibilities.

In the last few years, the concept of configuration has matured into a separate technology that is helping to drive sales automation and mass customization applications. A configuration model defines the rules and allowed values for assembling a system and specifying its data objects. A configuration engine uses the model to track user actions, to provide currently valid choices, and to offer explanations of why certain choices are not available, or others are recommended. For example, in an application for ordering a sport-utility vehicle, if the customer wants chrome wheels then only the "super" and "super duper" vehicle models are valid choices. If the customer also chooses the 20-liter V-16 Terminator engine, then only the super duper model is recommended, and the "afterburner" and "cryogenic cooler" option packages are also required. The user might ask why the lower cost models are not recommended (discommended), and the system would say that with the Terminator engine the more reasonably priced models will break down.

You may ask what this scenario has do with 3D user interfaces. In next-generation applications, 3D will provide the way to make visualization and manipulation of complex data more compelling and intuitive. Configuration will make the manipulation easier for the user to perform effectively and accurately. The ultimate goal of configuration is to prevent the user from specifying a product that can't be ordered or designing a system that can't be implemented. (This is yet another example of the designer and computer working harder to make life better for the user.) In the sports-utility vehicle example, as the user selects wheel and engine options, the specification is validated and the choices are seen immediately, in 3D, as they would appear on the actual vehicle. If, instead, the application is dealing with modifications to a chemical plant, as the user specifies processing capacities and space allowances, equipment satisfying those requirements would be presented. Selecting a piece of equipment would make it appear in a model of the plant, where the user can optimize its layout and finalize its hookup in 3D, just as if he or she were in the actual plant.

8.8 SUMMARY

Relational feedback elements address the needs of directly manipulating objects in a 3D scene. Elements such as feelers, outlines, and skirts allow the user to better see the 3D relationships of objects on a 2D display; tic mark and ruler elements assist the user in precisely placing objects; and snap elements aid in connecting objects together.

PTF is an offshoot of dynamic feedback that combines visual and audio feedback with discontinuities in eye-hand control as a substitute for tactile feedback, which is lacking in a POCS. PTF drag comes in several flavors, including marked, sticky, snap, and solid. Simulation of real object dynamics in the form of strong and weak drag grip could further enhance the tactile-like feel of the user's 3D experience.

An important aspect of direct manipulation involves getting objects together and keeping them together, as defined by snapping and attachment techniques. Snapping conveniently gets the objects together and attachment makes their connections persistent. Physical forms of attachment are gluing and sticking, the logical form is linking, and a special form is anchoring.

Specification is the internal manipulation of data objects, which comes in the form of dumb and smart shapes. Configuration refers to the notion of guided and constrained manipulation, which is becoming an important technology for next-generation applications, 3D and otherwise.

C H A P T E R   9

Access

With visions of killer 3D apps dancing in our heads, it's easy for us as designers to overlook some of the more mundane needs of the user. Before the user can navigate the 3D world and manipulate its 3D data, he/she has to decide what data to view and figure out how to get that data into the scene. Whether within the scene or without, it is often convenient to group data together for the user so that he/she can access it in larger units, such as a whole suite of furniture. Many applications also allow the user to create or modify data; in such cases the user will probably want to get the data out of the scene for safekeeping and later use. In fact, from a commercial perspective, e-commerce vendors might consider product selection from an e-catalog and order placement—not 3D navigation and manipulation—to be the most important aspects of an application, since those are the activities that close the sale. Whether the application is 3D, 2D, or even 1D, the issues and concerns regarding data access are similar. For 3D applications, however, the nature of the data offers some unique opportunities as well as some unique problems.

An important aspect of providing the user access to the data is the data's organization and presentation outside of the scene, whether by the vendor for marketing purposes, the designer for easy user access, or by the user for more personalized and effective use. The nature of 3D applications and 3D data can complicate matters. Is 3D or 2D the best format for presenting out-of-scene data for selection? Once the data objects are selected, how does the user get them into the scene? When in the scene, a data object can sometimes be difficult to find again because the user may not be looking in the right place, or the clutter in the scene may be hiding it. How can the user easily find the proverbial needle in the 3D haystack? Even if the user can see the object in the scene, it may be difficult to get at it because of its small apparent size or due to interference from nearby objects. How can the user easily and consistently access data objects in the scene? Not everything that the user might need to load or save can be strictly classified as a data object. How does the user access pre-defined data attributes or specifications and apply them to data objects already in the scene? How does the user save navigation and layout information for later use? These questions and more will be answered in this, the final chapter of part 2, which addresses the need for data access in next-generation 3D applications.

9.1 IN-SCENE GROUPING

Data grouping was mentioned in chapter 8 as being somewhat like attachment but in a less direct and often more abstract manner. Whereas object attachment involves direct one-to-one relationships between objects, grouping implies an often diffuse relationship among a set of objects. In other words, there can be more than two objects in the group, the objects do not have to be touching, and the constraints on the members of the group can be varied.

9.1.1 Physical versus logical

Physical grouping involves the spatial or geometric relationship among the target objects. Typically, objects that are physically grouped maintain their relative position and orientation within the group. Pulling on one object pulls the rest of them along, allowing the group to be manipulated as a whole. As with attachment, variations might selectively freeze the geometry, such as freezing the relative positions of the objects but allowing the user to individually rotate them. In many ways, physical grouping and physical attachment are similar. Physical attachment, however, requires the objects (more accurately, the snap elements) to touch, and allows more precise control over how the relative object geometry is maintained.

Logical grouping defines an abstract relationship for a set of target objects, with nothing implied about the set's geometry. In many ways, it is just a method for assigning an identifier to an arbitrary group of objects for convenient access and management. The logical relationship could be as general as the set of objects that are the target of some operation, such as delete or copy; or, it could be as specific as defining suites of furniture according to job function or salary grade. Being only logically grouped, the user would be free to manipulate and re-arrange the furniture pieces in such suites.

Physical and logical grouping can also be combined. For example, each suite of furniture (logical grouping with a label) might also have a fixed layout (physical grouping of geometry). Such hybrid groupings of pre-arranged objects are often used as templates in design applications to speed up repetitive layout, such as pre-defined modular furniture suites in an office layout application.

9.1.2 Grouping operations

Performing a group operation is easy compared to snapping and attachment, since jumping and pairing are not involved. A grouping operation involves selecting the objects and then designating them as a group, which for a logical group might also involve the user specifying a label for it. Group designation might be as simple as clicking on a toolbar button to establish a physical grouping of the selected items, or as involved as having to type in a logical group's name and attributes.

Multiselection

The most common form of grouping operation is *target multiselection*, where a selected group of objects serves as the target for some subsequent user action. Often the group designation occurs automatically according to the type of action the user performs; performing a drag designates the group as physical, and performing a command designates it as logical. As refined over the years, the normal selection action in a GUI is for any previously selected object(s) to deselect when a new object is selected. The user must do something special in order to perform multiselection. A common and somewhat standard approach is to allow the user to hold down the Control modifier key to override the normal single-selection action. This is shown in part 4 starting with the TargetSelecting example in section 20.2.5. Another approach is to define a tool or mode that adds each newly selected object to the current selection group. In any case, the user can make selections directly in the scene by clicking on objects or indirectly by clicking on entries in a list. The advantages of indirect data selection in a 3D application will be discussed later in section 9.2.2.

Lasso selection

Although the objects in a group do not have to be neighbors, they often are, in which case a *lasso* can be used to perform multi-selection. With 2D lasso selection, the user draws an outline such as a rectangle or circle around one or more objects to select them. Lasso selection in 3D is not quite as straightforward. One approach is to use 3D analogs to 2D lasso shapes. For example, using control WRM to map the 2D mouse coordinates into a 3D world position, the user clicks in the scene to define a corner point for a box or the center point for a sphere. As the user drags the mouse, the bounding volume grows as indicated by outline feedback, and all enclosed objects are shown as being selected. Another approach is to use a 2D lasso with a 3D presence. As the user stretches the 2D lasso on a 3D surface, such as the floor in a room, a skirt appears above the lasso and all the objects inside the skirt are selected, as shown in figure 9.1.

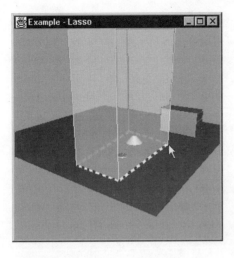

Figure 9.1
An example of in-scene object selection with a 3D lasso, with a skirt above the lasso defining an enclosing volume

Nesting

Making a group out of other groups, or a mix of objects and groups, is a common generalization of the grouping concept; many 2D drawing packages support nesting of groups. Nesting of groups comes naturally to users since it happens in the real world. Although nesting does not have to maintain the original groups, with all the elements of all the groups being thrown into a single large group, most users would expect the groups to be preserved. Making nested groups is easy—just lasso the items to be grouped. Maintaining them is another matter. The user must remember the nesting, discover it by trial and error, or be presented with a hierarchical representation of the grouping, such as in a tree widget or with nested 3D outlines.

Another issue concerning nesting is whether physical and logical groups can be mixed within a given group. Segregating the group types requires that the user be able to distinguish between the types with some sort of feedback decorating the groups, which tends to complicate the UI. This also brings up the bigger question of whether or not to allow both physical and logical grouping in an application, which can only be decided based on the application's requirements.

9.1.3 Ungrouping operations

Ungrouping, the reverse of grouping, involves selecting one or more groups (using one of the many grouping techniques described above) and commanding the selection to ungroup. If nesting of groups is allowed, there is the question of what happens when they are ungrouped. One possibility is to simply undo the topmost level of grouping; another possibility is to undo all levels of grouping. Which is better depends mostly on what the user is likely to expect to happen.

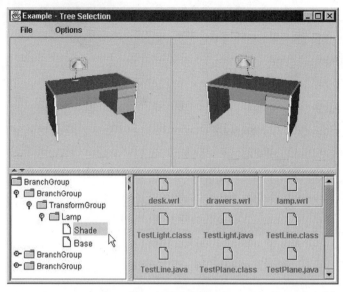

**Figure 9.2   An example of out-of-scene object selection with a tree.
The tree also shows in-scene object groupings.**

9.2   OUT-OF-SCENE ACCESS

When thinking of 3D user interfaces, often the last thing to be considered is what happens outside of the 3D scene. In next-generation applications, such as those for e-commerce, selecting and configuring products are the true goal for the designer, the user, and the vendor. If 3D needs to be a part of the user experience in order for the user to make the buy decision, then so be it; vendors will want it and designers will include it. Although 3D can be a medium for product selection and configuration, often 2D or 1D will suffice, as in an electronic catalog with photos of the products, or in a table listing product specifications. Even if selection occurs in 1D or 2D, 3D can allow the user to examine the selection more thoroughly and naturally. Also, 3D is a prime candidate for letting the user visualize a selection as part of some larger setting, such as the user's home, office, or manufacturing floor.

Beyond specific application needs, out-of-scene access to data can be important for helping the user to manage in-scene data. For example, to find an object in the scene, the user might look it up in a sorted list, a tree of object groupings, or perform a search for it based on its characteristics. When the user finds the object and selects it outside of the scene, the object would also appear selected in the scene, as shown in figure 9.2. With selection scroll navigation, the view would also center on the selected object. Out-of-scene data tree and graph presentations are excellent ways to create and maintain logical groups, such as for layout templates and complex object assemblies. Other access forms, such as a data object palette, can facilitate data transfer, such as through 3D drag-and-drop.

This section covers some of the basic techniques for presenting and accessing data out-of-scene in order to use it in the scene. To complete the picture, once the user can see the data choices and select one, the data needs to be transferred into the scene for presentation and manipulation in 3D. Data transfer will be covered separately in section 9.3.

9.2.1 Data presentation

Data visualization applies to both in-scene and out-of-scene data, but the requirements are generally different. In-scene presentation takes advantage of 3D's ability to show data in a more natural and realistic setting for concrete data, and a higher dimensional setting for abstract data. Out-of-scene presentations are more geared to data selection and configuration. For a product catalog, the vendor might present the data items in a flashy 2D layout with large colorful pictures to maximize sales. For a scientific visualization application, the data sets might be arranged as names in a 2D table that are sorted by factors such as time of capture and sensor settings. The specific data presentation can also reflect the internal structure of the application data, such as a data tree and its branches indicating nested object groupings.

In a 3D application, designers have the luxury of presenting data to the user in 3D, 2D, and even 1D. By definition, 3D holds reign over in-scene presentations, but any form of the data can be used for out-of-scene presentation. The following summarizes the pros and cons for using different presentation forms outside of the scene.

3D presentation

3D presentation outside the scene can show an object in isolation, as a preview, whereas in-scene presentation generally shows the object *in situ*, with the clutter of neighboring objects, in-scene controls, and assorted feedback elements. Although 3D presentation sounds good in principle, a 3D presentation requires some means for the object (or view) to move around. Otherwise, the presentation is simply a static 2D image on the POCS screen. The fact that the 2D image may have been rendered live from a 3D model is lost on the user, and might be considered a waste of processing power. Introducing an interactive 3D presentation outside the scene adds complexity to the application and requires more screen real estate, which may not be appreciated by the user. The use of 3D for out-of-scene data preview, with ways to avoid some of its disadvantages, will be covered in section 9.2.5.

2D presentation

For simple data selection, 3D presentation of the data is generally overkill. Often a 2D image or icon will do. 2D images afford the user an opportunity to see a photograph of the actual item or product. For more industrial applications, or less discriminating users, 2D hidden line drawings automatically generated from 3D CAD models might suffice. For situations where it is difficult to distinguish items according to their outward appearance, iconic representations might be preferred, especially if the icons are standardized, such as for many engineering and architectural components. 2D presentations are often more compact than 3D versions, since no space is wasted on 3D navigation and manipulation controls. A 2D iconic presentation would be an even better choice for saving space since icons are by nature small yet easy to distinguish.

1D presentation

For situations where space is at a premium, a 1D presentation might be the only choice. A 1D presentation uses traditional non-image GUI widgets, such as a list, table, or tree. Objects in a list might be represented by a short name, such as a model number, and possibly a description of the item. The ability to compactly present large amounts of descriptive information, such as in a scrollable table, can be a big advantage of 1D presentations over 2D and 3D choices. 1D widgets and their role in 3D applications are addressed in more detail in section 9.2.2.

Mixed presentation

For the purpose of idiomatic recognition, 1D and 2D presentations can be combined, with a small icon of the object or its class next to its name in a list or tree. Tooltips can provide transient but more detailed information about an item, whether the item is shown in 3D, 2D, or 1D. In the case of 3D or 2D items, the tooltip might provide a detailed textual description. For a 1D item, the tooltip might provide a detailed 2D image or 3D preview.

9.2.2 Non-spatial access

Some tasks, such as positioning and rotating data objects, are spatial in nature, requiring that the data be seen in 2D or 3D. Other operations do not require a spatial presentation and, in fact, might best be done without one, such as renaming objects or logically grouping them by product features. Nonspatial, or indirect, access through lists, trees, and other widget forms are extremely familiar to most users, and is ubiquitous in modern GUIs. Such access offers an alternative means for selecting objects and manipulating them. For example, if the target object is deeply buried among other objects in the scene, it may be difficult to see the target, much less unambiguously select and manipulate it.

Data lists and tables

The simplest and most compact form of presentation is the data *list*. Although humble in form and function, lists are ubiquitous and familiar to the user. For the designer they are easily generated on-the-fly without the need for much layout or design. A useful variation is the data *table*, with columns listing various details about the data object in each row, such as model number, manufacturer, description, physical attributes, available options, and the like. GUI table widgets have become quite

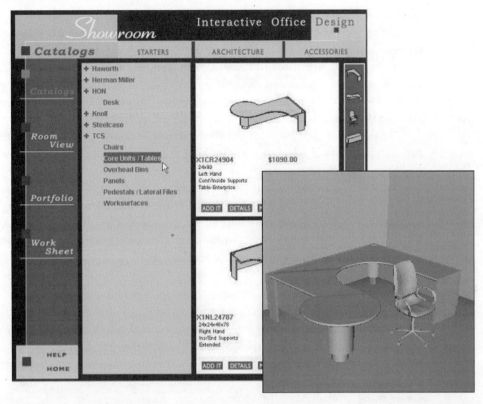

Figure 9.3   This application example shows many representations of the same data object, the curved desk: It is selected in a 1D tree, it is shown in a 2D image catalog, it appears as a data palette icon, and it is rendered in 3D in the inset. (Courtesy of TechniCon Corporation)

refined, offering various sorting options by column, bump scrolling, and editing capabilities for user customization of the table contents and, correspondingly, the data objects.

For users who can deal with nonspatial presentations, a table can be a compact and efficient way to perform data specification and configuration of data objects in the scene. The object can be selected in the table, and the scene autoscrolls to the selected 3D item, or it can be selected in the scene, and the table autoscrolls to the corresponding table entry. Either way, the user modifies the object by simply changing the values in its table cells. Taking this concept to the extreme results in a full-blown spreadsheet, with dropdown lists in the cells showing the available options for each specification.

Data trees

A data *tree* offers a convenient and familiar form for arranging items in some logical order and grouping, with data files and folders being a long-standing metaphor. Unlike spatial presentations, a tree offers the means for organizing spatial objects in one or more nonspatial ways, such as by name, manufacturer, and cost. They can also offer alternative presentations of spatial groupings, such as the nesting of geometric assemblies, assembly components, and object parts (vertices, edges, and faces). Such visualization would be useful for in-scene data as well as for previewing out-of-scene data prior to selection. Tree access can also be a very useful alternative for selecting a target object that may be spatially grouped with other objects, or in selecting a constituent element that comprises an object, such as a vertex, edge, face, snap, or attachment.

Trees offer a good way for the designer to pre-arrange the data objects so users can more easily find what they are looking for. For example, the levels in a product tree might reflect the manufacturer, product line, function, and model number. This subject will be covered more extensively under catalogs. As with lists and tables, the state-of-the-art in GUI tree widgets is quite mature, offering a host of editing capabilities and options for item presentation and selection. The ability of such widgets to let the user directly rename items in the tree offers an attractive means for letting the user specify and change logical group designation.

Data graphs

A more general form of tree-like access to in-scene and out-of-scene data is the *graph*, which is effective at presenting the data's generalized topology. (This form of graph should not be confused with the non-tree-like form, where data is plotted along two or more axes.) A graph is a collection of items arranged in some possibly nonhierarchical form, with lines, arrows, boxes, spatial clustering, color-coding, and so on indicating the relationships of the nodes. For data access, a graph might be preferred over a tree organization for data groupings that are not limited to being strictly hierarchical, such as a communications network like the one shown in figure 9.4. Also, a simple tree would be hard pressed to clearly show a nested physical grouping of objects where objects can be shared (same object in two different groups) or cloned (different objects with shared specifications). Not being limited to a strict hierarchy is a great feature, but this can also make graphs appear disorganized.

Graphs, as well as trees, tables, and lists can be presented in 3D using data visualization techniques, with full-blown 3D navigation and manipulation. The possibility might leave you wondering which aspects of an application are in-scene and which are out-of-scene. The answer to such questions is simple: Use whatever works, no matter what it is called.

9.2.3   Data palette

A technique popularized in 2D drawing applications is the drag-and-drop *palette*, where icons in the palette represent data objects that the user can drag and drop into a drawing. In a 3D application, the user would instead drop the data directly into the 3D scene. Typically, a palette appears as a 2D box containing a set of data items represented by 2D graphical icons or thumbnail images of the actual object. Often the items are labeled and include tooltip feedback, either as an alternative to the labels or

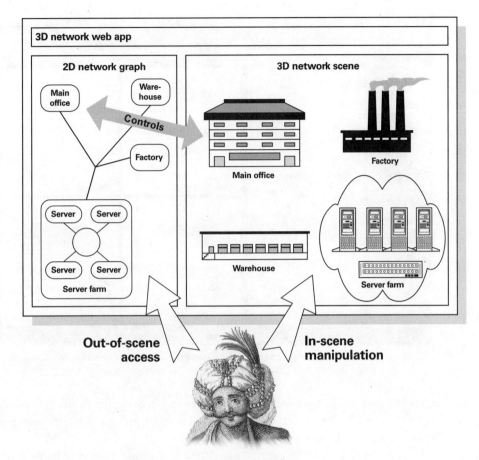

Figure 9.4 For some problems, a 2D graph is a better fit than a 1D list or a 2D tree for out-of-scene data representation and access.

to provide a detailed description. The user might be allowed to arbitrarily position palette items, or they may be restricted to a fixed grid and a particular order, such as for a more compact and consistent presentation.

Palettes can also be used to save data, with the user dragging objects from the scene and dropping them in a palette for safekeeping and later use. 3D drag-and-drop, whether dragging into or out of the scene, presents a number of challenges, which will be addressed in section 9.3.5 as part of data transfer.

9.2.4   Data catalog

The purpose of a mail-order catalog is clear: It provides a convenient means for potential customers to scrutinize a vendor's product offerings and to order them. The motives behind the organization of the catalog are a bit more subtle. Catalogs can be organized for easy user access, such as alphabetically by product class and product but

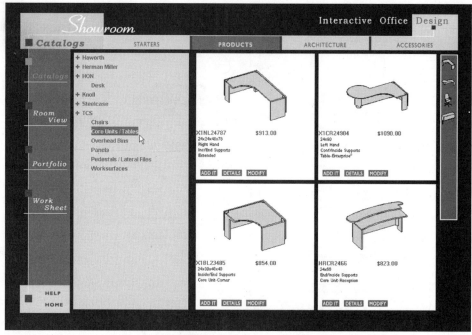

Figure 9.5 This e-commerce application presents the catalog with a tree for navigation and a page for product details. (Courtesy of TechniCon Corporation)

they can also be arranged for improving sales and maximizing profits. The discussion here will stick to the more utilitarian aspects of organizing and presenting out-of-scene data as a catalog.

A *catalog* is a visually oriented presentation of products or data items available to the user through the application. In e-commerce, the catalog has been anointed with the title of e-catalog to signify its prominent role in online business. In some sense, a palette could be considered as a primitive catalog, with all of its items on a single page. More typically, a catalog resembles its paper counterpart, consisting of multiple pages showing pictures of the items together with textual information about them. An example of a catalog in an e-commerce application is shown in figure 9.5.

Data organization

The simplest organization for a catalog is the same as for its paper-based ancestor, which is linear. In a linear organization, the catalog pages are arranged from front to back and are accessed in sequence, with perhaps a table of contents to jump the user to the start of particular sections in the catalog. Unless there is some overwhelming need to reproduce an existing paper catalog exactly, a vast improvement would be to use hyperlinking to arrange the contents hierarchically. The hierarchy can be derived from the sections in an existing linear catalog, or it can represent some inherent organization in the data. An interesting variation is to design the hierarchy to guide the user to the best solution for a given problem. Associating branches in the tree with item feature choices, such as for speed, operating temperature, life expectancy, price, and availability can provide such guidance. The branches can also take the form of questions and answers in a decision tree, with each branch narrowing down the definition of the user's problem and honing in on a particular item that can solve it.

Going beyond simple trees, in its most general form a catalog is a graph (network) of closely related information and data items. Using the full power of hypertext and the web, branches are allowed to converge as well as diverge, and branches and items in the catalog can be linked to collateral information, maintained locally or spread throughout the web. For example, links on a page could lead to sales information extolling the virtues of a product, or provide supporting scientific information about a data sample object in the form of graphs and tables. Crossing the line between in-scene and out-of-scene, links can also perform contextual navigation from the catalog to a 3D representation of an item in isolation, as a data preview, or to an existing item already in the scene, as data selection.

Data permanence

Catalogs can be immutable, being supplied as part of the application or as a standard offering from a vendor. Immutable in this sense refers to whether the user—not the supplier—is allowed to modify or re-arrange the catalog's contents. Aside from ease of access for the user, a major advantage of e-catalogs is that the supplier can easily update them so users are provided with the most current information. Not only is this good for the user, but it also helps to assure that the vendor receives valid orders that can be quickly fulfilled. In the past, e-catalogs were distributed and updated by CD-ROM. With the advent of the web, updates can be directly tied to company business systems with catalog updates occurring just as fast as business decisions are made and entered.

In terms of user access, catalogs can also be mutable. Frequent users of a catalog may wish to bookmark sections and items, which requires some form of state persistence associated with the catalog to save the user's links. Other users might prefer to construct their own mini-catalog containing just the items they use on a regular basis, which requires that the user be allowed to modify the catalog organization and perhaps even its contents, such as to preconfigure items. Another form of catalog mutability is to allow the user to save new and modified work in a personal catalog, separate from the supplier's catalog.

9.2.5 Data preview

Analysis and design applications, such as for engineering, architecture, and even online product selection, can be rich in data. The items involved can be complex and sometimes difficult to visualize, or they may require more detailed inspection before the user can commit to including them as part of the 3D scene. Such a commitment can be significant because the user must properly place the item in the scene and perhaps even to attach it to other objects. Also, once in the scene, an object may be difficult to examine because of its surrounding neighbors. Allowing the user to preview a selected item, up close and in isolation, can be a valuable and integral part of the data selection process. For the same reason, preview can also be used as an opportunity for the user to configure a selected item prior to transferring it into the scene. Such benefits of preview are true whether the application is allowing a customer to select furniture and arrange it in a mockup of his or her home office, or is allowing an engineer to select equipment and configure it in a virtual model of an actual chemical plant.

Although users can preview objects in 2D, as a blow-up of a picture in the catalog, and even 1D, as a table of item specifications, 3D can offer a more natural and intuitive medium for the user to quickly size up an item. As mentioned previously, for 3D to be 3D and not just a 2D image, the view or the data must be movable. Because the goal of preview is to offer the user a quick peek, fancy navigation and manipulation techniques are generally not called for. These techniques will be available once the data is transferred into the scene. Besides, they complicate the interface and can require additional screen space for the controls. If manipulation of the object is not required, such as for configuration, then first-person control of an orbit camera is a good choice for 3D preview. If the designer decides that no user interaction is needed, another possibility is a hands-off technique called "auto-examination," where the system automatically spins and twirls the object in-place, on the catalog page or in its palette, when the object is selected.

9.2.6 Search

Because catalogs, trees, and tables can be intimidating to the novice user, or their sheer size can be overwhelming even to the experienced veteran, a search capability is a must-have feature in applications with large volumes of data. *Search* is a familiar paradigm to most web users and any serious web site or application is expected to have a search capability. The capability can be provided as a simple keyword search against the item's attributes; or, for a more focused search, the user can be offered predefined sets of data features from which to choose, such as part number, manufacturer, physical characteristics, available options, and even pricing. Data items that match the search criteria are returned in a hit list that may be sorted alphabetically or by the degree of match. Clicking on a search hit contextually navigates the user to the out-of-scene catalog page of the found item or to the autoscrolled in-scene location of it.

9.3 DATA TRANSFER

After the user finds and selects a data item in a catalog or palette, the object must make a transition from being outside the scene to inside the scene. Although the focus here is on techniques for making the actual transfer happen, other issues that the designer must consider are what happens back in the catalog or palette after the object leaves, and what must happen in the scene for the object to appear. Consideration must also be given to the transfer of nonobject data, such as a navigation tour of the scene or a color scheme for a suite of furniture.

9.3.1 Data instantiation

After the user selects and possibly previews a data object, what happens to the object in the catalog or palette after the object is transferred? Depending on the application and what the data represents, a transfer could mean that the data object is first copied, and the copy is transferred into the scene. Another possibility is that objects are considered to be singletons, and only one instance is allowed to exist in the application. If this is the case, after the object is transferred, the catalog page or palette that held the object would be left showing a blank space.

The first interpretation, where the object is copied, is the more typical one. The latter one, where the object is moved, might be useful in situations where items represent unique real world instances that perhaps get passed along for sequential evaluation and processing. For example, in a business workflow application, each object might represent a unique case to be analyzed, or a customer order to be verified and processed. In an analysis/control application, each item in the catalog might represent an actual item that must be inspected, documented, and tracked through various stages of a manufacturing process.

9.3.2 Nonobject access

Applications often allow the user to create "nonobject" data. Such data is not normally recognized as being an object that can be viewed in a scene as a separate entity. It is generally not the focus of the application or the user's activities. An example would be the information defining a navigation tour through the scene, such as for a demonstration. The user may want to save the tour for later recall or perhaps to serve as a template for a different scene. Other examples of nonobject data would be object specifications, object layouts, navigation viewpoints, and grouping information. Although nonobject data may be closely associated with actual data objects, and perhaps this data can be viewed and handled as an object, such as dragging a color scheme from a catalog and dropping it on the furniture in the scene, it doesn't quite fit into the normal notion of an application data object. In any case, applications must make allowances for users to save, recall, and transfer such information for use in and out of the scene.

9.3.3 Data basket

In a supermarket, it would be somewhat inconvenient if you had to purchase an item immediately after taking it off the shelf. Instead, we use shopping baskets to hold the items until we are ready to pay for them. When you get your groceries home you may put them in the cabinet or refrigerator to get them out of the way until you are ready to prepare them for dinner. This notion of selecting and caching items until you are ready to use them is a familiar one in real life and on the web, such as for online sales.

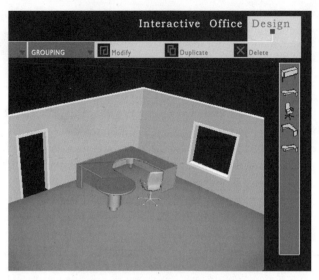

Figure 9.6 **The shopping basket on the right serves as a cache for items selected from the catalog and as a drag-and-drop palette. (Courtesy of TechniCon Corporation)**

It also addresses the need for people to focus on one type of task at a time—first we make our grocery selections, then we purchase them, and finally we work in the kitchen to prepare them into a meal.

For many 3D applications, the task of finding and selecting objects from a catalog can be quite different from placing those objects in the scene and attaching them to other objects. Selection involves contextual navigation and searching, whereas transfer into the scene involves manipulation and navigation. A *basket* offers the user a convenient place to temporarily save selected items before transferring them to the scene. This allows the user to focus first on object selection; and, when ready, to shift attention to the task of getting the items from the basket into the scene. Of course, the basket could also be used in the reverse direction, with the user dragging objects out of the scene and into the basket, such as to create an order. If there is room for it, the basket might appear as a special palette on the same page as the scene display. Objects selected from the catalog might appear automatically in the basket, perhaps as icons to minimize space. From there drag-and-drop could be used to get the objects into the scene, the same as for any other data palette. Figure 9.6 shows a basket that serves as both a catalog item cache and as a drag-and-drop palette.

Some of the details to consider about baskets are their lifetimes and whether objects dragged from them are copied or moved, which is similar to the question discussed earlier concerning object instantiation in general. For example, if the basket is simply a means to transition from the task of picking to the task of placing, then basket items would likely be moved, and the basket would exist only until it is emptied. If, however, the basket serves as a cache of most recently selected objects, then items might be copied, and the basket would exist for the duration of the session or as long as the user desires, perhaps being saved as nonobject data in a mutable catalog. In this case the basket could serve as the user's personal minicatalog.

9.3.4   Teleport

Conceptually, the simplest approach to data transfer, whether directly from a catalog or indirectly through a basket, is to *teleport* it. With teleport, the selected item immediately appears in the target container. Teleport is likely a good choice between the catalog and basket because the user probably doesn't want to be burdened at this stage with the details of drag-and-drop. Also, there are no serious issues concerning placement of items in a basket because a palette is 2D. Perhaps the items are simply auto-arranged in the basket in the sequence they are chosen. Teleport into the scene is a different matter.

When a selected item, whether from the catalog or the basket, suddenly appears in the scene, where does the system place it? The world origin is always a good place to start, but perhaps that is in the middle of a structure, behind a wall, or underground. Although teleport is a simple concept, the designer nevertheless has to put some serious effort into the details to get it to work effectively and consistently. If the scene and the way it is used are rather simple, such as a single room where furniture is placed, then the application might be able to follow some simple rules. For example, the application could try to place the teleported furniture in the center of the room; if an object is already there, then it would place it nearby, but away from any existing furniture. If the user wants to select a lot of furniture before laying it out, a problem could arise as the furniture piles up in the center of the room. It can be hard to generalize this use of teleport because the system is trying to guess where the user might want the data objects.

Another variation on teleport is simple cut-and-paste, where the user goes to the catalog or palette, cuts or copies an item, positions the mouse in the scene, and then pastes the object at a particular location. This shifts the decision to the user as to where the object goes in the scene, which is generally a good thing, but the designer may have to give the user a bit more instruction on how to do it. A variation on the classic cut-and-paste paradigm is for the user to select a target item in the scene to which the pasted object will be snapped or attached. This can work well as long as there is plenty of feedback to tell the user which object is the target and what will happen when the paste occurs. Generalizing this approach leads to drag-and-drop, where instead of cutting and pasting, the user drags and drops. 3D drag-and-drop and issues such as target feedback are covered in the next section.

9.3.5   3D drag-and-drop

Drag-and-drop (DnD) is a powerful and intuitive form of data transfer involving direct WYSIWYG manipulation of data objects. Although seemingly innocuous because of its common use, it touches on a wide range of user interface concepts and techniques, and can be difficult to implement well in cross-application and cross-platform situations. drag-and-drop's acceptance in 2D drawing applications took a while; but it is now considered standard practice thanks to its popularization through applications such as Visio. Such applications use drag-and-drop palettes in which data appears as icons that can be dragged onto the drawing and dropped.

In recent years, drag-and-drop has started to make inroads into 3D user interfaces. Perhaps its slow adoption is due in part to the difficulties involved in performing 3D drag-and-drop using a 2D mouse in a 2D POCS display. But wait, you say, hasn't the problem of dealing with 2D in a 3D world already been addressed? Yes, it was covered back in chapter 4 on control, in the form of DRM and WRM but not in the context of drag-and-drop.

Drag-and-drop basics

DnD is typically used for situations where the user needs to move an object from one place to another, spatially or contextually. The object can represent an abstract set of data, such as a data file, a single concrete object such as a desk, or a group of objects such as all the furniture in an office cubicle. In a GUI desktop, the user can drag an icon representing a data file from the left side of the desktop and drop it on the right side. This is simply a spatial repositioning of the icon, perhaps to suit the user's desire to keep his desktop tidy. Typically, using the modifier keys, the user can control whether the drag-and-drop operation is a move, a copy, or a link. (A link allows the same object to be in two or more places at the same time; changing the object in one place changes all the other instances of the linked object.) The user can also drag an icon representing a data file and drop it on a word-processing application open on the desktop. This has the effect of opening the file in the application for editing. This is contextual movement of the object, in contrast to spatial movement.

As with any use of drag-and-drop, good practice requires a generous dose of user feedback at every step of the operation. Before the drag starts, the source object over which the cursor is positioned could highlight indicating that the object may be dragged. During the drag, the cursor shape could change to indicate when the cursor is over a valid drop target, and the drop target could also highlight to reinforce this situation. When the drop occurs, the dropped object could be highlighted so the user can see that the object was truly dropped at the specified location, and the dropped object could be left selected so the user can easily adjust its position or orientation if needed, such as nudging it with the arrow keys.

Drag-and-drop environment

A typical use of drag-and-drop in graphics applications, 2D and 3D, is to provide the user with a palette of icons that represent graphical models. Often the palettes are arranged with tabs or in a tree to form a catalog. Dragging an object from the palette and dropping it on a view display has the effect of loading the object's model into the graphics world, where the user can view it and possibly manipulate it. This is analogous to dropping the data file on the word processor to open it for editing. Just as reasonable but less typical, the user can drag an object from the display view and save it in a palette. In an e-commerce application, this might be used to build an order in a basket before submitting it. As with the desktop, the user can organize the palettes by moving and copying objects in and between them.

While an object is in the virtual world, the user can drag it around, positioning and orienting it using various control and manipulation techniques. If these operations involve dragging an object and dropping it on another object in the world, perhaps to attach them together, the operation would be more like drag-and-drop than simple target object manipulation. The distinction can be subtle and is not important for this discussion. If there are multiple worlds or multiple views of the same world, then the user might be able to move and copy objects from one world or display to another by simply dragging and dropping the objects.

2D-3D transition

For 3D drag-and-drop, the 2D-in-a-3D-world problem becomes visible, literally, when an object is dragged from a 2D palette and into the 3D world in a view display, which can raise a number of questions. At what point in the operation does the object change from appearing as a 2D icon to appearing as a 3D model? When it does change into a 3D model, what form does it take? When the drop occurs, where does the object get placed?

Taking this one step at a time, one simple and obvious approach is to preserve the object as an icon until it is dropped. When the drop occurs the icon is replaced by its 3D model equivalent, but where in the world does it go? Taking the easy way out, the 3D object could appear at some predefined 3D location, such as the world origin, which would be a DnD operation with a teleport result. This may be simple for the designer to implement, but it is not very useful or intuitive for the user. Always placing the dropped object at the world origin or some other fixed spot means that the object will likely jump to some place in the virtual world nowhere near the mouse cursor, possibly not even in the display. The power of drag-and-drop is that in one simple mouse gesture, the user can select an object and place it exactly where it is needed in the target space. Using teleport ignores a major benefit of using drag-and-drop. What is needed is some way to figure out where the 2D mouse cursor is in the 3D world. WRM and its partner, object picking, offer a solution.

WRM to the rescue

WRM provides 3D drag-and-drop with the means for figuring out where the drag cursor is in the 3D world. This is useful during the drag, to determine if the drag cursor is over a potential drop target, and after the drop, to determine where in the world to place the 3D model of the object. In the office layout example, users drag furniture objects from a 2D palette in the product catalog and drop them into a model of their offices in the 3D world. Using object picking, the application knows which item the mouse cursor is being dragged over in the 3D world. If a desk is

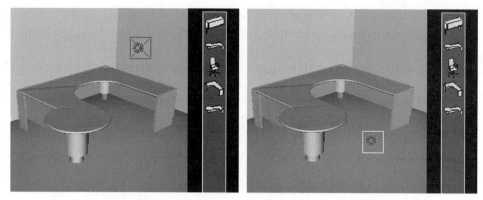

Figure 9.7   During drag-and-drop from the basket, a "no-drop" indicator appears while the cursor is over the wall (left), and turns into a "drop" indicator when over the floor (right). (Courtesy of TechniCon Corporation)

being dragged over a wall, door, window, another piece of furniture, or the world background, then a "no-drop" indicator might appear. If it is being dragged over the floor and there is adequate surrounding clearance, then a "drop" indicator would appear. Figure 9.7 shows examples of no-drop and drop during a basket DnD operation. When the drop occurs, through the miracle of WRM, the 3D object model would appear in the world exactly where the user placed it: on the floor directly under the mouse cursor. All of your problems are solved—or are they?

When to switch

As to the question of when to make the target object change from a 2D icon into a 3D model, part of the answer involves aesthetics and the other part entails practical considerations. One approach, the *late switch*, is to use the icon throughout the drag-and-drop operation, with the model only appearing after the fact, when the drop occurs. A second approach, the *early switch*, is to change the icon into the 3D model when the mouse cursor first enters the 3D display.

An icon is small and does not obscure very much of the work area in the scene around where the mouse is being dragged. Being a 2D icon instead of a 3D model, it must live in the display space and therefore appear overlaid in the display rather than as part of the virtual world. This can be good because the user can always see the icon, even if there are other objects in the work area that might otherwise obscure it. In the late switch approach, however, this can be bad, since the user will not be able to see how the object fits into its 3D surroundings until after the object is dropped. Figures 9.7 and 9.8 show a DnD sequence using late switch. Note that because late switch was used, there was no way to see that the chair was backward until after the drop occurred (figure 9.8).

With early switch, the switch to the 3D model occurs before the drop; and, the user can see exactly how the object will appear in the world while dragging it. Because

the object turns into its 3D model counterpart, depending on where the cursor
falls in the scene, the target object can
appear quite large or quite small when
the switch occurs. Beside being unexpected to the user, the model may
obscure the work area completely or disappear from view entirely, making it
difficult to proceed with the drag-and-
drop operation. Even if size were not a
problem, because the target is a member
of the virtual world, it may become hidden behind other objects in the work
area, again making it difficult to conduct the drag-and-drop operation.

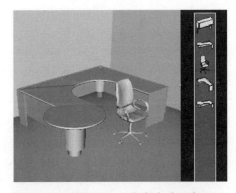

**Figure 9.8   With late switch during drag-
and-drop, there is no way to tell that the
chair will appear backward in the scene
until after the drop. (Courtesy of TechniCon
Corporation)**

There is no right solution to the problem of when to switch from a 2D to a 3D
representation. As with most decisions in UI design, you have to understand what the
problem is, come up with a solution that best satisfies the requirements, and iterate
the design with real user testing until you get it right.

9.4   SUMMARY

With the subject of data access out of the way, all the bases have been covered for
next-generation 3D user interfaces. Data access techniques can be described as allowing out-of-scene versus in-scene access to the application's data. Data grouping, which
is commonly used for in-scene data selection, is a diffuse relationship among objects
that can have physical as well as logical implications. Out-of-scene access comes in
3D, 2D, and non-spatial varieties such as trees and lists, with data palettes allowing
iconic drag-and-drop access to application data.

Next-generation applications will likely include some form of visually oriented
data catalog—an e-catalog—from which the user can select data items or products. An
alternative would be to present the data items in a drag-and-drop palette. In any case,
showing the user a preview of the item, preferably in 3D, can be helpful in finalizing
the selection. The preview can also serve as a convenient place to configure the item,
in private and away from the clutter in the scene. A data basket offers a convenient
way to collect selected objects before the user has to switch mental gears for placing
them in the scene. And, finally, an intuitive solution for getting objects into the scene
from the 2D world is 3D drag-and-drop.

From here the book will take a sharp turn from the conceptual to the practical.
The rest of this text concentrates on the implementation and demonstration of many
of the techniques presented in this part of the book, starting with an introduction to
Java 3D and ending with examples implemented using a lightweight 3D UI framework
in Java 3D.

PART 3

Java 3D user interface essentials

With the advent of Java, developers were provided with a rich range of sophisticated functionality capable of dealing with the challenges of modern computing. Even better, the various Java packages were developed to work together from the start. Along the way, though, there have been a few bumps in the road, particularly, the handling of the user interface. When Java was first developed, it came equipped with the AWT toolkit, which was inadequate for supporting the kinds of sophisticated user interfaces to which application developers and users had grown accustomed. From these halting baby steps evolved a full-featured toolkit that goes by the name of Swing.

What Java did for the world of general application development, Java 3D is trying to do for the more narrowly defined world of 3D graphics. As with any new generation, Java 3D benefits from the many prior years of research and development within the graphics community. A major accomplishment of such efforts was that 3D graphics came into the realm of the common developer, with even a few offerings to the common user. Most of the heavy lifting for this was done by OpenGL, OpenInventor, and most notably VRML, which made 3D available to the masses over the web. As was the case with Java, Java 3D is now taking its baby steps and feeling its way along in the big, wide 3D world. In many ways, Java 3D is weakest in the very same area in which Java was lacking when it was first introduced—user interface support.

This part of the book introduces Java 3D and describes those aspects of the API that serve as a foundation for the kinds of 3D user interface techniques presented in part 2. This introduction to Java 3D lays the groundwork for part 4, which describes a framework built on top of Java 3D to demonstrate many of the 3D UI techniques. Portions of the framework will be used to illustrate many of the Java 3D API features covered here.

C H A P T E R   1 0

Java 3D introduction

There is no better way to introduce you to a new API than with a discourse on what it is, what it is not, and where to go for more information. Although this is a traditional approach, it is useful but brief. To help guide you from the earlier conceptual parts of the book to the more practical side of 3D UI development, a roadmap is provided summarizing how Java and Java 3D can support the implementation needs of 3D UI techniques.

10.1   WHAT IS JAVA 3D?

Quoting the official Sun statement on the matter, "Java 3D is a network-centric, scene-graph-based API for developing 3D applets and applications." As with the rest of Java, Java 3D is bred for "write once, run anywhere" application development. It was designed to scale from low-end laptops to high-end supercomputers while taking advantage of the native capabilities of each host platform. In a major advance over its predecessors, Java 3D also supports the latest in virtual reality-sensor and display devices, including head-mounted displays and immersive computer-assisted virtual environment (CAVE) systems. Of course, in a POCS we are only dealing with a mouse and a monitor, but it's reassuring to know that as the level of POCS hardware sophistication advances, Java 3D is there to support it.

Java 3D is considered to be a mid- to high-level fourth-generation 3D API. What sets a fourth-generation API apart from its predecessors is the use of scene-graph architecture for organizing graphical objects in the virtual 3D world. Unlike the display lists used by third-generation APIs, scene graphs mercifully hide a lot of the rendering detail from the programmer while offering opportunities for more flexible and efficient rendering.

Java 3D has benefited greatly from the successes and failures of its predecessors, which include VRML, OpenInventor, and OpenGL. Because Java 3D is part of the Java pantheon, it assures developers ready access to a wide array of application and network support functionality. With Java 3D standing on the shoulders of such giants, what more could the 3D application developer ask? Having a "Swing 3D" would be nice.

10.2   *WHERE IS SWING 3D?*

Although Java 3D does many things well, it seems to be lacking in a few areas. One is in supporting the kinds of user interfaces discussed earlier in the book. The parallels between the introductions of Java and Java 3D with respect to UI support are noteworthy. When Java was released, user interface developers and users were accustomed to tear-off menus, copious drag-and-drop, and editable tree diagrams. With the introduction of Java's AWT toolkit, however, developer and user alike were reduced to using basic windows, menus, and buttons—the GUI equivalents of stone knives and bear skins. Matters have improved considerably with the maturing of Swing, Java's answer to the demands of the modern GUI. Not only does Swing offer a full complement of modern GUI widgets; its strong embrace of the MVC pattern clearly pushes it beyond its predecessors.

In terms of 3D user interface support, Java 3D's closest predecessor is VRML. Although VRML has its own problems, not the least of which is the lack of basic 2D GUI support and integration, it did have a mature outlook on the need for sophisticated in-scene control and feedback. Built right into the core of VRML are controls for in-scene object translation and rotation, and sensors for 3D mouseover detection and control activation. As you'll see, Java 3D can also support this type user-interface functionality and more, but the developer has to work at it.

Some might argue that Java 3D is doing exactly what it should be doing with respect to user interface support and related areas such as object picking and collision detection; it provides all the necessary building blocks for developers to formulate higher levels of functionality. Although this is good in principle, it falls short in practice. A good example is 3D mouseover detection, which is vital to good 3D UI feedback. In a side-by-side comparison, a VRML TouchSensor in any of the popular VRML players doing mouseover detection far surpasses the functional equivalent in Java 3D using its picking model and primitives.

Java 3D, however, has much to offer and its developers have ensured it can wear its fourth-generation label proudly. It also seems to be the best bet for providing a foundation for next-generation 3D applications, especially those that are web-based. Let's see how far we can get with Java 3D toward closing the gap between it and "Swing 3D."

10.3   JUST AN INTRODUCTION

In keeping with the central theme of the book, this introduction to Java 3D deals only with those aspects of the API and its Java API relatives that pertain to 3D user interface support. As such, it does not cover all aspects of Java 3D as would a tutorial. It also does not cover many of the getting started basics that a tutorial would cover, such as how to install the Java 3D software. Instead, it assumes that the reader is familiar with Java and 3D graphics, and is capable of installing and running the Java 3D application examples.

The main purpose of this introduction is to familiarize the reader with the basics of Java 3D and to highlight those areas of the API that will be used in the next part of the book. In the next part we'll see how to build a framework that demonstrates many of the 3D UI techniques presented earlier in the book. As with most APIs, there is often more than one way to get something done. Time and space do not permit exploration of alternative implementations, but the more significant ones will be noted.

The coverage here of the Java 3D API and its Java relatives is highly selective. Some areas are covered in great detail and others receive only a passing mention. The purpose is to focus on what is necessary for 3D UI development. This still leaves plenty of Java 3D to be covered in this part of the book and plenty of new concepts and code to be covered in the next, without having to deal with some of the more specialized areas of Java 3D. In practical terms, this introduction touches on most of what people just starting out in Java 3D need to know: the practical steps to getting a window up that displays a 3D world with which they can interact.

10.4   3D UI ROADMAP

Although the gap between Java 3D and Swing 3D is appreciable, table 10.1 attempts to map the basic functionality provided by Java 3D to the various 3D UI techniques described in the previous part of the book. The left column categorizes the techniques, and the right column describes the key classes and class methods, or groups of them (indicated by square brackets), that best support the techniques. In some sense, this table provides a roadmap describing how to get from Java 3D, the right column, to Swing 3D, in the left column. Unfortunately, the roads provided by Java 3D for this journey do not extend very far. The software presented in part 4, a 3D UI framework, will significantly extend many of the roads started by Java 3D.

Although all the techniques are shown in the table as supportable—something is put in all of the rows in the right hand column—the actual support provided by Java and Java 3D can be rather remote. As such, some of the entries may leave you wondering just how it is that the framework will get from, say, a Java 3D `Transformgroup` to the DRM UI technique (sixth row under Control). You may also notice that there is a lot of redundancy in the support column, which is indicative of the fact that Java 3D provides only the most fundamental capabilities when it comes to UI support. It is up to the application, or in this case, the UI framework, to use them to build a specific solution for a particular need. Note that the square brackets in the left column of the table identify low-level UI techniques that use a common and recognizable set (pattern) of API functionality, which is used to support higher-level techniques as indicated later in the table. Also, note that in spite of the right column being filled, the framework does not implement all of the techniques.

Some Java 3D capabilities that you might expect to be in the table, such as those dealing with collision and other more sophisticated behaviors, are absent, which is mainly attributable to design or implementation deficiencies in the API. This situation will hopefully improve with future releases of Java 3D.

Table 10.1 Java/Java 3D support for 3D UI techniques

3D UI Technique	Java/Java 3D Support
Control	
• Mouse, keyboard devices [devices]	Behavior, WakeupOnAWTEvent, EventListener, javax.swing.Timer
• Input origin, action, gestures	javax.swing.Timer
• Target actuation	TransformGroup, Transform3D, Vector3d, AxisAngle4d
• Coordinate mapping	TransformGroup, Transform3D
• Object picking [picking]	Canvas3D.getPixelLocationInImagePlate(), PickRay, BranchGroup.pickAllSorted(), Shape3D.intersect()
• DRM	Node.getLocalToVworld(), TransformGroup, Transform3D
• WRM	[picking], Node.getLocalToVworld(), TransformGroup, Transform3D
Feedback	
• (all visual elements) [visuals]	Shape3D, Appearance, TransparencyAttributes, Texture, Geometry, Toolkit.getDefaultToolkit().getImage()
• Basic elements (identifiers, indicators)	[visuals], sun.j3d.util.Text2D, Text3D, Billboard
• Basic elements (cursor)	java.awt.Cursor
• Basic elements (sounds) [sounds]	Sound, JavaSoundMixer, MediaContainer
• Simple dynamics	[devices], [picking], javax.swing.Timer

Table 10.1   Java/Java 3D support for 3D UI techniques (continued)

• Interaction states	[devices], [picking]
• Multi-shape	Switch, [visuals], [sounds]

Visualization

• (display and view changes) [changes]	Behavior, WakeupOnAWTEvent, Canvas3D, View, Canvas3D.getImagePlateToVworld(), Toolkit.getDefault-Toolkit().getScreenSize()/getScreenResolution()
• Display space techniques	[changes], OrderedGroup
• World space techniques	[changes], Node.getLocalToVworld(), TransformGroup, Transform3D
• LOS revealment	[picking]
• Multiple views	Canvas3D, View

Navigation

• Cameras (manual)	[picking], TransformGroup, Transform3D
• Cameras (assisted)	[devices], [picking], Bounds, Node.getLocalToVworld(), Transform3D, javax.swing.Timer
• Cameras (scripted)	[devices], [picking], Behaviors, PathInterpolator

Manipulation

• Feedback elements (passive)	[visuals], Bounds, Node.getLocalToVworld(), Transform3D
• Feedback elements (active)	[devices], [picking], Bounds, Node.getLocalToVworld(), Transform3D
• PTF	[devices], [picking], Java
• Snapping, attachment	[devices], [picking], Java
• Specification, configuration	[devices], [picking], Java, Swing

Access

• In-scene grouping	[devices], [picking], Java, Group, BranchGroup, TranformGroup
• Out-of-scene access	Java, Swing, Java 2D
• Data transfer	[devices], [picking], java.awt.datatransfer, java.awt.dnd, SharedGroup, Link, Node.cloneNode(), Node.cloneTree()

10.5 JAVA 3D AND ITS FRIENDS

Java 3D is part of the Java Media suite of APIs. These APIs provide capabilities for integrating with various multimedia and Internet technologies including audio, video, and 2D and 3D graphics. Java 3D also works with parts of the standard Java 1.2 platform to provide integration with the windowing system and input devices such as the mouse and keyboard. Some of this cooperation is indicated in the preceding UI Roadmap table with references to Java, Swing, and Java 2D packages.

The Java 3D core is found in the `javax.media.j3d` package. Java 3D relies heavily on the `javax.vecmath` and `java.awt` packages. The former provides support for point, vector, and matrix data constructs and operations, and the latter provides access to the Java windowing and input event systems. You will be seeing a lot of the `javax.vecmath` classes in Java 3D programming. The more common data constructs are points and vectors, which come in 2D, 3D, and 4D versions. All data constructs come in single- and double-floating point precision. For example, `Point2d` and `Point3d` represent a 2D and 3D point, respectively, with double precision, as indicated by the "d" in the class name. `Vector4f` represents a 4D vector with single precision, as indicated by the "f" in the name.

Outside of the Java 3D API are a set of utilities commonly referred to as the "Sun utilities." They are located in the `com.sun.j3d.utils` package shipped as part of the Java 3D release. Whereas the Java 3D core classes are relatively low-level, the utility classes provide higher levels of functionality, including some basic 3D objects such as a box and a sphere, and operations such as picking. Often used in conjunction with Java 3D, are the Java Swing, drag-and-drop, and data transfer packages. These are found in `javax.swing`, `java.awt.dnd`, and `java.awt.datatransfer` respectively.

10.6 JAVA 3D RESOURCES

Because this is only an introduction to Java 3D, you will likely need outside help. For more information about 3D computer graphics in general, as well as detailed explanations of various mathematical concepts, such as matrix multiplication and geometric transformations, you can refer to the book *Computer Graphics* by Foley, van Dam, et al. Many consider this book to be the bible of computer graphics. For more general information about Java 3D, several tutorial books are on the market.

Another place to look for help is on the web. The following sites should be useful, and many lead to a number of other useful sites:

- **Sun's Java 3D Homepage**
  http://java.sun.com/products/java-media/3D/
  From here the Java 3D software can be downloaded, and the Java 3D documentation can be viewed online or downloaded. Of special note on this site is Java 3D application specification.

- **Sun's JDK Homepage**
  http://java.sun.com/products/jdk/
  The Java 1.2 JDK and documentation can be downloaded from here. Java 1.2 or higher is required to run Java 3D.
- **Sun's Java 3D Tutorial**
  http://sun.com/desktop/java3d/
  This site includes Java 3D news and information, and in particular an online tutorial.
- **Java 3D FAQ**
  http://www.j3d.org
  This FAQ is maintained by Steve Pietrowitcz of NCSA with the help of Justin Couch of ADI Ltd.
- **Java 3D Loaders**
  http://www.billday.com/Java3DArchive/
  This site, which is maintained by Bill Day, provides links to the latest model loaders, such as for VRML files. To run many of the book's examples you will have to download and install a VRML 97 loader, which can be obtained from this site.

Of course, all the source code presented in this book is available through the publisher's web site at www.manning.com/barrilleaux. The same, unfortunately, can not be said of Java 3D itself. Unlike Java or Sun's Java 3D utilities, Sun has not released the source code for Java 3D. When things go wrong and a bug is suspected, there is no definite way to verify it in the source code. This, together with its limited documentation, is why the discussions here on Java 3D have a "might be this, or might be that" tone; divining what Java 3D is really doing requires poking an input into the API and seeing what comes out the other side.

10.7 A MOVING TARGET

These days, businesses and APIs alike are all operating on "web time." Both have become fast-moving targets. Java is very much a work in progress that is continuing to expand, improve, and stabilize. Java 3D, one of the younger Java progeny, is no exception. Books that discuss APIs are unavoidably a generation behind the standard. The first half of this book, which is conceptual in nature and not based on any specific API, is impervious to the work-in-progress juggernaut. The second half, starting with this part, is not so fortunate. As a point of reference in your reading, the Java 3D introduction here and the framework and examples in the next part are based on version 1.2 of the Java SDK and version 1.1.2 of the Java 3D API, which are the most recent versions available at the time of writing.

The nature of the UI techniques described in the book are such that you quickly find yourself out in the fringes of the API, where the majority of developers seldom go or haven't yet had the need to go. Also, the techniques tend to generate a lot of internal interaction between the various capabilities and models in the API, which can expose additional soft spots. This was true in the early 3D UI prototypes done in VRML, and it has proved to also be true with Java 3D. Specific UI techniques often rely on specific API capabilities. The framework has to deal with these problems, and so will you if you want to use these techniques. So, rather than avoiding the soft spots in the API, the book indicates where the more critical bumps in the road can be found and occasionally suggests changes to the API that could make our lives as UI developers easier. Keep in mind as you try your hand at programming some of the UI techniques that the next version of Java 3D, version 1.2, may fix some of the ills described here. Most likely, however, it won't fix all of them.

10.8 SUMMARY

Although Java 3D seems to come up short in its treatment of 3D user interfaces, it has a lot to recommend it for the types of 3D applications that are on the world wide web horizon. Here, we saw a roadmap that indicated which 3D techniques were supported by which portions of the Java and Java 3D API. We also saw how Java 3D fits in with other useful Java packages, and where to go on the web for more help.

Let's start off this introduction to Java 3D with a bit of practical how-to advice: Before trying any of the Sun or book examples, make certain your display card's drivers are up to date. Any bugs in your OpenGL or DirectX (depending on which flavor of Java 3D you have chosen) graphics drivers will be manifested in Java 3D, because it relies heavily on the underlying drivers for rendering support. Although highly specific to card type and driver version, some of the problems caused by older drivers include flickering, incorrect lighting, and incorrect rendering of geometric primitives.

C H A P T E R   1 1

UI spaces and the
scene graph

A good place to start a discussion of 3D UI implementation is with the coordinate and conceptual spaces described in the first part of the book and elaborated on in subsequent chapters. To make the transition into implementation, however, these rather abstract constructs must be mapped into something a lot more concrete, which in Java 3D is the scene graph. The scene graph is the backbone of the Java 3D architecture and API, and should be familiar if you have any experience with OpenInventor or VRML. Because OpenGL does not use a scene graph, experience with it is useful but not to the same degree as with the other programs.

A number of Java 3D classes will be introduced in this chapter that relate to the 3D UI spaces and Java 3D's scene graph architecture. To help you understand the relationships, several figures are provided along the way. Another approach for following this discussion is to point your browser at the Java 3D API specification and `javadoc` documentation. This will help you to begin making the association between the abstract concepts presented in the text and the actual classes that you will need to use if you want to start programming in Java 3D. You can access the documentation directly online or download it from Sun's Java 3D homepage, which was listed in chapter 10.

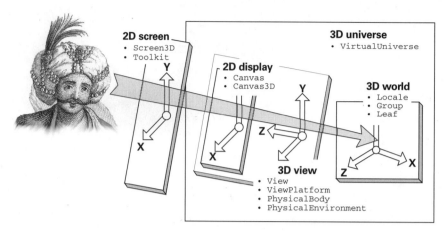

Figure 11.1   The associations between 3D UI spaces and high-level Java/Java 3D classes

If you are so inclined, you may also want to take a look at some of the classes from the UI framework in the next part of the book as examples of how to use the Java 3D classes. A good place to start for seeing how the UI spaces can be implemented in the context of an application is the `j3dui.utils.app` package. The `SingleFrame` class is an example of how the framework's various space classes—`AppWorld`, `App-View`, and `AppDisplay`—are used in a very simple application.

11.1   3D UI SPACES

As introduced in earlier chapters, it is often convenient to describe a 3D UI in terms of its coordinate and conceptual spaces: world, view, display, and screen. Java 3D introduces yet another space, the universe, which is like the world space, only bigger. Here, the Java 3D counterparts to these spaces are identified and discussed in terms of their general role in UI development, which is illustrated in figure 11.1. The progression is from the largest and most abstract space, the universe, to the smallest and most concrete one, the screen.

There is a bit of a chicken-and-egg dilemma here in trying to discuss the UI spaces and their classes before presenting the Java 3D scene graph, or vice versa. Many of the classes define the spaces, and the scene graph arranges the spaces and class instances—the objects. Perhaps the best approach is to read through this section, about spaces and classes, and the next one, on scene graphs, and then to come back and re-read this section. To help bridge the two sections, figure 11.2 provides a class hierarchy of the classes discussed in this section and the next. A complete version of the Java 3D class hierarchy can be found at http://java.sun.com/products/java-media/3D/collateral/j3dclass.html.

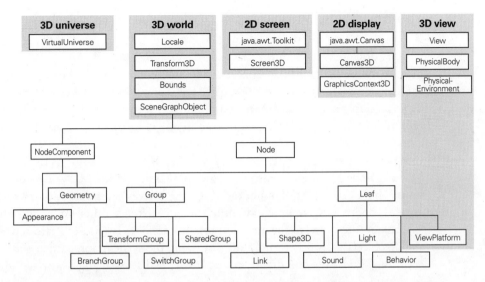

Figure 11.2   Class hierarchy of the main Java/Java 3D classes discussed in this chapter

11.1.1   The universe

In Java 3D the `VirtualUniverse` class defines the highest level of object aggregation. Everything that is to exist in a Java 3D scene must eventually end up connected to a `VirtualUniverse`, where "everything" includes: visible objects, nonvisible objects, such as sounds and behaviors (they need a home), and view objects, like cameras floating in space. Although an application can have more than one universe, often one is enough. If more than one universe is used it is important to note that objects can exist only in one universe at a time and that objects can be seen only by a view from that universe (there is no Java 3D equivalent of a wormhole between universes, at least not yet).

As its name implies, a universe can be a big place. To help in the precise placement of objects that may be located on opposite ends of the universe, literally and figuratively, as might be the case in an astronomical application, Java 3D provides a `Locale` class. A `Locale` provides a local frame of spatial reference for the objects it contains. The `Locale` is positioned in the universe with high precision and the objects in the `Locale` are positioned with lower and more computer-friendly precision. Unlike a universe, objects in two different locales can be seen in a single view.

The relationship between locales and universes is simple. A `VirtualUniverse` contains none, one, or more `Locale` objects, and a `Locale` contains one or more scene graphs. Scene graphs are what actually hold the universe's objects and maintain their spatial and conceptual relationships.

11.1.2 The world

In terms of UI spaces, there is no world class in Java 3D. Instead, the world is defined by a set of closely cooperating classes. The `VirtualUniverse` and `Locale` classes provide the world coordinate space, and the scene graph holds the objects that live in the virtual world. So where is this elusive scene graph class? There is a `SceneGraph-Object` class but it is fairly abstract and not very interesting in the context of the current discussion. We are interested instead in one of its subclasses, the `Node` class.

A scene graph is a tree-like data structure built from subclasses of `Node`. Nodes come in two flavors, represented by the `Group` and `Leaf` classes. As its name implies, a `Group` node provides the means for grouping other `Nodes`. A `Group` node can have none, one, or more children nodes, which themselves can be `Group` or `Leaf` nodes. A `Leaf` node can have no children, but it can reference other nodes and objects for special purposes. One of the more important leaf nodes is `Shape3D`, from which most visible objects derive. Let's hold off discussing the scene graph further until we have accounted for all the coordinate spaces. It will be discussed and illustrated in detail in section 11.2.

11.1.3 The view

You may recall that the view space is that portion of the world space that appears in front of the user's virtual eyeball. Objects placed in the view space are positioned and manipulated relative to the view's coordinate space, not the world's. Because of the nature of the Java 3D scene graph, the UI concept of a view space is defined by a set of cooperating classes instead of a single class.

View space

The `ViewPlatform` class is a `Leaf` node that defines the view coordinate space. Moving the `ViewPlatform` moves your eyeball in the virtual world, which is done by geometrically manipulating some `Group` node above the `ViewPlatform` in the scene graph. You'll see more about such spatial transforms in a later section. Because the `ViewPlatform` is a `Leaf` node, it can't have any children (otherwise it wouldn't be a leaf). To add an object to the view space, you must instead add it to a `Group` node above the `ViewPlatform` in the scene graph. To assure that the added object is actually in the view space, and not in some intermediate space you should generally add view objects to the same `Group` node to which the `ViewPlatform` belongs.

The next major player in the view story is the `View` class. It provides the logical and spatial association between the view space and the display space. Java 3D's view model is rather complex because it is intended to satisfy a variety of VR display and tracking configurations, and as such it encompasses both virtual and physical world characteristics. Because of the relatively primitive nature of a POCS display you can ignore—or try to ignore—most of the model. As will be discussed in part 4 of the book, the Java 3D view model surprisingly does not seem to allow the full range of control over the display and view spaces described in chapter 3, which were simplified for use in a POCS.

View model

In a `View` object the spatial association between the view and display space is defined by references to `PhysicalBody` and `PhysicalEnvironment` objects as well as a host of view policy and view parameter attributes of `View`. The two classes address physical world model parameters, and their default configurations are generally adequate for a POCS. The View attributes cover such matters as the type of view projection (perspective or parallel), the field of view (degree of perspective), and how to handle display window movement and resizing. The default settings of `View` are generally adequate although some applications might want to make some adjustments, such as for projection and field of view.

A more important function of the `View` is its role in establishing the logical association between view and display space. Java 3D supports the simultaneous display of multiple views of the same world (technically, the same universe). To do this you simply add more `ViewPlatform` objects to the scene graph with associated `View` objects and displays. Note that a `View` can only be associated with one `ViewPlatform` at a time. A variation on the multiple-view theme is to create multiple `ViewPlatform` objects as prepositioned viewpoints in the world. Then, under user or program control, a `View` object and its associated display can be conveniently detached from one `ViewPlatform` and reattached to another. To the user this will appear as an instantaneous teleportation to another place in the world.

11.1.4   The display

For a POCS, the display space is the plane on which the visible contents of the view space is projected, with or without perspective as defined by the view attributes. To refresh your memory, the 2D display space can be thought of as living in the world at the position of the view and facing in the direction of the view. The user sees the display as an image in a portion of the computer's display screen. As with the view space, objects placed in the display space (2D, or 3D projected as 2D) are positioned and manipulated relative to the display's coordinate space, not the world's.

Display space

The `Canvas3D` class serves as the display window image, and for the most part, represents the display space. (As we saw in the previous section, `View` also manages a few of the display-related characteristics.) `Canvas3D` is an extension of the AWT `Canvas` class. As with any other AWT component it maintains window-related state information such as its size and position on the display screen. Although we don't have to worry about it in a POCS, it is interesting to note that a `View` can have multiple `Canvas3D` objects associated with it. This corresponds to a VR display system where a large tessellated display is made up of multiple individual display elements.

Display overlay

In an ideal world, virtual or otherwise, we'd like to maintain separate image spaces for the projected view contents and the overlaid display contents. Such a separation would allow world and display space objects to appear over- or underlaid with respect to their neighbors. Unfortunately, Java 3D does not directly support such separation of spaces, nor does it directly support image layering or display overlay.

One alternative is to interpose the `Canvas3D` rendering cycle and generate the display overlay in "immediate" rendering mode, object by overlaid object. `Canvas3D` provides the hooks for detecting where in its cycle the renderer is, and for drawing an object in immediate mode through its `GraphicsContext3D` object. This approach also requires the designer to explicitly transform and draw each object in the display, sacrificing many of the benefits of using a scene graph-based architecture. Another alternative is to use the geometry transformation tricks described in chapter 6, on Visualization. As you may recall, PDO and PWO make view and world objects, respectively, appear as though they are overlaid in front of or underlaid behind their fellow objects.

Each approach has advantages and disadvantages. Rendering the overlay contents directly to `Canvas3D` guarantees that nothing else in the view space will be in front of the overlay, but there are aesthetic and performance concerns regarding Java 3D's immediate mode rendering in general, and for world overlay in particular. Using the geometry transform trick has definite computational advantages when world overlay is involved but, as you may recall, special care must be taken to assure that an overlaid object remains overlaid in all viewing conditions. For the purposes of this book, the PDO and PWO approaches have been chosen for overlay implementation, which will be described and demonstrated as part of the software framework in part 4.

Display picking

`Canvas3D` serves a central role in display-based picking operations. Display picking involves determining over which objects in the world the mouse cursor appears. Through `Canvas3D` methods you can determine the position and orientation of the display in the world space, and account for any view perspective in the view's projection, which affects the mouseover determination. Picking will be covered in detail later.

Display printing

Java 3D has no native capability for printing a `Canvas3D` display image. Instead, you have to coerce the contents of a `Canvas3D` into a Java `Image`, and then hand it over to an object that implements the Java `Printable` interface for the actual printing. The framework class `j3dui.utils.app.AppDisplay` supports display image capture, and the `j3dui.utils.app.ImagePrinter` class supports printing. The use of these classes is demonstrated in the FancyApp example.

11.1.5   The screen

Canvas3D uses the Screen3D class to define physical world model characteristics, which include head tracker attributes in addition to display screen characteristics. The only attributes we are interested in for a POCS are the screen's physical size, in meters, and its resolution, in pixels. As with the rest of the Java 3D view model, the defaults for the physical model are adequate for a POCS.

As it turns out, Java itself provides a way to obtain the physical attributes of the display screen; and Java's notion of the display screen is exactly that of a POCS. Access to the screen attributes is through the Toolkit class, specifically the getScreen-Size() and getScreenResolution() methods. Unlike Java 3D, which assumes a standard screen size and resolution, Java accesses the system's understanding of its underlying hardware, which presumably reflects the current settings for the system's display hardware. For this reason the framework uses Toolkit to obtain the screen geometry instead of the canvas' Screen3D object.

11.2   SCENE GRAPH AND MORE

The scene graph serves as a home for all objects in the virtual world. For an object to have a presence or effect in the world, whether visible or nonvisible, it must be in a scene graph. This includes concrete objects such as desks, jumbo jets, and chemical plants, as well as less tangible objects such as lights, views, and behaviors. The scene graph paradigm was well established by the time Java 3D came along. It helps both the system and the developer to keep track of the bookkeeping involved in maintaining and presenting a 3D virtual world.

11.2.1   Scene graph basics

In general terms, a scene graph is made from nodes arranged in a hierarchical parent-child tree structure. The topmost nodes are called root nodes, the middle-level nodes are called branch nodes, and the bottom most nodes are called leaf nodes. (The structure does indeed resemble a tree, only the tree is upside down, with the root at the top.)

The purpose of the branch nodes is to group descendant nodes related through some common association or set of characteristics. As such, branch nodes are also called group nodes. All branch nodes provide some form of logical grouping. Many also provide special grouping properties, such as for geometric grouping, where changes to the group's geometric state can affect the overall geometry of its children; and for rendering purposes, where the group's children can be selectively rendered or not. For example, to keep things tidy, an office layout application may contain one group under which all the architectural elements live—floor, walls, doors—and another group under which all furniture objects live—desks, chairs, lamps. The architecture may be static and not subject to user modification; but to enhance visibility, the system may need to selectively hide a wall or two. Thus, the architecture subgraph would be constructed

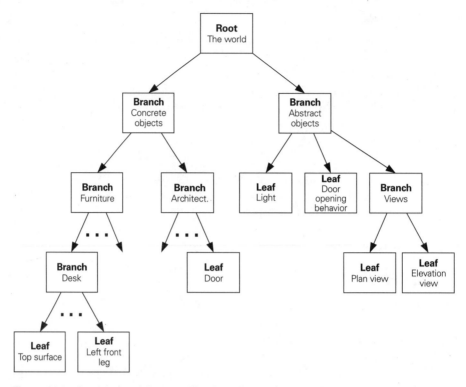

Figure 11.3 A scene graph is a tree-like data structure that maintains logical and spatial relationships for all objects in the virtual world—concrete as well as abstract.

using "geometric" and "rendering" group nodes. The furniture is a different matter. The user is meant to move it around and group it into ensembles. As such, its subgraph would be constructed using "geometric" and "logical" group nodes.

Leaf nodes are where the substance in the virtual world resides. For visible objects, such as a desk, leaf nodes collectively provide its geometry and the visual characteristics of its components, such as color and shininess. Leaf nodes also provide substance to less concrete objects. A leaf view node would define the internal view geometry and display characteristics. A light node might define the direction, color, and size of the lighting effect. And, a behavior node might specify the events that stimulate it and the nature of its response to those stimuli. For example, the office door may open when the user's view approaches it.

In Java 3D, the ultimate root of the scene graph is the `VirtualUniverse`, the branch nodes below it must be `Locale` objects, and the branch nodes below them must be `BranchGroup` objects. `BranchGroup` objects have the unique distinction of being the only group node that can be detached and re-attached in a scene graph at run time. As such, in practical terms, `BranchGroup` objects serve as root nodes, but only of a subgraph. Below the topmost `BranchGroup` level in the scene graph,

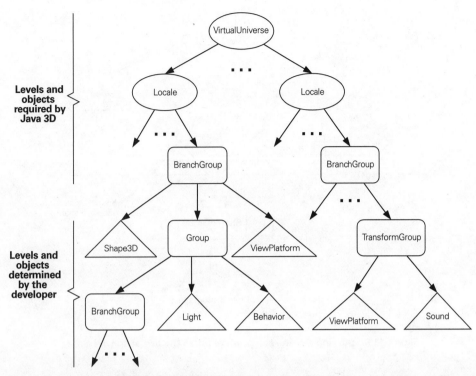

Figure 11.4 Below the topmost BranchGroup level there are few restrictions on how a Java 3D scene graph can be organized.

the structure of the tree and the choice of objects to use in it are up to the discretion of the developer. Any subclass of `Group` can serve as a branch node, and any subclass of `Leaf` can serve as a leaf node in the tree. Also, Java 3D imposes few restrictions on how many of a given node type is present in the tree. For example, the scene graph can contain multiple `ViewPlatform` leaf nodes anywhere in the tree, which represent multiple views of the virtual world.

11.2.2 Sharing subgraphs

Although a scene graph is frequently referred to as a tree, technically it is a directed acyclic graph (DAG). This is important to know because it means that portions of the scene graph can be shared by two or more `Group` nodes. A strict rule of Java 3D scene graphs, however, is that a `Node`, regardless of its type, can have only one parent. The mechanics for sharing a subgraph get a bit complicated in order to satisfy the one-parent rule. To get around this restriction, Java 3D uses the `Link` and the `SharedGroup` classes.

A `Link` is a leaf node with the unique ability to reference a `SharedGroup`. A `SharedGroup` is a group node with the unique property that it cannot have a parent node but it can be referenced by a `Link`. What all this means is that in order to share

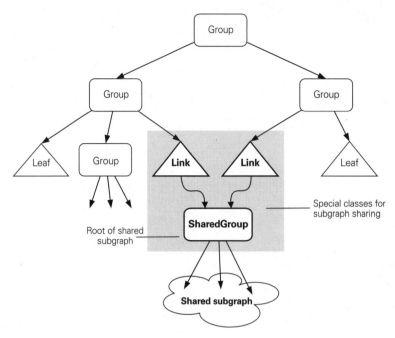

Figure 11.5   Sharing a scene subgraph requires the use of special classes.

a portion of the scene graph (a subgraph), the topmost or root node of the subgraph must be a SharedGroup; and, the SharedGroup must be connected to the rest of the scene graph with one or more Link nodes. This is shown in figure 11.5. In terms of 3D UI support, subgraph sharing facilitates object linking as part of data transfer, as indicated in the UI roadmap in table 10.1.

11.2.3   Group nodes

So far only the structural roles of Group and Leaf nodes have been discussed. Beside providing the relational glue for the scene graph elements, Group nodes can impose logical and spatial relationships. The more interesting ones for our needs are the SwitchGroup and the TransformGroup.

The SwitchGroup allows some or all of its children to not be rendered, as if they did not exist. This is useful if an object is supposed to have multiple forms that are selected dynamically at run time. It is this quality that allows the SwitchGroup to form the basis of the multi-shape interaction-state feedback technique, as indicated in the UI roadmap.

The real workhorse among group nodes is the TransformGroup. The Trans-formGroup handles geometric relationships among objects in the scene graph. Specifying a rotation in a TransformGroup has the effect of rotating its children, as a group, and all of their descendants. The same goes for translation, scale, and any other form of geometric transformation. The effect of nested TransformGroup objects is cumulative. The soul of a `TransformGroup` is the `Transform3D` class. In order to make a `TransformGroup` perform you have to manipulate its `Transform3D` object.

11.2.4 Spatial transforms

Earlier discussion focused on how views are positioned and oriented in world space using `Group` nodes. It should be clear now that the specific node in question was the TransformGroup, where rotating some `TransformGroup` above the `ViewPlatform` has the effect of rotating the `ViewPlatform` and correspondingly its view space.

The `Transform3D` class supports a host of geometric operations ranging from basic translation and scale to quaternion rotation. `Transform3D` also provides ready access to raw matrix manipulation, which can be handy for building complex pre-defined geometric transformations by multiplying them together as a single `Transform3D` object. The ubiquitous nature of the `TransformGroup` and its `Transform3D` homunculus accounts for their strong showing in the UI Roadmap table. These two classes form the basis of all interactive target object manipulation, of which there is a lot in most 3D user interfaces. You may have noticed in the table a third member that usually accompanies the "transform gang," the `getLocalTo-Vworld` method of `Node`.

A `Node` has the wonderful ability to divulge its position and orientation in the world space, which it does by providing the asker with a `Transform3D` object. This information can be used to re-interpret an object's position and rotation from the local space to that of the virtual world. Such coordinate transformation is vital to intuitive control techniques such as DRM and WRM coordinate mapping. As is often the case in situations involving coordinate conversions, the inverse transform, to go from world space to that of the node's local space, is also needed, which `Transform3D` ably provides with its `invert` method.

11.2.5 Leaf nodes

Last but not least is the `Leaf` node, which provides the actual substance behind everything in the virtual world. `Leaf` nodes contain geometric and other attributes for anything that has a presence in the virtual world, such as shapes, lights, behaviors, sounds, and even views. Of particular note for 3D UIs are the `Light`, `Behavior`, and `Sound` classes, in addition to the `Shape3D` and `ViewPlatform` classes mentioned above. View-related classes have already been discussed; lights, shapes, behaviors, and sounds will be covered later.

The `SceneGraphObject` class was mentioned earlier. At the time we were only interested in its `Node` subclass. Java 3D uses the other subclass of `SceneGraph-Object`, the `NodeComponent` class, as the base class for defining most of a `Leaf` node's personality. For example, `Shape3D` leaf nodes are used to define visible objects in the world. The `Geometry` and `Appearance` subclasses of `NodeComponent` are used to respectively define the shape's geometry and visual appearance, which includes color, transparency, and texture.

11.2.6 Node bounds

An interesting attribute of a node is its bounds, which is specified via one or more component objects derived from the `Bounds` class. A bounds is like a geometric shell surrounding a node that serves as an alternate and simpler form of itself. Choices for bounds shapes, which are all subclasses of `Bounds`, are `BoundingSphere`, `BoundingBox`, and `BoundingPolytope`—a convex closed polygonal hull. Common operations performed with bounds shapes are intersecting primitive shapes and other bounds, combining bounds, and geometrically transforming them. Because the default for most bounds attributes is null, the developer must be careful to set the bounds on most leaf nodes, otherwise the node won't work—the light won't be seen and the sound won't be heard.

Geometric bounds

Through inheritance from the `Node` class, all nodes—whether a group or a leaf—have a geometric bounds. A geometric bounds is intended to enclose the geometric shape of the object represented by the node and all of its descendants in the scene graph. Java 3D uses this bounds as a surrogate for the object during spatial operations (such as picking) to improve performance. The idea behind this use of the proxy pattern is that it is more efficient to operate on a simple shape, such as a sphere or box, than it is to operate on a complex one made of many polygons, such as a desk or chemical factory. The tradeoff being made, however, is that spatial operations using bounds are less precise because the bounds are only an approximation of its host object. This is a classic struggle in computer graphics: Making the bounds fit its host more closely improves precision but generally requires a more complex shape, which takes more time to process.

Java 3D tries to make the use of geometric bounds convenient by allowing them to be computed automatically, by default. The API specification is vague about setting a bounds versus having it generated automatically. At the time of writing, there were also several bugs in how bounds were set, retrieved, and automatically computed. For example, no matter what shape you use to set a node's bounds, a group node always returns a spherical bounds and a shape node always returns a bounding box bounds, even if automatic computation is disabled. After setting the bounds, the size returned is not necessarily the size of the bounds that the system uses, such as for picking. And finally disabling automatic bounds and setting them manually sometimes interferes with picking and colliding.

Presumably the bugs will be fixed in a later release, but problems in the API will remain. API control over when bounds are automatically generated and whether they should override manually-set bounds seems inadequate. Also, there is no clear way to distinguish between a bounds used as a surrogate for geometric operations and a bounds computed automatically to determine the host node's extent, such as for creating a bounding box feedback element.

Bounding boxes

On the subject of bounding boxes for feedback, computing one is not easy. The scene graph must be live, and, because of the bugs, you can't get a bounding box from a group node. Instead, you have to preconfigure the capability bits of the subgraph, recursively walk it to the leaf shapes, spatially transform their automatically generated bounding boxes, and explicitly combine the individual bounding box results into a single composite bounding box. In the framework, this is performed by utility methods in the class `j3dui.utils.BoundsUtils` (scenegraph liveness and capability bits will be discussed in section 11.3).

Collision bounds

`Leaf` nodes that have a geometric shape, such as a `Shape3D` node, as well as `Group` nodes, can have a collision bounds. The documentation on it is very poor, and empirical evidence about it is ambiguous. In concept, one might think that the collision bounds would be used in colliding the same way that geometric bounds is used in picking; and it is, sometimes. If the collision bounds is left as null (the default), then the automatically computed geometric bounds will be used for colliding. Evidence indicates that if the collision bounds is larger than the computed geometric bounds, then the collision bounds will sometimes be ignored. Also, the API specification for collision refers to geometric bounds, and not collision bounds.

Influencing bounds

Leaf nodes that produce an effect over a region of the virtual world, such as the `Light` and `Fog` nodes, also have an influencing bounds. The bounds region serves two purposes. It defines a region over which the node's effect continuously decreases, as specified by the node's attributes, and it defines the absolute limit of the node's effect, which has performance benefits. By limiting the effect of a node to a given region, the system won't waste effort generating fog or lighting effects where they are not needed.

Application bounds

A variation on the influencing bounds is the application bounds, which is found in leaf nodes such as `Clip` and `Background`. Whereas the influencing bound involved the relationship of the bounds and any world objects inside that bounds, the application bounds only has an effect on the view. Also, the influencing bounds had a continuous and graduated effect over its region, whereas the effect of the application bounds is binary—off or on. For example, if the view wanders inside a background node's application bounds, then the node's background image will appear in the view's display.

Scheduling bounds

Yet another variation on the bounds theme is the scheduling bounds, which is associated with leaf nodes that require the system to generate an action over time, such as `Sound` and `Behavior`. When the view enters a scheduling bounds and certain other conditions are met, the system schedules the host node's activity for activation, such as playing a sound effect or making a door open automatically.

11.3 LOGISTICS AND OPTIMIZATION

Although this tour of Java 3D has been moving along rather quickly, hopefully you are gaining a sense for the immense breadth and depth of Java 3D in general, and an understanding of the Java 3D scene graph architecture specifically. Although most of the discussion so far has been about the scene graph and the nature of its elements, we're not quite done with the scene graphs yet. Important topics that haven't yet been discussed are the practical aspects of handling scene graphs and dealing with their rendering optimization.

11.3.1 Dead or alive

In order for Java 3D to render a scene graph, it has to take control of it and severely limit the user's access to it. This is partly because Java 3D needs to know the complete contents of the scene graph in order to best optimize its rendering; and partly because it is impractical to allow the user to arbitrarily alter the scene graph in the middle of the rendering. While Java 3D has control of the scene graph, it, and by implication each of its nodes, is said to be "live." The corollary is that any node that is not connected to a live scene graph is classified as being "dead." Dead nodes can be manipulated at will but the effect will never be seen or heard by the user.

What can be frustrating to the beginner is that a scene graph becomes live automatically when it is connected to a `Locale` in a `VirtualUniverse`. Often the beginner will add a `BranchGroup` to the `Locale` and then try to add a child node to the `BranchGroup` as shown in the following code.

```
// setup universe
VirtualUniverse vu = new VirtualUniverse();
Locale lo = new Locale(vu);

// create world contents
BranchGroup bg = new BranchGroup();
lo.addBranchGraph(bg);                  // becomes live
bg.addChild(new BranchGroup());         // exception thrown
```

The result is a `CapabilityNotSetException` and a message saying that the capability to append children has not been set. The problem is that the scene graph, consisting of one `BranchGroup` node, becomes live when it is added to the `Locale`. Once the `BranchGroup` is live, the user is prevented from adding a child node to it by default.

One way to deal with this situation is to build the scene graph first and then attach it to the `Locale`. This is fine for getting started, but at some point, you will find yourself needing to add a node or rotate a `TransformGroup` in a live scene graph. You could try to kill the scene graph first by detaching it from the `Locale`, and this would work if Java 3D would let you. By default, however, you can't detach a live scene graph—because it's live. The way out of this Catch-22 is with capability bits. (Or, you can just use the framework's `AppWorld` class, which makes killing and resuscitating the scene graph explicit and easy.)

11.3.2 Capability bits

The restrictions on a live scene graph are severe, and they have to be for Java 3D to work. By default, the user is not even allowed to traverse the scene graph—ask who a node's parent or children are. The way to gain permission for accessing and manipulating a live scene graph, such as to add a child or to change the transform in a `TransformGroup`, is through capability "bits."

Java 3D gives up control of a live scene graph grudgingly. Each required capability for each affected node has to be set with a separate call to the node's `setCapability` method. You're not allowed to OR them together in spite of their being called bits. Another "gotcha" for the beginner is that capability bits can not be set if the scene graph is already live, even to set the capability to detach the scene graph so you can kill it.

At the time of writing, there did not seem to be an appreciable penalty for choosing to set lots of capability bits. Hopefully this will change in the future so that some tangible benefit—improved performance—can be realized from having to deal with them.

11.3.3 BranchGroup and compilation

`BranchGroup` nodes are conferred a special status. Only a `BranchGroup` can be attached to a Locale, and only a `BranchGroup` can be detached from a live scene graph and reattached—that is, assuming the right capability bits have been set on all the affected nodes. Another privilege accorded a `BranchGroup` is that it can be compiled. Compiling a `BranchGroup` converts it and its descendants into an internally formatted unit optimized for rendering. Compilation offers the potential for the highest performance possible in Java 3D. A drawback of compilation, however, is that a compiled subgraph, even a dead one, must be handled similar to a live one: Access and interaction to it are forbidden unless appropriate capability bits are first set.

The amount of speedup realized through compilation, which can range from none to some, is dependent on the particular implementation of Java 3D and how compilation is used. The greatest benefit will be realized from compilation if a given subgraph is compiled and then reused as a single instance multiple times. Reports at the time of writing indicate that the speedup may not be that significant, but this may change with future releases as optimization of the compilation improves. Before investing a lot of time optimizing your scene graph with compilation or by limiting the use of capability bits, make certain that the expected benefit is real.

11.4 SUMMARY

This tour of Java 3D started by identifying how the API supports the various coordinate and conceptual UI spaces introduced earlier in the book. Java 3D's Virtual-Universe class and its attached scene graph provide the closest thing to the UI world space. The view space is supported collectively by a set of classes, the two main ones being the ViewPlatform and the View. The Canvas3D class and its host View class closely support the display and screen spaces.

Java 3D's backbone is its scene graph, which consists of Group and Leaf nodes arranged in a tree-like data structure. Anything that the user is to experience, such as shapes, sounds, and behaviors, must be in a live scene graph. The rules regarding live access to a scene graph and node sharing are strict. The TransformGroup class is a special form of group node that, together with the Transform3D class, forms the basis for all spatial manipulation. Nodes also have alternate forms expressed as bounds, which are used for functional control over a region as well as for performance. On a practical note, it is wothwhile to invest some time understanding the need to set capability bits in order to access a live scene graph.

CHAPTER 1 2

Lights, shapes, textures and sounds

Now that you have a good idea of what constitutes a scene graph, the next stop on your UI tour of Java 3D is learning how to create things to put in it. In Java 3D anything that the user experiences through sight or sound must eventually culminate in a live scene graph. This includes shapes, sounds, lights, views, behaviors, and other entities. Views were covered in the previous chapter as part of the UI spaces. The next chapter, on actions and interaction, will address behaviors. This chapter focuses on creating objects that the user sees and hears.

As you may have already come to expect, the focus will be on those aspects of the Java 3D API that support the 3D UI techniques described earlier, specifically the creation of feedback elements that will be needed for the next part of the book. Note, however, that although the presentation here is selective it will address many of the practical issues of getting Java 3D to do something useful, such as constructing simple geometric shapes, texture mapping and lighting them, and playing sounds. As an added bonus for the do-it-yourself minded developers, emphasis is on how to create objects with Java 3D, not the Sun utilities. Although the utilities can be useful, they can make it difficult to distinguish between what the API does and what the utility is trying to do. In any case, if you are using the utilities and things go wrong, it is helpful to understand what the API is doing inside of them (unlike Java 3D, the utilities are released with source code).

12.1 LIGHTS

Lights, which all derive from the `Light` leaf node class, come in a variety of forms, including ambient, directional, point, and spot light. Ambient light provides general diffuse lighting that is directionless and not very aesthetically appealing by itself. Directional lights are a computationally efficient way to give lighting more character by providing it with a direction from which to radiate. Point and especially spot lights provide nice lighting effects but are more expensive computationally.

Although lighting might be considered more of an aesthetic issue than a UI concern, there is a very practical reason for discussing it here. In Java 3D, the virtual universe is, like the real one, inherently dark. In order for you to see objects in your virtual world, light must be added. You can do this in a couple ways. You can make the visible objects emissive, so that they glow of their own accord; or, more typically, you can add lights to the scene to illuminate the visible objects. Common problems for the beginner include forgetting to add lights and properly configuring their influencing bounds and the lighting-related attributes of the objects they illuminate.

Sounds complicated? It can be, but only the first few times. The best way to get started with lighting and 3D model creation in general is to use the primitive object classes provided with the Sun utilities (e.g., `Box` and `Sphere`), which are already configured for lighting, and to study an example of a working light. In the following code fragment, `DirectionalLight` is extended and its influencing bounds set to infinity so that it shines on all objects in the world regardless of their distance from the light. This example is also a good way to start easing you into some Java 3D code. The `j3dui.utils.objects.TestLight` class in the framework is a more generalized version of this code.

```
import javax.media.j3d.*;
import javax.vecmath.*;

public class MyLight extends DirectionalLight {

        // creates a full intensity white
        // light pointing along the -Z axis
        public MyLight() {

          // make influencing bounds infinitely large
          BoundingSphere lightBounds = new BoundingSphere(
           new Point3d(0.0,0.0,0.0), Double.POSITIVE_INFINITY);

          setInfluencingBounds(lightBounds);
        }
}
```

12.2 SHAPES

Visible objects with which most developers will deal, whether for data or for feedback, will derive from the `Shape3D` leaf node. Because shapes are rather primitive, complex objects in the virtual world such as office desks and chemical factories are typically made of multiple `Shape3D` nodes gathered together hierarchically under group nodes. The `Shape3D` class itself is rather bland. Its lot in virtual life is to serve as a convenient container for component objects that define the actual geometry and visual appearance of the shape. The two main components are the `Geometry` and `Appearance` subclasses of `NodeComponent`. Java 3D provides a smorgasbord of `Geometry` derivatives to handle shape primitives, ranging from point arrays to extruded 3D text. It also provides a wealth of appearance attributes, ranging from line style to texture image filtering.

12.2.1 Geometry

Geometry is what gives an object its overall shape. In Java 3D, geometry can take the form of 3D text, a 3D image, compressed geometry, or an array of primitive elements. Of most immediate utility for UI purposes are the primitives, which are needed to define feedback element shapes, such as for tooltips, indicators, and drag handles.

Primitives can take the form of points, lines, or polygons; and polygons can be triangles (three-sided) or quads (four-sided), with the restriction that quads must be planar and convex. Because individual points and polygons are of little practical use, most geometry definition occurs through classes derived from the base class `GeometryArray`, which allows geometry to be specified as an array of primitives. Closely associated with the spatial qualities of geometry are the visual aspects of a shape that are dependent on geometry, such as texturing, coloring, and normals. Texturing is the most important one for UI work because it serves as the basis for the multi-shape technique, which offers an easy way to implement most multi-state feedback elements. Texturing will be covered in section 12.3.

Geometry is seldom defined as a set of disjoint primitives. Often the primitives are arranged in some regular and connected fashion. To this end, Java 3D supports simple arrays, arrays of strips, arrays of fans, and indexed versions of these forms. Not all combinations of primitives and data structures are supported, however. In the combinations that do exist, there is considerable regularity and consistency. If you know how to define triangles, being able to use quads, lines, and points is a short step away. For the purposes of this discussion the triangle polygon will serve as the primitive of choice.

Arrays and indexed arrays

In a simple array, defined by the `TriangleArray` class, each set of three vertices in the array defines a three-sided polygon. No connection between the triangles is assumed. In the indexed version, defined by the `IndexedTriangleArray` class, a level of indirection is introduced. Rather than using the vertices themselves to define the polygons, indices are used which in turn reference the actual vertices, which are sitting in a vertex pool. Using an indexed scheme allows vertices to be used multiple times in defining the geometry. For example, eight vertices define a cube. In an `IndexedTriangleArray` object, the 8 three-element (X, Y, Z) vertices would be defined, and then referenced multiple times using integer indices to define the 12 triangles that make up the cube's six sides. Using a `TriangleArray` object, 36 three-element vertices would have to be defined, three for each of the 12 triangles.

Strips and fans

If a shape's triangles need to be connected in a regular manner, then strips and fans can make the job of geometry definition a lot simpler. In a strip, defined by the `TriangleStripArray` class, consecutive triangles share a common edge. A fan, defined by the `TriangleFanArray` class, is like a strip, but all the triangles also share a common vertex. With both of these constructs, the first three vertices (or, in the case of indexed geometry, indices) define the first triangle, and each subsequent vertex defines a new triangle. In a strip, the two previous vertices form the common edge between the new triangle and the previous triangle. In a fan, the first vertex is common to all triangles, and it and the previous vertex form the common edge between the previous triangle and the new one. Also, no assumptions are made about the last edge connecting to the first one to form a closed shape. If you want to define a cone (closed fan) or cylinder (closed strip), then you have to define the last one or two vertices as being the same as the first one or two, respectively.

The strip and fan classes are intended to define *arrays* of strips and fans, and not just individual ones, hence the array in their class name. If you happen to take a look at the constructor for a strip or fan class you'll notice a parameter `stripVertexCount`. This parameter is an array of integers. The API documentation describing how to use it is rather cryptic and perhaps confusing. The role of this parameter is actually quite simple. Each integer in the `stripVertexCount` array corresponds to a single strip in the array of strips defined in the object; its value tells the constructor how many vertices are in the corresponding strip. For example, if a strip array object contains two strips, with the first one having four vertices and the second one having six, then the total number of vertices in the object is 10. The `vertexCount` constructor parameter for this object would be specified as 10, the total number of vertices in the object, and its `stripVertexCount` parameter would be specified as {4, 6}, the number of vertices from the total that are in each of the strips in the object. A better name for the `stripVertexCount` parameter might have been `vertexCountsPerStrip`.

Surface normal

When defining a polygon, the direction that the surface normal points is important. If a polygon's normal is pointing toward the user's virtual eyeball, then the polygon will be visible. Assuming of course that it is not transparent and is properly lighted. If the surface normal is pointing away from the view, then the polygon will not be seen. This is the reason why on most 3D platforms, Java 3D included, you get the single-sidedness revealment technique for free. For example, if the walls of a room were made of single polygons with their surface normals facing in, then only the far walls would be seen and the near ones would be invisible.

The default surface normal used for polygons in Java 3D is defined using a right-hand "winding" rule. If you curl the fingers of your right hand around the edges of a polygon with your fingers pointing in increasing vertex order, your thumb will point in the direction of the surface normal. For discrete triangles, such as in a `Triangle-Array` object, the surface normals are easy to determine using the right-hand rule because each one is considered in isolation. In strips and fans, things are less clear because edges and their vertices are being shared—seemingly in the wrong order for the right-hand rule to work. The easiest way to determine the surface normal for a strip or fan is to determine it for the first triangle using the right-hand rule, and then trust that the normals for the rest of the triangles will be pointing in the same direction.

Examples

The following table, table 12.1, indicates where in the framework specific examples can be found that use the Java 3D API, not the Sun utilities, to define various geometric primitives. Since these classes are fairly lightweight and don't rely on complex helper classes such as the Sun utilities it should be easier to see how the raw API is being used in them.

Table 12.1 Examples of Shape3D geometry definition in the 3D UI framework

Framework class/method	Java 3D API demonstrated
j3dui.feedback.elements.TextureRect.buildGeometry()	QuadArray
j3dui.feedback.elements.TextureCylinder.buildGeometry()	TriangleStripArray
j3dui.feedback.elements.TextureCone.buildGeometry()	TriangleFanArray
j3dui.manipulate.BoxOutline.buildGeometry()	IndexedLineStripArray

Another example in the framework that might be of interest is the j3dui.feedback.elements.TextureShape class. It serves as a base class for building feedback elements out of transparent textures. Many of its methods nicely encapsulate the Java 3D code used to set up the more common geometry and appearance attributes, which are described next, in a `Shape3D` object.

12.2.2 Appearance

The nongeometric aspects of an object's visual appearance are defined by an instance of the `Appearance` class, which contains a host of attributes. Making the most of the delegation pattern, these attributes are defined by component objects that specify the actual attributes, which include such characteristics as material, texture, texture attributes, coloring attributes, and transparency attributes. For UI work, we are most interested in the Texture and TransparencyAttributes component classes, which are needed to define transparent textured feedback elements, the workhorse of the multi-shape technique.

12.2.3 Transparency

Transparency is useful for allowing the user to see what might otherwise be hidden behind opaque objects. This is especially useful in feedback elements, such as indicators, handles, and skirts, which are artificially added to objects and could otherwise prevent the user from clearly seeing the target objects during manipulation. Object transparency is also used to create feedback elements using texture mapping. To make an arrow using a texture, for example, everything in the texture image and the underlying object that is not an arrow must appear transparent. Object transparency is controlled through its TransparencyAttributes component object. Texture transparency will be covered in section 12.3.

The TransparencyAttributes class is fairly simple in that it contains only two attributes: transparency value and transparency mode. Transparency value ranges from 0.0 to 1.0 and specifies the degree of transparency, with 0.0 being opaque and 1.0 being clear. The transparency value, however, will have an effect only if the transparency mode is set to any mode other than TransparencyAttributes.NONE. Because NONE is the default value, it must be set to something else, otherwise the host object will appear opaque. Any of the remaining modes will work (bugs not withstanding); which one to use depends on how fast or how well you want the transparency to be rendered.

12.2.4 Loading

Java 3D has no native file format. Without getting into the matter of scene graph serialization (which at the time of writing works or doesn't to varying degrees depending on to whom you listen) Java 3D also doesn't have any native ability to read model files other than that provided by the Java loader. Instead, Java 3D relies on the kindness of strangers to develop classes called loaders. A loader class reads a particular graphics file format and instantiates appropriate Java 3D objects in a scene subgraph. In its utilities, Sun has provided the LoaderBase base class for creating loaders, and the Loader interface, which LoaderBase implements. The load method in the Loader interface returns an object implementing the Scene interface, which is also provided with the utilities, through which the model subgraph can be obtained. Third parties have developed several loaders, many of which are referenced in the model loader web site listed in chapter 10.

As previously mentioned, object models can also be loaded using the Java loader. In this case the object model to be loaded must be in a Java 3D class file, with the Java loader loading the object class and instantiating it. In part 4, the FancyApp example demonstrates loading models from VRML and object class files. To see the VRML and

Java loaders in action, look in j3dui.utils.ModelLoaders in the framework code. The following code snippet summarizes how to use a model loader, in this case a VRML loader. The loader is constructed, and a model is loaded from file using its `load` method. The root of the model scene graph is then extracted as a `BranchGroup` using the `getSceneGroup` method of the loaded Scene object.

```
import javax.media.j3d.*;
import com.sun.j3d.loaders.*;
import com.sun.j3d.loaders.vrml97.*;

Scene scene = null;
BranchGroup group = null;

// construct loader object
Loader loader = new VrmlLoader();

try {
  // load model from file
  scene = loader.load(modelPath);

  // get the model root
  group = scene.getSceneGroup();
} catch (Exception ex) {
  …
}
```

12.3   TEXTURES

As proposed earlier in the book, constructing feedback elements using texture mapping and the multi-shape technique allows them to be designed, and for the most part implemented, by graphic artists, not programmers. Not only does this allow experts in visual design to create the elements, but it also simplifies revisions to the elements, requiring a paint package instead of a Java IDE. For most shaped feedback elements, such as arrow shapes, the host object being textured needs to be transparent, which was discussed above, and the texture image needs to have a transparent background, which is covered in this section.

The abstract `Texture` class serves as a base class for the concrete `Texture2D` and `Texture3D` classes. For feedback elements, we are interested only in 2D textures, which are textures based on 2D images, as opposed to 3D textures, which are based on 3D voxel images. As with other `Shape3D` attributes, `Texture` itself has a number of attributes, which include such things as mipmap mode, boundary mode, boundary color, and filtering modes. With a few exceptions as noted below, the defaults are fine for creating transparent texture maps for feedback elements.

12.3.1   Filtering

When a graphics renderer applies a texture image to an object, the pixels in the image rarely match the pixels in the display one-for-one. If the object appears far away in the scene, it is likely that multiple pixels in the texture image will bunch up under each pixel in the display. If, on the other hand, the object appears close by in the scene, then the pixels in the texture will likely be spaced far apart leaving nothing for the intervening display pixels to display. The renderer must perform a spatial filtering operation to address these issues. In the first case the renderer must perform subsampling, or minification, where multiple pixels in the source image, the texture image, are converted into a single pixel in the target image, the display image. In the second case, the renderer must perform supersampling, or magnification, where a single pixel in the source image is converted into multiple pixels in the display image.

Although renderers can perform most forms of magnification quite efficiently, good quality minification can be a problem as the degree of minification increases because the number of input pixels that must be processed to create a display pixel rises exponentially. The trick used to handle this problem is to use multiple versions of the same texture image, each at a different spatial resolution. This technique is called *mipmapping*. The first image is the original image; the second image is a minified version of the original image, typically by a factor of ½; the third image is a minified version of the second image, and so forth. Then, when the render needs to perform minification, it first determines which version of the texture image has the closest minification factor, and it uses that one (or a combination of the two closest ones) as the source image for the minification.

Unlike its graphics predecessors, which offered no options, Java 3D offers quite a rich variety of texture filtering options, including mipmapping and several flavors of magnification and minification. The net result is that, given sufficient processor horsepower, texture mapping can be done with very high quality. The default mode for filtering in the `Texture` class, `Texture.BASE_LEVEL_POINT`, is the fastest but also of the lowest quality, causing the texture details to appear blocky. If the constant size technique is used for a feedback element, then mipmapping is generally not needed; you just need to generate the texture image so that the spatial resolution of its pixels in display space (i.e., the number of pixels per meter) roughly matches that of the display screen. Without the need for mipmapping, which can slow things down, you might even be able to splurge and use the highest quality filtering mode for magnification and minification, `Texture.NICEST`.

12.3.2 Transparency

For a texture, or more precisely its background, to appear transparent, two factors are key: The texture image itself must support transparency, and the texture must be loaded and constructed with an alpha channel. Not all image formats support transparency. Of the more popular formats on the web, GIF and PNG support transparency, but JPEG does not. Java 1.2 alone cannot load PNG (but rumor has it that Java 1.3 will be able to). This leaves GIF. Although GIF does not have a true alpha channel like PNG, GIF allows a single color, such as the background color, to be designated as transparent. As long as an alpha channel is maintained in the image data throughout the loading process, the transparent GIF image should appear in Java 3D as a transparent texture image.

12.3.3 Loading

When it comes to loading media, you might think that in comparison to loading a model or a sound that loading an image would be the easiest; but it's not. It's the most complex. The reason for this is that between Java and Java 3D, several layers of image data translation are required. Also, in Java, images cannot be loaded as a single, simple operation. Instead, the loading is started asynchronously and the status of the loading must be explicitly monitored until the loading is complete. The Texture class requires that the width and height dimensions of the texture image be a power of two. If you start with an image that is not a power of two in size, then it needs to be resampled to make it one before using it as a texture. It is small wonder that the Sun utilities provide a TextureLoader class to hide all of this from you, but what's the fun of that?

If you are interested in seeing how to get Java and Java 3D to load a simple Texture object, specifically one that contains a transparent image, take a look at the method j3dui.utils.LoadUtils.loadTexture2D in the framework code, which is provided below in an abridged form. In this method, the image loading is started with the default toolkit's getImage method, which returns an Image object. Using Java's image observer pattern, the loader must loop until the observer's checkImage method returns a status code indicating that all the image bits have been loaded. Next, the raw image must be converted to a BufferedImage object, which can then and only then be converted to a Texture2D object. Note that the image formats used in these conversions—BufferedImage.TYPE_INT_ARGB and Texture.RGBA—are full color, with an alpha channel to preserve any transparency information.

```
/**
Loads a texture image from file.  If there is a problem
it is reported and null is returned.
@param texturePath The path of the file containing the
texture image.  Never null.
@return A new texture.  Null if there was a problem.
*/
public static Texture2D loadTexture2D(String texturePath) {

  // load image from file
  Image image = Toolkit.getDefaultToolkit().getImage(
    texturePath);

  /// make sure its loaded, loop until done
  Component observer = new Component() {};
  observer.prepareImage(image, null);

  int status;
  while(true) {
```

```
      status = observer.checkImage(image, null);

      if ((status & ImageObserver.ALLBITS) != 0) {
        // image done, quit checking
        break;
      }

      try {
        Thread.sleep(100);
      } catch (InterruptedException ex) {}
    }

    // convert image to buffered image
    int width = image.getWidth(observer);
    int height = image.getHeight(observer);

    BufferedImage bufImage = new BufferedImage(
      width, height, BufferedImage.TYPE_INT_ARGB);

    Graphics g = bufImage.getGraphics();
    g.drawImage(image, 0, 0, null);
    g.dispose();

    // convert buffered image to texture
    ImageComponent2D image2D = new ImageComponent2D(
      ImageComponent.FORMAT_RGBA, bufImage);

    Texture2D texture = new Texture2D(Texture.BASE_LEVEL,
      Texture.RGBA, width, height);
    texture.setImage(0, image2D);

    return texture;
}
```

12.4 SOUNDS

As with the Java 3D view model, which is intended for use with sophisticated VR display devices, the sound model is also primed for VR success. It includes such capabilities as soundscapes, Doppler effects, reverberation, and sometime in the near future, spatialized sound. As with everything else in Java 3D that the user experiences, sounds are represented by leaf nodes in the scene graph. All sound nodes derive from the abstract Sound base class. For feedback elements in a POCS, the most basic sound capability will do, which is provided by the BackgroundSound subclass of Sound. The default attributes for this class are to play the sound once when its setEnable method is set to true, which is perfect for sound feedback, whether a sound effect or an audio message. The sound data itself is supplied to a sound node via a Media-Container object.

Once a BackgroundSound node is loaded with data, you might think that you are ready to hear the sound, but one more piece of the puzzle must be accounted for:

the device that will physically play the sound. Just as the view model had to account for physical display devices and specify which one to use, so too must the Java 3D sound model account for and specify the physical sound device. At the time of writing there is only one sound device available for use with Java 3D, which is provided by the `JavaSoundMixer` class. To use this device, it must be associated with Java 3D's model of the physical environment, which is embodied by the `PhysicalEnviron-ment` object. As you may recall, a `PhysicalEnvironment` object was associated with the `View` object. The following code fragment demonstrates how to set up the audio device. It also serves as a reminder that, similar to light's influencing bounds, the sound won't be heard unless the view is inside the sound's scheduling bounds, which here is set to infinity. In the framework, the class j3dui.feedback.elements.SoundEffect encapsulates the loading and playing of a simple sound effect.

```
View = new View();
...
// build audio device based on view physical environ
PhysicalEnvironment host = view.getPhysicalEnvironment();
JavaSoundMixer mixer = new JavaSoundMixer(host);

// MUST initialize the device
mixer.initialize();

// set infinite bounds
BoundingSphere bounds = new BoundingSphere(
 new Point3d(0.0,0.0,0.0), Double.POSITIVE_INFINITY);
_sound.setSchedulingBounds(bounds);
```

12.4.1   Loading

Loading sounds in Java 3D is quite easy using the MediaContainer class. In the framework, the method j3dui.utils.LoadUtils.loadSound, which is provided below in an abridged form, demonstrates the process. Unlike with texture loading, the `Media-Container` class does everything for you when it is constructed: It reads the file, makes sure it is loaded, and gets it into the right format.

```
/**
Loads a sound from file.  If there is a problem
it is reported and null is returned.
@param soundPath The path of the file containing the sound.
Never null.
@return A new sound.  Null if there was a problem.
*/
public static MediaContainer loadSound(String soundPath) {
   if(soundPath==null) throw new
     IllegalArgumentException("<soundPath> is null.");

   MediaContainer sound = null;

   try {
```

```
    // load sound from file
    File file = new File(soundPath);
    URL url = file.toURL();

    sound = new MediaContainer(url);
  }
  catch(Exception ex) {
    System.out.println("LoadUtils.loadSound:" +
      " Error while loading sound file.");
    return null;
  }

  return sound;
}
```

12.5 SUMMARY

The focus of this chapter was on creating tangible objects—ones that can be seen and heard—to put into the scene graph. In keeping with the theme of this book, only those portions of the Java 3D API needed to support the user interface were covered in detail, although most everything covered in this chapter—lighting, geometric shape definition, texture mapping, and sounds—is applicable to non-UI development. Although lighting is more of an aesthetic issue than a UI concern, it is nevertheless a necessary one for being able to see objects because the virtual universe, like the real one, is a dark place. For model building, Java 3D supports several types of geometric shape primitives—points, lines, and polygons—and several ways to assemble them to form more complex shapes—arrays, strips, fans, and indexing. A good way to develop visual feedback elements is with texture mapping, which allows graphic artists to do most of the work with a paint package. The key to this approach is the use of textures with transparent backgrounds. Transparent texture mapping requires the host object to be transparent, and it requires special attention as to how the texture is loaded. Compared to textures, loading and using sounds, such as sound effects and instructional feedback, can be quite easy.

C H A P T E R   1 3

Actions and interactions

System action and user interaction in a 3D application can take many forms. Actions are automatic manipulations of an object or the view by the system, such as turning an object in a preview or blinking the eyes on an avatar to make it seem more lifelike. Actions are also called animations, where objects in the scene appear to move of their own volition. With actions the user is a passive observer; there is no two-way dialogue between the system and the user as in interaction. With interaction the user's involvement is usually direct and explicit, such as in-scene mouseover feedback and object dragging. Actions and interactions can occur in the 3D scene as well as outside of it, in the 2D area surrounding the 3D display in the application's window frame. With Java 3D the focus is on in-scene activities, which is the subject of this chapter. Associations between Java 3D and out-of-scene interaction will be covered in chapter 14.

This chapter roughly divides Java 3D actions and interactions into spatial transformations, object picking, and behaviors. Spatial transformations are the basis for all geometric manipulation of objects and views in the virtual world; object picking identifies what the user is pointing to in the scene; and, behaviors, as embodied by the `Behavior` class, are the basis for Java 3D event handling, especially collision and change detection.

All of these capabilities play (or should play) major roles in UI work. Unfortunately, picking and colliding in particular are rather poorly documented and loosely defined in the API specification. This, together with the fact that source code is not included with Java 3D means that a lot of the details about these areas can be obtained only through a process of trial and error. Rather than ignore these important UI capabilities or to only treat them lightly, I've chosen to dig into the details, so be warned. Any details covered here about these subjects could easily change with future releases of Java 3D.

13.1 SPATIAL TRANSFORMS

Any time the system slides an object in the scene or rotates one, either as a result of a programmed action or a user interaction, a `TransformGroup` group node is likely to be involved. This node, together with its associate, the `Transform3D` class, is at the heart of all geometric manipulation in Java 3D. Being a group node, it can have child nodes; but its distinction among group nodes is that any change to its `Transform3D` component object influences the geometry of its child nodes, as a group. For example, specifying a 10-meter shift in a `TransformGroup` node would cause its child objects, as a group, to move 10 meters relative to the node. If the node's parent was itself a `TransformGroup` node with a 10-meter translation in the same direction, then the net result on the child objects would be a 20-meter translation—the combination of the two translations.

Although the framework in the next part of the book uses spatial transforms extensively, it does so in a manner that does not lend itself to nice, clean code samples. The details of why this is so will be left for the discussions in part 4 about the framework. For now, code fragments at the end of this section will illustrate how to use `TransformGroup` and `Transform3D` in some practical UI situations. If you are curious and can't wait until the next part, spatial transformation in the form of generalized actuation and actuators can be found in the `j3dui.control.actuators` package in the framework.

13.1.1 Local coordinates

Another way of looking at a `TransformGroup` node is that each one defines a local 3D coordinate system inside the virtual world space, and its child nodes live within this local space. As the local space is moved, rotated, and stretched by the host node's transform, so too are the child nodes. The implication of nesting transform groups in the scene graph is that their coordinate systems become nested. For example, causing a transform node that is high up in the scene graph to perform a rotation has the effect of rotating the local space of its children and, correspondingly, that of any lower-level nodes. Any visible leaf node descendants in these nested coordinate systems, high or low, will also appear to rotate. This is shown in figure 13.1 where three north-pointing arrow shapes are placed under three different groups, each with a different local coordinate space. The bottommost shape receives the combined effects of the 90-degree rotations from its parent and grandparent `TransformGroup` nodes, with a combined rotation of 180 degrees as seen by the user.

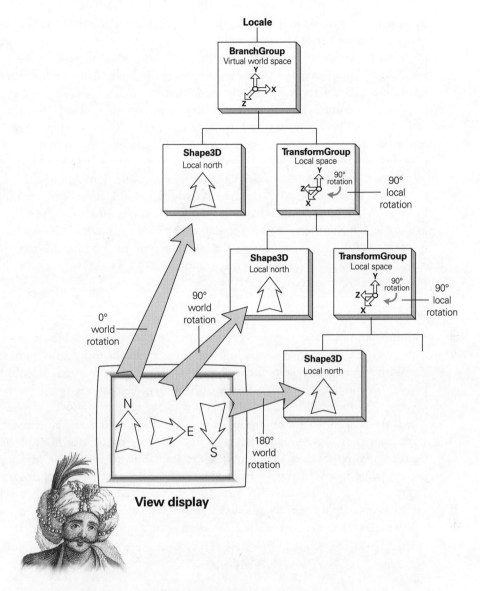

Figure 13.1 The effects of local space transformations in the scene graph are cumulative when viewed as a whole in the world space.

13.1.2 Transform3D

The `Transform3D` class represents a generalized geometric transform that is represented internally by a 4×4 matrix. The `transform` method applies the transformation to a data point or vector, in essence transforming the entity from one coordinate system to another. The other methods provided by `Transform3D` allow access to the state of the transformation in many different ways, both as a matrix and as individual transformation components—translation, rotation, and scale. As a matrix, transformations can be added, multiplied, normalized, transposed, and inverted. As transformation components, translation, rotation, and scaling can be set individually and in combination. Most of the methods also come in different versions for different parameter types—float and double.

There is some symmetry and consistency among the methods, but they are far from complete. Some of the transformation component methods affect only a portion of the transformation, preserving the rest of it. Others reset the complete transformation and then set the component. For example, `setRotation(AxisAngle4d)` and `setRotation(Quat4d)` preserve the original non-rotational portions of the transformation, but `setEuler(Vector3d)`, which sets the transform's rotation using Euler angles, does not. And, although there are methods for setting the rotation as an axis-angle, a quaternion, or as Euler angles, the only get method for rotation is for a quaternion. (Note that `AxisAngle4d` provides a set method for `Quat4d`, which in a round-about way allows the rotation component of a Transform3D to be converted into an `AxisAngle4d`.)

Matrix multiplication

Multiplying transforms together concatenates and combines their individual effects. This offers an alternative to nesting transform nodes in order to achieve complex transformations. For example, to achieve the 180-degree rotation described in the previous section, the two transforms with 90-degree rotations could be multiplied together and the resulting transform applied to the bottommost shape. The order in which the transforms are multiplied is significant. To reproduce the effect of nested transforms in a scene graph, start with the topmost transform, multiply it by the transform corresponding to the next lower transform in the graph, and repeat the process while accumulating the transform until the bottommost transform is reached. In general, using nested transforms is easier to conceive but multiplying transforms is often easier to implement because fewer scene graph elements are involved.

This code fragment uses nested transform groups to turn and slide the target object.

```
// Create a scenegraph with a "turner" at the top, a "slider" in the
// middle, and a "thing" at the bottom.

TransformGroup turner = new TransformGroup();
TransformGroup slider = new TransformGroup();
MyThing thing = new MyThing();

turner.addChild(slider);
slider.addChild(thing);

// manipulate the Thing using nested transforms
Transform3D change = new Transform3D();
```

CHAPTER 13 ACTIONS AND INTERACTIONS

```
/// turn 45 degrees about Y axis
change.set(new AxisAngle4d(0, 1, 0, Math.PI/4.0));
turner.setTransform(change);

/// slide 2.0 along X axis
change.set(new Vector3d(2, 0, 0));
slider.setTransform(change);
```

This code fragment uses chained matrix multiplication to achieve the same geometric effect on the target object as the first code fragment.

```
// Create a scenegraph with a "mover" at the top and a "thing"
// at the bottom.

TransformGroup mover = new TransformGroup();
MyThing thing = new MyThing();

mover.addChild(thing);

// manipulate the Thing using chained matrix multiplication
Transform3D change = new Transform3D();
Transform3D total = new Transform3D();

/// turn 45 degrees about Y axis (topmost transform first)
change.set(new AxisAngle4d(0, 1, 0, Math.PI/4.0));
total.mul(change);     // total = total * change

/// slide 2.0 along X axis (bottommost transform last)
change.set(new Vector3d(2, 0, 0));
total.mul(change);     // total = total * change

/// apply total change transform matrix to mover
mover.setTransform(total);
```

A situation where transform multiplication is superior to nested transforms is incremental updates to an object's geometry. For example, if an existing object in the scene graph needs to be rotated 90 degrees relative to its last transformation—rotation, translation, or scale—having nesting transforms wouldn't help. Instead, the transform in the transform group that performed the operation could be read, multiplied with a transform representing a 90-degree rotation, and the result written back to the transform group. Both the SMTransformGroupPlugin and MMTransformGroup-Plugin classes in the framework's j3dui.control.actuators package use this form of incremental update.

Access by value

Access to the Transform3D component object in a TransformGroup is strictly by value and not by reference. When the transform in a TransformGroup object is set or gotten, the Transform3D value is copied instead of the reference to the value being transferred. This means that each time you want to change an object's position or rotation you have to create a new `Transform3D` object or modify a previously created one, and then explicitly set it in the target `TransformGroup`; you can't simply associate the two objects and then just update the `Transform3D`. This can be an inconvenience at times, and beginners can easily forget to do it.

Point versus vector

There are quite a few `transform` methods associated with `Transform3D`, but the main distinction among them is between transforming points and transforming vectors. When a point is transformed, in essence, the full transformation is applied, with the position of the point being re-interpreted in a different and possibly translated, rotated, and scaled space. When a vector is transformed, the transformation is interpreted differently: Only rotation and scale are applied because translation of a vector, which by definition defines only direction and magnitude, doesn't mean a whole lot. The distinction between these two forms of transformation, which is actually defined by the data being transformed and not the transformation itself, can be subtle but important. Transforming a ray, which has a position as well as a direction, is a different matter, but a ray isn't a primitive element defined by the `javax.vecmath` package or handled directly by `Transform3D`.

13.1.3   getLocalToVworld

Whether nested in the scene graph or concatenated through multiplication, the composite transformation of a node can sometimes be difficult to track, especially if changes to the transform chain in the scene graph can be made by different parts of the application at the same time. To address this problem, Java 3D imbues all scene graph nodes with the ability to divulge their absolute geometry in the virtual world. The `getLocalToVworld` method of the `Node` class allows you to obtain a `Transform3D` defining how to convert from the node's local space to that of the virtual world, which works no matter how nested or concatenated an object's transformation is. Note that for a transform group node, its `getLocalToVworld` method returns the transform for the space in which the node itself lives, not that of its children. In other words, the transform state of a `TransformGroup` node has no effect on the transform returned by its `getLocalToVworld` method.

The local-to-Vworld transform has many uses. It can be used to determine the absolute world position of a shape object's vertex, or to determine the direction of "forward" in the world relative to a view object. For example, in first-person navigation, movement of the user's view occurs relative to the view. To correctly move the view in the world, you have to be able to interpret local view-relative control inputs such as forward, right, and left, into absolute movements in the world space. To move the view forward by 10 meters you would start with a 10-meter long vector pointing straight ahead in the view's local coordinate system, which would correspond to a vector of $(0, 0, -10)$. Using the `ViewPlatform` object's local-to-Vworld transform, you would translate this locally defined vector into an absolute world direction and magnitude. Multiplying the transform defining the world position of the view by the transformed vector concatenates the two transforms into one, which has the effect of moving the view forward by 10 meters relative to the view's current position. This example is illustrated in the following code fragment:

```
// create the world space
VirtualUniverse universe = new VirtualUniverse();
Locale locale = new Locale(universe);
BranchGroup root = new BranchGroup();
locale.addBranchGraph(root);

// create the view space
ViewPlatform view = new ViewPlatform();
...

// build a view actuator
/// create a view actuator and add the view to it
TransformGroup actuator = new TransformGroup();
actuator.addChild(view);

/// add the view actuator to the world's root node
root.addChild(actuator);

// arbitrarily manipulate the view using its actuator
...

// move the view forward relative to itself by 10 meters
Vector3d forward = new Vector3d(0, 0, -10);

/// get the view's local transform
Transform3D xform = new Transform3D();
view.getLocalToVworld(xform);

/// transform the forward vector from local to world space
xform.transform(forward);

/// get the current view actuator state
Transform3D current = new Transform3D();
actuator.getTransform(current);

/// apply the change vector to the view actuator state
Transform3D change = new Transform3D();
change.set(forward);
current.mul(change);

/// don't forget to set the new transform
actuator.setTransform(current);
...
```

In case you are wondering what the difference is between the // and /// comments, this is a convention used to indicate levels or nesting of comments and associated code functionality. If you read the top-level // comments and skip the code and lower-level comments you should get a pretty good overview of what is going on. The lower-level /// comments within a given top-level comment section provide details about the code and its functionality.

13.1.4   Inverse getLocalToVworld

Situations can arise where you need the Vworld-to-local transform, instead of the local-to-Vworld transform returned by a node. In such case, you can use the inverse method of Transform3D to convert the transform. Because this situation comes up fairly often when performing in-scene manipulation and the pseudo-overlay visualization techniques, it is worth exploring this subject in more detail.

For example, using world-relative mapping (WRM) control you may want to slide a desk in a room toward a window, which is north of the desk. Normally, the world-relative output from the WRM technique would be used to manipulate the desk's "actuator" transform group directly. If, however, the desk is a member of a group, such as in a suite of furniture, then the group itself is likely to have an actuator transform allowing the group as a whole to slide and rotate. Because the desk's actuator is not in the world space but in the local space of the group, you can't simply apply the world-relative movement from WRM to the desk's actuator. Instead, you have to first convert the world-relative movement, a vector pointing north, into a group-relative movement. This requires getting the desk actuator's local-to-Vworld transform, inverting it into a Vworld-to-local transform, and transforming the north-pointing vector with it. The result is a north-pointing vector expressed in terms of the desk actuator's local space, which is defined by the group's actuator. Because the coordinate space of the vector and the desk's actuator now match, they can be multiplied together to update the desk actuator's transform state while leaving the rest of the group alone.

The following code fragment illustrates the salient points of this example:

```
// build a desk and group with actuators
/// create the desk object
MyDesk desk = new MyDesk();

/// create a desk actuator and add the desk to it
TransformGroup deskAct = new TransformGroup();
deskAct.addChild(desk);

/// create a group actuator and add the desk actuator to it
TransformGroup groupAct = new TransformGroup();
groupAct.addChild(deskAct);

/// add the desk to the world's root node
root.addChild(groupAct);

// arbitrarily manipulate the group and desk
...
```

```
// move the desk north in the world by 10 meters
Vector3d northward = new Vector3d(0, 0, -10);

/// get the desk actuator's local transform
Transform3D xform = new Transform3D();
deskAct.getLocalToVworld(xform);

/// transform the northward vector from world to local space
xform.invert();
xform.transform(northward);

/// get the current desk actuator state
Transform3D current = new Transform3D();
deskAct.getTransform(current);

/// apply the change vector to the desk actuator state
Transform3D change = new Transform3D();
change.set(northward);
current.mul(change);

/// don't forget to set the new transform
deskAct.setTransform(current);
```

13.1.5 Local-to-local

In the most general case of coordinate-space transformation, conversion is needed to go from one local space to another. A simple example would be DRM control of a target object in a group, where display-relative local space inputs are translated into their world-relative equivalents, which are then converted for use in the local space of the target object actuator. To perform this two-legged coordinate-space transformation, imagine combining the two previous coding examples into one, with the first half going from local to world space, and the second half going from world to local space. Generalized versions of local-to-local transformation—from a source space to a target space—are provided by the `j3dui.control.mappers.Mapper.toTargetSpace` methods in the UI framework. One method is for point transformation and the other is for vectors.

13.2 OBJECT PICKING

Although spatial transformation plays a leading role in UI development, it is played out mostly behind the scenes. Object picking also plays a leading role, but it is positioned center stage in full view of the user right under his mouse's nose. Any time mouseover feedback is generated in the scene or a drag operation is performed, picking is required, whether it is for first-, second-, or third-person control, or for navigation or manipulation. In a POCS, 3D UI picking is the process of translating the 2D mouse position on the display screen into an in-scene object selection, a hit, and optionally the 3D position of the hit on the object. The process requires casting a ray into the scene through the mouse position and determining which objects, if any, are hit.

Picking can serve other needs besides those in the UI, and Java 3D can support them. In situations where the application needs to determine the relationship among objects in the scene, ray-based picking can determine the objects that lie in a particular direction and their distance. Such in-scene picking can be used in active relational feedback, such as limiting the length of a skirt to the nearest underlying object or measuring the distance between two objects like a tape measure. Other forms of in-scene picking might use a volume instead of a ray, such as to determine which objects are nearest the target object. Variations of volume-based picking could be used to determine the approximate visibility of an object in the scene, which is needed because Java 3D provides no native capability for this sometimes-essential operation. The following discussion will focus on ray-based UI object picking, but keep in mind that the same basic operation is useful for many other 3D application needs.

13.2.1 Picking overview

Picking, in Java 3D, is a process supported by a number of cooperating classes. There is no single "pick" class, method, or event trigger for the general case. Picking occurs in several stages, with the earlier stages getting you close, and the later stages providing spatial precision to the hit determination. The following is an overview of the full precision process, which is the one that best supports the UI techniques described in this book.

- Throw a pick ray from the user's virtual eyeball, through the mouse position in the view's display plane, and on into the scene. This is shown in figure 13.2.
- Intersect the pick ray with the bounds surrounding the shape objects (leaf scene graph nodes) in the scene, sorting the hits from closest to farthest.
- Test each hit candidate, starting with the closest, for intersection between the pick ray and the candidate's actual geometric shape (defined by a geometry array).
- If no shape is hit, or the hit object owning the shape is not a designated target object, quit the process without a real hit.
- Determine the hit point on the hit object using the distance of the hit ray to the point of intersection.

The picking process and the issues surrounding it can be technical. You may want to refer back to this list and to figure 13.2 occasionally to maintain your bearings as you read through the following sections.

13.2.2 Picking quality

Java 3D offers the designer plenty of features and flexibility for performing object picking. Translating this from marketing to engineering terms, you as a designer have some serious tradeoffs to make that affect the quality and performance of picking. As with many aspects of UI design, the Goldilocks principle reigns supreme (not too much, not too little, use just the right amount): Picking needs to be precise enough to maintain an intuitive WYSIWYG effect, but not so much so that poor performance

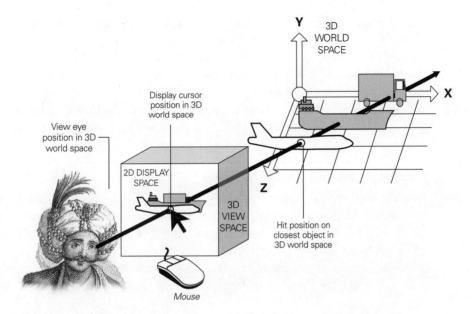

Figure 13.2   The pick ray starts at the eye position and projects through the mouse cursor into the scene.

rates make it unusable. Before diving into the details of the Java 3D picking process, let's consider some of the picking quality issues.

Continuous versus discrete picking

In general, object picking occurs continuously. As the mouse moves, the pick status is continuously updated. *Continuous picking* is the basis of mouseover feedback, such as for interaction highlighting, and world-relative control inputs, such as during a WRM drag. A more restrictive form of mouse picking performs hit testing only when a mouse button is pressed or released. Such *discrete picking* is often used in 3D applications because it is easier to implement and much less demanding on the designer and the system. It is also generally inferior to continuous picking because any feedback it provides to the user occurs after the fact; by the time the user presses the mouse button to attempt a drag, any feedback the pick provides is too late to be of much benefit. For example, the object may not be draggable, in which case the user's drag action is simply wasted effort; or the drag operation may be the wrong kind, in which case the user is required to undo it, which can interrupt the user's task and concentration. Discrete picking is also incapable of providing feedback during a drag, such as for WRM control or highlighting of drag-and-drop targets.

Discrete picking is the form provided by the Sun utilities. The UI framework, on the other hand, uses continuous picking throughout, but it pays a price for such extravagance. Unlike earlier 3D platforms such as VRML, Java 3D does not seem very well tuned for continuous precision picking. Part of this may be the efficiency of

Sun's implementation, but a more significant factor seems to be the Java virtual machine's garbage collector (GC), which causes moving objects to stutter during intensely interactive operations, such as continuous picking. Still, the advantages of continuous picking are many and its performance with Java and Java 3D can only improve with future releases.

➤ In part 4, discrete picking is first demonstrated in the OverEnabling example in section 19.1.4, and continuous picking is first demonstrated in the MultiShaping example in section 20.1.6.

Geometry versus bounds picking

As mentioned in the picking overview previously, Java 3D offers two levels of spatial precision in its picking process. The first level performs hit testing against the geometric bounds associated with the eligible target shapes, and the second level uses shape geometry intersection. Bounds-based picking is generally faster but can be imprecise, depending on how close the fit is between the bounds and the shape of its host leaf node. The speedup difference between the two is noticeable, especially if large numbers of eligible targets are in the scene, although GC stutter is still an issue.

Geometry picking assures the highest quality of picking. With it, what the user sees, the user gets—precisely. With bounds picking the user can place the cursor over an object to start a drag only to have another object highlight and move. Such behavior in the UI is unexpected, confusing, and definitely not intuitive. As a concession to performance, the framework uses a slightly watered-down version of full-precision geometry picking. Even so, the framework still pays a hefty price in performance. As with continuous picking, the hope is that future releases of Java 3D will offer picking that is better tuned for high quality use.

13.2.3   Picking model

As already mentioned, picking in Java 3D is a diffuse process. It is spread over a number of cooperating classes and capabilities. This section will attempt to bring some structure to the picking process by identifying and organizing key concepts and entities. Such a model for picking can help to integrate and explain its details, and help you to make design decisions.

By exposing such a diffuse process for such an important capability as picking, Java 3D allows plenty of opportunity for fine-tuning—or does it? For the kinds of techniques presented in this book, which stress high-quality intuitive user interfaces, the flexibility offered by the API is of limited use because most of it concerns obtaining faster but less precise results. Also, it seems that exposing so many of the intermediate stages of the picking process in the API would interfere with the optimization of the full, high-precision picking process, which should be a top priority in next-generation 3D applications.

In any case, picking is important, and understanding how the API supports it is crucial if you will be doing any interactive UI code development. In the UI framework, most of the picking process and several of its variations are gathered in the j3dui.control.mappers.PickEngine class. The heart of the process starts with the method `pick-TargetFair`, and the full precision portion of it uses the `pickTargetGeometry` method. The Sun utilities also support picking, but their emphasis is on discrete picking under controlled circumstances. Also, the documentation is slim when it comes to integrating the details, describing the model, and explaining the choices made.

Pick targets

Because of the complexity of the picking process, we need to refer to two different levels of target entities that are involved. The low level target, or *shape target*, is the one determined directly by the Java 3D picking apparatus. Bounds and geometry intersection only work on leaf nodes, specifically ones with a geometric shape such as `Shape3D` and `Morph`, hence the name "shape target." The high-level target, the *object target*, is the one in which the application is really interested. It may be a shape leaf node, but typically it is a group node high up in the scene graph that represents some complex object, such as a desk, possibly made up of nested components, such as a desk top, two sides, and a set of drawers. Ultimately, objects and their components are comprised of individual leaf nodes defining actual geometric shapes—the shape targets.

Shape pickability

Shape leaf nodes have an attribute called pickability, which is not shared by group nodes because they are not pickable, at least not directly. A leaf shape node can only be picked in a bounds intersection if it is pickable. The API provides the `Node.setPickable` method, which sets or resets the pickability of a leaf shape or, if used on a group node, the pickability of all the group's descendant leaf shapes. Leaf shape nodes are pickable by default. One odd feature of pickability is that if you directly set a leaf shape's pickability to false, to make it pickable again you have to explicitly set it; you can't use an ancestral group node to do it. Because the API seems focused on picking shape targets, you may be wondering how to get some useful work out of it, such as picking an object target.

Pick reporting

To perform object target picking you must use a capability called *pick reporting*, which is a capability that is separate from the pickability of a shape target. The result of a shape target bounds intersection is returned in a `SceneGraphPath` object. This object includes the shape target and possibly the scene graph path leading to it. For a group node above the shape target to appear in the `SceneGraphPath` result, the group's `Node.ENABLE_PICK_REPORTING` capability must be set. By default, pick reporting is disabled. It is important to note that pick reporting applies only to group nodes; the leaf shape node will always be reported in the `SceneGraphPath` result.

The key concept here is that, although picking can occur only on leaf shape nodes, any group nodes in the path leading to a shape target can also be reported in the bounds hit result. One approach for translating the result's shape target hit into an object target hit is efficient, but can be used only if certain conditions are met. If the application has the good fortune to have only group node object targets, and if it has the agility to enable pick reporting only on the object targets under the pick root in which it is interested, and if the object targets are not themselves nested, then any `SceneGraphPath` shape target that is hit will contain a single group node, which is the object target containing (or sharing) the shape target.

If those conditions cannot be met or an application doesn't care to deal with setting and resetting capability bits throughout the scene graph, there is an alternative approach, which uses an explicit object target list. The reporting capability is set on all of the nodes under the pick root, and, a list is kept that identifies the object targets in which the application is currently interested in being able to pick. When a bounds pick hit occurs, the `SceneGraphPath` nodes, including the shape target, are compared against the object target list and, if a target is found, it becomes an object target hit. Although a bit less efficient than relying solely on pick reporting to determine the object target, the target list approach affords a large degree of flexibility and requires a lot less finesse in setting up the scene graph. This is the approach used by the framework. The target list is established using the `j3dui.control.mappers.Pick-Engine.setTargets` method, and it can be seen in use in the `pickTarget` and `findHitTarget` methods.

Pick ray

Rather than limiting picking to using only a ray, Java 3D allows the operation to use a number of different picking shapes. The `PickShape` class serves as a base class for all picking shapes, which include points, rays, line segments, and any shape based on a `Bounds` object, which includes spheres, boxes, and polytopes. Future releases promise to add cone and cylinder pick shapes. For UI work, ray-based picking is good for picking polygonal shapes, but can prove difficult to use if attempting to pick individual vertices or edges on an object. A better picking shape for these situations would be one with a non-zero cross section, such as a long skinny box or one of the future shapes.

Regardless of the pick shape used, you still have to figure out how to position and orient it in the virtual world. For mouse-based UI picking, the shape needs to be ray-like with an origin position and a vector direction. The origin is set to the position of the user's eyeball in the world space, which is typically the view position; and the direction is set such that the ray projects through the position of the mouse cursor in the view's display plane. This arrangement was shown in figure 13.2.

In Java 3D, computing the ray geometry is easier said and illustrated than done. Depending on how the view model is configured, the eye position may not be exactly where the view is located. Also, the eye and mouse cursor positions are returned relative to the "image plate" space, which corresponds to the 3D view space, not the world space. To use these positions you have to first spatially transform them from local to world space. This is shown in the code sample below, which assumes perspective projection, and in a more generalized form in the framework utility method `j3dui.control.mappers.Mapper.buildPickRay`.

```
Canvas3D canvas;
int mouseX, mouseY;
...

Point3d rayOrg = new Point3d();
Vector3d rayDir = new Vector3d ();

// get the eye position in view space
Point3d eyePos = new Point3d();
canvas.getCenterEyeInImagePlate(eyePos);

// translate the mouse canvas position to view space
Point3d mousePos = new Point3d();
canvas.getPixelLocationInImagePlate(
 mouseX, mouseY, mousePos);

// get the view-to-world transform
Transform3D xform = new Transform3D();
canvas.getImagePlateToVworld(xform);

// transform eye and mouse from view to world space
xform.transform(eyePos);
xform.transform(mousePos);

// save the world pick ray origin
rayOrg.set(eyePos);

// build the world pick ray direction
rayDir.sub(mousePos, rayOrg);
rayDir.normalize();
```

To build a pick ray object, you use the computed ray origin and direction as parameters in the `PickRay` constructor. If, instead, you want to use a bounds shape for the picking ray, you have to first construct the bounds shape, then spatially transform it to the correct world position and orientation, and then use it to construct a `Pick-Bounds` object.

Pick root

Bounds intersection, which is the low precision and first portion of the picking process, is performed relative to a *pick root* node in the scene graph. The operation itself is executed using one of the pick methods in the `Locale` or `BranchGroup` classes, which limits your candidates for pick root in the scene graph to being one of these types. Your pick root choice is important because only the leaf shape nodes under the root will be considered. Also, the fewer nodes, especially pickable leaf nodes, that you have under the pick root, the better the overall picking performance will be.

Bounds intersection

Bounds intersection is low precision and is performed using one of the pick methods in the pick root object. These methods take a `PickShape` object as a parameter. Your choice of pick method determines how thoroughly Java 3D will search the pick root subgraph and how the hit results will be sorted. The methods `pickAll`, `pickAllSorted`, and `pickClosest` perform an exhaustive search of the subgraph for shape target hits, whereas the `pickAny` method searches only until the first one is found. As their names indicate, `pickAny` and `pickClosest` return a single `SceneGraphPath` hit result, which may be null if no shape target was hit, and `pickAll` and `pickAllSorted` return an array of hits, which could be null.

If all you are interested in is low-precision bounds picking, then `pickClosest` will probably do, which returns the single closest hit. The closest hit is the one that the user sees as being immediately under the cursor (or should be under the cursor but may not be because of the imprecision of bounds-based picking). In figure 13.2 the closest hit would be the jet object, as shown. If, however, you need high-precision geometry picking, then `pickAll` or `pickAllSorted` is needed. The `pickAll` returns all the hits—the ship, the truck, and the jet—and `pickAllSorted` returns them sorted closest to farthest—jet, then ship, then truck.

The following code fragment shows a simple example of how to use `pickAllSorted` for bounds intersection as the first stage in picking, and to combine it with geometry intersection and hit point determination in the second stage, which will be covered next. The pick ray origin and direction are obtained as described in the previous code sample.

```
// establish pick root
BranchGroup root;
...

// build pick ray
/// compute ray parameters from eye and mouse position
Point3d rayOrg = new Point3d();
Vector3d rayDir = new Vector3d ();
...

/// build pick ray object from ray origin and direction
PickRay ray = new PickRay(rayOrg, rayDir);

// throw the pick ray into the scene at all the leaf shape
// nodes under the pick root
SceneGraphPath paths[] = root.pickAllSorted(ray);

if(paths==null) {
   System.out.println("no hits");
```

```
} else {
  // shape target bounds were hit, check for real hits
  for(int hitI=0; hitI<paths.length; hitI++) {
    System.out.println("hit [" + hitI+ "]=" + paths[hitI]);

    // intersect pick ray with shape target geometry
    Node shape = paths[hitI].getObject();

    double dist[] = {0.0};
    boolean isRealHit = ((Shape3D) shape).intersect(
     paths[hitI], ray, dist);

    if(isRealHit) {
      // compute hit point from hit distance and pick ray
      Point3d point = new Point3d();
      point.scaleAdd(dist[0], rayDir, rayOrg);

      System.out.println("  real hit at " + point);
    }
  }
}
```

Geometry intersection

The second portion of the overall picking process is geometry intersection, which provides high precision picking by determining whether or not the pick shape actually intersected the hit node's geometry and not just its bounds. It is performed using one of the `intersect` methods on the hit leaf nodes returned by the bounds, picking process. These methods take the pick shape and the hit's scene graph path as parameters. Conveniently, bounds intersection returns only leaf nodes containing shape geometry, which are the only types of leaf nodes capable of performing geometry intersection. This was shown in the previous code sample. Note, however, that the shape was assumed to be a `Shape3D` object, but in general it could also be a `Morph` object.

One of the `intersect` methods takes a `PickShape` object as its parameter. The other one takes only a `PickRay` object, but returns the hit distance. Thus, you have to choose between using a general purpose pick shape, and determining the 3D hit point. Neither bounds nor geometry intersection depends on the direction of the shape's surface normals. This may seem like a *non sequitur*, but not if you are trying to perform picking while looking through a backward facing shape, such as an invisible wall in a room. Although the shape is invisible, it can still be picked, and will be if it is a shape leaf under the pick root that is pickable.

In order for a node's `intersect` method to work, the `Geometry.ALLOW_INTERSECT` capability bit must be set on it's geometry component object. Unlike pick reporting, however, there is no `setIntersect` method in the API; so, you must either set it in every shape leaf that you create and want to pick, or recursively walk the scene graph and set it. The methods in the framework utility class j3dui.utils.PickUtils should help with the latter approach.

Pick closest or all

Earlier it was mentioned that `pickAll` or `pickAllSorted` would be needed to perform bounds picking if geometry intersection were to follow. For the highest quality picking, the `pickAll` method should be used, and the hit that is closest as determined by its `intersect` method hit distance would be deemed the closest hit. This form of picking is also the slowest because all the bounds hits must be intersected for geometry. A much faster but slightly less precise approach is to use the `pickAllSorted` method and stop checking the bounds hit list when the first geometry intersection is found. This compromise approach is used in the framework, which can be seen in the `j3dui.control.mappers.PickEngine.pick-TargetGeometry` method.

At this point in the picking process, what you have found is the closest shape target whose geometry intersects the pick shape. What you really want, however, is the object target that was hit. As described above under pick reporting, if you took the pains to set up the scene graph properly then the single group node in the hit shape's `SceneGraphPath` object is the hit object. If not, then you will need to test the hit shape's scene graph path nodes to see if any match the object targets in the target list. If a shape hit is found but it doesn't contain an object hit, you can either quit (because the closest object under the cursor was not a designated target object), or you can keep looking. For direct manipulation, you probably want to quit if the object that the user sees and is trying to drag is not an object target. For WRM, however, you probably want to ignore all non-object target hits and, instead, keep hit testing until you find the first (closest) valid target object that is hit.

13.3 BEHAVIORS

The Java 3D model for detecting and reacting to system events is based on the `Behavior` class, which is a scene graph leaf node. It forms the basis for detecting object interactions, such as collisions, and for performing automatically generated actions, such as animations. It can also be used for accepting user inputs, such as from the mouse and keyboard.

13.3.1 The behavior model

In concept, the behavior model is quite simple. When a Behavior object becomes live in the scene graph, its `initialize` method is called, and when an event occurs, the Java 3D scheduler calls the object's `processStimulus` method. To perform an action or interaction, you extend the `Behavior` class or one of its derivatives, and override the `initialize` and `processStimulus` methods. Sounds easy, right? Of course the devil and a whole lot more are in the details.

Activation

For a behavior to fire, two conditions must be met: The behavior must be active and its wakeup conditions must be satisfied. You may remember from the earlier discussion on node bounds that one type was called the scheduling bounds. This is the kind of bounds that is associated with `Behavior` nodes. A behavior is only active if the activation volume associated with a `ViewingPlatform` object intersects its scheduling bounds. The intent of this spatial enabling scheme is to conserve system resources and thereby improve performance by enabling behaviors only when they are needed, which is presumably when the view is around to see them. If you want the behavior to be active all the time, construct a spherical scheduling bounds with an infinite radius. If you want all behaviors to be active all the time, set the view's activation volume to infinite radius. Because the default bounds for a behavior is null, you have to set it for the behavior to work.

Wakeup

An active behavior means only that it is receptive to receiving stimuli from the system. For the behavior to fire, its wakeup criteria must be met, which are set with its protected `wakeupOn` method. Behavior firing is a one-shot process. Setting the wakeup conditions cocks the trigger. When all the wakeup criteria are met, the system pulls the trigger by calling the `processStimulus` method, and the behavior is expended. A behavior can't fire unless wakeup conditions have first been set, which is typically done as part of the `initialize` method; and it won't fire again unless you re-cock its trigger by setting its wakeup conditions again, as part of the `process-Stimulus` method. Although this seems complicated, it is actually quite easy to do and allows the behavior to change its wakeup criteria between firings.

Conditions

Specifying a behavior's wakeup criteria and checking them in the `process-Stimulus` method can be confusing to the beginner because of the somewhat ambiguously named classes involved and the possibly nested data structures defining the criteria. Wakeup conditions are set using a `WakeupCondition` object in the `wakeupOn` method. Subclasses of `WakeupCondition` include the `WakeupCriterion` class and several other classes for building boolean combinations of conditions, such as the `WakeupAnd` and `WakeupOrOfAnds` class. This is a classic use of the composite pattern, with the boolean *condition* classes serving as group nodes in a condition tree, and the *criteria* subclasses serving as the leaves. When the behavior fires, its `processStimulus` method is called with an `enumeration` object listing the wakeup criteria that caused the triggering. Some criteria subclasses, such as `WakeupOnAWTEvent`, contain event elements. Thus, you may find yourself having to dig through an enumeration of arrays to get to the triggering events.

Criteria

Java 3D provides quite a wide variety of wakeup criteria from which to choose, including behavior activation and deactivation, AWT events, collision between objects, a transform change, elapsed time, elapsed number of display frames, a manual event posting, and more. AWT events, collisions, and event posting will be covered in detail in the following sections.

The breadth and depth of behaviors and their wakeup criteria offer a lot of potentially useful functionality that can be employed in 3D UI implementation. Unfortunately, at the time of this writing, serious bugs in a number of the behavior criteria, especially the collision and posting criteria, prevent their widespread use in the UI framework (and the need for a few rather unsightly hacks). Some problems are straightforward, and, thus fixes are promised in the next release; but others are more subtle. One in particular is the synchronization of behavior event handling and the rendering of any resulting scene graph changes, which will be discussed in a later section. Nevertheless, once the kinks are worked out, behaviors should play a major role in Java 3D UI development.

13.3.2 User inputs

One way to handle mouse and keyboard input is through the Java 3D event model, using behaviors and the `WakeupOnAWTEvent` criterion class. Another way to handle it is through the AWT event model, by creating AWT event listeners and registering them with a view's `Canvas3D` display, which is a subclass of an AWT `Canvas`. Going the AWT event route may be a lot more familiar if you've done any Java UI programming, and it is also simpler to implement. Using the AWT event model to handle events that will likely affect the scene graph may not seem quite legitimate, but the latest word from Sun is that it poses no problems (and in practice, it seems to be less prone to bugs).

The UI framework uses mostly behaviors for its mouse and keyboard input sensors, which can be found in the package `j3dui.control.inputs.sensors`. This was a result of early concern about event synchronization. An example of using the AWT event model can be found in the j3dui.control.inputs.sensors.AwtKeyboardArrowSensor class, which was forced out of necessity due to a minor bug in how key repeats are handled by behaviors.

If you do decide to use behaviors, keep in mind that the scheduling bounds size is ignored and is assumed to be infinite. This is an undocumented but confirmed feature. Thus, if you have two separate views, each with its own behaviors for display interaction, all behaviors associated with both displays will wake up when display interaction from a particular device type—mouse or keyboard—occurs. This is true regardless of the spatial separation of the views and no matter how small the scheduling bounds are, as long as it is non-zero.

13.3.3 Interpolators

Automatically generated actions that occur over time, such as animations, are performed using the `Interpolator` subclass of `Behavior`, which takes a single parameter in its constructor, an `Alpha` object. Animations are useful in UI feedback to show transitions and to draw the user's attention. Each interpolator is capable of controlling a specific kind of target object in a particular way, including color, transparency, position, rotation, scale, and others. For example, the position, rotation, and scale interpolators all target a `TransformGroup` object, but each controls its `Transform3D` in a particular manner. The `Alpha` object specifies how time is translated into a changing and possibly repeating value between 0.0 and 1.0, which all interpolators use to drive their target object from one action extreme to another, such as from 90 degrees to 180 degrees of rotation.

You can think of an interpolator as a control actuator whose input is time, and only time. Interpolators do some nifty things and make it really easy to do constrained spatial transforms and other actions. It's too bad that `Alpha` wasn't defined as an interface; then, an interpolator could be used as a general purpose control actuator that could be controlled by time, programmatic input, or even user interaction. This was a major reason why the framework developed its own model for control actuators, which is described in the next part of the book and embodied in the `j3dui.control.actuators` package.

13.3.4 Collision detection

The ability to detect collisions in the virtual world is an important building block for some of the more advanced UI techniques, such as PTF, the walk-around navigation technique, and active relational feedback. In all of these, the system is required to detect the presence of objects in relation to some target object and to act accordingly. Collision detection in its most general form can also serve as the basis for spatial change detection, which is a basic requirement for PWO and other visualization techniques, where view and object motion detection is required.

Collision behavior

The Java 3D collision model is built on the behavior model, and it folds in some of the concepts established in the picking model. As in picking, geometry bounds are used, and both bounds and geometry intersection are used. As you may recall from chapter 11, collision bounds can also be used for colliding. Collision detection uses an ordinary Behavior object, with special wakeup criteria for collisions that make it a collision detector. Keep in mind that, because you are using a behavior, you still have to view-activate it even though the collision you are trying to detect may have nothing to do with the view. A scheduling bounds with infinite radius might come in handy.

Collision criteria

The spatial conditions for performing the collision detection are established through behavior wakeup criteria. The `WakeupOnCollisionEntry` and `WakeupOnCollisionExit` criteria discretely detect when a collision condition begins and ends, respectively. The `WakeupOnCollisionMovement` criterion continuously detects when motion occurs between objects that are in collision. The constructors for all three of these criteria are the same. They allow a single collision *arming* object to be specified. Unlike in picking, the arming object can be a leaf shape or a group node. The constructor also lets you say whether you want collision detection to occur based on bounds or geometry intersection, with the default being bounds colliding.

Collision targets

A collision event is triggered when the collision wakeup criteria occur with respect to some *triggering* object, which can be the result of the triggering, the arming, or both objects having moved. For an object to serve as a triggering target it must be set collidable using the `Node.setCollidable` method. The collidable capability parallels that for picking, even down to the "feature" where leaf shapes can be set noncollidable from a group, but they can only be set collidable from the leaf itself.

There are a number of inconsistencies in the collision model when you start comparing the arming object versus the triggering object. For example, although the arming object can be a leaf shape or a group node, the triggering object will always be a leaf shape node. And, only triggering objects can be set collidable; arming objects are always collidable.

Collision reporting

Collision uses a reporting scheme somewhat similar to that used for picking. Collisions are reported for both the arming and triggering objects by means of `SceneGraphPath` objects, which can be obtained from the behavior's collision wakeup criteria. Similar to picking, there is a `Node.ENABLE_COLLISION_REPORTING` capability, which is separate from collidability. Note, however, that collision reporting only works for the triggering object's SceneGraphPath hit result; the one for the arming object will always contain just the arming object.

Collision dynamics

Both the collision enter and exit criteria exhibit a type of hysteresis effect where the first triggering object will cause the behavior to fire, but a second triggering object won't cause the behavior to fire unless all triggering conditions have first been cleared. For example, for a collision enter criterion, when an arming object encounters the first triggering object, the behavior will fire. If while still colliding with the first object, it encounters a second object, the second object will not cause the behavior to fire a second time. To make the behavior fire again, the arming object has to first be clear of all other objects, whether triggering or not. The bottom line is that a given collision detector can detect only a single collision at a time. This limitation is further reinforced by the fact that the API returns only a single `SceneGraphPath` hit result, not an array of them as in picking.

Because of what appears to be a serious bug in behavior scheduling involving movement detection in general, the collision movement criterion doesn't work. When a collision occurs it fires continuously, whether or not there is movement. The implications of this on the framework are far-reaching, and this accounts for the reason that behaviors aren't generally used in it except for input sensors (and even then they are not really needed).

Collision problems

Besides the problems already mentioned, there are a number of outright mysteries surrounding collision. For example, if bounds colliding is specified, and the collision bounds is set on the trigger object, then the collision bounds will be used, but only if it is smaller than the automatically generated geometric bounds of the trigger shape. With geometric colliding, sometimes the trigger and arming geometry is used, and sometimes only the trigger's geometry is used. Also, geometry colliding will sometimes fail to work depending on the relative sizes of autocomputed bounds of the arming and triggering shapes. More inconsistencies arise if a group is used for the arming object instead of a leaf. Keep in mind that this information was obtained through empirical evidence, and collision seems to be rather sensitive to how it is configured.

To say that collision and bounds have problems is an understatement. With the inconsistencies and vagueness of the API concerning these two areas, the problems described here concerning collision, and all the problems with setting and computing geometry bounds, create a real mess. It is no small wonder that tutorials have tried to steer clear of collision and even picking.

13.3.5 Change detection

Another low-level capability that is useful for UI work is change detection, which includes both spatial and nonspatial changes in target objects. External and internal geometry changes are needed for many of the visualization techniques. Nonspatial changes, such as appearance, the addition or removal of child components, or even application-defined changes such as selection and mouseover, are useful in coordinating object specification, configuration, and interaction states throughout the application. Detection of changes is also useful in synchronizing user and programmatic-initiated changes in the scene with renderer updates to the view display image.

Spatial changes

Detection of external geometry changes is a key aspect of the world overlay, display facing, and constant size visualization techniques. These techniques generally require immediate knowledge of any view and target object position and orientation changes.

Collision movement detection, discussed above, is an example of continuous external geometry change detection: Whenever a triggering object moves—translates or rotates—its external motion would be reported. As discussed earlier for spatial transforms, in Java 3D, external geometry changes are specified and reported through `Transform3D` objects. You may also remember that picking and collision results are provided in the form of `SceneGraphPath` objects. The API designers had the forethought to include the local-to-vworld transform of the target object as part of the `SceneGraphPath` class, which is obtained with the `getTransform` method.

Although many of the behavior criteria detect discrete movement, such as collision entry, the only one, other than collision movement, that detects continuous motion is `WakeupOnTransformChange`. Given the problems with collision movement detection and the collision model in general, you might think that it would be a perfect alternative. Unfortunately, this criterion detects only geometry changes that are local to its target `TransformGroup` object, specifically any changes to its `Transform3D` component object. Such changes affect only the spatial geometry of its child nodes as a whole, which are external to the children but internal to the target group. Although such local motion detection is useful for certain situations, movement of the transform group relative to the world space, as expressed by its local-to-Vworld transform, is what is needed for the visualization techniques.

Although not much help in general purpose spatial change detection, Java 3D provides a few behavior subclasses that incorporate change detection of external view geometry, such as `Billboard` and `LOD` (level-of-detail). Keep in mind that if you are trying to use such view dependent behaviors in a multi-view application that they will work correctly only with a single designated view. The next release of Java 3D promises to address this shortcoming. So, what does the framework do for general purpose spatial change detection? The next section describes how Java 3D lets you handle changes that are not specifically covered by the API, as a developer's means of last resort.

Nonspatial changes

Even if external geometry changes could be correctly detected, the visualization techniques also require internal geometry change detection. They specifically need to be notified of changes to the internal state of the view, display, and screen spaces, which include such parameters as display size, field-of-view, view and display scale factors, and screen resolution. Some of these could be handled as AWT events, such as display window size, but there is no specific way to handle the other changes. The same goes for nongeometric changes, such as an object's appearance, constituent members, and interaction state. To accommodate generic change detection and notification, Java 3D provides a scheme for manually posting events to behaviors. To use it, the application would explicitly detect a change, such as when the user interacts with a virtual control or the application programmatically generates a change; and post that change, such as a change in field-of-view, to interested target behaviors, such as a visualization technique.

Behavior posting is handled through the `WakeupOnBehaviorPost` criterion, which is constructed with a source `Behavior` object and an arbitrary post ID. When the target behavior receives a post from the specified source behavior and/or with the specified post ID, it fires. A post is sent with the `Behavior.postId` method. Although the assumption is that a post will be generated only by another behavior, situations can arise outside of the behavior model that require a post, such as in response to a direct AWT event. For such cases, a static version of the post method would be useful.

Unfortunately, there is a serious bug in behavior posting (confirmed by Sun) that allows the target behavior to fire only once, with any subsequent postings to it being ignored. This factor eliminated the final hope for using behaviors in the framework. As an alternative, a nonbehavior form of posting had to be developed for the framework, which is embodied in the `j3dui.visualize.ChangePoster` class. These and other aspects of the framework are discussed in more detail in the next part of the book.

Update synchronization

Any time a visual change occurs to the scene graph or to the state of one of its nodes, the change must be reflected in the view display. For this to happen, the Java 3D renderer, which converts the 3D model represented by the scene graph into a 2D image in the view display, must be notified of the change so that it can re-render the display. Coupled with rendering update is the update to the scene graph itself. For all practical purposes, in Java 3D, change notification to the renderer and commitment of changes in the scene graph occur automatically; you as designer have no control over them.

The implications for change detection might seem subtle but the consequences can be dramatic. For example, if the user turns a virtual knob on the display to rotate the view of the scene, the following events would have to occur: The mouse drag would be detected and a corresponding change to a transform group above the view in the scene graph would be made. As a result of a scene graph node being changed, the renderer would be notified automatically to update the display image. When the image updates, the handling of the original event stimulus—the drag—is completed. So far so good; but, what if you are using some visualization technique that depends on knowing where the view is at all times, such as world overlay?

Expanding on the previous example, when the view's transform group changes, the world overlay handler must be notified that the view's external geometry is changing. When it receives this change notification, it goes to the view object in the scene graph and gets its local-to-Vworld spatial transform, which the overlay handler in turn uses to update the overlay position of its target object. Java 3D's update model is such that, when a spatial transform is changed, even though the new state can be read back immediately, it is not actually committed in the scene graph until the renderer starts its display update. This means that when the overlay handler goes to get the view's local-to-Vworld transform, the wrong value is returned. This is because the view movement won't be committed until all scene graph changes are completed and the renderer update begins.

The bottom line is that secondary event handlers that query the scene graph state, such as world overlay, could be working with old information. Any changes they make to the scene graph will appear out of sync with the rest of the display update—and the overlaid object will appear in the wrong place. There is no work-around for this problem, and its effects can be seen plainly in the WorldOverlaying example in section 21.2.4, where the overlaid objects jerk and jump around to catch up with their moving host objects.

Update synchronization can be a hard problem to identify, especially because it is only exposed in applications that are pushing the envelope, like the 3D techniques described in this book. (I have always found it amusing that UI techniques are generally not recognized as pushing the implementation envelope, but they do because they are so intimately tied to the platform's event handling and nongeometric performance.) It can be an even harder problem to solve, especially if you are also trying to avoid event loops, which would be an even worse problem than out-of-date scene graph information. Many graphics platforms have tried to tackle this problem and its subtleties, and most have failed, Java 3D included. The next release of Java 3D promises to fix this problem. As the saying goes, hope for the best but prepare for the worst.

For a future release of the Java 3D API, some have suggested breaking out interactions as separate subsystems with well-defined but general purpose interfaces. Thus, if the default picking, collision, or change detection subsystem were not up to the task due to lack of precision, time resolution, or performance, third parties or developers could conceivably write their own. Exposing such interfaces would also require that the update/synchronization model be better defined and exposed.

13.4 SUMMARY

For a 3D application, action and interaction are the lifeblood of its 3D UI. Without spatial transforms, picking, and change detection, the virtual world would be a pretty static place and the user would quickly become bored with the application. The `TransformGroup` class and its closely associated `Transform3D` class form the basis for all spatial manipulation. These classes, together with the `getLocalToVworld` method of the `Node` class, are vital to many of the 3D techniques, such as DRM, WRM, and world overlay. Picking in Java 3D is a rather decentralized process that generally occurs in two stages, the first one getting you close and the second one adding spatial precision. The behavior model, as embodied by the `Behavior` class, provides the basis for automatic actions (interpolators), collisions, and general change detection in Java 3D.

As Java extensions go, Java 3D is still quite young, which is evident from the problems discussed here. Future releases will no doubt fix the bugs and even address some of the API problems. Although one might question the specific approaches taken for such critical UI functions as picking, collision, and event handling, Java 3D has definitely tried to cut a wider swath through these important areas than previous 3D platforms, and offers the greatest potential for quality support of 3D user interfaces.

C H A P T E R   1 4

In a Java world

Given that Java 3D is an extension of Java, developers are expected to take advantage of the many capabilities that it provides to supplement those of Java 3D. This is certainly true in the case of 3D application development, where there must be a melding of 2D and 3D UI techniques and layout. Some of the more important aspects of merging Java 3D into a Java world are addressed in this chapter.

14.1   SWING

The Swing 2D GUI components offer a wealth of widgets and functionality for use in a 3D application window. For example, the number and types of 3D views presented to the user might be selectable from a menu, toolbar, or with buttons underneath the view area. Swing popup dialogs could be used for instantiating and configuring 3D data objects in the scene. And, Swing table and tree widgets could be used for out-of-scene access to in-scene data objects. Mixing Java 3D and Swing makes obvious good sense; in practice, however, you have to contend with something called the "heavyweight versus lightweight" problem.

14.1.1   Heavyweight versus lightweight

The original AWT components are referred to as *heavyweight* components. This means that each AWT component is represented by a corresponding native GUI component, a peer, in the underlying operating system. An AWT frame, menu, and

266

button corresponds to a native frame, menu, and button. As such the native component owns and controls the pixels on the screen covered by component, not Java; and it dictates how events on a component, such as mouse clicks, are reported. This limits what Java can do with the component screen pixels and events.

Swing, on the other hand, uses *lightweight* components, in which Java exclusively manages the pixels and events. This allows Java to do some pretty fancy things such as overlaid tooltips and glass pane event capturing. To do this, Java starts with a single heavyweight component, such as a blank frame, on which it paints lightweight components, like an artist on a canvas. In this way Java can maintain complete control over how the pixels and events within the hosting component are managed. Such control is necessary to provide cross-platform support for advanced GUI features that may be available only natively on some platforms.

The Java 3D canvas, `Canvas3D`, is a heavyweight component, extended from Java's heavyweight `Canvas` class instead of something lightweight such as Swing's `JPanel` class. This is not due to lack of foresight on the part of the API designers. Java 3D requires a heavyweight canvas to take advantage of any native 3D rendering capability, such as that provided through OpenGL. Such native capabilities need to directly own the screen pixels. Although this complicates matters somewhat, with care much of the functionality offered by Swing can be used in application windows that also contain Java 3D view displays.

14.1.2 Mixing Java 3D and Swing

When lightweight and heavyweight components are mixed, strange things can happen when the components try to overlap. In general, the lightweight components will fail to appear, the heavyweight component will suddenly pop to the front, or the lightweight component behind the heavyweight one will flash during any interaction. This is simply because the heavyweight components own the screen pixels where they live, not Java. When Java tries to paint the lightweight component's pixels, such as for a pop-up menu or tooltip, the heavyweight component is unaware of this and will just paint right over them.

Although there is not much that can be done for static Swing components that overlap a Java 3D canvas, such as placing Swing buttons and icons inside of the view display, Java does give the UI designer a break when pop-up menus and tooltips are involved. Before building any Swing components, set the static methods `JPopupMenu.setDefaultLightWeightPopupEnabled` and `ToolTipManager.sharedInstance().setLightWeightPopupEnabled` to false, which indicate to Java that it should use heavyweight components to build pop-up menus and tooltips. Then, when a Swing menu or tooltip overlaps a Java 3D display, it will (usually) always appear on top. Note that some developers have warned that *any* overlapping of Java 3D displays and Swing components can be unreliable.

14.1.3   Examples

➤ The FancyApp example in part 4 incorporates dual Java 3D views with a Swing menu bar, data tree, and data palette. The following code fragment is taken from the example. Although not specifically a Swing issue, notice how the content of the frame is packed using the frame's `pack` method just before showing the frame with its `show` method. If you want to set the size of your GUI components and then have the frame shrink to fit them, rather than explicitly setting the frame size, then you have to first pack the frame contents. It is easy for beginners to forget to do this. Without the packing, the frame will implode on itself with only a titlebar showing.

```
import java.awt.*;
import java.awt.event.*;
import javax.swing.*;
import javax.media.j3d.*;
import javax.vecmath.*;

public class FancyFrame extends JFrame {

    public FancyFrame() {
        // kill the window on close
        addWindowListener(new WindowAdapter() {
            public void windowClosing(WindowEvent winEvent) {
                System.exit(0);
            }
        });
        ...

        // tell Swing to use heavyweight popups
        JPopupMenu.setDefaultLightWeightPopupEnabled(false);
        ToolTipManager.sharedInstance().
         setLightWeightPopupEnabled(false);

        // build Swing window components with 3D displays
        buildMenuBar();
        buildContentPanel();
    }

    // sizes and shows the frame.
    public void showFrame() {
        ...
        // size contents THEN show frame
        pack();
        show();
    }
}
```

14.2   DRAG-AND-DROP

Drag-and-drop is an easy and often intuitive way to move data objects around, within, and between applications, whether those applications are Java or native to the hosting operating system. Java provides such capabilities for performing drag-and-drop and its cousin, clipboard cut-and-paste, through the `java.awt.dnd` and `java.awt.datatransfer` packages.

Currently, there are very few examples available on how to use drag-and-drop in Java, much less Java 3D. The example DndApp in section 23.2.2 demonstrates how to use Java's drag-and-drop capabilities to perform 2D and 3D drag-and-drop within and between Swing and Java 3D components in a single application.

14.2.1   Drag-and-drop model

A drag-and-drop operation occurs in two steps: a *drag*, which starts the operation, and a *drop*, which terminates it; and it involves two major players: a *drag source* object and a *drop target* object. Typically, a drag starts when the user starts dragging with the left mouse button while over an object registered as a drag source; and, a drop occurs when the user releases the mouse button while the cursor is over an object recognized as a drop target. Although within Java the drag source and drop target objects must be AWT `Component` objects, there are sufficient events and information generated by the drag-and-drop operation to allow refinement of the operation to entities within an AWT component, such as objects in a 3D scene.

The code fragments in the two sections below on dragging and dropping are taken from the DndApp example. The first sample is from the `DragSourceJLabel` class, which is an example of a drag source object, and the second one is from the `DropTargetJPanel` class, which illustrates how you might build a drop target object. Both classes can be found in the `J3duiBook/examples/DndApp` directory (they did not make it into the framework). For the following discussion you may also want to refer to the UML-like class diagram, figure 23.2, provided with the example.

Drag-and-drop dragging

To allow for generalization of how the user initiates a drag operation, which could be performed using other mouse buttons or even other input devices, the drag "gesture" is detected using an object of the class `DragGestureRecognizer`. The recognizer monitors input events on the drag source object and, when it determines that the user has initiated a drag operation on the object, it will notify its registered gesture handler, implementing the `DragGestureListener` interface. The gesture handler will, in turn, start a drag operation with the `DragSource.startDrag` method.

A `DragSource` object serves as a drag-and-drop operation's drag manager. When the drag is started the `startDrag` method is handed a data object implementing the `Transferable` interface, which serves as a proxy for the drag source object, and which will be transferred to the drop target when a valid drop occurs. The `StringSelection` class is such a data object, which represents the source object as a text string, such as its name.

The start method also registers a drag handler, which implements the `Drag-SourceListener` interface. During a drag. the manager tells this handler what is happening, such as the drag cursor being over a drop target or that a drop has taken place and the operation is done. Such notification is typically used to provide user feedback in addition to that provided through the drag cursor appearance, which the drag manager controls. If the underlying operating system supports it, a drag image such as an icon can also be provided when the drag starts.

Example of a draggable JLabel

Filename: J3duiBook/examples/DndApp/DragSourceJLabel.java

```java
import java.awt.*;
import java.awt.dnd.*;
import java.awt.datatransfer.*;
import javax.swing.*;

import j3dui.utils.Debug;

/**
A JLabel capable of initiating drag operations.

@author Jon Barrilleaux,
copyright (c) 1999 Jon Barrilleaux,
All Rights Reserved.
*/
public class DragSourceJLabel extends JLabel
 implements DragSourceListener, DragGestureListener {

   // public interface ========================================

   /**
   Construct a DragSourceJLabel with default drag actions.
   */
   public DragSourceJLabel(String text) {
     this(text, DnDConstants.ACTION_COPY_OR_MOVE |
       DnDConstants.ACTION_LINK);
   }

   /**
   Construct a DragSourceJLabel with the specified drag actions.
   @param actions Flags specifying the types of drag actions
   this object will provide (DnDConstants.ACTION_???).
   */
   public DragSourceJLabel(String text, int actions) {
     super(text, CENTER);
     _dragSource = new DragSource();
     _dragGesture = _dragSource.
       createDefaultDragGestureRecognizer(this, actions, this);
   }

   // implements java.awt.dnd.DragGestureListener

   public void dragGestureRecognized(DragGestureEvent evt) {
```

```
      // use label name as transfer data, start drag
      StringSelection item = new StringSelection(getText());

      _dragSource.startDrag(
        evt, DragSource.DefaultCopyNoDrop, item, this);
    }

    // implements java.awt.dnd.DragSourceListener

    public void dragDropEnd(DragSourceDropEvent evt) {}
    public void dragEnter(DragSourceDragEvent evt) {}
    public void dragExit(DragSourceEvent evt) {}
    public void dragOver(DragSourceDragEvent evt) {}
    public void dropActionChanged(DragSourceDragEvent evt) {}

    // personal body =========================================

    private DragSource _dragSource;
    private DragGestureRecognizer _dragGesture;

}
```

Drag-and-drop dropping

Defining a drop target object is simpler than defining a drag source object because only a single handler is involved. A DropTarget object monitors input events occurring on a drop target object and notifies a registered drop handler, implementing the DropTargetListener interface, about any drag-and-drop activity that pertains to the target object, such as the drag cursor being over it or a drop having occurred on it. In essence, the DropTarget object serves as a drop target manager, which coordinates the drag-and-drop operation with the active drag source manager.

Normally when the drag cursor is over a drop target object, the default is for it to be receptive to a drop, which is reflected in the drag cursor appearance. If, however, the drop target needs to actively decide whether or not to permit a drop, the drop handler can use the acceptDrag and rejectDrag methods of a received DropTargetDragEvent object. Such action is conveyed back to the drag source manager, which updates the drag cursor shape accordingly.

If the drop handler has accepted the drag and the user performs a drop, such as by releasing the mouse button, then the drop target manager notifies the handler that a drop has occurred. In response, the drop handler must decide whether to accept the drop or to reject it, which it does using the DropTargetDropEvent object's acceptDrop and rejectDrop methods. A drop might be rejected because the handler cannot handle the type of data in the transfer, as defined by its "data flavor." Upon accepting the drop, the handler typically instantiates an object defined by the transfer data and adds it to the drop target in some appropriate manner. In the example, for a drag-and-drop drop on a list, a `DragSourceJLabel` object is created whose name is specified by the transfer data, and it is added to the `DropTargetJPanel` drop target.

Example of a JPanel acting as a drop target

Filename: J3duiBook/examples/DndApp/DropTargetJPanel.java

```java
import java.util.*;
import java.awt.*;
import java.awt.dnd.*;
import java.awt.datatransfer.*;
import java.io.IOException;
import javax.swing.*;

import j3dui.utils.Debug;

/**
A JPanel capable of accepting drop operations.

@author Jon Barrilleaux,
copyright (c) 1999 Jon Barrilleaux,
All Rights Reserved.
*/
public class DropTargetJPanel extends JPanel
  implements DropTargetListener {

  // public interface =========================================

  /**
  Construct a DropTargetJPanel with default drop actions.
  */
  public DropTargetJPanel() {
    this(DnDConstants.ACTION_COPY_OR_MOVE |
      DnDConstants.ACTION_LINK);
  }

  /**
  Construct a DropTargetJPanel with the specified drop actions.
  @param actions Flags specifying the types of drop actions
  this object will accept (DnDConstants.ACTION_???).
  */
  public DropTargetJPanel(int actions) {
    _dropTarget = new DropTarget(this, actions, this);
    setLayout(new BoxLayout(this, BoxLayout.Y_AXIS));
  }

  /**
  Adds a component item to this panel and updates its
  presentation.
  @param item Item to be added.
  */
  public void addItem(Component item) {
```

```
      add(item);
      revalidate();
   }

   /**
   Removes a component item from this panel and updates its
   presentation.
   @param item Item to be removed.
   */
   public void removeItem(Component item) {
      remove(item);
      revalidate();
   }

   // DropTargetListener implementation

   public void dragEnter (DropTargetDragEvent evt) {}
   public void dragExit (DropTargetEvent evt) {}
   public void dragOver(DropTargetDragEvent evt) {}
   public void dropActionChanged (DropTargetDragEvent evt) {}

   public void drop(DropTargetDropEvent evt) {

      // if unsupported action, no drop
      if(evt.getDropAction()==DnDConstants.ACTION_NONE) {

         evt.rejectDrop();
         return;
      }

      // if unsupported transfer data, no drop
      Transferable tr = evt.getTransferable();
      if(!tr.isDataFlavorSupported(DataFlavor.stringFlavor)) {

         evt.rejectDrop();
         return;
      }

      // good drop, do it
      try {
         evt.acceptDrop(evt.getDropAction());

         // user transfer data as drop source object name
         String item = (String)tr.getTransferData(
          DataFlavor.stringFlavor);

         // add source object to this list
         addItem(new DragSourceJLabel(item));

         // done with drop
         evt.getDropTargetContext().dropComplete(true);
      } catch (IOException io) {
```

```
        io.printStackTrace();
        evt.rejectDrop();
    } catch (UnsupportedFlavorException ufe) {
        ufe.printStackTrace();
        evt.rejectDrop();
    }
}

// personal body =============================================

private DropTarget _dropTarget;

}
```

Drag-and-drop actions

In the preceeding code samples, you may have noticed mention of actions and action flags. The Java drag-and-drop model supports three basic drag-and-drop *actions*: move, copy, and link. The bit flags corresponding to these actions are found in the DnDConstants class. Each defines a standard action that will occur if the drag-and-drop operation is successfully completed; with the drag source object being moved, copied, or linked to the drop target container. The definition of a system-mediated link is platform dependent, but generally it allows the same object to live in two different locations, such as the same file being shared in two different directories. Regardless of the operation, the drag source and drop target objects, whether in Java or outside in the native operating system, are responsible for the actual interpretation and implementation of the transfer semantics.

If the entire drag-and-drop operation occurs in the same context, such as all within the same Java Virtual Machine (VM), then the actions can be implemented using the actual object, with the object reference being moved or being used to clone the source object. If the drag-and-drop operation is occurring between two different Java VMs then the object might be transferred in serialized form through a special Transferable data flavor for this purpose. If the transfer is between Java and the native operating system, the Java side still uses Transferable and data flavors, the same as would be used for clipboard cut-and-paste, but the transfer is mediated by the native platform.

Aside from defining the semantics of the transfer, the action flags also serve as action filters for accepting or rejecting a particular phase of the operation. Regarding actions, there are three players: the drag source object, the drop target object, and the user drag gesture. In general, the source and target are assigned action flags defining the types of operations they support. For the drag source, this is specified when the drag gesture recognizer is constructed; for the drop target, this is specified when the drop manager is built. The user determines the gesture's action (there can only be one at a time) during an operation, which can be changed on the fly. For example, the

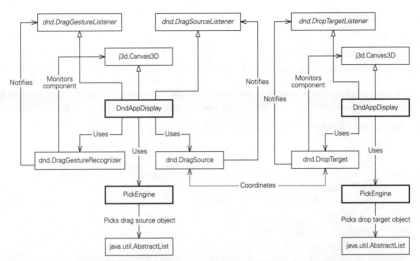

Figure 14.1   Relationship of classes and interfaces related to Jave 3D-based drag sources and targets

default action might be Move; with the control key held down the action might be Copy; and with the shift and control keys down the action might change to Link. The current action of the operation is typically reflected in the shape of the cursor, such as a small plus sign appearing if the operation will result in a copy.

For a drag operation to start, the intersection of the drag source actions and gesture action must be non-null; for a drop to occur, the intersection of the drop target actions and the gesture action must not be null. If a drag is underway and the combination of gesture and source flags, or gesture and drop flags is null, then the no-drop cursor will appear and the drop will not be allowed.

14.2.2   3D drag-and-drop

Within Java, drag-and-drop operations occur at the AWT component level, such as a `Canvas3D`. In order to use drag-and-drop within a Java 3D scene, the drag-and-drop handlers must monitor and interpret the drag cursor position and actions within the canvas. Essentially, as the cursor moves over the 3D scene, the handlers perform object picking to determine if the cursor is over a valid drag source or drop target 3D object in the scene. The DnD model provides plenty of events and information to make this fairly easy to do as long as you have a good object picker.

The following code sample is taken from the `DndAppDisplay` class in the DndApp example, which combines drag and drop handling into a single class with provisions for 3D object picking. Figure 23.3, which is reproduced here as figure 14.1, illustrates how the drag-and-drop and picking are used in this class. Because the structure of the handlers is similar to that shown earlier for the `DragSourceJLabel` and `DropTargetJPanel` classes, only the portions specific to 3D drag-and-drop are shown here. All picking is done with the framework's pick engine class. All data transfers are based on the object name, which is simple and effective, but limited. An apparent conflict between Java DnD and Java 3D behaviors, at least under Windows NT, causes DnD to freeze up when dragging from out-of-scene to in-scene. For this reason no in-scene user feedback or view interaction is provided in the example.

Example of a 3D Display containing draggable objects and a drop target

Filename: J3duiBook/examples/DndApp/DndAppDisplay.java

```
/**
Construct a DndAppDisplay.
@param world Host world serving as the root for all scene
picking and object instantiation.
@param dragSourceList List containing references to nodes
that can act as drag source objects.
@param dropTargetList List containing references to nodes
that can act as drop target objects.
@param dropSourceList List containing references to nodes
that can act as drop source objects.
@param dragActions Flags specifying the types of drag actions
this object will provide (DnDConstants.ACTION_???).
@param dropActions Flags specifying the types of drop actions
this object will accept (DnDConstants.ACTION_???).
*/
public DndAppDisplay(AppWorld world,
 ArrayList dragSourceList, ArrayList dropTargetList,
 ArrayList dropSourceList, int dragActions, int dropActions){

   _world = world;

   // setup dragging
   if(dragSourceList != null) {
     _dragSourceList = dragSourceList;

     _dragSource = new DragSource();

     _dragGesture =
     _dragSource.createDefaultDragGestureRecognizer(
     this, dragActions, this);

     _dragSourcePicker = new PickEngine(
     _world.getSceneRoot(), _dragSourceList);
   }

   // setup dropping
   if(dropTargetList != null && dropSourceList != null) {
     _dropSourceList = dropSourceList;

     _dropTarget = new DropTarget(
     this, dropActions, this);
```

```
      _dropTargetPicker = new PickEngine(
        _world.getSceneRoot(), dropTargetList);
  }
}

// DragGestureListener implementation

public void dragGestureRecognized(DragGestureEvent evt) {

  // if over valid source, start drag
  DndNodeInfo source = pickDragSource(
    evt.getDragOrigin().x, evt.getDragOrigin().y);

  if(source != null) {
    // get drag source object name
    StringSelection text = new StringSelection(
      source.getName());

    // use name as transfer data
    _dragSource.startDrag(evt,
      DragSource.DefaultCopyNoDrop, text, this);
  }
}

// DragSourceListener implementation
…
// DropTargetListener implementation

public void dragEnter(DropTargetDragEvent evt) {
  dragOver(evt);
}

public void dragOver(DropTargetDragEvent evt) {
  // if over valid target, accept drag
  DndNodeInfo target = pickDropTarget(
    evt.getLocation().x, evt.getLocation().y);

  if(target != null) {
    evt.acceptDrag(evt.getDropAction());
  } else {
    evt.rejectDrag();
  }
}

public void drop(DropTargetDropEvent evt) {
  // if unsupported action, no drop
  …
  // if unsupported transfer data, no drop
  …
  // good drop, do it
  try {
    evt.acceptDrop(evt.getDropAction());
```

```
        // user transfer data as drop source object name
        String name = (String)tr.getTransferData(
         DataFlavor.stringFlavor);

        // add source object at hit point in world
        Node source = buildDropSource(evt.getLocation().x,
         evt.getLocation().y, name);

        // add source object to list so draggable
        if(source != null) _dragSourceList.add(source);

        // done with drop
        evt.getDropTargetContext().dropComplete(true);
      } catch (IOException io) {
        io.printStackTrace();
        evt.rejectDrop();
      } catch (UnsupportedFlavorException ufe) {
        ufe.printStackTrace();
        evt.rejectDrop();
      }
  }
}
```

14.3   APPLETS

The promise is that Java and its extensions, such as Java 3D, can be used to develop
commercial web-based applications. In theory this is correct. In practice, however, the
answer requires a few qualifications before saying that this is perhaps correct. Let's
take care of applets first, and then step back and take a look at the bigger picture with
which an applet in a commercial 3D application will have to live.

14.3.1   Java 3D in applets

Using Java 3D in an applet is in principle no different than using Java in an applet. In
practice there are a few things to be aware of. For starters, Java 3D requires a fully
compliant Java 1.2 VM—nothing short of it will do. Therefore, the client program
running the applet must use a Java 1.2 VM, such as appletviewer that comes with
the Java developers' kit (JDK), although most users would prefer to use their browsers
to access the applets instead.

Java Plug-in and HTML converter

In general, browsers such as Internet Explorer and Netscape do not come with a Java
1.2 VM. Instead, the latest versions of these browsers are capable of using a VM plug-
in in order to become Java 1.2 capable. To take advantage of the browser VM plug-in
you, the designer, have to first convert the HTML referencing the applet to also reference the plug-in, and the user has to have the plug-in installed. Installing Sun's JDK
or JRE (Java runtime environment) on the client machine will (usually) automatically
install the plug-in to work with Internet Explorer and Netscape. The JDK comes with

a converter to help you convert the HTML. The converter is in the form of a class file, `HTMLConverter.class`, that you run from Java.

This is the original version of the `HelloUniverse.html` file that comes with Sun's Java 3D examples.

```
<HTML>
<HEAD>
<TITLE>Hello, Universe!</TITLE>
</HEAD>
<BODY BGCOLOR="#000000">
<applet align=middle code="HelloUniverse.class" width=256 height=256>
<blockquote>
<hr>
If you were using a Java-capable browser,
you would see Hello Universe! instead of this paragraph.
<hr>
</blockquote>
</applet>
</BODY>
</HTML>
```

Following next is the same file converted using the utility. Seeing it, you can understand why Sun has provided a utility to help you.

```
<HTML>
<HEAD>
<TITLE>Hello, Universe!</TITLE>
</HEAD>
<BODY BGCOLOR="#000000">
<!--"CONVERTED_APPLET"-->
<!-- CONVERTER VERSION 1.0 -->
<OBJECT classid="clsid:8AD9C840-044E-11D1-B3E9-00805F499D93"
WIDTH = 256 HEIGHT = 256 ALIGN = middle  codebase="http://java.sun.com/prod-
ucts/plugin/1.2/jinstall-12-win32.cab#Version=1,2,0,0">
<PARAM NAME = CODE VALUE = "HelloUniverse.class" >

<PARAM NAME="type" VALUE="application/x-java-applet;version=1.2">
<COMMENT>
<EMBED type="application/x-java-applet;version=1.2" java_CODE = "HelloUni-
verse.class" WIDTH = 256 HEIGHT = 256 ALIGN = middle   pluginspage="http://
java.sun.com/products/plugin/1.2/plugin-install.html"><NOEMBED></COMMENT>
<blockquote>
<hr>
If you were using a Java-capable browser,
you would see Hello Universe! instead of this paragraph.
<hr>
</blockquote>
</NOEMBED></EMBED>
</OBJECT>

<!--
<APPLET  CODE = "HelloUniverse.class" WIDTH = 256 HEIGHT = 256 ALIGN = middle >
```

```
<blockquote>
<hr>
If you were using a Java-capable browser,
you would see Hello Universe! instead of this paragraph.
<hr>
</blockquote>

</APPLET>
-->
<!--"END_CONVERTED_APPLET"-->

</BODY>
</HTML>
```

Java 3D runtime and security

In order for the client to run a Java 3D applet, the user must have the Java 3D extension installed. At the time of writing there were problems with the Java 3D installer that would sometimes prevent all of its components from being put in the correct places for running applets. Some people have also reported problems with the classpath. These problems will no doubt be fixed in a future release but in the interim, consult the Java 3D FAQ web site for guidance on how to rectify matters.

Another issue with running applets, whether Java 3D or just Java, is the possibility of having to run the Java security gauntlet. If your applet accesses resources, such as sound and texture image files from the server then there should be no problem. If, however, you want to download resources to the client along with your applet so that they can be used locally, which avoids downloads over the web at run time, then you will have to deal with security. In order to access files locally from an applet, the files must be bundled into a Java Archive (JAR) file and the file must be signed. The JDK comes with several utilities that will allow you to sign your own files, but, if you are contemplating commercial release of your application to the public, you may have to consider certification from a third party so that users downloading your application can trust it.

No example applets

For all the above reasons, the examples in the next part of the book are provided as applications, not as applets. This approach should greatly improve your chances of successfully running the examples. Hopefully the overall situation regarding Java 3D applet development and deployment will improve with the maturing of Java, Java 3D, and the consistent support for Java and its nuances in web browsers in general. The following section addresses these and other practical issues concerning 3D application deployment on the web.

14.3.2 Real-world issues

Users have grown accustomed to accessing the web and any applications found there by means of their web browsers. It is their sole portal to the cyber world and most users have become quite proficient at using their particular flavor of browser. In corporate environments, the browser vendor and version may even be dictated for cost and maintenance reasons. For commercial web application development this probably means that you will have to support both the Netscape and Microsoft browsers, and deal with the particulars of each.

Much for the user to do

The vast majority of browsers installed on machines today are very old versions. Older versions of browsers do not support Java 1.2 out of the box; many do not even support Java 1.1; and they provide no way to upgrade to a newer version of Java. Although some applications stick to Java 1.1 or 1.0 for this reason, Java 3D requires Java 1.2, which leaves many users no choice but to get a new browser. The latest browser versions do not come with a Java 1.2 VM out of the box either, but they are capable of using a Java plug-in, which comes with Sun's JRE. This was a great step forward in deploying Java content on the web because a browser with an older VM could be updated with the most recent one simply by installing a new plug-in. The latest browsers also do not come with the Java extensions and neither does the JRE. A user wanting to use Java 3D would have to download and install it separately. Because Java 3D relies on OpenGL, it is highly recommended that the target machine use the latest drivers for its specific display card, which is yet another download and install.

Much for the developer to do

Because of limited bandwidth and appreciable network delays, web applications have to be carefully constructed to avoid high bandwidth interaction between the application client, on the user's machine, and the server on the other side of the wire (fiber, ether, or whatever). For interactive 3D, this usually means that the client side tends to be heavyweight (large with many local resources), and might even require a separate user download and installation. As already mentioned, if you go the applet route you have to contend with the Java 3D installer not always getting everything in the right place; and whenever you deal with applets you have to grapple with differences between browsers as to when and whether they invoke the applet's `init`, `start`, and `stop` methods. For web applications that are visually intensive and utilize cooperating applets, this can be problematic relative to synchronization, state maintenance, and presentation refreshing. Also, if the applet will be loading files locally for speed, such as sounds, models and texture images, you will have to package them in a signed JAR file to satisfy security restrictions.

Half empty or half full?

So, what does all this mean to you as a Java 3D web application developer? What does this mean to your users? This means that a typical user will likely have to download and install a new browser, download and install the 1.2 JRE, download and install the

Java 3D extension; and they may have to download and install the latest OpenGL drivers and a Java 3D client viewer. Even if a user could find everything, and would take the time to download more than 25 megabytes of software, the current state of Java and Java 3D installation would probably leave most users swearing at their machines (perhaps more so than they do now). And, if your users could get all the software installed properly, they may still have to run the Java security gauntlet and deal with certificates and such in order to access content through an applet locally as part of the application. And this is the cyber future we are all rushing toward?

In all fairness to Java-based applications, many of the same issues would exist even if you chose a different 3D platform with the same kinds of capabilities as Java 3D (although with VRML a lot of vendor effort went into making the installation as simple, easy, and reliable as possible). Given this reality, what do we as developers do? We do what everyone else does who is caught up in the dot-com craze; we strengthen our resolve that things will get better, real soon. And they are getting better. DSL and cable modems are bringing bandwidth to the masses; each release of the JRE gets simpler and more reliable to install, and presumably the same will be true of Java 3D; browsers are becoming more accommodating when it comes to security configuration; developers and installers are getting a lot better at bundling up everything for easy installation; and there is even some hope that browsers will come bundled with a JRE and maybe even the Java extensions.

14.4   SUMMARY

Good design for 3D applications is not limited to the 3D virtual world. It must extend outside of the 3D display and into all the applications areas surrounding it. For this you can take advantage of a lot of what Java has to offer. Swing provides a rich set of 2D GUI functionality that, with care, can be mixed with Java 3D. Java DnD and the clipboard provide users the ability to easily and intuitively access data inside the scene, outside the scene, and even outside of your application, in the host operating system. And, applets and Java's networking support in general offer the promise of being able to deploy serious commercial web-based applications that provide significant capability for support of intuitive 3D user interfaces. Although the situation regarding 3D application deployment to the masses over the web is still in its infancy, and there are still many hurdles to run, the future of e-commerce on the web seems certain. The future of 3D in e-commerce seems a bit less certain but the issues are not so much the technology as they are the ability of developers to use it effectively.

This brings to a close part 3 of the book, which was a very UI-centric introduction to Java 3D and its friends. The next part will build on this Java 3D foundation to develop a lightweight framework for demonstrating many of the 3D UI techniques discussed in part 2.

PART 4

Java 3D framework and examples

This final part of the book will complete your journey from the abstract concepts of 3D applications and user interfaces to concrete demonstrations of those techniques in Java 3D. Although Java 3D is an able-bodied 3D graphics API, it extends few favors to the serious user interface developer. As seen in the previous part of the book, Java 3D provides all the necessary underpinnings for sophisticated 3D user interfaces but there is a significant gap between what Java 3D offers and what is required for functionality that approaches a Swing 3D. This leaves us with two choices: I can continue to expound on how one should go about using Java 3D to implement 3D user interfaces, or we can move to a framework that actually demonstrates some of the concepts described in the book. I choose the latter. Hopefully, you will too.

Staying true to the stated intent of this book not to get involved in the highly subjective issue of defining what is a good UI or a bad one, the examples presented here and the framework to back them up are rather simple and utilitarian. For the examples in the last few chapters one could even say that, although the techniques and their combination are rather sophisticated, the overall user experience is a bit clumsy. The purpose here is to show how the techniques can be implemented and to show possibilities. It is not to dictate what is the proper selection and combination of manipulation handles, interaction states, and feedback elements for all occasions.

Instead, such matters are left to the UI designer to figure out how best to assemble the techniques for his/her specific application and target audience. Perhaps in the not too distant future, as 3D begins to make serious inroads into everyday web applications, conventions for 3D UI design will unfold, bringing 3D cyber-consistency to the lives of designers and users alike.

CHAPTER 1 5

Why a framework?

The software framework presented here serves as a means to an end, which is to demonstrate many of the book's 3D UI techniques, and to show the reader how it is done using Java 3D. Although few designers cherish the thought of having to learn yet another framework, especially if they are already trying to learn one as complex as Java 3D, there is really no other way of getting there—Swing 3D—from here—Java 3D. It's just too big a leap. In order to reach the higher levels of UI functionality discussed in this book, there needs to be a significant support structure on top of the Java 3D foundation established in the previous part, and the framework provides it. If a bit of low-level generalization can be brought to the picture to enhance reuse, then so much the better.

To keep things simple and the pace moving, the framework will be lightweight, with just enough support to demonstrate the more significant and utilitarian concepts in the book. You might want to think of the framework as being more like scaffolding than an industrial strength framework. In any case, it does have vigor and substance, which is exemplified by its use to construct some rather sophisticated examples of proto-applications toward the end of the book. Besides showing you how to make Java 3D perform UI tricks, you should also find the framework useful for exploring and prototyping 3D UI additions to your own applications, as a UI toolkit.

One final note: I'm reluctant to suggest that the framework could serve as the basis for a Swing 3D because of its lightweight and somewhat incomplete nature. I am comfortable, however, in suggesting that it is substantial and general enough to serve as a decent prototype for what such an extension to Java 3D might resemble.

15.1 APPROACH

The following sections lay out a few guidelines and rules-of-thumb used in developing the framework. They are based on results from early exploration of Java 3D, and prototyping of the UI techniques in VRML and Java 3D. Some of these lessons learned might be good to keep in mind as you develop approaches and solutions to your own 3D UI needs.

15.1.1 Stick to the basics (when possible)

Although it's easy to get carried away while developing a framework that addresses such abstract and high-level concepts as those presented in this book, I've tried to restrain myself and stick to the underlying Java and Java 3D classes and concepts as closely as possible. For example, early on I developed a package for implementing an approximation of VRML routes, which allows the developer to easily wire up event connections between objects. In the end, however, I decided that it wasn't making a direct enough contribution to the end-goal of demonstrating the 3D techniques to justify its departure from the standard Java patterns for event handling.

This does not mean that new implementation concepts and paradigms are excluded from the framework. With such a large distance between Java 3D and some of the demonstrated UI techniques, innovation and abstraction in the framework is required. For example, the abstract concept of a control actuator is formalized in the framework, which encapsulates and generalizes the mechanism for interactively or programmatically manipulating a target object, much as an interpolator in Java 3D encapsulates time-based manipulation of objects.

15.1.2 Sun utilities

Java 3D was developed to host a wide range of applications, which is good. This, however, means that novices and veterans alike have to wade through a fair amount of boilerplate to get seemingly simple things done. To help, Sun has provided a set of utility packages under com.sun.j3d.utils. Included are such aids as a pre-configured universe in the SimpleUniverse class, interactive picking classes such as the Pick-RotateBehavior class, and primitive geometry objects such as the Box and Sphere classes.

Some of these are used in the framework and examples, in particular the geometry primitives. Many are not. The UI related utilities are structured for a somewhat different conceptual framework than that needed to support the 3D techniques in this book. They are also limited in their flexibility, being defined for a particular style of interaction. Another factor is that the Sun utilities are not part of Java 3D. As such, they are subject to change or even discontinuation.

15.1.3 Application utilities

What better way to demonstrate the UI techniques than in an application? Because of their generality, Java, Java 3D, and Swing require a fair amount of code and attention to detail to set up an application. Such boilerplate code provides opportunity for error and detracts from focusing on the real problem at hand. Some application convenience classes are in order, similar in spirit to those provided by the Sun utilities. To keep the framework relatively clean, these utility classes are segregated out and are (for the most part) not specifically required in order to use the core portion of the framework. In other words, much of the framework is usable even if you want to use the Sun application utilities, or even your own ones.

15.1.4 Progression of examples

The framework presentation is organized to correspond to that of the 3D UI techniques presented in part 2. The correspondence is by necessity only approximate because the concrete needs of a software framework do not readily conform to the tidy but abstract organization of the earlier presented concepts. Nevertheless, this organization allows the framework presentation and its examples to evolve from simple concepts to more complex ones. Such a progression of examples from simple to complex affords a certain efficiency in the presentation. Also, the parallel organization with the earlier presentation should lend an air of familiarity to the discussion, assuming of course that you've already explored the earlier parts of the book rather than diving directly into the code here.

15.1.5 Javadoc and UML

By necessity, not every aspect of the framework code is discussed. Only the more interesting and challenging aspects of making Java 3D perform are covered. Also, the emphasis of the discussion is on the 3D techniques and the Java 3D used to implement them, not the specifics of the framework implementation. Only enough of the framework is presented here to understand and use it. The rest is left for the source code and supporting `javadoc` documentation to explain. To help in understanding how the techniques are implemented, Universal Modeling Language (UML)-like class diagrams are provided to show how classes are derived and how they cooperate.

15.2 SOFTWARE ORGANIZATION

The software consists of four pieces: the framework, the examples, their documentation, and a small set of resource files. All are available as a single download and live under a common file directory, `J3duiBook`. The framework is organized as a set of Java packages, which are located in the directory `J3duiBook/lib`, and are summarized in table 15.1. The package directories include both source and class files.

Table 15.1 Java packages in the 3D UI framework

j3dui.utils	Miscellaneous utilities for testing, debugging, and application support, including model and resource loading, and picking and bounds setup. Not part of the framework core
j3dui.utils.app	Convenience classes for application support, including world, view, and display space classes, and support for printing
j3dui.utils.blocks	Functional building blocks used by the examples. Reusable and somewhat general, but too specific to be included in the framework core
j3dui.utils.objects	Pre-configured test objects, including light, thing, plane, line, and tic mark
j3dui.control	Support for UI techniques related to control
j3dui.control.actuators	Actuation events and target-specific actuator plug-ins, including translation, rotation, and scale
j3dui.control.actuators.groups	Actuator groups, including affine, center-affine, orbit, and spherical rotation
j3dui.control.inputs	Input device events, triggers, and filter plug-ins; including drag, move, button, modifier, cancel, and pause events
j3dui.control.inputs.sensors	Input device sensors for mouse and keyboard; including mouse button, move and drag, and keyboard arrow and modifier
j3dui.control.mappers	Input coordinate mapping, including object picking and overenabling.
j3dui.control.mappers.intuitive	Source space events, filter plug-ins, and mapping, including DRM and WRM
j3dui.feedback	Support for UI techniques related to feedback and group selection. Feedback events, triggers, multi-shapes, and selection managers
j3dui.feedback.elements	Basic feedback elements, including sound and transparent texture shapes for rectangle, cylinder, and cone
j3dui.visualize	Support for UI techniques related to visualization. World and display technique groups, change sensors, and change posters
j3dui.manipulate	Support for UI techniques related to manipulation. Relational feedback elements, including box outline and skirt

The examples are provided under the directory J3duiBook/examples. Each example directory and its class are named for the UI technique or framework component it demonstrates. Each directory includes both source and class files. Documentation for the framework and examples, other than provided herein are in the form of javadoc documentation, which can be accessed locally with a web browser starting with the index.html file in the J3duiBook/docs/lib and J3duiBook/docs/examples directories, respectively. In support of the examples a directory of resource files is included under J3duiBook/resources, which contains a small model catalog and some sound effects and texture images.

15.3 RUNNING THE EXAMPLES

The examples are provided under the directory `J3duiBook/examples`, with one per subdirectory. To run the examples you will need a Java 1.2 VM, the Java 3D 1.1.2 (or greater) extension, the book's j3dui library, and a VRML 97 class loader. The section on Java 3D resources in chapter 10 included links to sites for Java 3D resources. You can obtain all of the Java and Java 3D prerequisites from these sites. One of the links is a site where you can download the latest Java 3D model loaders. To run many of the examples provided with the book, you have to first download and install a VRML 97 loader; one is not included with Java 3D. A note included in the introduction to this book describes how to download the book's software from the publisher's web site.

You can execute each example from the command line or your favorite development tool, but first you have to either include the book's class library, `J3duiBook/lib`, in your classpath, or specify it on the command line for the Java interpreter. If you are running under Windows or NT, you can simply double-click from the file Explorer on the .bat file included in each example directory. It will take care of including the book's library on the command line for you.

15.4 DESIGN PATTERNS

User interfaces are by their nature event-driven: The user moves the mouse or presses a key and the system responds with a visual display change and perhaps an audio sound effect. As such, events and their handling form the nervous system of the framework. Another major characteristic of the framework is its use of building blocks. Many of the low-level UI techniques presented earlier in the book can be packaged as small functional components—building blocks—that are not too particular about where data comes from or where it goes to. Building blocks can easily be swapped in or out of the event chain to customize the nature of the UI control, feedback, and visualization.

The rest of this section describes the general patterns and naming conventions used in the framework. Specific classes will be covered in the chapters that follow. Because there are only so many good names to go around, some names here mean what the pattern "standards" say they should mean, and others are close but the specific meaning or the particular mechanics have been adapted for a different purpose. In any case, the patterns that are used are straightforward, so any deviations from the standards should be easy to follow.

15.4.1 Event model generalities

Because events and their handling are so prevalent in the framework, it's worth spending time discussing the particulars of the framework's event model. The building block nature of the framework cries out for an event model based on the Filter design pattern, specifically the push or sink form. In this pattern, the source object holds a reference to the target (sink) object, and an event and its data are sent (pushed) to the target when the source calls a set method in the target's event interface. This makes framework event-handling fairly lightweight and generic, with event types being defined by simple interfaces instead of with separate event classes as in the AWT. Also, any building block can connect to another building block so long as the source can delegate to the same event interface that the target implements (i.e., the output and input event interfaces match). You'll see more about the structure of building blocks later.

With this event model, the focus is on the UI action itself and its data, instead of the physical nature and ultimate source of the event as in an AWT event. In other words, the framework is more concerned with the fact that a drag gesture occurred than with identifying how it was generated and the specific button presses and releases that were used. This higher level conceptualization of events affords them a certain anonymity, which helps to keep generic the events and the building blocks that process them. It also removes any distinction between device-generated events and those generated by the system programmatically.

In concept and purpose, but not form, the framework's event model is not unlike that used by VRML. In VRML, connections between building blocks are called *routes*. Routes are unidirectional and possess both an event quality (something happened) and a data message quality (complete self-contained data package). It is the responsibility of whoever creates the route to determine the semantics of the event and its data (why was it sent and what should be done with it), which is accomplished by selecting specific fields (interfaces) on specific objects as the source and target ends of the route.

15.4.2   Event model specifics

In the framework an event comes from an *event source* object and goes to an *event target* object. Unlike the Java AWT, framework events are not objects. Instead, an event is simply a method call that the source makes on the target object. An event "connection" consists of a lightweight event target interface—many have only one method. As with VRML routes, the interface methods are designed to have qualities of both an event and a self-contained data package. Consistent with their function, the names of event target interfaces end in target, such as in `EnableTarget`, which is the interface for an enable event, whose data is a single boolean value. Event connections are typically established between building blocks when the source building block is constructed, with the event target being the first argument in most building block class constructors.

In the following code fragment, `EnableTarget` is the event target interface, `EnableFilter` is a building block, and `MyExample` is a test class. The filter implements `EnableTarget` as its event input and accepts an `EnableTarget` argument as its event output. Notice how `MyExample` chains one filter as the target of the next filter. You will see this pattern often in the framework, where the ultimate source in an event chain is at the *bottom* of the code segment, and the ultimate target is at the *top*.

```
// target interface for "enable" events
public interface EnableTarget {
  public void setEnable(boolean enable);
}

// building block with EnableTarget input and output
public class EnableFilter implements EnableTarget {
  private EnableTarget _target;

  // EnableFilter constructor
  public EnableFilter(target) {
    _target = target;
    ...
  }

  public EnableTarget getEventTarget() {
    return _target;
  }

  // EnableTarget implementation
  setEnable(boolean enable) {
    // handle input event and process data
    ...

    // send result as output event to target
    _target.setEnable(enable);
  }
}

// test example with chained building blocks
public class MyExample {
  // build filter chain with last block first
  ...
  EnableFilter filt2 = new EnableFilter(filt3);
  EnableFilter filt1 = new EnableFilter(filt2);
  EnableFilter filt0 = new EnableFilter(filt1);
  ...
}
```

15.4.3 Building blocks

Consistent with the framework event model, *building blocks* are generally based on the push Filter pattern. The building-block inputs are the event interfaces that it implements, and its outputs are to delegated event interfaces of the same or different type. You saw the basic structure for a building block in the previous code fragment. In that case both the input and output event type was EnableTarget.

To keep implementation simple, the convention for building blocks is that they have a single event target that is passed as an argument only in the constructor. There are no setEventTarget or addEventTarget methods, but there is a getEvent-

`Target` method. Another convention is that the event target can not be `null`, which avoids having to test for null at runtime.

15.4.4 Splitters

Because by convention building blocks have only a single target (a fan-out of one), a separate *splitter* building block (a.k.a., a multi-caster) must be used. Conceptually a splitter splits a single event connection into many. It does this by re-sending its input event to all the event targets registered in the splitter's target list.

Splitter names end in "splitter," such as `EnableSplitter`. Splitter base classes include the usual list modifier methods: `addEventTarget`, `removeEventTarget`, and `clearEventTargets`. They also include the method `getEventTargets` that returns a target list iterator, which parallels the function of the `getEventTarget` method in other types of building blocks.

15.4.5 Triggers

A *trigger* is a building block that monitors one type of event for a particular condition or set of conditions. When the condition is met, an output event of a different type is generated, typically in the form of an enable event. Trigger names end in "trigger," such as `InputModifierTrigger`. Triggers typically include an `initEventTarget` method to initialize the event target during trigger setup, after the event chain has been established.

15.4.6 Filters

As used in the framework, a *filter* specifically refers to a building block whose input and output event type is the same. Filter names end in "filter," such as `EnableFilter`. In general, the filter class itself is only a shell that implements the common building block methods, such as those in the event target interface. The specific filtering algorithm is provided as a plug-in.

15.4.7 Mappers

Most building blocks that convert one event type to another are called *mappers*. As with filters, mappers are implemented as a building block shell with a plug-in providing the specific type of mapping performed. Mapper names end in "mapper," such as `InputDragMapper`. The term "mapper" is in recognition of the fact that most event translation in the framework is a result of spatial or data coordinate transformation. In the framework, mapping also includes *picking*, which can be thought of as a conversion from spatial mouse location to logical object identification.

Mappers tend to be the most complex type of building block in the framework. This is because data conversion is often under- or overspecified, which means there is either not enough or too much information available to completely or uniquely transform data from the source to the target space. As such, mappers often require the designer to state certain assumptions about the mapping that is to be performed, such as the object the source space is defined relative to, or the 3D vector representing the axis for a scalar rotation.

15.4.8 Plug-ins

A *plug-in* class and the classes that use it, such as filters and mappers, are based on the Strategy pattern. In the Strategy pattern, the host object is provided with an object that encapsulates the strategy or algorithm needed by the host to perform a service for a client. In certain situations this pattern helps to avoid a proliferation of classes that would otherwise result if every type of host class had to be combined with every type of algorithm as a separate class. A good example of the Strategy pattern is the AWT layout manager, which allows different window layout strategies to be plugged into a window container.

In the framework, a building block host class provides the common event handling, but can't really do anything useful without a plug-in. In some sense the plug-in host is like an empty shell of a building block, with the plug-in providing it with its reason for being. Although plug-ins are usually specific to a particular type of host class, the host type is often dropped from the name because the association is clear. Plug-in names end in "plugin," such as `RelativeInputDragPlugin`, which is a plug-in for an `InputDragFilter`.

15.5 CONVENIENCE

One of the principles guiding the development of the framework is that, where reasonable, the framework should take care of the boilerplate code needed to get Java 3D to do common or reasonably expected things. The application utility classes mentioned previously are an example of this. Another area that the framework addresses regarding convenience is the setting of capability bits and spatial bounds.

In general, it is not a good idea to go around automatically setting capability bits for the user because this could have an adverse affect on performance. In the framework, however, there are situations where it is clear from the function of a building block that the objects it references must be accessed in a particular way for the building block to work. In these situations the framework can safely assume that it is OK to set capability bits automatically. For example, the way picking is done in the framework is that the pick engine is supplied with a list of candidate target nodes to monitor. A target node can only be picked, however, if its capability bits are set for pick reporting. When the picking engine is given the target list, the engine automatically sets pick reporting on each target node.

The case for automatically setting scheduling bounds is less clear. By default, the scheduling bounds of a Behavior is null, which means it won't work unless the scheduling bounds is set. In building blocks that involve display interaction, such as dragging the mouse or pressing a keyboard key, the framework automatically sets the scheduling bounds of the Behavior base class.

15.6   OPTIMIZATION

Another guiding principle used in the development of the framework is that optimization is good, but only up to a point. A corollary is that, if a feature doesn't adversely affect performance, then use it. As is often the case with optimization, most of the gain will come from implementing the few improvements that have the largest effect. Optimization can be difficult to implement and generally complicates your code. Make certain that whatever optimization you do is really worth it. Similarly, before dismissing a desirable approach or feature because of suspected poor performance, make sure that the performance hit is real.

Unfortunately, there does not seem to be much hard information available in the community regarding what really counts when it comes to Java 3D optimization. This is understandable because setting up good benchmarks and apples-to-apples comparisons across platforms are no small undertakings. As Java 3D matures, such conventional wisdom should develop. In the meantime, the following sections describe how the framework addressed—or chose not to address—various concerns regarding optimization. Decisions were based on a bit of experimentation, a bit of community feedback, a bit of conventional wisdom, and a bit of guessing as to how Sun may have implemented parts of Java 3D.

15.6.1   Garbage collection

Garbage collection (GC) can be a real problem for user interface intensive applications. The effect can be perceived as significant "stuttering" as the view or objects in the view are manipulated interactively. As with Java VMs, GCs can be designed to optimize certain performance characteristics. Unfortunately, the GC used in Sun's standard run time environment is not very charitable when it comes to Java 3D interaction. (At the time of writing, Sun's Java 1.3 Hotspot VM, which is in beta, seems to run a bit better than the 1.2 VM, but GC still seems to be a problem. GC may be better tuned for interactive use in a future release.) The stutter occurs when the GC wakes up every so often to clean house. Because the GC has a higher execution priority than anything Java 3D or your code has, Java 3D and your code have to wait. The quantity and frequency of garbage generation affects the length and frequency of the stutter (but in some indirect and nonlinear way). Even if you were able to eliminate all garbage generation from your code, keep in mind that the Java 3D API itself can generate garbage, so GC stutter can't be entirely eliminated. Each release of Java 3D has made strides towards minimizing its internal garbage generation, and no doubt future releases will continue this trend.

The best way to avoid GC stutter is to avoid generating garbage. Garbage is created every time a temporary object is created with new, and the object subsequently goes out of scope, such as at the end of a method call. The object then becomes a candidate for cleanup by the GC. The nature of programming in Java 3D is that it is conducive to the creation of temporary variables. For example, as part of geometrically manipulating an object, you might do something like the following:

```
Transform3D xform = new Transform3D();
xform.setEuler(new Vector3d(0, rotY, 0));
xform.setTranslation(new Vector3d(posX, 0, -10));
TransformGroup mover = new TransformGroup(xform);
```

In this seemingly innocent code fragment, four objects have been created (count the number of times new appears) that will likely become garbage. If this garbage were created only once in setting up a static world, then there wouldn't be much of a problem because you would take a GC hit only once at startup. If, however, this were done every time the mouse moved, then you likely would see GC stutter as you interactively manipulated objects in your Java 3D application.

In general the framework avoids the creation of temporary objects in methods that are subject to repetitive calling, such as in the implementation of the event interface methods. The way to avoid temporary objects is to create them once, ahead of time, as a dummy instance or class variable. Because a dummy object is not intended to maintain the state of an instance, it can and perhaps should be declared as a class variable, unless of course threading is an issue (which the framework gingerly sidesteps—everything executes in the initiating system event's thread).

Experimentation has shown that the use of dummy objects can have a significant effect on reducing GC stutter. Also, the impact on code complexity and clarity is not too severe. For these reasons the framework uses dummy objects whenever possible. The following code sample shows the previous one redone with dummy objects to inoculate it against GC stutter.

```
public class MyClass {
    // dummy class objects
    private static final Transform3D _xform = new Transform3D();
    private static final Vector3d _vector = new Vector3d ();
    ...
    public moveIt(double rotY, double posX,
     TransformGroup mover) {
        _vector.set(0, rotY, 0);
        _xform.setEuler(_vector);
        _vector.set(posX, 0, -10);
        _xform.setTranslation(_vector);
        mover.setTransform(_xform);
    }
}
```

15.6.2   Many small building blocks

When it comes to efficiency, everything is relative. What may in isolation seem like an expensive practice might, in the bigger picture, be a minor factor in overall performance. With this in mind, the framework uses many small building blocks strung together in event chains to achieve a particular UI effect. A first impression upon seeing these long building block chains might be that this is an inefficient way to do things. However, in the larger context, the contribution from all the method calls and argument passing in the interface connections between the building blocks is insignificant compared to activities elsewhere in the system. The execution overhead of a dozen or so building-block connections pales in comparison to the execution load from Java 3D's scene rendering, or the application's spatial transformations for in-scene object manipulation.

15.6.3 Dragging, keying, and picking

Experimentation, with confirmation from Sun, indicates that Java 3D handles display-related events, such as dragging the mouse or hitting a keyboard key, rather efficiently. This fact together with the philosophy of lots of little building blocks means that the framework does not shy away from using plenty of input sensors that monitor specific conditions on specific events in a specific display. For example, if an application needs to monitor two different displays for mouse drag and arrow key input to drive in-scene object manipulation, then four sensors might be used: one for the mouse, plus one for the arrow keys, times two for the two displays. Picking is another matter.

Picking is a very expensive operation in Java 3D (more expensive than it needs to be, but that may be addressed in future releases of Java 3D). If picking is performed only when a mouse button is clicked—discrete picking—then the cost of the pick will likely go unnoticed. If, however, continuous picking is needed, such as for mouse-over feedback or in-scene WRM object manipulation, then the pick cost will be clearly evident in the interactive performance, even for relatively simple scenes. As a consequence, the framework tries to disable picking whenever it is not needed, which is generally not the case for other less expensive operations—it is usually not worth the trouble. Also, the framework tries to include cheaper alternatives where possible, such as using relatively inexpensive ray-plane intersection to compute in-scene mouse position in lieu of full-blown object picking.

15.6.4 Double versus float

With a few good guesses, and confirmation from Sun, it seems that there is not much to be gained by using `float` instead of `double` type variables and methods, at least where shape geometry is not involved. As it turns out, Java 3D performs all geometry rendering using float arithmetic, but it performs most other computation, such as matrix-based spatial transformations, using double arithmetic. Because the framework doesn't deal with shape geometry directly, for the sake of simplicity and consistency throughout, it uses `double` type variables and methods parameters exclusively.

15.6.5 Capabilities and compiling

Although not much experimentation was done regarding the benefits of capability bits and scene compilation, feedback from others is that there is not much of a penalty for setting capabilities, nor much of a gain for compilation. This is supposed to change with future releases, so the framework generally avoids setting capability bits unless necessary. It avoids using compilation, however, because it complicates scene graph configuration even when the subgraph is dead.

15.7   SUMMARY

This chapter pleaded the case for developing a lightweight but rather lofty framework on top of Java 3D for supporting the 3D UI techniques discussed in the first half of the book. Although the primary goal of the framework is for it to serve as a vehicle for developing 3D UI examples and for demonstrating Java 3D in action, it might also serve as a good starting point for a future Swing 3D extension. A respectable amount of effort has been invested in organizing the framework, tying it to design patterns, and documenting it with `javadoc` and UML-like diagrams. The framework's approach to optimization is intentionally limited. Only those aspects that offer the most bang for the buck (while not unduly obfuscating the code) are addressed, such as avoidance of temporary objects. The framework takes a building-block approach to UI development, with small functional modules being strung together to achieve more sophisticated functionality.

The remainder of the book will introduce you to the framework proper, and describe and demonstrate how it uses Java 3D to implement many of the previously introduced 3D UI techniques.

Framework utilities

The framework is roughly divided into core functionality and utilities. The core provides low level 3D UI support in a general manner that is intended not to be specific to a given application or UI style. The utilities, on the other hand, provide a mixture of high- and low-level convenience classes, some of which are general in nature and others are quite specific to the application-like needs of the examples. They cover such diverse topics as test objects, display printing, data loading, debug message generation, and the application UI spaces. They also include most of the application-specific building blocks used to build the examples. Strictly speaking, the core does not rely on the utility classes (or, at least not much), but they can certainly make things easier for you, the designer, and can give you a head start in understanding how to use the core functionality.

Before diving into the framework core, this chapter takes a look at the utilities that accompany it. As with the introduction to Java 3D in the previous part of the book, you may want to follow along in the `javadoc` documentation, for this chapter as well as for the others about the framework. All of the framework classes discussed in this chapter are found in and under the package `j3dui.utils`.

16.1 TEST OBJECTS

A set of standard test objects is provided with the utilities, which are used in many of the framework examples. They encapsulate some of the boilerplate configuration code associated with setting up visible and nonvisible objects, and have been specifically configured for general use under a wide range of conditions. These classes are found in the package `j3dui.utils.objects`.

16.1.1 Shapes

The `TestThing`, `TestPlane`, and `TestTic` visible objects are based on the `Box` and `Sphere` primitive objects provided with the Sun utilities. The `TestLine` object is a simple line constructed directly as a shape node using a `LineArray` geometry object. The objects are configured for geometry picking (their leaf shape geometry can be intersected), for lighting (normals are generated, shapes are colored or configured for lighting), and for live color change (appearance can be written).

The test tic can be positioned in the local coordinate space and is intended for marking a host object. The test line's endpoints can be arbitrarily set, which makes it a good shape for measuring in-scene distances during debugging. The `TestPlane` class defines a thin box that can be sized and colored, and is used in the examples as a floor or wall.

The `TestThing` class defines an object consisting of a ball embedded in a thin box with small tic marks at its *X*, *Y*, and *Z*-axis extents. It is used in many of the early examples, and provides a nice 3D shape that works well for testing placement, rotation, and scaling. The box and ball components can be colored independently. Included with the class are sets of standard test colors representing feedback interaction states, with the box colors indicating status and selection states, and the ball colors indicating action state. For example, `BOX_NORMAL_0` is the box color used in the examples for when the object status is "normal" and its selection state is "0" (normal); and `BALL_PAUSE` is the ball color used when the object action state is "pause." If large numbers of `TestThing` objects are used in the scene, then rendering can start to get sluggish because the spherical ball contains quite a few polygons. For faster rendering, `TestThing` supports a fast version of the ball, which is a simple cube. Use the `setFast` class method to set the ball shape prior to instantiating any `TestThing` objects.

16.1.2 Lights

The `TestLight` class is a thin wrapper around the Java 3D `Light` class. The wrapper enables the light and sets its influencing bound to infinity so that the light affects all objects in the world no matter how far away from the light they are. The default light is a medium intensity white `PointLight`, but you can pass in your own light if you want a different type light or set of attributes. If the light can be positioned, such as a `PointLight`, then it can be included with a view and used as a "headlight" to illuminate the objects seen in the view, which is what the example utility blocks do.

16.2 APPLICATION SPACES

Included in the utilities is a set of useful classes that correspond to the application UI spaces introduced earlier in the book. Besides providing software analogs to the conceptual coordinate spaces, they take care of some of the boilerplate code needed to set up Java 3D. These classes are found in the package j3dui.utils.app. An example at the end of the section shows you how to construct a simple Java 3D application using them.

16.2.1 AppWorld class

The AppWorld class represents an application's *world space*. It extends VirtualUniverse, contains a single scene graph, and includes a dim ambient "nightlight." The night light allows you to see objects in the world even if you forget to add room lights or head lights, which is more helpful than leaving you staring at a black screen wondering what might be wrong. (This assumes that the scene objects are configured with an ambient light appearance, such as is done in the framework's visible test objects.)

The scene graph is divided into *scene* and *view* branches, which are useful if you need to clear the world's scene without clearing its views. You can also put nonvisible objects in the view branch that you don't want cleared with the scene, such as behaviors. The methods getSceneRoot and getViewRoot get the root BranchGroup objects of the two subgraphs; addSceneNode and addViewNode add nodes to the two roots; and clearScene clears all nodes under the scene root while leaving the view subgraph intact. (At the time of writing, clearing the scene graph eliminated the objects from the scene and scene graph, but Java 3D fails to free the memory associated with them, which is a bug.) Note that the distinction between the view and scene branch is by convention only. As far as Java 3D is concerned, there is no difference between them.

The "liveness" of the scene graph is explicitly managed through the setLive method. A value of true causes the object's scene graph root to attach to the universe's single Locale, thereby making the scene graph live. Setting it false causes the scene graph to detach, making it dead and, because no compilation is used in the framework or examples, readily accessible. Many of the methods in AppWorld automatically control the liveness of the scene graph so that scene graph operations such as adding or clearing nodes can be performed without having to first set capability bits. Because of the liveness management, nodes should only be added and accessed through the methods provided with this class rather than through the API. AppWorld will not manage nodes that you add directly to its Locale.

16.2.2 AppView class

The AppView class represents an application's *view space*. It extends BranchGroup and includes the view's display, in the form of an AppDisplay object. In order to see the virtual world you have to create an AppView, add it to the view branch in AppWorld, and add its display to the application's window. An application can have more than one view of the virtual world by using multiple `AppView` objects. Keep in mind that, by default, Java 3D adds objects to the world at the world origin, including views. To see an object located at the origin you will have to first move the view back away from the origin using a transform group above the view in the scene graph, which is easy for beginners to forget to do.

The view space is represented by a subgraph separate from the `ViewPlatform` itself. Keeping objects that are in the view space, such as a headlight or an avatar body, under a separate view root allows them to be added and cleared without affecting the `ViewPlatform`, its attached view, or the view's attached display. The method `getRoot` returns the view root, `addNode` adds a node to the root, and `clearView` clears the view root subgraph. (Note that the Java 3D API declares the `addChild` method as final, which prevents its use here and in other classes that extend API classes for adding child nodes.) To maintain the integrity of the view subgraph, nodes should be accessed only through the methods provided. They should not be added directly to `AppView` using `addChild`.

Several methods allow access to the view object's internal geometry as it is defined in chapter 3, including VSF, DSF, DVO, and FOV. Due to bugs and complications with the Java 3D view model, there appears to be no way to cleanly determine or decouple VSF, DSF, and DVO. Until the situation improves, the framework assumes a DSF of 1.0 and a DVO of (0, 0). Also, the VSF is computed assuming that the image plate is 1 meter from the user's virtual eye, and that the view scale tracks the display window size, which is the view model default.

16.2.3 AppDisplay class

The `AppDisplay` class represents an application's *display space*. It extends `Canvas3D` and includes several methods for obtaining internal display and screen geometry, including the display and screen size in pixels, and the screen resolution in pixels per meter. It also includes the means for capturing the display image, which is necessary for printing the display, which is covered in a later section.

The `Canvas3D` superclass provides the internal display geometry but, as already discussed in chapter 11, the Java `Toolkit` class is used to obtain the screen geometry instead of the Java 3D `Screen3D` object associated with `Canvas3D`.

16.2.4   Example: SimpleApp

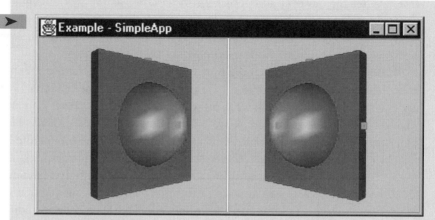

Figure 16.1   Screen shot of the SimpleApp example

This example demonstrates how to build a simple Java 3D application using the framework UI space application utility classes. (See chapter 15 for details about running the book's examples.)

> ➤ See

The application window contains dual 3D displays of the virtual world, which contains a single test object. Each view contains its own headlight. The displays show the target object from left and right vantage points. A screen shot is provided in figure 16.1.

> ➤ Do

- Study the source code (included below).
- Run the example with debugging enabled (described in the Debug class section).

> ➤ Observe

- Because each view has its own headlight, you may see two glints on the test object ball.
- A significant amount of the code is spent positioning and orienting the static views. The framework can simplify such operations and make them interactive.
- If debugging was enabled, debug messages should have printed to the console.

The code for the SimpleApp example is shown below. Notice how the virtual world is created using AppWorld, the two 3D views are constructed using AppView, and their displays are added to the window using AppDisplay. The content of the virtual world is a single TestThing object and the two view objects. The "debug" statements in main will be explained in a later section, as part of the discussion about the Debug class.

Filename: J3duiBook/examples/SimpleApp/SimpleApp.java

```java
public class SimpleApp extends Frame {

   public static void main(String[] argv) {
      Debug.loadAllProperties();
      Debug.println("hello.world", "Hello world!");
      Debug.println("hello.sun", "Hello sun!");

      new SimpleApp();
   }

   // public interface ========================================

   public SimpleApp() {
      super("Example - SimpleApp");

      new HelpDialog(this, "Help - SimpleApp",
       "An example of a 'simple' application with dual " +
        ...
      );

      // kill the window on close
      addWindowListener(new WindowAdapter() {
         public void windowClosing(WindowEvent winEvent) {
            System.exit(0);
         }
      });

      // build the UI spaces
      AppWorld world = new AppWorld();
      AppView viewL = new AppView();
      AppView viewR = new AppView();

      // add the displays to the window
      setLayout(new GridLayout(1,2,2,2));
      add(viewL.getDisplay());
      add(viewR.getDisplay());

      // build and add the scene objects
      world.addSceneNode(new TestThing());

      // build and add the view objects
      world.addViewNode(
       BasicBlocks.buildView(viewL,
       new Vector3d(-3.3, 0, 8),
       new Vector3d(0, -Math.PI/8, 0)
      ));

      world.addViewNode(
```

```
    BasicBlocks.buildView(viewR,
      new Vector3d(3.3, 0, 8),
      new Vector3d(0, Math.PI/8, 0)
    ));

    // make the scene graph live
    world.setLive(true);

    // size and show the window
    setSize(400, 200);
    show();
  }
}
```

Each view is constructed using the utility building block method `buildView` found in the `BasicBlocks` class. This class is a repository for common high-level utility methods used in the basic framework examples here and in the next chapter. The `buildView` method is shown below. It builds a transform group and adds the view object passed in with the constructor to it. It also adds a `TestLight` headlight to the view. Thus, each view in the example contains its own headlight, which is why you might see two light glints on the `TestThing` ball in the displays. Notice that a significant portion of the code for the example is in the `buildView` method, which statically positions and orients the view. As we get further into the framework you'll see ways to simplify such operations and to make them interactive.

Building block for positioning and orienting a view

Filename: J3duiBook/lib/j3dui/utils/blocks/BasicBlocks.java:
```
...
/**
Attaches the view to a TransformGroup, positions and
rotates it, and adds a headlight.
@param view View to be attached.
@param pos Position of view.
@param rot Euler rotation of view.
@return TransformGroup with view attached.
*/
public static final TransformGroup buildView(
  AppView view, Vector3d pos, Vector3d rot) {

    // create group, add view.
    TransformGroup group = new TransformGroup();
    group.addChild(view);

    // rotate and position the group.
    Transform3D xform = new Transform3D();
    xform.setEuler(rot);
    xform.setTranslation(pos);
    group.setTransform(xform);
```

```
    // add a headlight to the view.
    view.addNode(new TestLight());

    return group;
}
...
```

16.3 OTHER UTILITIES

The framework provides a number of other utilities and helper classes as part of the
`j3dui.utils` packages. Some are high-level and others are low-level. All provide
common functionality that falls outside of the framework's UI core. The higher-level
ones are covered here. The lower-level ones will be covered in later chapters, as they
are needed in the examples.

16.3.1 Building blocks

The examples are developed as simple applications that demonstrate progressively
more sophisticated and complex UI techniques. The intent of the framework core is
to be general in nature—without prejudice as to UI style. Its classes serve as general
purpose UI building blocks. Specific examples, however, require specific combinations and configurations of the framework core functionality. These needs are satisfied by sets of somewhat application-specific building blocks, which greatly simplify
the implementation of the examples. They also serve as examples of how to use the
framework core classes to satisfy specific UI needs. Many are general enough to be
used as-is in other applications, perhaps giving you a further head start in your own
3D UI work. An example of such a building block, the `buildView` method from the
`BasicBlocks` class, was shown in the previous code sample.

Each utility class in the `j3dui.utils.blocks` package provides class methods
that are used to implement closely related examples in a chapter. To keep pace with
the examples, these application-specific building blocks become progressively more
sophisticated with each chapter. Although not the most object-oriented of approaches
in that the methods are not easily extended, they are easy to use and can be readily
combined to form more sophisticated building blocks. For example, the `Actua-
tionBlocks` class, which is introduced in chapter 18, contains a method called
`buildRelativeDragger` that provides a somewhat generalized version of a direct-
action, relative-origin, input-control primitive that handles both mouse and keyboard
input. This building block is sufficiently general and high level enough that it is used
in subsequent examples as-is. Another method, `buildDirectMapper`, is from the
same class and is also general in nature, but it is a much lower-level building block.
It is used in many of the higher-level building blocks developed for later examples.

16.3.2   Display printing

Although Java 3D will likely include built-in support for printing in the future, at the time of writing it does not. The framework provides utility classes which, when used in conjunction with AppDisplay, provide support for previewing and printing a Java 3D display image. They are found in the package j3dui.utils.app. The FancyApp example, which is covered later, demonstrates how these classes can be used in an application.

The ImageCanvas class extends Canvas to provide support for loading an image and displaying it. Consistent with the notion of an image intended for printing, it preserves the display image aspect ratio regardless of the canvas size. One of its constructors accepts an AppDisplay object, whose getImage method is used to capture a snapshot of its 3D display image. The ImagePrinter class implements Printable to provide printing support. It prints the image passed to it during construction, such as the image maintained in an ImageCanvas object. Before initiating the print job, ImagePrinter pops up a dialog box allowing print parameters to be entered by the user.

The PrintFrame class extends Jframe and pulls all of these classes together into a print preview frame. It uses an ImageCanvas object provided during construction to display the print image. Pressing the frame's Print button causes an Image-Printer object to be built from the canvas image and printed.

16.3.3   Debug class

The Debug class found in the j3dui.utils package provides generalized support for debug message generation, and is used throughout the framework. Debug messages are placed in your code with the print and println class methods.

A nice feature of Debug is that you can tag print statements with a key string so that the message is printed only if its tag is enabled. With this feature you can leave debugging statements in your code and selectively turn them on at run time. Tags and other debugging controls can be specified programmatically or through -D properties that you pass to the Java interpreter on the command line when you execute your code. The debug.enabled property value specifies whether or not debugging is enabled. The debug.tags property specifies a list of comma or semi-colon delimited tags whose corresponding messages will be printed. Use the loadAllProperties method at the beginning of your code to conveniently load these property values into Debug.

The SampleApp example above showed how to set up Debug and contained two tagged messages. To run the example so that it prints both of its debug messages, tagged with hello.world and hello.sun, you would enter the following on the command line (or use the .bat file included in the example directory):

```
> java -Ddebug.enabled=true -Ddebug.tags=hello.world,hello.sun SimpleApp
```

When the program runs it prints the following:

```
Debug: Enabled...
Debug: Adding tags [hello.world,hello.sun]...
Hello world!
Hello sun!
```

For even finer control over printing, provisions are included to associate an object instance with a debug statement, which allows debugging of objects instead of classes. Then, when that instance is included for debugging using the `setObj` class method, any debug messages associated with it are printed. Debug tags and objects can be combined such that messages are printed only if both conditions are satisfied.

Although `Debug` has provisions for disabling printing, this does not prevent your code from spending time processing the arguments passed to the print methods. If performance is a concern then you should always place `Debug` print method calls inside of a conditional block, such as in the following code sample. In it the debug message `Actuator.initActuation: input=<value>` will be printed if debugging is enabled, and the message's `this` object and `Actuator.init` tag are specified for debugging.

```
if(Debug.getEnabled()){
   Debug.println(this, "Actuator.init",
     "Actuator.initActuation: input=" + value);
}
```

16.3.4   Assert class

The `Assert` class allows you to assert that a condition in your code should be true. If the asserted condition is false, then, depending on the particular print method used, a message might be printed, a stack trace might be generated, and/or an exception might be thrown. As with `Debug`, `Assert` is enabled through system properties.

16.3.5   ModelLoader class

The `ModelLoader` class in the `j3dui.utils` package provides a single convenient source for loading models from various sources, including VRML files and Java 3D model classes referenced through their corresponding ".java" and ".class" file names, such as `TestThing.java` and `TestThing.class`.

The `ModelLoader` class uses trial-and-error to locate and load the named model file. For example, the `loadModelFromName` method first attempts to load the model as VRML and, if that fails, then as a class. In all cases the name is tried as a URL and, if that fails, then as a file path. Class loading is a bit more complicated because the class name must be inferred from the URL/file path. First the name is converted to a package name. Then, each time the load fails, the head element in the package name is removed and the load is again attempted. Although crude and not foolproof, it is nevertheless convenient.

Note that in order for VRML loading to work, which is used in many of the examples, you *must* first install a Java 3D VRML loader because, at the time of writing, one does not come with Sun's Java 3D installation. Refer to section 10.6, on Java 3D resources, for a web site where model loaders can be downloaded.

16.4 SUMMARY

Before digging into the framework core, this chapter introduced the framework utilities. The utilities are separated from the core because the core does not rely on them. They are provided more as a convenience, with general support for some of the more common 3D application needs, such as printing; and with specific support for all the framework examples, mostly in the form of functional building blocks specific to a given example. Of particular note are the classes that support the UI application spaces—world, view, and display. They take care of much of the Java 3D boilerplate code for setting up an application. As a special bonus, utilities for printing, debugging, and model loading are also included. Several of the utility classes, which are more special-purpose in nature, will be introduced later, as they are encountered in the examples.

Control basics

This chapter begins the presentation of the 3D UI framework core. The core provides the architectural building blocks that support implementation of the UI techniques described in the first half of the book. It is also by far the largest portion of the framework. The order and organization of the coming chapters roughly parallel that of the 3D UI techniques described in part 2. As there, the discussion here starts with control. Control is the portion of the UI that lets the user interact with an application. It is the first half of the interaction dialog that occurs between the user and the application. The other half is Feedback.

Control is a fun subject because there is a lot to do and see. It is also a complex subject that requires a significant amount of "scaffolding" to reach such lofty goals as DRM and WRM in a somewhat generalized manner. This chapter covers the basics of control. These start with getting events from input devices and end with using those events to perform simple target object manipulation, such as translation, rotation, and color change. The next chapter will generalize the notion of target control in the form of actuation and actuators, which, although basic in concept, are advanced in implementation.

The framework's event model was described earlier as forming its nervous system. The control basics covered in this chapter and the next constitute its backbone. Both the event model and control basics are covered in some detail because they are important to establishing a working knowledge of the framework. Don't be put off by the length of the first few chapters, however. The framework concepts and patterns presented here are straightforward, but there are many of them. Also, because this is your first chance to see real framework building blocks and examples in action, the discussion starts out simply. In later chapters, as more and more of the framework is established, and as you become familiar with it, the pace of the discussion will increase accordingly. All of the classes covered in this chapter can be found in and under the `j3dui.control` package.

17.1 INPUT SENSORS

Control interpretation starts with user input provided through input devices. In a POCS, physical input devices are few and simple—the mouse and the keyboard. In the context of UI software, it is helpful to break out device inputs into several input event types. The Java AWT does this by organizing events by physical device (mouse, keyboard) and physical device action (mouse move, button down, key pressed). The framework, with a somewhat different agenda, sets its sights higher.

In the framework, we are more interested in the intent of the user action than in the physical activity that initiated it. For example, AWT reports that "a key was pressed" and provides the key code, whereas the framework reports that "the modifier state changed" and provides the new collective modifier state. This isn't too radical a change, but for the framework it provides an approach to event classification and handling that is focused more on functional control interpretation than on low-level device handling.

17.1.1 Input class

Closely associated with input event handling is the `Input` class, which is found in the `j3dui.control.inputs` package. This simple class provides many of the low-level utilities and constants used by the framework to resolve and specify input device state. Partly to simplify state definition, partly because of usability considerations for the POCS user, and partly because of the way Java overloads mouse buttons and modifier keys, the framework defines the mouse button and modifier key states as single-valued choices instead of the usual multi-valued bit flags. For example, the mouse button state can have a value of BUTTON_NONE, BUTTON_FIRST, BUTTON_SECOND, or BUTTON_THIRD. It can not have a state value of BUTTON_FIRST *and* BUTTON_THIRD.

As you'll see, some combinations of buttons and keys (not states) are supported, such as MODIFIER_SHIFT_CTRL, but many are not. If a constant for a particular combination is not provided in the `Input` class, then the corresponding state for that combination is "none." For example, if both the first and third mouse buttons were down, then the resulting state would be BUTTON_NONE since there is no BUTTON_FIRST_THIRD state.

Button states

You may have noticed that the framework does not use the AWT button constants to name its mouse button states. This was done for three reasons: to acknowledge the UI prioritization of the buttons; to avoid ambiguity in situations where the left and right buttons may be reversed for other-handed configurations; and to emphasize the fact that the constants represent states, and not simply buttons. The framework mouse button states are defined as follows.

- MOUSE_NONE: No buttons are down, or the button combination is not recognized.
- MOUSE_FIRST: The primary button is active, which is Button 1 in the AWT. On most systems this is the left button by default.
- MOUSE_SECOND: The secondary button is active, which is Button 3 in the AWT. On most systems this is the right button by default.
- MOUSE_THIRD: The tertiary button is active, which is Button 2 in the AWT. On most systems this is the middle button by default.
- MOUSE_FIRST_SECOND: Alias for MOUSE_THIRD.

Not all mice are created equal when it comes to their buttons. The number of buttons on a mouse typically ranges from one to three. The Java AWT approach to supporting these variations is to assume a one-button mouse and to use modifier combinations to define equivalents for the other mouse buttons. Unfortunately, these button equivalencies do not seem to be reliably implemented across platforms. As a partial solution to this problem, the framework defines the combination of the first and second mouse buttons as a reliable alias for the third button (at least it is reliable for mice with at least two mouse buttons). Therefore, if you are using a two-button mouse and an example calls for use of the third (middle) button to perform some operation, use the first and second buttons together, instead.

Modifier states

Unlike mouse buttons, modifier key combinations are in more common use. For example, the MODIFIER_SHIFT, MODIFIER_SHIFT_CTRL, and MODIFIER_SHIFT_ALT states are recognized. Because of mouse button and other platform-dependent conflicts, the CTRL+ALT modifier combination is not recognized, nor is any combination with the META modifier. Although ALT is recognized, on at least Windows platforms, it can conflict with key-based menu selection. To be on the safe side, stick to using only the SHIFT and CONTROL modifiers which, for a POCS user, shouldn't be a problem because these are by far the most familiar and commonly used ones in existing applications.

Means of escape

Included among the modifier state values is MODIFIER_ESC, which indicates that the ESCAPE key is pressed. Although technically not a modifier key (i.e., it cannot be used in combination with other keys), the ESCAPE key and some of the real modifier keys play important roles in drag-and-drop, and so the framework gives it a home as part of the modifier state.

Precedence rules

The mouse button and modifier key states can have only one value, but rules of precedence must be established because it is possible for more than one mouse button or modifier key to be down at one time. These are implemented by the whichButton and whichModifier class methods (utilities). The whichButton utility can accept an AWT InputEvent object as input, and returns the corresponding choice for mouse button state.

One version of the whichModifier utility acccpts an AWT InputEvent object as input, and another accepts an AWT KeyEvent. The former one considers only the true modifier keys in determining the modifier state. The latter one, which is the more general one, also takes into account the ESCAPE key.

Bit flags too

If you looked at the javadoc and source code for Input you may have noticed a few odd constants, such as BUTTON_ALL, and that all the state value constants are defined in hex—the same as for bit flags. This is because the state constants serve as both state choices and parameter flags for input event handling. For example, BUTTON_ALL, which conveniently ORs together all the possible button state flags, indicates to the MouseDragSensor class (which will soon be discussed) that any mouse button state can initiate a drag. ORing together BUTTON_FIRST and BUTTON_SECOND specifies that only the first or the second button state will initiate a drag.

BUTTON_NONE corresponds to no buttons down, and is a separately recognized state. It means that all buttons must be up for the trigger condition to be true. BUTTON_IGNORE is a special value meaning that no buttons or button combinations will trigger an event, effectively disabling the corresponding action.

Cooking the mouse

One last job for the Input class is "cooking" raw mouse coordinates. In AWT, all screen-based coordinates, mouse or otherwise, increase down and to the right. This is neither a right-hand nor a left-hand coordinate system. Because Java 3D uses a right-hand coordinate system for everything but the display space, display-based coordinates have to be converted to a right-hand system at some point. The framework does this as soon as possible, before the rest of the framework gets hold of it. For generality and consistency with the rest of the framework UI spaces, cooking also includes conversion of the position data from type int to type Tuple2d.

The cookMouse utility provides the standard method for the framework to convert a display coordinate from AWT to right-hand coordinates. To handle the rare situation where the inverse is needed, the uncookMouseX and uncookMouseY utilities are also provided. To keep the conversion as simple as possible, cooking does not try to do anything nice about the origin—it still remains at the upper left corner of the display space. What this means in practical terms is that within the display area the *Y* coordinate is *negative*.

17.1.2 InputSensor class

Framework events from input devices are generated by *input sensors*, which are all found in the j3dui.control.inputs.sensors package. Most input sensors are named for the input device they monitor and the type framework event they output. For example, the MouseDragSensor monitors the mouse device for input events and, in response, is capable of outputting events to an InputDragTarget object. Table 17.1 summarizes the input sensor building blocks provided by the framework.

Table 17.1 Summary of framework input sensors

Class/*Interface*	Description	Input Events	Output Events
MouseButtonSensor	Monitors the mouse buttons for clicks and specified button state changes		InputButtonTarget
MouseDragSensor	Monitors mouse movement and specified button state changes for drag gestures		InputDragTarget
MouseMoveSensor	Monitors mouse movement while no buttons are down		InputMoveTarget
KeyboardModifierSensor	Monitors the keyboard modifier and escape keys for specified modifier state changes		InputModifierTarget
KeyboardArrowSensor	Monitors the keyboard arrow keys for drag gestures		InputDragTarget
AwtKeyboardArrowSensor	Monitors the keyboard arrow keys for drag gestures. Uses AWT event model instead of the Java 3D behavior model		InputDragTarget

All but one input sensor uses InputSensor as its base class, which extends the Java 3D Behavior class and therefore gets involved in the rather complex world of wakeup conditions, criteria, and events. InputSensor monitors a particular Canvas3D display for certain AWT events, with a method for each possible AWT action, such as mouseDragged and mousePressed. Subclasses of InputSensor override its buildWakeup method to specify which AWT events to monitor. They also override one or more of its AWT action methods as needed to formulate a framework input event. This approach insulates the developer and most of the framework from having to deal with behaviors and wakeups (which are overkill for handling AWT events and, as mentioned in the Java 3D introduction, not even necessary). Because of problems encountered with the way that Behavior handles arrow key repeats, the `AwtKeyboardArrowSensor` class was developed. It is a purely AWT input sensor that is not a subclass of `Behavior`.

Although it might seem that dedicating a sensor to a single display and a limited set of AWT events is inefficient, in the bigger picture the additional overhead is insignificant. This is consistent with the framework's approach to optimization as described in chapter 15, which is to optimize only things that have a significant benefit, especially if the alternative introduces complexity. Another reason not to gratuitously monitor more than one display with a given sensor is that some events are state-sensitive. This sometimes makes the building blocks that handle them source-sensitive, with the restriction that they monitor only one source display at a time. In any case, as a convenience, if the input sensor's source display is set to null, then events from all displays will be reported.

Before leaving `InputSensor`, one word of caution: Do not use the `setEnable` method of the `Behavior` superclass. It will not have the desired effect and may corrupt some of the framework input events. The framework does allow for enabling and disabling input events, which is handled through a separate filter class that is covered in a later section.

17.1.3 MouseDragSensor class

The `MouseDragSensor` class senses planar drag gestures generated by the mouse in a source display canvas. The AWT definition of drag is mouse movement while a mouse button is down. The framework augments this definition with a "deadband" and a start delay timer. The deadband requires that the mouse move a minimum distance after the button is pressed for a drag operation to start. This helps to prevent mouse clicks and especially double-clicks from inadvertently becoming drags, which can be quite confusing and annoying to users. There are situations, however, where just the button press should start the drag, such as in a rate action control. The delay timer takes care of this situation by starting the drag after a brief pause even if the mouse hasn't moved beyond the deadband.

Mouse buttons

Another departure from the AWT model for input device handling is that the framework does not pass along low-level information such as which mouse button or key was pressed. Instead, device inputs are treated more like gestures, with the mouse button state being only an enabling criterion; it is not passed on as part of the event. The `setButtons` method of `MouseDragSensor` establishes which buttons will initiate a drag gesture. Its argument is one or more of the mouse state flag constants from the `Input` class or'd together.

InputDragTarget interface

The operation of the mouse drag sensor, as with all the input sensors, is largely defined by its output event target interface. For the `MouseDragSensor`, this interface is the

InputDragTarget class, which consists of three methods, each defining a particular phase in a planar drag gesture: startInputDrag, doInputDrag, and stopInputDrag. The event data packet passed by all of these methods includes the source display and the (cooked) drag position relative to the source display space. Because it is possible for there to be more than one display in the application, the source display is needed by handlers to determine the event's display space and geometry, such as for picking.

Note that the framework's approach to event interfaces assures a certain degree of anonymity with respect to how the event was generated and by whom. Nothing in the event interface specifies the device that caused the action; it could have been the mouse, the application program, or as we'll see in the next section, the keyboard arrow keys. This addresses the goal of being able to develop functional building blocks that can be wired up without regard to how the events were generated.

InputDragSplitter class

Closely allied with InputDragTarget is the InputDragSplitter class. Splitters divide an event connection into multiple output connections (i.e., a multi-caster). InputDragSplitter implements InputDragTarget as its event input. When an input method is called, InputDragSplitter in turn calls that method on all the event targets that are registered to it as outputs. Event targets are registered with the addEventTarget method. Methods are also provided to remove a target, clear the target list, and to access the target list through an Iterator.

17.1.4   KeyboardArrowSensor class

Because the arrow keys as a group are a significant means of input control, the framework treats them as a separate device with its own drag sensor. The KeyboardArrowSensor class senses planar drag gestures generated by the keyboard arrow keys in a source display canvas. (For consistency, this class should instead be called KeyboardDragSensor.) As with the other drag sensor, MouseDragSensor, this one also uses the InputDragTarget class as its output event interface.

Pressing an ARROW initiates a drag operation. Unlike the mouse, which has an explicit position in the display space, the ARROW keys have an inherent relative origin. Pressing an arrow key always starts a drag operation (the startInputDrag event method is called) at display position (0,0). The initial key press increments this position by one in the appropriate direction. Holding the key down and thereby causing it to autorepeat causes the drag position to continue incrementing (the doInputDrag event method is called repeatedly). Releasing the ARROW key terminates the drag operation (the stopInputDrag event method is called).

17.1.5   MouseMoveSensor class

In the framework, the distinction between a mouse drag and a mouse move, in terms of gestures, is significant. A mouse move, as opposed to a drag, is used in the framework for mouseover sensing. As you'll see, mouseover sensing is an extremely important aspect of in-scene direct manipulation and feedback. The `MouseMoveSensor` senses mouse movement only while all the mouse buttons are up, therefore there is no button criterion or any need to wrestle with AWT over the definition of a drag.

Related classes

The output event target interface for `MouseMoveSensor` is the `InputMoveTarget` class. Unlike a drag gesture, mouse movement has no phases and therefore the event interface requires only a single method, `setInputMove`. As with a drag event, the move event "data packet" includes the source display and the (cooked) position relative to the source space.

As with all event target interfaces, there is a corresponding splitter. For the `InputMoveTarget` event interface, the splitter is `InputMoveSplitter`.

17.1.6 KeyboardModifierSensor class

The KeyboardModifierSensor class senses modifier state changes generated by the keyboard in a source display canvas. The `setModifiers` method establishes which modifiers the sensor recognizes, which is similar in purpose to the `setButtons` method in `MouseDragSensor`. The argument to `SetModifiers` is one or more of the modifier state flags OR'd together.

For example, if `MODIFIER_SHIFT` and `MODIFIER_SHIFT_CTRL` are or'd together as the event trigger criteria, then the sensor will report any modifier state changes involving the SHIFT key alone, or the SHIFT and CONTROL keys in combination. If the user presses the SHIFT key and holds it, a single modifier event will be generated. If the user then presses the ALT key while still holding the SHIFT key, no event will be generated because `MODIFIER_SHIFT_ALT` was not included in the event trigger criteria. If, instead, the user had pressed the CONTROL key while holding down the SHIFT key, an event would have been generated because the SHIFT-CONTROL combination became active and that combination was specified as a trigger condition. An event is also generated when the user releases a triggering modifier key or combination. Similarly, `MODIFIER_NONE` is a separate state used to identify the condition when no modifier keys are down, and `MODIFIER_IGNORE` signifies that the sensor should ignore all modifier states, thereby disabling the sensor.

An important feature of KeyboardModifierSensor is that modifier state change events are generated immediately, as the user presses and releases keys. This means that modifier keys can have an immediate effect on the current UI operation, not just when an operation begins or ends. For example, if in the middle of a mouse drag to position an object the user presses the SHIFT key, the drag might immediately change from a translation to a rotation operation. Releasing the SHIFT key would change the same drag operation back into a translation. Such immediacy is convenient and, once learned, intuitive.

Related classes

The output event target interface for `KeyboardModifierSensor` is the `Input-ModifierTarget` class. As with mouse movement events, there are no phases and therefore the event interface requires only a single method, `setInputModifier`. The event "data packet" includes only the new modifier state choice. The source display is not needed because modifier state requires no spatial interpretation. The corresponding splitter class is `InputModifierSplitter`.

17.1.7 Example: InputSensors

**Figure 17.1
Screen shot of the
InputSensors example**

This example demonstrates the framework's mouse and keyboard input sensors.

➤ **See**

The virtual world contains a single target object (figure 17.1).

➤ **Do**

- Move (do not drag) the mouse in the upper left portion of the display to translate the target along the world *X-Y* axes.
- Use the arrow keys to translate the target along the world *X-Y* axes.
- Drag the mouse (left button) up-down in the display to rotate the target about the world *X* axis.
- Drag the mouse (right button) left-right in the display to rotate the target about the world *Y* axis.
- Drag the mouse (middle button, or left and right buttons together) left-right in the display to rotate the target about the world Z axis.
- While moving or dragging the mouse, press the MODIFIER and ESCAPE keys to change the target colors.

➤ **Observe**

- Target manipulation is offset from the mouse cursor.
- The arrow keys work much like a drag sensor.
- Different mouse buttons trigger different drag gestures.

The implementation of this and the next few examples may seem complicated despite their functional simplicity and the use of a UI framework. This is because the examples use only framework classes that have already been introduced, and so far very little of the framework has been introduced. As more of the framework is covered, the sophistication of the examples will increase significantly without unduly complicating the implementation, which is one of the benefits of using a framework.

Because this is your first opportunity to see the framework core in action, let's spend some time studying how the example is put together. Although a good bit of the implementation is based on code developed specifically for the example, instead of on actual framework building blocks, the coding techniques and patterns that are used are the same. The application-specific building blocks used in this and the rest of the examples in the chapter can be found in the j3dui.utils.blocks.BasicBlocks class.

buildTarget building block

In this example, the target object, a framework `TestThing`, is underneath a chain of two Java 3D `TransformGroup` objects constructed with the `buildTarget` utility found in the `BasicBlocks` class. The chain is returned as an array of `Transform-Groups`, with the target object attached to the second (tail) group. To actuate these target transforms and the target object's color, BasicBlocks provides three nested utility classes: `Translator`, `Rotator`, and `Colorer`. Each implements a different type input event interface and performs a particular type of manipulation on its target object. You'll see more about actuators and how such actuator classes can be generalized in the next chapter. The following code sample shows the example's transform chain creation and its connection to the actuator classes:

Transform chain creation using utility blocks

Filename: J3duiBook/examples/InputSensors/InputSensors.java

```
...
// setup manipulation targets
/// create transform chain
TestThing thing = new TestThing();
TransformGroup target[] = BasicBlocks.buildTarget(thing);
getWorld().addSceneNode(target[0]);

/// connect chain to actuators
BasicBlocks.Translator xlt =
 new BasicBlocks.Translator(target[0]);
BasicBlocks.Rotator rotX =
 new BasicBlocks.Rotator(target[1], 0);
BasicBlocks.Rotator rotY =
 new BasicBlocks.Rotator(target[1], 1);
```

```
BasicBlocks.Rotator rotZ =
 new BasicBlocks.Rotator(target[1], 2);
BasicBlocks.Colorer col =
 new BasicBlocks.Colorer(thing);
...
```

■

Translator, rotator, colorer building blocks

The `Translator` nested utility class implements the `InputMoveTarget` and `InputDragTarget` interfaces as event inputs, and it updates the translation state of its target `TransformGroup` according to the input event position. The `Rotator` class also implements the `InputMoveTarget` and `InputDragTarget` interfaces as event inputs, but it uses the input event position to update the rotation state of its target `TransformGroup`. A constructor parameter specifies which axis to use for the rotation. The `Colorer` class uses the same building-block pattern, but its input event interface is `InputModifierTarget`, and it changes the color of its target `TestThing` object according to the input event modifier state.

Following is the whole `BasicBlocks.Translator` utility block. It makes no attempt to preserve the target transform state between operations. Because of its simplicity, all of its event interface methods can use the same code to update the target state. An update starts by setting the state of a `Transform3D` object with the desired geometric manipulation, which is the scaled input position. Then, the transform in the target `TransformGroup` is set to this configured transform object. `BasicBlocks.Rotator` and `BasicBlocks.Colorer` use the same basic structure, except in the case of the latter, as the target's color is being set instead of its geometry.

Notice that, as a convenience, during construction the capability to write the target's transform is set while the target is live. Also note the use of dummy objects in lieu of new objects to avoid GC stutter during interaction. Both of these techniques were discussed in chapter 15. You'll see these patterns in use throughout the framework.

Utility class for basic translation

Filename: J3duiBook/lib/j3dui/utils/blocks/BasicBlocks.javaNested
```
/**
Example building block that connects its input events to a
TransformGroup target such that the target translates as
input position changes.
*/
public static final class Translator implements
 InputMoveTarget, InputDragTarget {

    // public interface ======================================

    /**
    Constructs a Translator.
    @param target Manipulation target.
```

```
*/
public Translator(TransformGroup target) {
  _target = target;
  _target.setCapability(
    TransformGroup.ALLOW_TRANSFORM_WRITE);
}

/**
Sets the translation scale factor.
@param scale Translation scale factor.
*/
public void setScale(double scale) {
  _scale = scale;
}

// InputMoveTarget implementation

public void setInputMove(Canvas3D source,
 Vector2d pos) {

  _vec3d.set(_scale*pos.x, _scale*pos.y, 0);

  _xform.setIdentity();
  _xform.setTranslation(_vec3d);
  _target.setTransform(_xform);
}

// InputDragTarget implementation

public void startInputDrag(Canvas3D source,
 Vector2d pos) {
  setInputMove(source, pos);
}

public void doInputDrag(Canvas3D source,
 Vector2d pos) {
  setInputMove(source, pos);
}

public void stopInputDrag(Canvas3D source,
 Vector2d pos) {
  setInputMove(source, pos);
}

// personal body =======================================

/** Manipulation target. */
private TransformGroup _target;

/** Scale factor. */
private double _scale = .025;

/** Dummy Vector3d.  (for GC) */
private final Vector3d _vec3d = new Vector3d();
```

```
/** Dummy Transform3D.  (for GC) */
private final Transform3D _xform = new Transform3D();

}
```
∎

Input sensors

Input sensors are created for each type of input for user interaction. The sensors are in turn connected to the appropriate target actuators. This is shown in the code sample below. The `MouseMoveSensor` and `KeyboardArrowSensor` input sensors both connect to `xlt`, the target `Translator`, which was shown being constructed in an earlier code sample. A `MouseDragSensor` input sensor is created to control each `Rotator` associated with the three axes of rotation. Notice that each sensor is configured to trigger with a different mouse button state—the first (left) button for the *X* axis, the second (right) button for the *Y* axis, and the third button (middle) for the *Z* axis. Completing the suite of input sensors, the `KeyboardModifierSensor` connect to `col`, the target `Colorer`.

Input sensors for each type of user interaction

Filename:J3duiBook/examples/InputSensors/InputSensors.java

```
...
// setup manipulation controls
AppDisplay disp = getView().getDisplay();
Group root = getWorld().getViewRoot();

/// move translation
new MouseMoveSensor(xlt, disp, root);

/// arrow translation
new KeyboardArrowSensor(xlt, disp, root);

/// drag rotation
MouseDragSensor dragger;

//// rotate X
dragger = new MouseDragSensor(rotX, disp, root);
dragger.setButtons(Input.BUTTON_FIRST);

//// rotate Y
dragger = new MouseDragSensor(rotY, disp, root);
dragger.setButtons(Input.BUTTON_SECOND);

//// rotate Z
dragger = new MouseDragSensor(rotZ, disp, root);
dragger.setButtons(Input.BUTTON_THIRD);

/// modifier color
```

```
KeyboardModifierSensor modifier;
modifier = new KeyboardModifierSensor(col, disp, root);
modifier.setModifiers(Input.MODIFIER_ALL_ESC);
...
```

What's missing?

As you play with the example, notice that the target manipulation states are not pre-served between operations. Each time an arrow key nudge starts, the target object jumps back to the world origin (center of display). Each time a mouse drag starts, the target jerks to some seemingly random orientation. Also notice how the target action is offset from the mouse cursor. This is because the origin of the cooked mouse space is the upper left corner of the display area, not the display space origin at the center of the display window. (Move the cursor to the upper left corner of a display and notice that the target object moves to the world origin, which appears at the center of the display.)

Being able to manage the input interpretation and preserve the state of control operations in a generalized manner are the first big steps in going from UI toy to UI tool. You'll soon see how the framework makes both of these important steps toward generalization, with flexible input interpretation in the following sections, and state preservation in the next chapter, as part of generalized actuation.

17.2   INPUT ENABLING

In the previous example you saw how using a given mouse button rotated the target object about a different axis. This was implemented using three MouseDragSensor objects, each with a different button state specified for its trigger condition. What if, instead of using the mouse button to differentiate the control operation, we wanted to use a modifier key? For example, dragging with no modifier keys would translate the target object, but holding down the SHIFT key would instead rotate it.

For starters, we would need a KeyboardModifierSensor object to sense the modifier state; but how do we use that state to select the control action? What we need is some way to test the modifier state against a trigger condition, and for the result to selectively enable and disable event "connections" between building blocks. With this approach we could set up dragging to control both translation and rotation, but only one of these actions would be enabled at a time, according to the modifier state. This technique is called *input enabling*.

Table 17.2 lists the framework's enable event interface and classes, and the filter classes used for basic input enabling. Table 17.3 summarizes all of the framework's input event interfaces and related classes, including enable triggers.

Table 17.2 Summary of classes and interfaces related to input enabling

Class/*Interface*	Description	Input Events	Output Events
EnableTarget	Event interface for reporting enable state change		
EnableSplitter	Enable event splitter	EnableTarget	EnableTarget
EnableTrigger	Base class for generalized enable event triggering	EnableTarget	EnableTarget
EnableFilter	An enable filter based on an enable trigger that can change the sense of an enable event (i.e., logical "not")	EnableTarget	EnableTarget
EnableInputDragFilter	An input drag filter for enabling (EnableTarget) an input drag (Input-DragTarget). Includes provisions for canceling the drag (InputCancelTarget)	InputDragTarget InputCancelTarget EnableTarget	InputDragTarget

Table 17.3 Summary of input events, splitters, and triggers

Class/*Interface*	Description	Input Events	Output Events
InputMoveTarget	Event interface for reporting input movement		
InputMoveSplitter	Input move event splitter	InputMoveTarget	InputMoveTarget
InputDragTarget	Event interface for reporting input drag gestures		
InputDragSplitter	Input drag event splitter	InputDragTarget	InputDragTarget
InputButtonTarget	Event interface for reporting input button state changes and clicks		
InputButtonSplitter	Input button event splitter	InputButtonTarget	InputButtonTarget
InputButtonTrigger	A trigger that monitors for specified input button state changes and clicks	InputButtonTarget EnableTarget	EnableTarget
InputPauseTarget	Event interface for reporting input motion pausing		
InputPauseTrigger	A trigger that monitors for pauses in input movement	InputMoveTarget EnableTarget	InputPauseTarget
InputModifierTarget	Event interface for reporting input modifier state changes		
InputModifierSplitter	Input modifier event splitter	InputModifierTarget	InputModifierTarget
InputModifierTrigger	A trigger that monitors for specified input modifier state changes	InputModifierTarget	EnableTarget
InputCancelTarget	Event interface for reporting input cancellation (e.g., ESCAPE key press).		
InputCancelSplitter	Input cancel event splitter	InputCancelTarget	InputCancelTarget

Table 17.3 Summary of input events, splitters, and triggers (continued)

Class/*Interface*	Description	Input Events	Output Events
InputCancelTrigger	A trigger that monitors input modifier state changes for cancel	InputModifierTarget	EnableTarget

17.2.1   InputModifierTrigger class

The InputModifierTrigger class satisfies the first of our needs for input control enabling, which is the capability to monitor the modifier state against a trigger condition. The event "input" for this building block is the InputModifierTarget interface, which is what the KeyboardModifierSensor class outputs. Its event output is the EnableTarget interface, which you'll learn more about shortly. The setModifiers method establishes the trigger condition, which consists of one or more modifier state constants from Input OR'd together. When the input modifier state matches any of the modifier state values in the trigger condition, the building block outputs an enable event whose value corresponds to a condition met result.

17.2.2   Enable classes

The InputModifierTrigger class uses EnableTrigger as its base class. EnableTrigger is a trigger whose event output is the EnableTarget interface. This event interface is as generic as they come: it has a single method, setEnable, with a single boolean parameter. Its associated event splitter is EnableSplitter.

EnableTrigger has two particularly interesting methods, which are of course inherited by InputModifierTrigger. The setOutputSense method specifies whether "true" or "false" is output when the trigger condition is met. The init-EventTarget method is used to initialize the building block chain downstream from the trigger so that their states are consistent with that from the trigger at startup. This can only be done reliably after the application has established the processing chain, which may not be completed until after the trigger is constructed.

The EnableFilter class extends the EnableTrigger class. Depending on how the filter sense is set, input events will pass through without change (true in, true out) or their sense will be flipped (true in, false out), achieving the logical equivalent of a "not" operation.

17.2.3   EnableInputDragFilter class

The EnableInputDragFilter class satisfies the second of our needs for enabling input control events, which is the capability to enable and disable an input drag event. Being a filter building block, its event input and output have the same type, which is the InputDragTarget interface. It receives its control orders by also implementing the EnableTarget interface, which is what the InputModifier-Trigger class outputs. Because of its internal complexity, however, it does not derive from the base class InputDragFilter (which is discussed in the next section). The complexity of this class stems from the fact that, unlike the other input event interfaces, `InputDragTarget` has distinct time-dependent phases: start, do, and stop. The framework uses these phases to perform internal bookkeeping, such as preserving the manipulation state of the target between operations.

What is a drag?

The difficulty with drag enabling arises when we start to ask important questions: What does it mean to disable a drag operation? If a drag operation is currently underway and the order to disable it is received, does that mean the drag was stopped? Or, does it mean that drag is just temporarily suspended? Although suspending the drag operation is by far the simpler approach to implement, it often does not have the desired effect. This is because suspending the drag operation in the virtual world does not also suspend the user's finger in the real world. While the virtual drag is suspended it is quite possible for the user to release the mouse button, and to even start a new drag. When the virtual drag is resumed, its state is likely to be out of sync with recent real world events.

For example, the user may have started a drag operation to slide a target object along a floor plane. In the middle of the drag, the user presses a modifier key to change the meaning of the drag from horizontal sliding in *X-Z* to vertical lifting in *Y*. When the user releases the modifier key to change back to sliding, the original drag operation, which was suspended, knows nothing about the object's *Y* position being changed. Without cooperation between the two operations, the resumed first drag operation will set the object at its original *Y* position, thereby negating the effect of the lift operation. One way to solve the problem is to split the control of the target object's translation state in some application-specific manner, such as one drag controlling only *X-Z* and the other only *Y*; but, there is a more general and perhaps easier way to handle this.

A tale of two drags

To achieve the desired result from input drag enabling, the `EnableInputDrag-Filter` class must keep track of both the real world (source) drag state and the virtual world (target) drag state. When it receives the disable order, it artificially terminates the target drag operation by calling the `stopInputDrag` method of its output `InputDragTarget` interface. When it receives the enable order, it checks the current source drag state and, if a source drag is in progress, it artificially initiates a target drag operation by calling the `startInputDrag` method on the event target object. If, however, no source drag is in progress, then no target drag is initiated.

In terms of the previous example, when the user indicates a switch from sliding to lifting, the first target drag is ended and the second target drag is started. When the manipulation switches back to sliding, the lifting target drag (the second one) is ended, and the sliding target drag is started anew. Note that during all of this there has been only a single source drag—the user never released his finger from the mouse button.

By stopping one drag before starting another, the framework (specifically, an actuator building block from the framework) has a chance to preserve the intermediate manipulation state of the target object. There will be much more on actuation and state preservation in the next chapter.

Sole source enabling

Because of its unique requirements and complexity, the framework provides only one place for enabling input drag events: the `EnableInputDragFilter` class. As you'll see later, with other event types that are not state dependent, the framework allows multiple building blocks to enable and disable them, as a convenience.

17.2.4   Example: InputEnabling

 This example demonstrates input drag enabling as controlled through modifier keys. It also demonstrates the use of event splitters.

> **See**

The virtual world contains a single target object (as did the InputSensors example).

> **Do**

- Drag the mouse (left button) in the display to translate the target along the world *X-Y* axes.
- Drag the mouse (left button with SHIFT key) left-right in the display to rotate the target about the world *Y* axis.
- Drag the mouse (left button with CONTROL key) left-right in the display to rotate the target about the world *Z* axis.

> **Observe**

- Different modifier keys trigger different control operations.
- Modifier state changes occur immediately, even during an active drag operation.
- Target manipulation is offset from the mouse cursor.
- The target manipulation state is not preserved between operations.

This example uses the same utility building blocks that you saw in the previous example. Because the same mouse button is used for all drag operations, an event splitter is used to connect the input sensors to multiple targets. The following code sample from the example shows the creation of the common sensors and their splitters.

Creation of common sensors and input event splitters

Filename: J3duiBook/examples/InputEnabling/InputEnabling.java

```
...
// setup manipulation sensors
AppDisplay disp = getView().getDisplay();
Group root = getWorld().getViewRoot();

/// draggers
InputDragSplitter dragSplt =
 new InputDragSplitter();

new MouseDragSensor(dragSplt, disp, root);
```

```
/// modifiers
InputModifierSplitter modSplt =
 new InputModifierSplitter();

new KeyboardModifierSensor(modSplt, disp, root);
...
```

For each type of control operation in the example—translation, rotation Y axis, rotation Z axis—the same basic processing chain is used, as shown in the next code sample from the example. The drag sensor connects to an `EnableInputDragFilter` object, enabler, via the drag splitter, `dragSplt`. The enabler in turn connects to multiple target actuators, such as the `rotY` and `rotZ` Rotator objects. Control for the enabler starts with the modifier sensor, which connects to an `InputModifierTrigger`, called `trigger`, via the modifier splitter, called `modSplt`. The trigger in turn connects to the enabler. Note that the trigger sense is set to `true` signifying that the trigger output will be `true` when the trigger condition is met, thereby enabling the rotation control. Also note that the processing chains downstream from the rotation triggers, towards the enabler, are initialized to `false` because at startup the trigger conditions—SHIFT and CONTROL key down, respectively—won't be met.

Processing chain for control of target translation and rotation

J3duiBook/examples/InputEnabling/InputEnabling.java

```
...
// setup manipulation targets
/// create transform chain
TestThing thing = new TestThing();
TransformGroup target[] = BasicBlocks.buildTarget(thing);
getWorld().addSceneNode(target[0]);

/// connect chain to actuators
BasicBlocks.Translator xlt =
 new BasicBlocks.Translator(target[0]);
BasicBlocks.Rotator rotY =
 new BasicBlocks.Rotator(target[1], 1);
BasicBlocks.Rotator rotZ =
 new BasicBlocks.Rotator(target[1], 2);
...
// setup manipulation controls
InputModifierTrigger trigger;
EnableInputDragFilter enabler;

/// translation, if None
enabler = new EnableInputDragFilter(xlt);
dragSplt.addEventTarget(enabler);

trigger = new InputModifierTrigger(enabler,
 Input.MODIFIER_NONE, true);
trigger.initEventTarget(true);
```

```
modSplt.addEventTarget(trigger);

/// rotation Y, if Shift
enabler = new EnableInputDragFilter(rotY);
dragSplt.addEventTarget(enabler);

trigger = new InputModifierTrigger(enabler,
 Input.MODIFIER_SHIFT, true);
trigger.initEventTarget(false);
modSplt.addEventTarget(trigger);

/// rotation Z, if Ctrl
enabler = new EnableInputDragFilter(rotZ);
dragSplt.addEventTarget(enabler);

trigger = new InputModifierTrigger(enabler,
 Input.MODIFIER_CTRL, true);
trigger.initEventTarget(false);
modSplt.addEventTarget(trigger);
...
```

17.3 INPUT FILTERING

In part 2 of the book, the discussion on control input interpretation included such topics as control origin, control actions, and control gestures. One approach for handling these techniques is to create a drag sensor for each combination of input device and input interpretation. A more general approach is to use an InputDragTarget filter with a different plug-in for each type of input interpretation. This is the strategy pattern that was discussed in chapter 15 and is used throughout the framework.

The InputDragFilter class is the base class for most filters implementing the InputDragTarget interface. It uses plug-ins based on the InputDragFilter-Plugin base class. In keeping with the plug-in pattern, the InputDragFilter class is essentially a hollow shell. It implements the InputDragTarget interface, with the same basic structure for each interface method: Call the plug-in's method to generate the output value, and then call the corresponding event method in the output event target. You'll see this simple formula for all other filter classes in the framework that use plug-ins. Its simplicity, however, is the reason why InputDragFilter can not be used as a base class for EnableInputDragFilter. It can not readily handle state or time-dependent processing, where output events are not generated one-for-one with input events.

The class diagram in figure 17.2 illustrates the framework model for input drag filtering with a plug-in. The framework classes related to input drag filtering based on the InputDragFilter class and its plug-ins are summarized in table 17.4. Input drag filter classes not based on the use of plug-ins are listed in table 17.5.

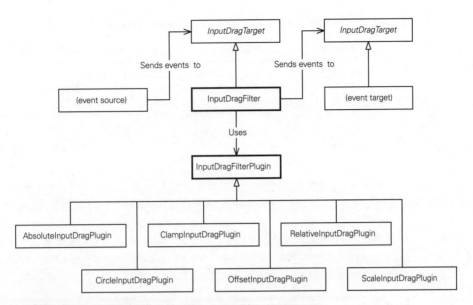

Figure 17.2 Class diagram of input drag filtering with plug-ins

Table 17.4 Summary of classes related to plug-in-based input drag filtering

Class/*Interface*	Description	Input Events	Output Events
InputDragFilter	An input drag filter that uses a plug-in to perform a specific filtering operation	InputDragTarget	InputDragTarget
InputDragFilterPlugin	Abstract base class for input drag filter plug-ins		
AbsoluteInputDragPlugin	An input drag filter plug-in that interprets the drag with an absolute drag origin		
CircleInputDragPlugin	An input drag filter plug-in that interprets the drag as a circular gesture (angle and radius)		
ClampInputDragPlugin	An input drag filter plug-in that limits the drag output position to a range		
OffsetInputDragPlugin	An input drag filter plug-in that offsets the drag position by a constant value and/or a dynamic one (InputMoveTarget)	InputMoveTarget	
RelativeInputDragPlugin	An input drag filter plug-in that interprets the drag with a relative drag origin		
ScaleInputDragPlugin	An input drag filter plug-in that scales the drag input position by a constant value		

Table 17.5 Summary of input drag filtering classes *not* based on plug-ins

Class/*Interface*	Description	Input Events	Output Events
EnableInputDragFilter	An input drag filter for enabling (EnableTarget) an input drag (InputDragTarget). Includes provisions for canceling the drag (InputCancelTarget)	InputDragTarget InputCancelTarget EnableTarget	InputDragTarget
RateInputDragFilter	An input drag filter that interprets input drag position as a rate of output change	InputDragTarget	InputDragTarget

The code sample following shows the filter class's implementation of its `Input-DragTarget` interface. Notice that the `startInputDrag` method implementation calls the plug-in's `startInputDrag` method. This method tells the plug-in that a drag is starting, which some plug-ins use to save the starting position, such as for computing a relative-origin drag.

Details for use of the filter plug-in

Filename: J3duiBook/lib/j3dui/control/inputs/InputDragFilter.java

```
...
// InputDragTarget implementation

public void startInputDrag(Canvas3D source, Vector2d pos) {
    _plugin.startInputDrag(source, pos);
    _plugin.toTargetValue(source, pos, _pos);
    _eventTarget.startInputDrag(source, _pos);
}

public void doInputDrag(Canvas3D source, Vector2d pos) {
    _plugin.toTargetValue(source, pos, _pos);
    _eventTarget.doInputDrag(source, _pos);
}

public void stopInputDrag(Canvas3D source, Vector2d pos) {
    _plugin.toTargetValue(source, pos, _pos);
    _eventTarget.stopInputDrag(source, _pos);
}

// personal body =============================================

/** Event target. */
private InputDragTarget _eventTarget;

/** Personality plugin.  Never null. */
private InputDragFilterPlugin _plugin;

/** Dummy position value.  (for GC) */
private final Vector2d _pos = new Vector2d();
...
```

17.3.1 Framework

Because a major goal of the framework is demonstration and not completeness, only the most common forms of input interpretation filter plug-ins are implemented. Nevertheless, quite a wide variety of input interpretations are achievable by combining the provided filters in series, such as an absolute origin filter followed by a rate action filter followed by a clamp filter, which will be demonstrated in the next example.

Control origins

The `AbsoluteInputDragPlugin` class and the `RelativeInputDragPlugin` class perform absolute and relative interpretation of the input drag space origin, respectively. As you may recall from chapter 4, absolute origin interpretation is where the drag position is interpreted relative to some point in the space that does not have to be the true origin of the space. For example, it may be the center of a third-person control widget at the bottom of the display area. Relative origin is where the drag position at the start of the drag is interpreted as the origin of the drag operation (a perfect job for the `startInputDrag` method in the filter plug-in).

Control actions

By default, a drag event without any processing is a direct control action: When the mouse moves five units, the drag target position changes by five units. For a rate action, however, moving the mouse five units results in a proportional change in drag target position with time, such as a five-unit change in position per second—a rate of position change. The `RateInputDragFilter` class provides simple rate-based drag control. Its `setCurve` method establishes the shape of the exponential curve used to interpret source position as a target position rate. Note that, because of its time-dependent nature, this function can not be implemented as a plug-in, nor can it easily be derived from `InputDragFilter`.

Control gestures

By default, a drag event without any processing is a planar drag gesture: Mouse movement is interpreted as the output from two one-dimensional sliders. For support of circular gestures, the framework provides the `CircleInputDragPlugin` class, which is a filter that interprets planar drags in terms of angle about and distance from the origin. By using an origin filter, you can shift the reference point for the gesture to wherever it is needed in the source space, such as at the center of a third-person virtual control knob.

Miscellaneous processing

As part of the general plumbing needed to wire up custom control input interpretations, the framework also provides several filters that perform arithmetic vector processing (i.e., the same operation is applied to each element in the data vector). The

`ScaleInputDragPlugin` class multiplies the input value by a constant; the `Off-setInputDragPlugin` class adds a constant to the input value, and the `Clamp-InputDragPlugin` restricts the input value to min/max limits.

17.3.2 Example: InputFilters

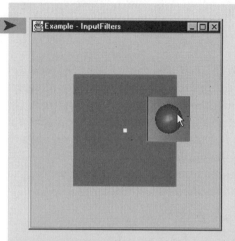

Figure 17.3
Screen shot of the
InputFilters example

This example demonstrates the framework's input interpretation filters.

> See

The virtual world contains a single target object with a background control plane for visual reference. A screen shot is provided in figure 17.3.

> Do

- Drag the mouse (left button) in the display to translate the target along the world X-Y axes.
- Drag the mouse (right button) left-right in the display relative to the center tic, or just hold down the button, to rotate the target about its world Y axis.
- Drag the mouse (middle button) in a circle around the center tic in the display to rotate the target about its world Z axis.

> Observe

- The translation drag is "relative direct," meaning that the drag always starts at zero position (the middle of the control plane) and controls the position of the target.
- During translation, the target position is "clamped" to the area defined by the control plane.
- The Y-axis rotation drag is "absolute rate," meaning that the drag starts at a value proportional to the distance from its origin (the middle of the control plane) and controls the rate of target spin.
- The Z-axis rotation drag is "absolute direct" meaning that the circular gesture reference point is fixed (the center of the control plane).
- The target manipulation state is not preserved between operations (but the drag offsets seen in earlier examples are gone for the most part).
- If you resize the display window, the position of the rotation reference points (which are specified in absolute mouse space) will no longer appear at the center of the control plane.

The code sample following is from the example. It shows how the filter building blocks are connected in series to achieve more complex filtering operations. For example, the drag sensor for translation connects to a relative origin filter formed by plugging a `RelativeInputDragPlugin` object into an `InputDragFilter` object. The origin filter, in turn, connects to a clamp filter, created using a `Clamp-InputDragPlugin` object. The clamp limits are set such that they match the size of the control plane (after taking into account the default translation scale factor in the `BasicBlock.Translator` class). Note how the control origins for rate and circle rotation are specified as being absolute. Setting the origins relative to the display space (e.g., middle of the display window or flush with its lower right corner) is a much more difficult problem because it requires display geometry change detection, which will be covered later.

Input drag interpretation with filter chains

Filename:J3duiBook/examples/InputFilters/InputFilters.java

```
...
// setup manipulation controls
MouseDragSensor dragger;
InputDragTarget filter;

/// relative clamped translation, first button
filter = new InputDragFilter(xlt,
 new ClampInputDragPlugin(new Vector2d(-100, 100)));
filter = new InputDragFilter(filter,
 new RelativeInputDragPlugin());

dragger = new MouseDragSensor(filter, disp, root);
dragger.setButtons(Input.BUTTON_FIRST);

/// absolute rate rotation, second button
filter = new RateInputDragFilter(rotY);
filter = new InputDragFilter(filter,
 new AbsoluteInputDragPlugin(new Vector2d(150, -150)));

dragger = new MouseDragSensor(filter, disp, root);
dragger.setButtons(Input.BUTTON_SECOND);

/// absolute circle rotation, third button
filter = new InputDragFilter(rotZ,
 new CircleInputDragPlugin());
filter = new InputDragFilter(filter,
 new AbsoluteInputDragPlugin(new Vector2d(150, -150)));

dragger = new MouseDragSensor(filter, disp, root);
dragger.setButtons(Input.BUTTON_THIRD);
...
```

17.4 SUMMARY

In this chapter, you saw the framework core for the first time. The discussion started with input sensors and their related event interfaces. The sensors provide the bridge between physical input devices and the framework's building block event model. The framework provides input sensors for mouse movement, mouse dragging, ARROW key dragging, and modifier key state. Next you saw how to control input events by combining a drag enable filter with a modifier trigger. This configuration allows you to use the MODIFIER keys to select which control operation is active. The chapter ended with a respectable sampling of input drag filters that covered origin, action, and gesture control interpretation. The flexibility of the building-block model was demonstrated when several of the filters were strung together to form custom control interpretations, such as "relative planar translation" and "absolute circular rotation."

One of the problems you saw with these early examples is the lack of target state preservation between drag operations. Whenever a new operation was started, the target object would jump back to the origin or jerk back to its initial orientation. In the next chapter, you'll see how the framework addresses this issue as part of a generalized implementation for actuators.

CHAPTER 18

Control actuation

Since part 2 of the book was conceptual in nature, the discussions there tread lightly over messy details concerning implementation. One such detail was how to actually make a target object move. The discussions described all kinds of wonderful UI techniques to tell the target object what it should do. How the object was supposed to carry out these orders was mentioned, but details were in short supply—until now.

In the previous chapter, we kept bumping up against the problem of how to make objects do something. In the discussion and examples you saw a few utility blocks that could take a drag position and convert it into target object translation and rotation. In a sense, these building blocks were serving as the target object's actuators. As with their mechanical counterparts, actuators can be stateless, ignoring any actions to the target that may have come before, or they can attempt to preserve the manipulation state, with the next operation continuing where the previous one left off. It was obvious from using the actuators in the previous examples that they made no attempt to preserve their state. Each time a drag started the target object made an unsightly jump or jerk. This was certainly something that we didn't worry about in part 2.

The first half of this chapter is difficult because it has to lay down a hefty layer of groundwork. It will prepare you, though, for the next example.

18.1 TARGET ACTUATION

The closest thing to an actuator in Java 3D is the `Interpolator` class. An interpolator accepts a time value as input and performs some time-dependent operation on its target object, which might affect its position, color, or even transparency. The framework takes this basic idea and generalizes it to work with its input event interfaces for programmatic control of target objects. To avoid having to create a unique event interface and actuator type for each specific action, the framework uses a generic actuator base class and actuation event type, and leaves it to the surrounding building blocks to use them in a specific manner. This approach is analogous to that taken by Java's collection classes, which maintain all data as instances of the most generic of all objects, `Object`. It is up to the designer to figure out how to use and access these generic object collections in some application-specific manner.

All of the classes covered in this section about target actuation are found in and under the framework package `j3dui.control.actuators`.

18.1.1 Actuator class

Appropriately enough, all actuators in the framework are based on the `Actuator` class. This class has much in common with the framework's implementation of the input filter class in that it is mostly an empty shell that accepts a plug-in to give it a personality. The plug-in defines both the target type and operation of the actuator, including whether or not it is capable of maintaining state between operations. The `Actuator` class implements the `ActuationTarget` and the `EnableTarget` event interfaces as input. Its constructor accepts a single `ActuatorPlugin` argument. It provides methods for getting the plug-in, getting the enable state, and getting the target object that it is actuating.

Base and event classes related to actuation are listed in table 18.1. Figure 18.1 is a class diagram of the basic actuator model showing its use of an abstract actuator plug-in.

Table 18.1   Summary of classes and interfaces related to actuation

Class/*Interface*	Description	Input Events	Output Events
ActuationTarget	Event interface for target actuation via a 4D state vector		
ActuationSplitter	Actuation event splitter.	ActuationTarget	ActuationTarget
Actuator	Controls an attached target object according to actuation events. The type of actuation and target are determined by its plug-in	ActuationTarget EnableTarget	
ActuatorPlugin	Abstract base class for actuator plug-ins		

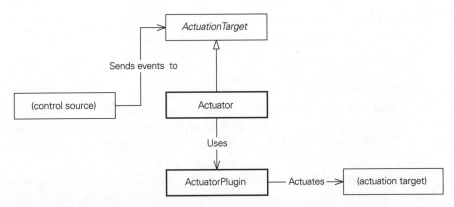

Figure 18.1 Framework actuation model with an abstract actuator plug-in

Related classes

The `ActuationTarget` interface serves as the generic event input to all actuators. What helps to make it generic is that its event data packet is a four-dimensional value represented by a `Tuple4d` object. As with all the other "tuple" classes and their relatives, the `Tuple4d` class is provided by the `javax.vecmath` package. Questions such as how many of the four values in the vector are used, and how, are left to the actuator, or more specifically its plug-in. The corresponding splitter class for `ActuationTarget` is the `ActuationSplitter` class. Although you won't need it for a while, the `PseudoActuator` interface provides the same event input interfaces as the `Actuator` class, which can be useful for hooking up building blocks to something that acts like an actuator but doesn't require the plug-in apparatus.

Actuation in action

The methods in the `ActuationTarget` interface are specifically designed to facilitate control of the actuation state. The `initActuation` method explicitly sets the actuation state of the actuator and, correspondingly, the state of the actuator's target. The internal actuation state provides a reference for subsequent actuation updates performed through the `updateActuation` method.

An actuation update is a "delta" or change to the reference state, with the result being a change in the target's state (the actuation reference state is unaffected). How the update is applied to the target's reference state depends on the actuator. For example, an actuator that performs spatial translation might simply add together the input and reference actuation values to obtain the new target state. An actuator that performs geometric scaling, however, would probably multiply the two values together to obtain the target state.

The last method in the `ActuationTarget` interface is `syncActuation`. It has no argument because it simply instructs the actuator to synchronize its internal actuation reference state to that of the target object. The new reference state might be inferred from the previous actuation updates, or it might be obtained directly by reading the state of the target object. The details are left to the actuator, or in the case of the `Actuator` class, its plug-in.

Have it your way

Using all these interface methods might seem complicated, but in actual practice it's not. If you want to directly set the state of the target, such as its initial position, then use `initActuation`. During an interactive operation use `updateActuation`, which will change the target's state relative to that set by `initActuation`. When the operation is done, you have the option of calling `syncActuation`, or not. If you want operations to be cumulative, starting where the previous one left off, then call it. If you don't call it, the next operation will start relative to the most recent reference state established by `initActuation`, and any changes to the target resulting from previous `updateActuation` calls will be lost. The `ActuationTarget` interface is simple but flexible enough to let you have it your way.

Actuator enabling

Although actuators maintain an internal state, the `ActuationTarget` interface does not. Its methods tell the event target to perform certain actions, but they do not establish an active and inactive state such as the start and stop methods in the `InputDragTarget` interface. What this means is that actuation is not very picky about how its events are enabled and disabled: There is no need for a special enabler class like `EnableInputDragFilter`. Thus, as a convenience, most classes that implement the `ActuationTarget` interface also implement the `EnableTarget` interface, including Actuator. Use this interface to enable and disable the associated actuator.

18.1.2 Outer and inner plug-ins

The `Actuator` class is purposely kept in the dark as to the type of object it actuates and the manner in which it actuates it. These concerns are the responsibility of its personality plug-in. The use of plug-ins avoids the need to define separate actuator classes for every combination of target type and operation, a feature that the framework takes full advantage of. To satisfy the somewhat independent needs of what is manipulated versus how it is manipulated, the framework implements all of its `ActuatorPlugin` subclasses as nested plug-ins, with the outer plug-in defining the specific type of target manipulated, and the inner plug-in defining the type of operation performed on it.

Figure 18.2 shows the outer and inner actuator plug-in classes provided by the framework, and how they cooperate.

18.1.3 ActuatorPlugin Class

The `ActuatorPlugin` class is the base class for all plug-ins used directly by an `Actuator`. Although this means that it also serves as the base class for all outer plug-ins, to keep it general, it has no knowledge of any inner plug-ins, or any of the inner

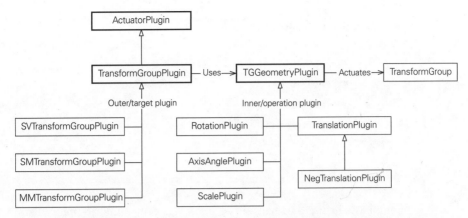

Figure 18.2   Outer/target and inner/operation actuator plug-ins in the framework

workings concerning the actuation target. In fact, its constructor doesn't even have parameters for specifying such details. Instead, it leaves such matters to its subclasses, which may require different parameters and plug-ins depending on the type of target and operation involved.

Through abstract methods, the `ActuatorPlugin` class defines the interface that the hosting `Actuator` class uses to communicate with it, and provides a template for its subclasses. Because its inner workings are hidden, one of these methods, `getTargetNode`, provides generic access to the target object that is being actuated. The other methods should seem familiar since they correspond to those in the `ActuationTarget` interface: `initActuation`, `updateActuation`, and `syncActuation`. This correspondence simplifies the structure of the `Actuator` class because each of its `ActuationTarget` interface methods simply calls the corresponding method on its plug-in. This is shown in the code fragment below from the `Actuator` class. Also notice how input event enabling is handled. If the actuator is disabled, it simply does not call its plug-in's methods.

Details of the internal plug-in interface for actuators

Filename: J3duiBook/lib/j3dui/control/actuators/Actuator.java

```
...
// ActuationTarget implementation

public void initActuation(Tuple4d value) {
   if(!_enable) return;

   _plugin.initActuation(value);
   ...
}

public void updateActuation(Tuple4d value) {
   if(!_enable) return;
```

```
    _plugin.updateActuation(value);
    ...
}

public void syncActuation() {
    if(!_enable) return;

    _plugin.syncActuation();
    ...
}
...
```

The emphasis in the first half of the book was on geometric manipulation, and the framework follows suit with its `ActuatorPlugin` subclasses. Although it could implement actuators for other types of targets, the framework only includes plug-ins for handling Java 3D `TransformGroup` objects. In spite of this narrow focus, the framework still manages to offer three distinct flavors of `TransformGroup` plug-ins. As you'll see, each plug-in makes different assumptions and satisfies different requirements about how the target object's state is maintained. Table 18.2 summarizes the outer/target actuation plug-ins provided by the framework.

Table 18.2   Summary of outer/target plug-in classes for actuation

Class/*Interface*	Description
ActuatorPlugin	Abstract base class for actuator plug-ins
TransformGroupPlugin	Abstract base class for outer/target actuator plug-ins whose target is a TransformGroup object
SVTransformGroupPlugin	Transform group actuator plug-in that assumes it is the only user of its target, and uses a 4D vector to maintain actuation state (single-user vector)
SMTransformGroupPlugin	Transform group actuator plug-in that assumes it is the only user of its target, and uses a matrix to maintain actuation state (single-user matrix)
MMTransformGroupPlugin	Transform group actuator plug-in that assumes its target is being used by multiple users, and uses a matrix to maintain actuation state (multi-user matrix)

Actuation value processing

The `ActuatorPlugin` class provides support for source (input) and target (output) side processing of event actuation values. Scale and offset factors can be applied to the actuation input value and, depending on how the actuation state is maintained, clamping (minimum/maximum limits) can be applied to the target actuation state. For example, typically when a drag starts, its control value is zero. If an actuator were performing geometric scaling, this would result in a scaling factor of zero. If, however, the input control value were offset by a value of one, then when a drag starts, the corresponding actuation value would be one, the normal starting point for a scaling operation, not zero. Continuing with the scaling example, clamping should also be applied so that the target scaling factor never goes to zero, which throws a Java 3D non-affine transform exception, or negative. Such an effect can be disorienting to the user.

The `setSourceScale` and `setSourceOffset` methods specify the source-side offset and scaling factors applied to source-side actuation input values. The `set-TargetClamp` method sets the minimum/maximum values that are applied to target-side actuation state values. Subclasses perform the source and target-side processing using the protected `toActuationSource` and `toActuationTarget` methods. Scale and offset can be applied by all plug-in subclasses; however, clamping can only be performed by plug-ins that maintain state as a 4D actuation value, a distinction that will become clearer in the following sections.

Because the implementation of the outer actuator plug-in is dependent on that of its inner plug-in, discussion of the outer plug-in's implementation will be deferred until after that of the inner plug-in.

TransformGroupPlugin class

The `TransformGroupPlugin` class is an abstract base class for all actuator target plug-ins that handle `TransformGroup` target objects. Its constructor accepts as its only argument a `TGGeometryPlugin` object, which is an inner/operation plug-in for handling geometric manipulation of `TransformGroup` targets.

SVTransformGroupPlugin Class

The `SVTransformGroupPlugin` subclass of `TransformGroupPlugin` is the simplest of the outer/target actuator plug-ins for handling `TransformGroup` target objects. Its distinguishing characteristics are that it assumes it is the sole user of its target object, and that the actuation state can be defined by a `Tuple4d` data vector. This accounts for the "SV" it its class name, which stands for "single-user vector." As you'll see, using this plug-in makes for the most efficient but least flexible form of actuator.

By assuming that it is the only user of its target object, it does not have to read the state of its target. Instead, it maintains the state of the target internally, and only writes the target's state when it determines that a change is needed. This avoids the overhead of reading the object's state, but it also requires that no one else change the target state, otherwise, the actuator will become out of sync with reality.

The plug-in's assumption that the target's state can be tracked with a 4D data vector makes implementation simple and efficient. A 4D vector is capable of maintaining the actuation state for most simple geometric operations, such as a series of translations, fixed-axis rotations, or scalings. A benefit of being able to use a vector to define the target state is that the state is well-behaved and amenable to measurement. For example, it can easily be tested against limits in order to clamp the value. Unfortunately, there are some operations that the framework requires which can not be maintained with a 4D vector, such as a mixed series of simple geometric operations. This is one of the reasons why there is more than one flavor of `TransformGroupPlugin`.

SMTransformGroupPlugin class

Like the previous plug-in, the `SMTransformGroupPlugin` subclass of `TransformGroupPlugin` assumes that it is the sole user of its target object. However, it takes a more sophisticated view of what is required to maintain the target object's state. Instead of a 4D vector it uses a 4×4 transformation matrix. Correspondingly, the "SM" in its name stands for "single-user matrix." By using a transform matrix, the actuator can track any sequence of geometric operations that a `TransformGroup` object is capable of performing, such as a mixed series of translations and rotations. Without getting too far into the details, the target's state is updated by converting the actuation update value into a transformation matrix, which is multiplied with the reference state matrix. In comparison to the previous plug-in, this one is less efficient because of the matrix multiplication, but it is more versatile.

The kind of versatility that the framework is looking for with this flavor of target plug-in is the ability to handle an arbitrary series of rotations in a general manner, such as with axis-angle rotations. An axis-angle rotation is one where the angle of rotation and the axis of rotation are specified together as a single operation, and are completely arbitrary. The `javax.vecmath` package defines a special 4-tuple for it, the `AxisAngle4d` class. For example, in a series of axis-angle rotations, the first actuation update might rotate the target about its X axis, the second update about its original Y axis, and the third about its original Z axis. In terms of actuation state maintenance, these transformations cannot be accumulated using a simple 4D vector as would happen in the `SVTransformGroupPlugin` class. Instead, a full transformation matrix is required.

MMTransformGroupPlugin class

There is only one more generalization left to make regarding `TransformGroup` target plug-ins, and that is to dispense with the single-user restriction. The `MMTransformGroupPlugin` class does just that, with the "MM" in its name standing for "multi-user matrix." To accommodate multiple users of the target, the actuator can not make any assumptions about the state of the target transform. The actuator, therefore, must read the target's state each time it needs to make an actuation update. As a convenience, the plug-in's constructor automatically sets the transform-read capability on the target `TransformGroup` object. In the bargain, however, the plug-in gives up its option to not preserve actuation state; otherwise, in the act of restoring some previous state, the plug-in might be negating the effect of some other user's actuation.

Because this plug-in must perform a transform read and a matrix multiplication, it is the least efficient of the set. What it loses in efficiency, however, it more than makes up in versatility. With this plug-in there is never the danger of one user negating the effect of another user. Instead, the second operation always picks up from where the first one left off, no matter who made the change or how it was made. As you'll see later in this chapter, this multi-user capability provides for some interesting operations that would be impossible with the single-user plug-ins.

18.1.4 TGGeometryPlugin class

The inner/operation actuator plug-ins that the framework provides all perform simple geometric operations on their `TransformGroup` target. All use `TGGeometryPlugin` as their base class, with the "TG" standing for "Transform-Group." Like its outer/target plug-in counterpart, the `ActuatorPlugin` class, all of its template methods are abstract. Its constructor, however, takes a parameter, which is the `TransformGroup` actuation target. As a convenience, the constructor sets the target node's transform-write capability, which is required by all `TGGeometryPlugin` plug-ins.

Geometry operations

The inner/operation plug-ins supported by the framework are summarized in table 18.3. Note that each plug-in is responsible for defining how the elements in the actuation event value are used. The `Tuple4d` value elements are named X, Y, Z, and W.

Table 18.3 Summary of inner/operation plug-in classes for actuation

Class/*Interface*	Description
TGGeometryPlugin	Abstract base class for inner/target transform group geometry plug-ins
TranslationPlugin	Transform group geometry plug-in that performs translation along the major axes relative to the target's local space. The actuation X, Y, and Z values specify the translation (W is ignored).
NegTranslationPlugin	Transform group geometry plug-in that performs negative translation along the major axes relative to the target's local space. The actuation X, Y, and Z values specify the translation (W is ignored).
RotationPlugin	Transform group geometry plug-in that performs rotation about an arbitrary but fixed axis defined relative to the target's local space. The actuation W value specifies the rotation in radians (X, Y, and Z are ignored). The rotation axis is established during construction and can not be subsequently changed (otherwise the actuation state would become invalid).
AxisAnglePlugin	Transform group geometry plug-in that performs rotation about an arbitrary axis defined relative to the target's local space. The actuation X, Y, and Z values specify the rotation axis, and the W value specifies the rotation about it in radians. Because of state maintenance requirements, this plug-in will not work reliably in an SVTransformGroupPlugin.
ScalePlugin	Transform group geometry plugin that performs scaling along the major axes relative to the target's local space. The actuation X, Y, and Z values specify multiplicative scaling factors (W is ignored).

TGGeometryPlugin implementation

Since this plug-in must serve the diverse needs of all of its host plug-ins, ranging from single-user vector to multi-user matrix, its methods must be equally diverse. Some are common to all host plug-ins, but others are specific to one or two of them. Shown below is a code fragment from the TGGeometryPlugin class that includes all the methods that must be overridden by its subclasses. Understanding what is required of its methods is key to understanding how the actuator's nested plug-ins work. The following method headers describe what the methods do, and note if a method is only used by certain host plug-ins. The next section will show the methods being used in the context of their host outer/target plug-ins, which should help to further explain the methods and their operation.

Template methods for TGGeometryPlugin subclasses

Filename: J3duiBook/lib/j3dui/control/actuators/TGGeometryPlugin.java

```
...
/**
Must be overridden to return the initial reference
actuation value.
@return Reference to an actuation value.
*/
protected abstract Tuple4d getActuationInit();

/**
Must be overridden to translate the actuation value
into an equivalent transform matrix.
@param value Actuation value.
@param copy Container for the copied return value.
@return Reference to <copy>.
*/
protected abstract Transform3D toActuationTransform(
  Tuple4d value, Transform3D copy);

/**
Must be overridden to translate the actuation input value
together with the actuation reference value into a new
actuation state value.  Only used by TransformGroupPlugins.
@param value Input actuation value.
@param reference Reference actuation value.
@param copy Container for the copied return value.  Unused
dimensions are unaffected.
@return Reference to <copy>.
*/
protected abstract Tuple4d toActuationUpdate(Tuple4d value,
  Tuple4d reference, Tuple4d copy);

/**
Must be overridden to compute a delta actuation value
given the new actuation value and the old actuation value.
Only used by SM and MMTransformGroupPlugins.
```

```
@param newValue New actuation value.
@param oldValue Old actuation value.
@param copy Container for the copied return value.  Unused
dimensions are unaffected.
@return Reference to <copy>.
*/
protected abstract Tuple4d toActuationDelta(
  Tuple4d newValue, Tuple4d oldValue, Tuple4d copy);
...
```

18.1.5 ActuatorPlugin Revisited

As promised, now that the inner/operation plug-in has been introduced, we can take a look at how the outer/target plug-ins use it to achieve their unique styles of actuation state management. The following code samples only show the implementation of the `ActuatorPlugin` methods, since that is where the `TGGeometryPlugin` is used. In the following code samples, note that the plug-in object, `_plugin`, is exposed in the `TransformGroupPlugin` super class for use by its subclasses.

SVTransformGroupPlugin implementation

The following code fragment is from the `SVTransformGroupPlugin` class. As you may recall, this plug-in uses a `Tuple4d` to maintain its action state, and it is single-user, meaning that it only writes the target's transform—it doesn't read it.

In the `initActuation` method, the input actuation value is pre-processed for scale and offset with the `toActuationSource` method, and the result, `_value`, is used to set the actuator's reference state, `_reference`, and its current state, `_state`. The state value is then post-processed for clamping with the `toActuationTarget` method to produce the final actuation state value. Using the geometry plug-in's `toActuationTransform` method, this value is converted to an equivalent transform matrix, `_xform`, which is then set as the target node's transform.

The structure of the `updateActuation` method is similar. Instead of setting the reference and current states, however, the plug-in's `toActuationUpdate` method converts the pre-processed input value into a new actuation state value relative to the reference value.

The `syncActuation` method simply sets the reference value to the current state value. This has the effect of preserving the current actuation state as the starting point for the next actuation operation. The next call to `updateActuation` will be performed relative to this new reference state, instead of the old original one.

Filename: J3duiBook/lib/j3dui/control/actuators/SVTransformGroupPlugin.java

```
...
/** Actuation reference value. */
private Vector4d _reference = new Vector4d();

/** Actuation state value. */
private Vector4d _state = new Vector4d();

/** Dummy actuation value.  (for GC) */
private final Vector4d _value = new Vector4d();

/** Dummy actuation transform.  (for GC) */
private final Transform3D _xform = new Transform3D();

// ActuatorPlugin implementation

protected void initActuation(Tuple4d value) {
   toActuationSource(value, _value);
   _state.set(_value);
   _reference.set(_state);
   toActuationTarget(_state, _state);
   _plugin.toActuationTransform(_state, _xform);
   _plugin._targetNode.setTransform(_xform);
}

protected void updateActuation(Tuple4d value) {
   toActuationSource(value, _value);
   _plugin.toActuationUpdate(_value, _reference, _state);
   toActuationTarget(_state, _state);
   _plugin.toActuationTransform(_state, _xform);
   _plugin._targetNode.setTransform(_xform);
}

protected void syncActuation() {
   _reference.set(_state);
}
...
```

SMTransformGroupPlugin implementation

The following code fragment is from the SMTransformGroupPlugin class. This plug-in uses a Transform3D (i.e. a transform matrix) to maintain its actuation state; and it is for single-user utility. Its structure is rather similar to that of the previous plug-in. In the initActuation method the input actuation value is converted to an equivalent transform matrix, which is saved as the actuator's new reference and current state. As before, the new state transform is written to the target. Note that the `toActuationTarget` method is absent. This is because the "value" of a state matrix cannot be clamped (at least in the sense of minimum/maximum limits).

In the `updateActuation` method, the input actuation value is again converted to an equivalent transform matrix, but here it is multiplied with the reference transform to obtain the new actuation state transform. The new transform is then written to the target. As in the previous plug-in, the `syncActuation` method simply sets the reference state to the current state, but here it is done with a `Matrix3D` object instead of with a `Tuple4d`.

Implementation of SMVTransformGroupPlugin template methods

Filename: J3duiBook/lib/j3dui/control/actuators/SMTransformGroupPlugin.java

```
...
/** Actuation reference value. */
private Transform3D _reference = new Transform3D();

/** Actuation state value. */
private Transform3D _state = new Transform3D();

/** Dummy actuation value.  (for GC) */
private final Vector4d _value = new Vector4d();

/** Dummy actuation transform.  (for GC) */
private final Transform3D _xform = new Transform3D();

// ActuatorPlugin implementation

protected void initActuation(Tuple4d value) {
   toActuationSource(value, _value);
   _plugin.toActuationTransform(_value, _state);
   _reference.set(_state);
   _plugin._targetNode.setTransform(_state);
}

/**
Must be overridden if update is anything but matrix
multiplicative.
*/
protected void updateActuation(Tuple4d value) {
   toActuationSource(value, _value);
   _plugin.toActuationTransform(_value, _xform);
   _state.mul(_xform, _reference);
   _plugin._targetNode.setTransform(_state);
}

protected void syncActuation() {
   _reference.set(_state);
}
...
```

MMTransformGroupPlugin implementation

The following code fragment is from the `MMTransformGroupPlugin` class. This plug-in also uses a `Transform3D` to maintain its action state, but it allows for multiple users, meaning that it must read as well as write its target's state. As previously mentioned, this plug-in always accumulates its actuation state. As such, it assumes that the actuation state will always be sync'ed at the end of an operation, such as a drag. Its structure is different from that of the previous plug-ins in that the reference state must be obtained directly from the target object prior to each actuation update. This means the reference state is constantly being updated as the target's actuation is updated, which is a completely different definition of reference.

In the `initActuation` method, the `Vector4d` actuation value is saved as the old actuation value, `_oldValue`. As in the other plug-ins, the new value is converted into a transform and written to the target. The role of `_oldValue` is to preserve the actuation value of the previous actuation initialization or update. In the `updateActuation` method, the current input actuation value and the previous one provided by `_oldValue` are used by the geometry plug-in's `toActuationDelta` method to compute a delta actuation value. This delta value is then converted into a transform matrix and multiplied with the reference transform read from the target. The resulting transform is the target's new actuation state, which is written to the target. The effect on the target's geometric state is that the change (delta) from the previous (old) actuation value to the current (new) one is impressed upon the target's current state, whatever that may be.

The `syncActuation` method does even less than in the other plug-ins. Here it simply sets the `_needSync` flag. You may have noticed that this flag is used in `updateActuation` to make the delta actuation value zero by using the new value as both the new and old value arguments. The effect is for the first update after a sync, such as for a new drag operation, to update the old actuation value, while leaving the target state unchanged. All the methods are still called in case they need to track the state changes.

Implementation of MMTransformGroupPlugin template methods

Filename: J3duiBook/lib/j3dui/control/actuators/MMTransformGroupPlugin.java

```
...
/** Old actuation value.   (direct for speed)*/
Vector4d _oldValue = new Vector4d();

/** True if sync is needed.   (direct for speed)*/
boolean _needSync = true;

/** Dummy actuation value.   (for GC) */
private final Vector4d _value = new Vector4d();

/** Dummy delta actuation value.   (for GC)*/
private final Vector4d _delta = new Vector4d();
```

```java
/** Dummy transform state.  (for GC) */
private final Transform3D _state = new Transform3D();

/** Dummy transform reference.  (for GC) */
private static final Transform3D _reference =
 new Transform3D();

// ActuatorPlugin implementation

/**
Will destroy any existing multi-user state.
*/
protected void initActuation(Tuple4d value) {
  toActuationSource(value, _value);
  _oldValue.set(_value);
  _plugin.toActuationTransform(_value, _state);
  _plugin._targetNode.setTransform(_state);
}


/**
Must be overridden if update is anything but incremental
matrix multiplicative.
*/
protected void updateActuation(Tuple4d value) {
  toActuationSource(value, _value);

  // compute actuation delta
  if(_needSync) {
    _plugin.toActuationDelta(_value, _value, _delta);
    _needSync = false;
  } else {
    _plugin.toActuationDelta(_value, _oldValue, _delta);
  }
  _oldValue.set(_value);

  // update target transform by delta
  _plugin.toActuationTransform(_delta, _state);

  _plugin._targetNode.getTransform(_reference);
  _state.mul(_reference);
  _plugin._targetNode.setTransform(_state);
}

protected void syncActuation() {
  _needSync = true;
}
...
```

18.2 BASIC COORDINATE MAPPING

The discussion on UI control techniques in part 2 identified the need to associate input coordinate values with like or different target coordinates. Motivation for this was driven by the need for a 2D input device, like a mouse, to control target objects in a 3D space. Somehow, the two input coordinates must be converted or *mapped* into the three target coordinates. A different aspect of coordinate mapping involves changing the input-to-target mapping to provide a more intuitive user interface, with movement of the target object matching that of the mouse in the context of the scene view.

18.2.1 Basic requirements

As was the case with actuation, the framework not only has to deal with the conceptual aspects of the technique but also with its practical needs. In terms of coordinate mapping, this means having to handle situations where the source and target space units and origin are different, which requires the introduction of conversion factors for such operations as scaling and offset. Other situations may require a more radical mapping of coordinate spaces, as from positional coordinates to rotational ones. Yet another aspect of the mapping is conversion from one event type to another, such as from a drag event to one for actuation.

In the examples presented in the previous chapter, coordinate mapping issues were hidden. The utility block actuators had built-in scale factors and sign conversions, and offsets were for the most part ignored, except when it came to input interpretation filtering. The following sections introduce the framework's answer to generalized coordinate mapping between display-based `InputDragTarget` events and world-based `ActuationTarget` events, which is only the most basic form of coordinate mapping. More sophisticated mappings, including DRM and WRM, are addressed in chapter 19.

Chapter 17 covered input sensors, which is the first link in a control chain going from input device to target transform. Actuators are the last link in the chain; and coordinate mapping is the middle link. This means that you will have to wait a little longer before seeing the next example: there is no easy way to demonstrate an actuator unless there is something to generate actuation events, which is one of many jobs for coordinate mapping. At the end of this section, you will see an example of how to wire up a complete one-way control chain from starting sensor to ending actuator. All of the classes covered in the following sections on coordinate mapping can be found in the package `j3dui.control.mappers`.

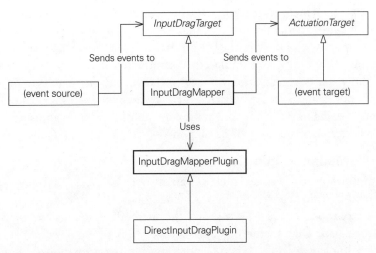

Figure 18.3 Relationship of input drag mapper and its plug-in

Table 18.4 Summary of classes for basic coordinate mapping

Class/*Interface*	Description	Input Events	Output Events
InputDragMapper	A coordinate mapper for input drag to actuation conversion. Uses a plug-in to perform a specific type of coordinate mapping.	InputDragTarget	ActuationTarget
InputDragMapperPlugin	The abstract base class for input drag mapper plug-ins		
DirectInputDragPlugin	An input drag mapper plug-in that performs source scale and target offset, and that statically maps individual source dimensions to none or more output dimensions		

18.2.2   InputDragMapper class

The `InputDragMapper` class is your first encounter with a building block type called a *mapper*. For all the good reasons that filters and actuators use personality plug-ins, so too does a mapper. Mappers are similar in structure to actuators in that they both implement an event interface as input, but its plug-ins must deal with a completely different type of output interface. The `InputDragMapper` class and its related classes and interfaces are shown in figure 18.3.

The `InputDragMapper` class implements the `InputDragTarget` interface as its event input, and uses the `ActuationTarget` interface as its event output. Its constructor takes two arguments: its output event target and its personality plug-in. It also has methods for getting the event target and for getting the plug-in. The `setCumulative` method controls how the output target's actuation state is managed. By default, the mapper assumes that each new input drag operation is meant to continue from where the last one left off. In other words, the drag and corresponding actuation operations are cumulative. If cumulative is set to false, when the next drag operation starts, its actuation will begin relative to the actuator's most recent initialization, not its most recent update, which is where the last drag operation left off.

Before getting into the implementation details of the drag mapper, you will need to have a better understanding of its plug-in.

18.2.3   InputDragMapperPlugin class

The `InputDragMapperPlugin` class is an abstract base class that serves as a lightweight template for concrete plug-ins. The following code fragment from the `InputDragMapperPlugin` class shows the methods that must be overridden by plug-in subclasses. Each method includes a header describing what is required of the subclass to implement the method. Understanding these methods is important to understanding how the `InputDragMapper` class works.

Implementation of InputDragMapperPlugin template methods

Filename: J3duiBook/lib/j3dui/control/mappers/InputDragMapperPlugin.java

```
...
/**
Transforms the starting input drag position into the target
actuation value (copy) relative to the target space.
@param source Source display canvas.
@param pos Input source position.
@param copy Container for the copied return value.
*/
protected abstract void startInputDrag(
  Canvas3D source, Tuple2d pos, Tuple4d copy);


/**
Transforms the continuing input drag position into the target
actuation value (copy) relative to the target space.
@param source Source display canvas.
@param pos Input source position.
@param copy Container for the copied return value.
*/
protected abstract void doInputDrag(
  Canvas3D source, Tuple2d pos, Tuple4d copy);


/**
Transforms the stopping input drag position into the target
actuation value (copy) relative to the target space.
@param source Source display canvas.
@param pos Input source position.
@param copy Container for the copied return value.
*/
```

```
protected abstract void stopInputDrag(
  Canvas3D source, Tuple2d pos, Tuple4d copy);
...
```

18.2.4 DirectInputDragPlugin Class

The `DirectInputDragPlugin` class is a mapper plug-in intended for situations in which the source event value needs to be wired directly to the target event value in some arbitrary but static manner. Static coordinate mapping for display space inputs is of limited use in most UI situations where the view is movable. As the view moves, what the user does with the mouse in the display will no longer match what is happening to the object in the scene. This plug-in is the only concrete subclass of `InputDragMapperPlugin` in the framework.

The parameters that make the connection between input and output dimensions are set with the `setSourceMap` method, with an argument for each source dimension. Each argument indicates to which target dimensions a given source dimension value contributes. Direct mapping also requires some means of specifying the sign of the mapped value. This is generalized in the form of a multiplicative source-side scaling factor, which is set with the `setSourceScale` method. To round out the mapping, an additive target-side offset is included, which is set with `setTargetOffset`. Including scaling and offset may seem redundant with that in the `ActuatorPlugin` class, but it allows parameters to be set where they are functionally needed, and it has negligible processing overhead.

The code fragment below is from the `DirectDragMapperPlugin` class. The first portion shows how the `setSourceMap` bit flag arguments are parsed and saved internally as boolean arrays, with one element per target dimension. The second portion shows the `toTargetValue` method, which performs the source to target mapping, and its use in the implementation of the plug-in's methods.

Setting and using direct coordinate mapping in DirectDragMapperPlugin

Filename: J3duiBook/lib/j3dui/control/mappers/DirectDragMapperPlugin.java

```
...
// public interface ==========================================
...
/**
Sets the mapping from source dimension to target
dimension by source dimension according to target
dimension flags (Mapper.DIM_???).
@param mapX The target dimensions (Mapper.DIM_???)
controlled by the source X dimension.
@param mapY The target dimensions (Mapper.DIM_???)
controlled by the source Y dimension.
*/
public void setSourceMap(int mapX, int mapY) {
  _mapX[0] = ((mapX & Mapper.DIM_X) == 0) ? false : true;
```

```
    _mapX[1] = ((mapX & Mapper.DIM_Y) == 0) ? false : true;
    _mapX[2] = ((mapX & Mapper.DIM_Z) == 0) ? false : true;
    _mapX[3] = ((mapX & Mapper.DIM_W) == 0) ? false : true;

    _mapY[0] = ((mapY & Mapper.DIM_X) == 0) ? false : true;
    _mapY[1] = ((mapY & Mapper.DIM_Y) == 0) ? false : true;
    _mapY[2] = ((mapY & Mapper.DIM_Z) == 0) ? false : true;
    _mapY[3] = ((mapY & Mapper.DIM_W) == 0) ? false : true;
}
…
// personal body ============================================

/** Scale factor applied to source values. */
private Vector2d _scale = new Vector2d(1, 1);

/** Offset factor applied to target values. */
private Vector4d _offset = new Vector4d(0, 0, 0, 0);

/** If true, the target dimension gets source X value. */
private boolean _mapX[] = {true, false, false, false};

/** If true, the target dimension gets source Y value. */
private boolean _mapY[] = {false, true, false, false};

/** Dummy source value.  (for GC) */
private final Vector2d _value = new Vector2d();

/**
Directly maps the 2D XY source space input value into a
4D XYZW target space actuation value, which affects all
output dimensions.  Output values are accumulated by
dimension.  Includes source scaling and target offset.
@param value Source value.
@param copy Container for the copied return value.
*/
protected void toTargetValue(Tuple2d value,
 Tuple4d copy) {

  _value.set(_scale.x * value.x,
   _scale.y * value.y);

  copy.set(_offset);

  if(_mapX[0]) copy.x += _value.x;
  if(_mapX[1]) copy.y += _value.x;
  if(_mapX[2]) copy.z += _value.x;
  if(_mapX[3]) copy.w += _value.x;

  if(_mapY[0]) copy.x += _value.y;
  if(_mapY[1]) copy.y += _value.y;
  if(_mapY[2]) copy.z += _value.y;
  if(_mapY[3]) copy.w += _value.y;
```

CHAPTER 18 CONTROL ACTUATION

```
}

// InputDragMapperPlugin implementation

protected void startInputDrag(Canvas3D source,
 Tuple2d pos, Tuple4d copy) {
   // do nothing
}

protected void doInputDrag(Canvas3D source,
 Tuple2d pos, Tuple4d copy) {
   // map coordinates
   toTargetValue(pos, copy);
}

protected void stopInputDrag(Canvas3D source,
 Tuple2d pos, Tuple4d copy) {
   // do nothing
}
...
```

18.2.5   InputDragMapper revisited

Now that you've been introduced to the InputDragMapperPlugin class, it is time to revisit the InputDragMapper class to see how it is implemented using this plug-in. The code fragment below shows the mapper's implementation of its InputDrag-Target event interface methods.

In the doInputDrag method, the input source value is converted to a corresponding actuation value using the plug-in's doInputDrag method. The new actuation value is used to update the target's actuation state by calling the event target's updateActuation method. Even though doInputDrag is the only interface method requiring a value from the plug-in, all interface methods call their corresponding plug-in method just in case the plug-in needs to internally track the drag state.

Because the ActuationTarget event interface is stateless, its output generation is simple. The mapper has no need to call the initActuation method because nothing in the input drag interface demands output initialization. If _cumulative is true, the syncActuation method is called when the input drag operation is done, signified when the drag source calls the input interface stopInputDrag method. And, as you already saw, the updateActuation method is called whenever the input drag position changes, which is indicated when the doInputDrag method is called.

Filename: J3duiBook/lib/j3dui/control/mappers/InputDragMapper.java

```
...
// InputDragTarget implementation

public void startInputDrag(Canvas3D source, Vector2d pos) {
  _plugin.startInputDrag(source, pos, _actuation);
}

public void doInputDrag(Canvas3D source, Vector2d pos) {
  _plugin.doInputDrag(source, pos, _actuation);
  _eventTarget.updateActuation(_actuation);
}

public void stopInputDrag(Canvas3D source, Vector2d pos) {
  _plugin.stopInputDrag(source, pos, _actuation);

  if(_cumulative) _eventTarget.syncActuation();
}

// personal body ============================================

/** Personality plugin.  Never null. */
private InputDragMapperPlugin _plugin;

/** Event target.  Never null. */
private ActuationTarget _eventTarget;

/** If true, drag effect is cumulative. */
private boolean _cumulative = true;

/** Dummy actuation value.  (for GC) */
private Vector4d _actuation = new Vector4d();
...
```

18.2.6 Example: Actuators

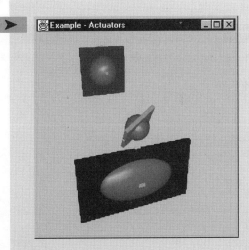

**Figure 18.4
Screen shot of the
actuators example**

This example demonstrates the framework's actuators using direct coordinate mapping.

> **➤ See**

The virtual world contains three target objects (red, green, blue) arranged vertically. A screen shot is provided in figure 18.4.

> **➤ Do**

- Drag the mouse (left button) in the display to translate the top (red) target along the world X-Y axes. Repeat the drag in different directions.
- Drag the mouse (right button) in the display to rotate the middle (green) target about the world X and Y axes. Repeat the drag in different directions.
- Drag the mouse (middle button) in the display to scale the bottom (blue) target along the world X-Y axes. Repeat the drag in different directions.

> **➤ Observe**

- The translation and rotation drags are relative cumulative, meaning that the drag always starts at zero and an operation continues from where the last one left off.
- The rotation drags are multi-user matrix, meaning that X and Y rotations occur independently but simultaneously, with the target being rolled like a trackball.
- The scale drag is relative non-cumulative, meaning that drag always starts at zero and the operation always starts from its initial value (unity scaling).
- During scaling the target scale is clamped to reasonable values.

The internal structure of this example has changed considerably in comparison to the previous ones. The following code samples from the example illustrate the more significant aspects of using actuators and mappers. Starting with the target setup section of the example, the following fragment shows how a transform chain is built for the translation target using the `buildTarget` utility block. The target object is initially positioned in the world at (0, 3, 0), which is at the top of a column of three manipulation targets. The second transform in the chain is attached to an

Actuator object that consists of a SV outer/target plug-in, and a translation inner/operation plug-in.

Transform chain for the translation actuator target

Filename: J3duiBook/examples/Actuators/Actuators.java

```
...
// setup manipulation targets
TransformGroup target[];

/// translation target
target = BasicBlocks.buildTarget(new TestThing(
 TestThing.BOX_TRANSLATION, TestThing.BALL_DEFAULT),
 new Vector3d(0, 3, 0));
getWorld().addSceneNode(target[0]);

Actuator xlt = new Actuator(new SVTransformGroupPlugin(
 new TranslationPlugin(target[1])));
...
```

The middle target demonstrates rotation, but not just simple single-axis rotation. Two actuators are connected to the same transform: one for X-axis rotation and the other for Y-axis rotation. Both are users sharing the same target transform, so MM (i.e., multi-user) target plug-ins must be used. This combination of rotation actuators driving the same target allows the target object to be rolled like a trackball. You'll see this pattern formalized as a framework building block in a later section.

Transform chain for the rotation actuator target

Filename: J3duiBook/examples/Actuators/Actuators.java

```
...
/// rotation target
target = BasicBlocks.buildTarget(new TestThing(
 TestThing.BOX_ROTATION, TestThing.BALL_DEFAULT),
 new Vector3d(0, 0, 0));
getWorld().addSceneNode(target[0]);

Actuator rotX = new Actuator(new MMTransformGroupPlugin(
 new RotationPlugin(target[1], new Vector3d(1, 0, 0))));
Actuator rotY = new Actuator(new MMTransformGroupPlugin(
 new RotationPlugin(target[1], new Vector3d(0, 1, 0))));
...
```

The bottom target in the example is for scaling. Notice that the actuation state is clamped in all dimensions to a safe range for scaling. To do this, the plug-in is accessed through its actuator.

Filename: J3duiBook/examples/Actuators/Actuators.java

```
...
/// scale target
target = BasicBlocks.buildTarget(new TestThing(
 TestThing.BOX_SCALE, TestThing.BALL_DEFAULT),
 new Vector3d(0, -3, 0));
getWorld().addSceneNode(target[0]);

Actuator scl = new Actuator(new SVTransformGroupPlugin(
 new ScalePlugin(target[1])));
scl.getPlugin().setTargetClamp(Mapper.DIM_ALL,
 new Vector2d(.5, 4));
...
```

Each target control in the example uses similar processing: a mouse dragger connected to a relative drag filter, connected to a direct mapper. Following is the code for the scaling control. Notice how an offset of 1 is applied to the target side of the coordinate mapping. When performing interactive scaling with a relative input, an initial value of 1 is needed, instead of 0, as with translation and rotation. In order to demonstrate non-cumulative actuation, notice how the mapper's cumulative flag is set to false.

Filename: J3duiBook/examples/Actuators/Actuators.java

```
...
// setup manipulation controls
DirectInputDragPlugin plugin;
InputDragMapper mapper;
InputDragTarget filter;
MouseDragSensor dragger;
...
/// relative non-cumulative scale, third button
plugin = new DirectInputDragPlugin();
plugin.setSourceScale(new Vector2d(.025, .025));
plugin.setTargetOffset(new Vector4d(1, 1, 1, 0));
mapper = new InputDragMapper(scl, plugin);
mapper.setCumulative(false);

filter = new InputDragFilter(mapper,
 new RelativeInputDragPlugin());

dragger = new MouseDragSensor(filter, disp, root);
dragger.setButtons(Input.BUTTON_THIRD);
...
```

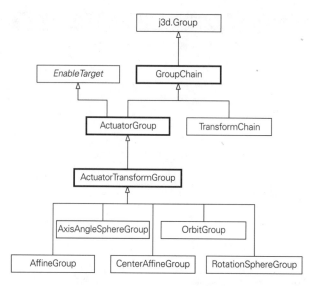

Figure 18.5 **Relationship of classes related to basic actuator groups**

18.3 ACTUATOR GROUPS

Because we covered sensors and filters in chapter 17, and actuators and mappers in sections 18.1 and 18.2, you finally have enough of the framework under your belt to start having fun (well, at least fun in a 3D UI sort of way). Earlier in the chapter, you saw how an actuator performs a single operation on an attached target transform group. In UI design, and 3D modeling in general, it is often desirable to bundle multiple related geometric functions into a single reusable object. This makes constructing and manipulating models easier and less prone to error. A good example is the VRML Transform node.

A VRML Transform node combines translation, rotation, scaling, centering, and a few other goodies into a single package. The node is placed in the scene graph, target nodes are attached as children, and you're off and running with the geometric manipulation equivalent of a Swiss Army knife. Taking this concept in the other direction, specialized sets of geometric transforms could be grouped together to achieve complex and constrained geometric operations, such as view orbiting.

To achieve such a degree of functional integration the framework generalizes the pattern for actuator target chaining that you saw in the previous example, where a chain of transforms is created and specialized, and pre-configured actuators are attached to them. The result is an *actuator group*. The base classes used to derive actuator groups are in the `j3dui.utils.control.actuators` package, and the actuator group classes themselves are in the `j3dui.utils.control.actuators.groups` package. The derivation of the framework's actuator group classes is shown in figure 18.5.

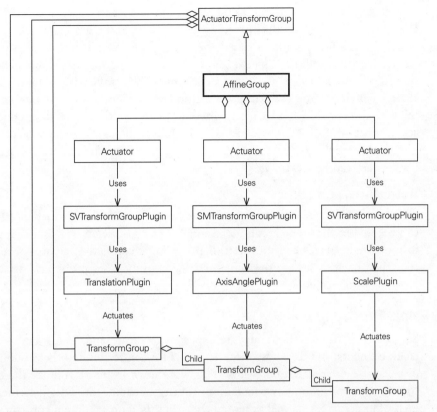

Figure 18.6 Relationship of actuators and transform groups in the AffineGroup class

Figure 18.6 illustrates how actuators and transform groups are used in the `Affine-Group` actuator group class, which is similar in function to the VRML Transform node.

18.3.1 GroupChain Class

The skeleton for an actuator group is the `GroupChain` class, which contains a chain of groups configured parent-to-child. It is similar in concept to the `MultiTrans-formGroup` class provided in the Sun utilities, but with a bit more specialization and a bit less exposure of (and protection for) its inner workings. The chain elements are provided with a modicum of privacy by extending the `GroupChain` from the Java 3D `Group` class and adding the chain elements to it, as opposed to using the group itself as the head element in the chain. Limiting access to the groups inside the chain is important so that their internal states, which actuators control, are not inadvertently corrupted by outside influences. Using `Group` for the chain and the chain elements instead of a `TransformGroup` permits a bit more flexibility when it comes to including custom elements in the chain, such as for nesting group chains, in a composite pattern.

A `GroupChain` object consists of any number of `Group` elements. The group closest to the host group (its immediate child) is called the head, and the one farthest down the chain subgraph is called the tail. If the chain length is zero (an empty chain), the `GroupChain` object itself serves as the tail group. In general, child nodes should only be added to the chain's tail group. The `getTail` method returns the chain's tail group, and the `addNode` method conveniently adds a node to it. (Ideally the `Group` class `addChild` method would be overridden for adding children, but at the time of writing it is declared final.) Both of these methods accommodate groups that are themselves `GroupChain` objects, with recursion occurring as needed (to get the "tail of the tail").

18.3.2 ActuatorGroup class

The `ActuatorGroup` class extends the `GroupChain` class, which means that it can be used in the scene graph like a single `Group` node, as well as a chain element in some higher-level `GroupChain`. If the group chain is the actuator group's skeleton, then its muscles are the actuators that its subclasses create and attach to the chain's group elements.

ActuatorGroup model

Subclasses of `ActuatorGroup` are expected to create and attach actuators to the chain elements, and to expose those actuators for connection to other building blocks by means of their actuation events. This was shown in figure 18.6 for the `AffineGroup` actuator group. By convention, subclasses should provide "get" methods for each of its actuators, as well as several constructors: a no-argument constructor, a single-argument constructor whose argument is the first child node, and a constructor allowing all of its actuators to be initialized.

Subclasses are required to implement the `setEnableGroup` method, which conveniently controls the enable state of its constituent actuators, and the group as a whole. Subclasses can also implement their own input actuation interface, in which case the actuator group itself becomes an actuator, or more specifically a `PseudoActuator`, which is the next best thing. An example of this is the `OrbitGroup` subclass described below.

18.3.3 ActuatorTransformGroup class

The `ActuatorTransformGroup` class extends the `ActuatorGroup` class. As its name implies, its chain elements are specifically made from `TransformGroup` objects. This class serves as a lightweight abstract base class for most of the framework's actuator groups. Its simplest constructor takes two arguments: the length of the transform chain and the first child node, which can be null if there is none.

To help protect the transform state of the chain elements, the `getTransformGroup` method, which gets the transform group at a specified index in the chain, is protected. The functionally similar method `getGroup` in the `GroupChain` base class is public, but it returns the chain elements as Group objects. Accessing individual chain elements is useful for attaching child objects to intermediate levels in the chain, such as including a Look-At-Point (LAP) object in the head group of a chain that performs view orbiting.

18.3.4   ActuatorTransformGroup subclasses

The following sections describe the more basic actuator groups provided by the framework, which are derived from ActuatorTransformGroup. They are summarized in table 18.5. Other actuator groups are located in more functionally specific packages, such as for visualization, and will be covered in later chapters.

Table 18.5   Summary of actuator transform group classes

Class/*Interface*	Description	Input Events	Output Events
ActuatorTransformGroup	The abstract base class for actuator groups that operate on transform group chains	EnableTarget	
AffineGroup	A transform actuator group providing translation, rotation, and scaling	EnableTarget	
CenterAffineGroup	A transform actuator group providing translation, rotation, scaling, and center point specification for rotation and scaling	EnableTarget	
RotationSphereGroup	A transform actuator group providing multi-axis rotation like rolling a ball. The rotation axes correspond to the major axes and are fixed.	EnableTarget	
AxisAngleSphereGroup	A transform actuator group providing multi-axis rotation like rolling a ball. The rotation axes are arbitrary and can be set dynamically.	EnableTarget	
OrbitGroup	A transform actuator group providing Euler angle-based rotation (heading, elevation, twist) for orbiting about a point	EnableTarget ActuationTarget	

AffineGroup class

The AffineGroup class provides basic translation, rotation, and scale functionality, applied in that order, with a separate transform group in the chain for each operation. For efficiency, the translation and scale actuators use SVTransformGroupPlugin as their outer/target plug-ins, and TranslationPlugin and ScalePlugin for their inner/operation plug-ins, respectively. The rotation actuator is of the axis-angle variety, which is provided by its AxisAnglePlugin inner/operation plug-in. As required for axis-angle rotation, its outer/target plug-in is a matrix-based SMTransformGroupPlugin. The AffineGroup class is close in geometric functionality to the VRML Transform node, but the next class is even closer, which it pays for by being a bit more complicated and a little less efficient.

CenterAffineGroup class

The `CenterAffineGroup` class provides everything that the `AffineGroup` provides, but it also includes actuators for controlling the center position about which rotation and scaling occur. This actuator group is a fairly close approximation to a VRML Transform node.

The code fragment below is the main constructor for this actuator group. It shows the order of the transforms. Starting from the head, they are translation, center, rotation, scale, and negative center. Center and negative center are inverse translations that bracket the rotation and scale transforms in order to provide them with a center point separate from the local space origin. This code fragment also reveals some of the more interesting wiring found in any of the actuator groups. Notice how the center and negative center actuators are connected together through a single `ActuationSplitter`, which is the only access provided to these actuators. This scheme assures that the associated actuators are always updated in unison when provided with a single center position value.

Group chain actuator construction and wiring for CenterAffineGroup

Filename: J3duiBook/lib/j3dui/control/actuators/groups/CenterAffineGroup.java

```
...
/**
Constructs a CenterAffineGroup with a child node.
@param node First child node of this group.  Null if none.
*/
public CenterAffineGroup(Node node) {
  super(5, node);

  // build actuators
  _translation = new Actuator(new SVTransformGroupPlugin(
    new TranslationPlugin(getTransform(0))));

  _center = new Actuator(new SVTransformGroupPlugin(
    new TranslationPlugin(getTransform(1))));

  _rotation = new Actuator(new SMTransformGroupPlugin(
    new AxisAnglePlugin(getTransform(2))));

  _scale = new Actuator(new SVTransformGroupPlugin(
    new ScalePlugin(getTransform(3))));

  _centerNeg = new Actuator(new SVTransformGroupPlugin(
    new NegTranslationPlugin(getTransform(4))));

  // build center splitter
  _centerSplit = new ActuationSplitter();
  _centerSplit.addEventTarget(_center);
  _centerSplit.addEventTarget(_centerNeg);
}
...
```

RotationSphereGroup class

The `RotationSphereGroup` class is a generalized version of the trackball-like rotation demonstrated in the previous example. Here, three actuators using multi-user `MMTransformGroupPlugin` and fixed-axis `RotationPlugin` plug-ins are all connected to the same transform group in the transform chain. The axes for the three rotations are set to the major axes: *X*, *Y*, and *Z*.

AxisAngleSphereGroup class

The `AxisAngleSphereGroup` class also uses a single transform group in the group chain with three actuators. The actuators also use `MMTransformGroup-Plugin` outer/target plug-ins, but they use `AxisAnglePlugin` inner/operation plug-ins to perform the rotation. Unlike in the previous group, the three rotation axes are arbitrary and can be changed dynamically. As you'll see in chapter 19, axis-angle rotation is what is needed to achieve dynamic coordinate mapping for rotations since the axis is passed along with the event, and can therefore be subjected to local geometric transformation.

OrbitGroup class

The `OrbitGroup` class is specialized for orbiting child objects about a point. As such it is much more constrained and specialized than the previous actuator groups. Its three actuators perform fixed-axis rotation, but in a specific order that is not the same as for standard Euler angles. The angles used for orbiting and the order of their transforms are: heading (*Y* axis), elevation (*X* axis), and twist (*Z* axis). All angles are right-handed. This actuator group also implements the `PseudoActuator` interface so that it can act like an actuator with respect to event handling. Its `ActuationTarget` interface allows its three orbit angles to be specified in a single actuation value in an input event.

18.3.5   Example: ActuatorGroups

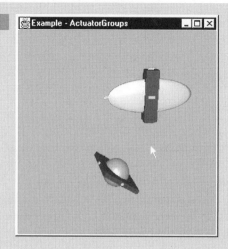

**Figure 18.7
Screen shot of the
ActuatorGroups example**

This example demonstrates the framework's actuator groups using direct coordinate mapping.

> See

The virtual world contains two target objects (orange, olive green), one above the other. A screen shot is provided in figure 18.7.

> Do

- Drag the mouse (left button with SHIFT) in a display to orbit the view in heading and elevation about the world origin.
- Drag the mouse (left button) in a display or use the arrow keys to translate the top (orange) target along the world X-Y axes. Repeat the drag from different view directions.
- Drag the mouse (right button) in a display to rotate the top (orange) target about its Z-axis tic mark. Repeat the drag from different view directions.
- Drag the mouse (middle button) in a display to scale the top (orange) target along the object X-Z axes relative to its Z-axis tic mark. Repeat the drag from different view directions.
- Drag the mouse (left button with CONTROL) in a display or use the arrow keys (with CONTROL) to roll the bottom (olive green) target like a trackball. Repeat the drag from different view directions.

> Observe

- View orbiting is performed using the OrbitGroup actuator group.
- Operations on the top target are handled through a single CenterAffineGroup actuator group whose center point is set to correspond to the target's Z-axis tic mark.
- Operations on the bottom target are handled through a single RotationSphereGroup actuator group.
- All coordinate mapping is static, meaning that manipulation of targets will seem non-intuitive if the view is not head-on.

Besides demonstrating many of the actuator groups, this example also introduces some powerful utility blocks that make the UI coding easier. They are found in the `ActuationBlocks` class in the `j3dui.utils.blocks` package. For your own work you can use the utility blocks as they are, or use them as a template. As promised, the sophistication of the examples is increasing, but the complexity of the code is, in many respects, getting simpler. The following code from the example shows how the new utility blocks are used to conveniently wire up display drag sensors to the top target's center affine actuator group for rotation. A similar configuration is used for all the control operations for both targets, including translation, rotation, scale, and spherical roll.

The `buildRelativeDragger` utility block bundles together a mouse drag sensor and a keyboard arrow sensor together with a relative drag filter. It also includes an independent modifier enabling for each sensor. Notice below how `MODIFIER_NONE` is specified for the mouse buttons, but `MODIFIER_IGNORE` is used for the arrow keys. This means that no modifier keys should be pressed to perform rotation using the mouse buttons, and that the arrow keys are completely ignored, which is necessary otherwise it would interfere with translation using the arrow keys with no modifiers. The `buildDirectMapper` utility block offers an input drag mapper with a plug-in for direct coordinate mapping. Its event target is the center-affine group's axis-angle actuator, which is obtained using the group's `getAxisAngle` method.

Dragging and mapping for rotation using the CenterAffineGroup

Filename: J3duiBook/examples/ActuatorGroups/ActuatorGroups.java

```
...
// setup manipulation targets
/// center affine target
CenterAffineGroup affine = new CenterAffineGroup(
 new TestThing(TestThing.BOX_DEFAULT,
 TestThing.BALL_AFFINE));
getWorld().addSceneNode(BasicBlocks.buildTarget(
 affine, new Vector3d(0, 2, 0))[0]);
...
// setup manipulation controls
InputDragMapper mapper;

...
/// rotation Y, second button
mapper = ActuationBlocks.buildDirectMapper(
 affine.getAxisAngle(), new Vector2d(.025, .025),
 Mapper.DIM_W, Mapper.DIM_NONE, true);

ActuationBlocks.buildRelativeDragger(mapper,
 getView(), Input.BUTTON_SECOND,
 Input.MODIFIER_NONE, Input.MODIFIER_IGNORE);
...
```

Another utility block used in the example is the `buildViewOrbiter` method. It uses `buildRelativeDragger` together with an `OrbitGroup` actuator group to provide convenient view orbiting. You may have noticed while playing with the view orbiter that the other controls may not seem to work right unless the view is head-on. This is because direct coordinate mapping is used, which is static. All manipulation is occurring in absolute world space. In the next chapter you'll see how to make the coordinate mapping dynamic, with both display and world-relative mapping.

18.4 SUMMARY

The chapter started by identifying the practical requirements involved in making target objects do something. The framework refers to this as actuation, and performs it using actuators. An actuator accepts an event input and, in turn, manipulates its target object in some constrained manner, such as translating it along or rotating it about a given axis. It also takes care of maintaining target state between drag operations and allowing multiple users to manipulate the same target. Next, coordinate mapping was introduced as the final piece of the puzzle in getting from input sensor to target actuator. Here we only saw the simplest form of mapping, which directly and statically connects 2D drag coordinates to 4D actuation coordinates. As seen in the last example, this form of mapping, when combined with view movement, can result in non-intuitive control actions, with the mouse going one way and the target object going another way.

The chapter ended with the introduction of the actuator group, which is a class that can be used in a scene graph as a group node, but which is manipulated through built-in actuators. The final example introduced several new utility blocks that conveniently bundle together sensors, filters, mappers, and actuators to form convenient high-level building blocks for target manipulation. With relatively simple example code, some rather sophisticated UI control techniques were demonstrated. Chapter 19 will introduce more intuitive forms of coordinate mapping as well as mouseover enabling of control operations.

C H A P T E R   1 9

Control intuition

As you saw in the previous chapter, trying to control a target object with static control mapping can produce reasonable results, but only if you, the designer, carefully control the position of the user's view in the world. For some applications this might be acceptable, but for many it is not. When static control mapping is combined with general forms of navigation, situations often arise where the controls seem wrong or backward. Another practical aspect of trying to control objects in the scene is designating which object is the target. In the previous examples this was handled by assigning a different mouse button, or button and modifier key combination, to each object in the scene. Such an approach obviously won't work for more than a few objects, and even then it is impractical for the user to have to remember which button-modifier goes with which object. Object picking is the technique needed to handle this problem.

The previous chapters described how the framework handles the fundamental aspects of the control chain, including device input and enabling, input filtering and mapping, and target actuation. This chapter will explore those aspects of the control chain needed to achieve more intuitive control of the situation, including control enabling based on picking, and dynamic forms of coordinate mapping, specifically DRM and WRM.

19.1 OBJECT PICKING

Object picking is the workhorse of a 3D UI. For the most part, little happens of an intuitive nature in a 3D scene without object picking. Although the framework supports picking in its various forms—discrete and continuous, bounds and geometric—the emphasis is on continuous geometric picking. Picking can be employed in a number of ways in a UI. This section introduces a general-purpose picking engine, and then describes how it can be used for target control enabling. Later chapters will describe how to use picking for other UI needs, such as for feedback and selection.

With a few minor exceptions, the classes used in picking and picking-based control enabling are found in the package j3dui.control.mappers. Table 19.1 summarizes the classes and event interfaces related to picking and enabling, and figure 19.1 illustrates how they cooperate.

Table 19.1 Classes and interfaces related to object picking and enabling

Class/*Interface*	Description	Input Events	Output Events
ObjectPickTarget	Event interface for reporting pick target changes		
ObjectPickSplitter	Object pick event splitter	ObjectPickTarget	ObjectPickTarget
PickEngine	Consolidates core picking functionality into a single class. Based on target list picking.		
ObjectPickMapper	Maps input movement and drags into object picks using a pick engine	EnableTarget InputMoveTarget InputDragTarget	ObjectPickTarget
OverEnableMapper	Maps object picks into target enables	ObjectPickTarget	EnableTarget (list) EnableTarget (any) EnableTarget (none)

19.1.1 PickEngine class

The complete Java 3D picking model was described in detail in chapter 13. As you may recall, the Java 3D picking process is complex and decentralized. To achieve a degree of flexibility and generality in what can be a target object for picking, the framework uses an approach where the candidate pick objects are specified explicitly in a target list. Only objects, or more specifically scene graph Node objects, that are in the list can be picked, and then only if the objects and their descendants have been properly configured, with which the framework also assists.

The heart of the framework's picking capability is the PickEngine class. The constructor requires a root BranchGroup object in the scene graph under which the pick search will be performed, and a list of pick target objects that will be sought. A pick operation is performed when the method pickTarget is called, which requires specification of the source display and the pick cursor position in that display. The

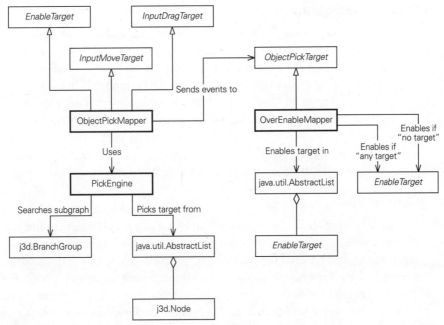

Figure 19.1   Relationship of classes and interfaces related to object picking and enabling

method returns the index of the target in the target list that was hit, if any, and optionally the 3D hit position on the target object. The method `getPickTarget` can be used to convert the pick index result into its equivalent pick object reference. After construction, the pick root and target list can be changed with the `setRoot` and `setTargets` methods, respectively.

Target pickability

For a target node to be pickable, it must lie under the pick root in the scene graph, its pick reporting capability must be set, its leaf shape nodes must be set pickable, and the capability to intersect the leaf shape geometry must be set. By default, Java 3D enables leaf nodes for picking, but pick reporting and geometry intersection must be explicitly enabled. As a convenience, objects in the target list are automatically configured for pick reporting, but not for leaf node picking. For explicit control of leaf node picking, you can use the utilities in the `PickUtils` class found in the `j3dui.utils` package. Also, many of the framework shape objects include the ability to set full leaf pickablity.

Engine configuration

By default, a pick engine performs geometry picking, and quits searching after the first pickable object is hit, whether or not it is in the target list. Bounds-only picking can be specified with the `setUseBounds` method, and hit testing of all objects under the pick cursor can be requested with the `setHitAll` method. Because picking performance is crucial to good UI design, the pick engine also includes provisions for assessing picking performance. A cheat mode, enabled with the `setUseCheat` method, allows side-by-side comparison of in-scene picking performance with and without Java 3D picking. This way, any difference in performance is due to the picking process itself, not the application overhead of handling input events and actuating targets.

Target order

The order of targets in the target list can be significant. If a parent and a descendant object, such as a desk and a drawer in the desk, are both targets in the target list, pick reporting will be enabled for both nodes. If a pick occurs on the descendant, both the parent and the descendant will be included in the hit's scene graph path. For each hit, the pick engine searches the scene graph path for each target in the target list, starting with the first target, which defines the order of pick precedence. When a hit on a list target is found, the search quits. Thus, for the descendant (the drawer) to be picked instead of its parent (the desk) in this situation, the descendant must be in the target list before the parent.

19.1.2   ObjectPickMapper class

The pick engine is truly only an engine; it does not handle or generate any events. Event generation is, instead, the duty of the `ObjectPickMapper` class, which converts input movement and drags into target object picks, including "no target" picks. The picking itself is handled through delegation to a `PickEngine` object configured with the desired pick root and target list. Both continuous and discrete picking modes are supported. For continuous picking, pick events are reported only when the target object changes, and not when the pick cursor moves, which helps to keep event handling overhead to a minimum.

Picking modes

To accommodate various flavors of discrete and continuous picking, several methods are provided. These methods affect only the mode of pick reporting for input drag events. Continuous pick reporting, as a result of input movement events, is not affected by these modes. The different modes can be combined, with the result being an ORing of object pick events. The `setDoPick` method specifies that the pick target is reported when a drag starts, and no target is reported when the drag stops. This is the default mode. The `setDoDrag` method specifies that the pick target is reported only when the drag starts, which is useful for triggering the drag portion of a drag-and-drop operation. The `setDoDrop` method specifies that the pick target is reported continuously during the drag, and when the drag stops, which is useful for tracking drop targets.

ObjectPickTarget interface

Pick reporting requires a new event interface. The `ObjectPickTarget` interface reports both the pick index and the pick object. In general, the pick index should be used if the event target has knowledge of the pick engine's target list, because it uniquely identifies the object in the list (and the object reference may not). If the event target is not privy to the target list, or if the pick event originates from a pick process that does not use a list, then the pick object must be used. It is important to keep these alternative uses of the event in mind when generating or handling `ObjectPickTarget` events because some event targets use one or the other exclusively. As with all other framework events, the event has a corresponding `Object-PickSplitter` class.

19.1.3   OverEnableMapper class

Knowing which object was picked using a pick engine and an object pick mapper is only two thirds of the solution when it comes to mouseover object control. The framework provides the last third of the solution in the form of the `Over-nableMapper` class. To use this class, you have to create a list of control targets that implement the `EnableTarget` interface, with a one-to-one correspondence between the event targets in this list and the pick targets in the pick engine's target list, such as that used by an `ObjectPickMapper` object. When a new target is picked, as indicated by the input `ObjectPickTarget` event interface, any previous enable target is disabled and the one corresponding to the new pick is enabled. Note that `OverEnableMapper` uses only the index parameter in its input event interface.

For convenience, two special-purpose control targets can be set in addition to, or in lieu of, the event list targets. The `setEventTargetAny` method establishes an enable target that is notified when any target is picked; the `setEventTargetNone` method establishes an event target that is notified when no target is picked.

19.1.4   Example: OverEnabling

Figure 19.2
Screen shot of the
OverEnabling example

This example demonstrates object picking and mouseover enabling of control inputs.

➤ See

The virtual world contains four target objects. As it initially displays, three are in a central column (red, green, blue) and one is to the right (magenta). A screen shot is provided in figure 19.2.

➤ Do

- Drag the mouse (left button with SHIFT) in the display or use the arrow keys (with SHIFT) to orbit the view in heading and elevation about the world origin.
- Drag the mouse (left button) on the top (red) target or use the ARROW keys to translate it along the world X-Y axes.
- Drag the mouse (left button) on the middle (green) target or use the ARROW keys to rotate it about the world Y axis.
- Drag the mouse (left button) on the bottom (blue) target or use the ARROW keys to scale it along the world X-Y axes.
- Drag the mouse (left button) on the right (magenta) target or use the ARROW keys to roll the target like a trackball.
- Repeat the drag operations from different view directions.

➤ Observe

- All target operations use mouseover to enable the operation.
- Target picking can differentiate between parent (green thing) and child (magenta thing) in the scene graph.
- All target operations use the first mouse button and no MODIFIER keys.
- All coordinate mapping is static, meaning that manipulation of targets will seem nonintuitive if the view is not head-on.

The general structure of the code for this example is similar to that in the previous example, which demonstrated actuator groups, but with one important difference. In this example, the utility building block `buildOverEnabler` from the `IntuitiveBlocks` class is used to perform overenabling of the target actuators.

The first code sample below is from the `OverEnabling` example class. It shows those portions that deal with the translation target and overenabling. The second sample is from the utility class. It shows how the utility building block combines the framework's core building blocks for picking with move and drag sensors into a single convenient module for overenabling.

Translation control and overenabling in the OverEnabling example

Filename: J3duiBook/examples/OverEnabling/OverEnabling.java

```
...
// setup manipulation targets
/// translation target
AffineGroup affineXlt = new AffineGroup(new TestThing(
 TestThing.BOX_TRANSLATION, TestThing.BALL_DEFAULT));
getWorld().addSceneNode(BasicBlocks.buildTarget(
 affineXlt, new Vector3d(0, 3, 0))[0]);
...
// setup manipulation controls
InputDragMapper mapper;

/// translation, first button
mapper = ActuationBlocks.buildDirectMapper(
 affineXlt.getTranslation(), new Vector2d(.025, .025),
 Mapper.DIM_X, Mapper.DIM_Y, true);

ActuationBlocks.buildRelativeDragger(mapper,
 getView(), Input.BUTTON_FIRST,
 Input.MODIFIER_NONE, Input.MODIFIER_NONE);
...
// setup over management
ArrayList pickList, enableList;

pickList = new ArrayList();
pickList.add(affineXlt);
pickList.add(sphere);
pickList.add(affineRot);
pickList.add(affineScl);

enableList = new ArrayList();
enableList.add(affineXlt);
enableList.add(sphere);
enableList.add(affineRot);
enableList.add(affineScl);

IntuitiveBlocks.buildOverEnabler(getView(),
 getWorld().getSceneRoot(), pickList, enableList);
...
```

Filename: J3duiBook/lib/j3dui/utils/blocks/IntuitiveBlocks.java

```
...
/**
Creates mouse move and drag sensors, an object picker, and
an over enabler and connects them together for continuous
target picking and enabling, whether during mouse movement
or dragging.  All enable targets will be initialized as if
no target was picked.
@param view Source display.
@param pickRoot Scene graph pick root.
@param pickList List of pick targets.
@param enableList List of enable targets corresponding to
the targets in the pick list.
*/
public static final OverEnableMapper buildOverEnabler(
 AppView view, BranchGroup pickRoot, ArrayList pickList,
 ArrayList enableList) {

  // setup over target enabling
  OverEnableMapper enabler = new OverEnableMapper();
  enabler.setEventTargets(enableList);

  enabler.initEventTargets(-1);

  // setup continuous target picking
  ObjectPickMapper picker = new ObjectPickMapper(enabler,
   new PickEngine(pickRoot, pickList));

  /// generate mouse position for any move or drag
  MouseDragSensor dragger = new MouseDragSensor(picker,
   view.getDisplay(), view.getRoot());
  dragger.setButtons(Input.BUTTON_ALL);

  MouseMoveSensor mouseMove = new MouseMoveSensor(
   picker, view.getDisplay(), view.getRoot());

  return enabler;
}
...
```

19.2 INTUITIVE MAPPING

As described in chapter 4, intuitive coordinate mapping, such as DRM and WRM, utilize control source and target spaces. In many respects, the InputDragMapper class described in an earlier chapter was a shortcut that went from 2D device input straight to 4D actuation output, completely bypassing the intermediate 3D source and target spaces required for intuitive mapping. The resulting control chain got things moving, so to speak, but not in a very intuitive manner. This section takes a more in-depth look at source and target spaces, and describes the framework's support for a longer and more effective control chain, with additional links that permit more generalized and, as a result, more intuitive interpretation of control inputs.

19.2.1 Source and target spaces

The seeds for understanding the role of the source and target space in intuitive mapping were planted in both parts 2 and 3 of the book. Chapter 4 discussed the general problem, and chapter 13 addressed the specific notion of world versus local spatial coordinates, and how local-to-local transforms can be useful. The matter boils down to one of spatial interpretation. When the user drags a mouse in the display, is the drag simply a change in mouse X and Y value, or should it be interpreted as a drag across a horizontal floor or a vertical wall in the context of the scene? When the control input is applied to an actuator, is it simply applied with respect to the target's local coordinate system, or should it be applied relative to the floor that the object is sitting on, or the wall to which it is attached?

Source space

When the user drags the mouse over a floor or wall in the scene, rather than thinking of the drag as a change in mouse X and Y value, it can be interpreted relative to the 3D space defined by those objects. Depending on which object is under the mouse, the 2D drag can be interpreted as being parallel to the horizontal floor or the vertical wall, in 3D space. This 3D motion could be considered a generalized form of drag input, as if we weren't dealing with a POCS and the user had waved a 3D mouse through the scene, over the floor or along the wall. As with its 2D counterpart, this generalized 3D drag input can be filtered, such as for absolute and relative origin, clamping and scaling, and even gestures, only in 3D.

An example using third-person controls might help to further illustrate the role of the 3D source space in the control chain. Normally we think of third-person controls as being virtual knobs and sliders in the application window. The user is expected to manipulate these controls as if they were pasted to the display screen. Now imagine that these controls were instead pasted to the floor and walls in the 3D scene. Using a "3D mouse," the user could reach into the scene and turn a knob on the floor or slide a knob on the wall. Although the user interaction is occurring in 3D, the effect on the actuation targets of the controls is the same as in the 2D case. The notion of a source space is simply a more generalized way to specify what a control drag is in reference to. Instead of the source space always being the display plane, it can now be any plane in the virtual world. In fact, it doesn't even have to be a plane. It could be the rolling surface of 3D terrain or the surface of an arbitrarily complex 3D shape.

Target space

As defined in the previous chapter, the actuation space is a 4D space that directly controls the actuator target's dynamic state. In a translation actuator connected to a transform group, when the actuation X value changes by 10 units, the target's transform state is modified accordingly, with the target group's children moving 10 units in a direction defined by the group's local coordinate space. If you instead wanted the X input to move the target relative to some other space in the scene, such as that of the floor or a wall, then a spatial transform would be needed, with the target space defined by the local coordinate system of the target object. In the general case, a local-to-local transform would convert the input source value from its local coordinate space to that of the target's.

19.2.2   Control chain spaces

Putting the source and target pieces together, there are a total of four spaces: 2D input, 3D source, 3D target, and 4D actuation. Correspondingly, there are three coordinate mappings: The 2D device input is interpreted relative to some 3D source space, converting it into a 3D source input. In turn, this generalized 3D source value is converted into a generalized 3D target value by means of a local-to-local spatial transform, such as that defined in chapter 13 using the `getLocalToVworld` methods of a source and target Java 3D `Node` object. The target value is then mapped into an actuation value, similar to that done by `InputDragMapper`, only here it is from 3D to 4D space instead of from 2D to 4D space. To simplify things, the framework exposes only the source space for processing with filter blocks, and the target and actuation transformations are combined into a single building block, with only the input source and output actuation interfaces exposed.

All of the classes discussed here are located in the `j3dui.control.mappers.intuitive` package. Table 19.2 summarizes the basic classes and interfaces that the framework provides for generalized intuitive coordinate mapping. Figure 19.3 shows the relationship of the building blocks.

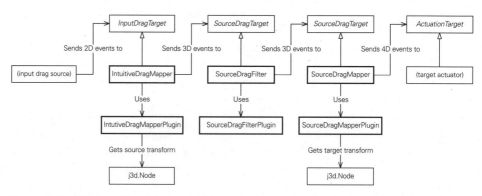

Figure 19.3   Relationship of classes and interfaces related to intuitive coordinate mapping

Table 19.2   Classes and interfaces related to intuitive coordinate mapping

Class/*Interface*	Description	Input Events	Output Events
IntutiveDragMapper	A coordinate mapper for input drag to source drag conversion. Uses a plug-in to perform a specific type of coordinate mapping	InputDragTarget	SourceDragTarget
IntuitiveDragMapperPlugin	The abstract base class for intuitive drag mapper plug-ins		
SourceDragTarget	Event interface for reporting source drag gestures		
SourceDragSplitter	Source drag event splitter	SourceDragTarget	SourceDragTarget
SourceDragFilter	The source drag filter, which uses a plug-in to perform a specific filtering operation	SourceDragTarget	SourceDragTarget
AbsoluteSourceDragPlugin	A source drag filter plug-in that interprets the drag with an absolute drag origin		
RelativeSourceDragPlugin	A source drag filter plug-in that interprets the drag with a relative drag origin		
SourceDragMapper	A coordinate mapper for source drag to target drag to actuation conversion. Uses a plug-in to perform a specific type of coordinate mapping	SourceDragTarget	ActuationTarget
SourceDragMapperPlugin	The abstract base class for source drag mapper plug-ins		
DirectSourceDragPlugin	A source drag mapper plug-in that performs source scale and target offset, and that maps source dimensions to none, one, or more output dimensions		
AxisAngleSourceDragPlugin	A source drag mapper plug-in that maps a rotation about a fixed source axis to a rotation about the corresponding target axis		

In the following discussion of the framework's building blocks for intuitive mapping, you'll notice a number of similarities with earlier building blocks. This should come as no surprise because many of the same operations still need to be performed, such as input drag mapping, output actuation mapping, and drag filtering, only here these operations involve 3D source space instead of 2D input space. Also, source and target spaces are defined in terms of nodes living in those spaces. The building blocks automatically configure such nodes for live access of their local-to-Vworld transforms, and make extensive use of the framework's local-to-local spatial transform utilities—the `Mapper.toTargetSpace` methods—to perform source-to-target spatial transforms.

19.2.3 IntuitiveDragMapper class

Conversion from 2D input space to 3D source space is performed by the `IntuitiveDragMapper` class. It uses an `IntuitiveDragMapperPlugin` to handle the details of translating between spatial coordinate systems and event types. Subclasses of this plug-in are provided to support DRM and several flavors of WRM. Each handles acquisition and use of source space reference nodes differently. Specifics will be covered in later sections on DRM and WRM. The internal interface between the mapper and its plug-in are similar to those between the `InputDragMapper` class and its plug-in, the `InputDragMapperPlugin`.

By definition, input to source mapping is a point mapping, meaning that the input position is mapped to a source position using a point transformation rather than a vector transformation. The distinction is subtle, but important when setting up an input drag filter chain to feed an intuitive mapper. The mapper's input event interface is `InputDragTarget`, and its output event interface is `SourceDragTarget`.

SourceDragTarget interface

The `SourceDragTarget` interface is essentially a 3D version of the 2D `InputDragTarget` interface, including methods for drag start, drag continuation, and drag stop. In place of a source display, the methods use a source scene graph node to define the local source space. The corresponding event splitter is the `SourceDragSplitter` class.

19.2.4 SourceDragFilter class

Source drag filtering is quite similar in form and function to that of input drag filtering. The `SourceDragFilter` class is the host for all filtering operations, with a plug-in giving it a personality. The plug-in base class, `SourceDragFilterPlugin`, has the same basic internal interface and is used the same way by its host as the `InputDragFilterPlugin` described for basic control interpretation. It also has the same limitation of being able to handle only the simplest forms of filtering, which do not involve state or time-dependent processing.

SourceDragFilterPlugin subclasses

Although all the same filter operations could be provided as for input drag filtering, the framework provides the two most common ones. The `AbsoluteSourceDragPlugin` class provides absolute filtering, with a 3D point specifying the origin of the drag operation The `RelativeSourceDragPlugin` class performs relative origin filtering, with the 3D origin being determined by the starting point of the drag. No source drag enable filter is provided because drag enabling can be handled from the input drag space—in a POCS there is no 3D mouse sensor to directly generate source drag events.

19.2.5 SourceDragMapper class

The `SourceDragMapper` class handles the conversion from source space to actuation space. Both the source-to-target and the target-to-actuation spatial conversions are included in this mapper. A method is provided to specify whether or not drags are cumulative. Consistent with other mappers in the framework, a plug-in, the `SourceDragMapperPlugin` class, handles the rest of the mapping details. The internal interface between the mapper and the plug-in is similar to that in the `InputDragMapper` class.

By definition, source-to-target mapping is a vector mapping, meaning that the source position value is treated as a vector, with direction and magnitude being transformed instead of position. As with intuitive mapping, the distinction is subtle but important when building a source drag filter chain to feed a source mapper. The mapper's input event interface is `SourceDragTarget`, and its output event interface is `ActuationTarget`.

DirectSourceDragPlugin class

The framework provides only for direct source mapping, with the `DirectSource-DragPlugin` class. It includes methods for specifying source value scaling and target value offset. All mapping is direct and by dimension, similar to that for input drag mapping, but here two separate mappings are used: one for source-to-source dimension mapping, and the other for target-to-actuation dimension mapping. Mapping occurs in three steps. First the source-to-source dimension mapping is applied to the source value, then the source value is spatially transformed to the target space, and finally the target-to-actuation dimension mapping is applied to the target value.

AxisAngleSourceDragPlugin class

To handle source drag rotations, the framework provides the `AxisAngleSource-DragPlugin` subclass of `DirectSourceDragPlugin`. To accommodate the generalized mapping from source to target space, a simple fixed-axis rotation can not be used. Instead, a fixed rotation axis is defined relative to the source space, and the axis is spatially transformed as a vector to the target space. The angle of rotation defined by the source value, however, is not spatially transformed as would normally be done in the superclass. Instead, it is mapped directly, by dimension, from source to actuation space using the combination of the source and target mappings.

19.3 DISPLAY-RELATIVE MAPPING

DRM is a dynamic coordinate mapping technique that controls a target object according to display relative inputs, such as from the mouse or arrow keys. In terms of source and target spaces, DRM generally uses the view itself as the source space node and the actuator's target transform group is used as the target space node.

At a conceptual level, the DRM process can be summarized as follows. When the user moves the drag cursor in the display, the intuitive drag mapper interprets that motion as occurring in 3D in the plane of the view's display. In turn, the source drag mapper obtains the view's local-to-Vworld transform, and transforms the local display movement into the equivalent motion expressed in absolute world space coordinates. The mapper then obtains the actuator target's local-to-Vworld transform, inverts it, and then transforms the world space movement into an equivalent motion in the target's local coordinate space. If, for example, the target actuator performs geometric translation, when the user moves the cursor left in the display, the target object will always appear to move left in the display regardless of the position or direction of the view.

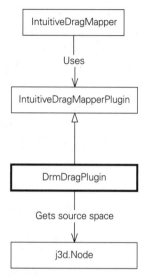

**Figure 19.4
Relationship of classes related to DRM drag mapping**

Table 19.3 summarizes the classes associated with DRM intuitive mapping. Figure 19.4 illustrates the relationship of these classes. The next example will demonstrate how to configure these and the rest of the intuitive mapping building blocks for DRM.

Table 19.3   Summary of classes related to DRM intuitive mapping

Class/Interface	Description	Input Events	Output Events
IntutiveDragMapper	A coordinate mapper for input drag to source drag conversion. Uses a plugin to perform a specific type of coordinate mapping	InputDragTarget	SourceDragTarget
IntuitiveDragMapperPlugin	The abstract base class for intuitive drag mapper plugins		
DrmPlugin	An intuitive drag mapper plugin that maps the 2D input drag to the Z=0 plane of the source space		

19.3.1   DrmDragPlugin class

For support of DRM, the framework provides the `DrmDragPlugin` subclass of `IntuitiveDragMapperPlugin`. The plug-in has very little to do. Because in DRM the intent is for the user's control inputs to be interpreted relative to the display space, the plug-in simply maps the 2D drag input to the Z=0 plane of the 3D source space. In other words, for DRM, the source space is the view space with the input drag confined to its display plane. (The intuitive drag mapper plug-in will play a more prominent role in WRM than it does in DRM.)

The constructor for `DrmDragPlugin` gives you a choice for how the source node is selected. Either you can let the input event's source display define it, in which case the source display's `ViewingPlatform` is used, or you can set it explicitly, such as with a node in the same space as the view. In any case, the source node is passed along with the mapper's output `SourceDragTarget` event for use by the source drag mapper.

19.3.2 Example: DrmMapping

Figure 19.5
Screen shot of the
DrmMapping example.

This example demonstrates DRM of control inputs.

➤ See

The virtual world contains four target objects. As it initially displays, three are in a central column (red, green, blue) and one is to the right (magenta). See figure 19.5.

➤ Do

- Drag the mouse (first button with SHIFT) in the display or use the ARROW keys (with SHIFT) to orbit the view in heading and elevation about the world origin.
- Drag the mouse (first button) on the top (red) target or use the ARROW keys to translate it along the display X-Y axes.
- Drag the mouse (first button) on the middle (green) target or use the ARROW keys to rotate it about the display Y axis.
- Drag the mouse (first button) on the bottom (blue) target or use the ARROW keys to scale it along the display X-Y axes.
- Drag the mouse (first button) on the right (magenta) target or use the ARROW keys to roll the target like a trackball relative to the display.
- Repeat the drag operations from different view directions.

➤ Observe

- All target operations use mouseover to enable the operation.
- All coordinate mapping uses DRM, meaning that manipulation of targets occurs relative to the display and will always seem intuitive regardless of view direction.

The first code sample below is from the `DrmMapping` example class. It shows only those portions pertaining to the translation target and DRM mapping. DRM mapping is provided by the utility building block `buildDrmTranslationMapper` from the `IntuitiveBlocks` class, which is shown in the second code sample. This block and others like it combine the framework's intuitive mapping blocks into individual modules specialized for a given type of geometric manipulation.

Notice in the example code how two different forms are used to specify the DRM mapper's source space reference node. The first case, for DRM translation, uses dynamic source node specification. It specifies the source node as null, indicating that the source node is to be defined by the view associated with the input drag event's source display. For this form, the local-to-Vworld read capability must be set on all the view platforms in the application from which the mapper might receive events. The second one, for DRM rotation, uses static source node specification. It sets the source node explicitly as the view object, in which case the transform read capability is automatically set on the view object by the DRM plug-in. This approach is simpler, but can only be used if the application has a single view.

DRM mapping, with dynamic and static source view specification

Filename: J3duiBook/examples/OverEnabling/DrmMapping.java

```
...
// setup manipulation targets
/// translation target
AffineGroup affineXlt = new AffineGroup(new TestThing(
 TestThing.BOX_TRANSLATION, TestThing.BALL_DEFAULT));

affineXlt.getTranslation().initActuation(
 new Vector4d(0, 3, 0, 0));
getWorld().addSceneNode(affineXlt);
...
// setup manipulation controls
/// manipulation draggers, first button
InputDragSplitter relDrag = new InputDragSplitter();

ActuationBlocks.buildRelativeDragger(relDrag,
 getView(), Input.BUTTON_FIRST,
 Input.MODIFIER_NONE, Input.MODIFIER_NONE);

/// manipulation mappers
InputDragTarget mapper;

//// Ex: let event source display define source node
getView().getView().getViewPlatform().setCapability(
 Node.ALLOW_LOCAL_TO_VWORLD_READ);

mapper = IntuitiveBlocks.buildDrmTranslationMapper(
 affineXlt, null, true);
relDrag.addEventTarget(mapper);
```

```
//// Ex: use view object as source node
mapper = IntuitiveBlocks.buildDrmRotationYMapper(
 affineRot, getView(), true);
relDrag.addEventTarget(mapper);
...
```

Utility block with mapping for DRM translation

Filename: J3duiBook/lib/j3dui/utils/blocks/IntuitiveBlocks.java

```
...
/**
Creates an intuitive drag mapper and corresponding source
drag mapper, configures them for DRM translation in view X-Y,
and connects them to the target object.
@param target Target object.
@param view Source display.  If null drag source is used.
@param cumulative True if drag actions are cumulative.
@return New building block.
*/
public static final InputDragTarget
 buildDrmTranslationMapper(AffineGroup target,
 AppView view, boolean cumulative) {

  // use target translation node as source space
  DirectSourceDragPlugin plugin =
   new DirectSourceDragPlugin(
   target.getTranslation().getTargetNode());

  // build source mapper for target X-Y translation
  SourceDragMapper mapper = new SourceDragMapper(
   target.getTranslation(), plugin);
  mapper.setCumulative(cumulative);

  // build DRM mapper
  DrmDragPlugin drmPlugin = new DrmDragPlugin();
  if(view!=null) drmPlugin = new DrmDragPlugin(view);

  IntuitiveDragMapper drmMapper = new IntuitiveDragMapper(
   mapper, drmPlugin);

  // scale input drag
  return new InputDragFilter(drmMapper,
   new ScaleInputDragPlugin(new Vector2d(.025, .025)));
}
...
```

19.4 WORLD-RELATIVE MAPPING

WRM is a dynamic coordinate mapping technique that controls a target object according to world-relative inputs, such as the projection of the drag cursor position onto a floor or wall in the scene. In terms of source and target spaces, the most general form of WRM uses object picking to determine the current source space node, and the actuator's target transform group as the target space node.

At a conceptual level, the WRM process can be summarized as follows: When the user moves the drag cursor over an object in the scene, the intuitive drag mapper interprets that motion as occurring in the scene relative to the object underneath the cursor, which is the source node. In turn, the source drag mapper obtains the source node's local-to-Vworld transform, and transforms the local movement on the node's surface into the equivalent motion expressed in absolute world space coordinates, such as movement in a northerly direction. The mapper then obtains the actuator target's local-to-Vworld transform, inverts it, and then transforms the world space movement into an equivalent motion in the target's local coordinate space. If, for example, the target actuator performs geometric translation, then the target object will always appear to move north in the world regardless of the position or direction of the view.

Table 19.4 summarizes the classes associated with WRM intuitive mapping. Figure 19.6 illustrates the relationship of these classes. The next example will demonstrate how to configure these and the rest of the intuitive mapping building blocks for WRM.

Table 19.4 Summary of classes related to WRM intuitive mapping

Class/*Interface*	Description	Input Events	Output Events
WrmPlugin	An intuitive drag mapper plug-in that uses a pick engine to perform the most general form of WRM. It also serves as the base class for less general WRM mappers		
QuasiWrmPlugin	A WRM plug-in that performs true WRM at the start of a drag, and uses a picking plane during the drag		
PseudoWrmPlugin	A quasi-WRM plug-in that performs a mapping that can approximate WRM. It uses a pick engine to place a picking plane on the target node for use during the drag		

19.4.1 WrmDragPlugin class

For support of WRM, the framework provides the `WrmDragPlugin` subclass of `IntuitiveDragMapperPlugin`. The class has several constructors. The single-parameter constructor is for the most general form of WRM. It uses the `PickEngine` object supplied to the constructor to select the source node lying under the drag cursor throughout the drag operation. The selected node serves as both the drag surface

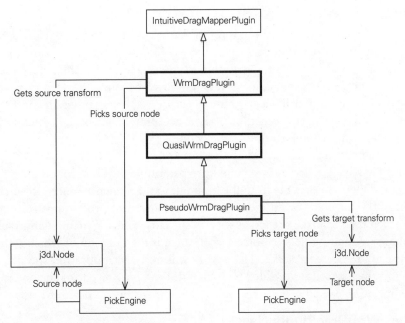

Figure 19.6   Relationship of classes related to WRM intuitive mapping

and the dynamic source reference space. The source space reference node is also passed along with the mapper's output `SourceDragTarget` event for use by the source drag mapper. The candidate source nodes with which the mapper is to work must be provided in the pick engine's target list. The mapper will generate output events only while the cursor is being dragged over a valid source target.

A second constructor, which takes a source node as its second argument, creates a WRM mapper that works much like the previous one, but the picked source nodes provide only the drag surface. The specified source node defines a static source reference space used for source mapping. A third constructor, which takes no arguments, serves as a special base class for pseudo-WRM, which is discussed in a later section.

Absolute input drag

An important note about WRM is that it will not work with a relative input drag origin. The input drag position for WRM must be absolute; otherwise, the picking that it performs will be incorrect. Because relative dragging is still a desirable feature, it must be performed after the WRM intuitive mapping, by a source drag filter, such as a `SourceDragFilter` with a `RelativeSourceDragPlugin`.

Sticky cursor

Because the source drag position is on the surface of the source node, by default, during a translation operation the target object's origin will appear to follow the drag cursor. With this arrangement, depending on the shape of the object and the angle of view, the target object may not always appear to be stuck to the cursor—the target object may appear to drift away from the cursor as the drag progresses and the relative viewing angle changes. Sometimes this is acceptable, but often a sticky cursor will seem more intuitive than a not-so-sticky one.

Although not included in the framework, one variation on WRM that would allow it to have a sticky cursor would be to determine the hit point on the target object first, and then project a ray from the hit point to the reference source object. The position of the hit point could then be computed relative to the source reference space, and then used to make the target stick to the cursor during manipulation. Of course, if there are multiple source objects, then there is the question of which source object to use as the reference space. The answer will likely be application-specific. As you'll see shortly, the technique called pseudo-WRM can provide cursor stickiness, although the operation overall is quite restrictive in comparison to true WRM.

19.4.2   QuasiWrmDragPlugin class

True WRM, as defined by the `WrmPlugin` class, can be expensive because it requires continuous picking. There are also situations where a less general and more constrained form of WRM might even be desirable. The solution to both of these problems is a picking plane.

Picking plane

A picking plane offers a cheap alternative to full blown object picking if all you are interested in is a hit point. The picking plane is positioned to approximate the drag surface on a picked object. Then, during a drag, the source space hit point is computed by intersecting the same picking ray used for normal picking with the picking plane, which is significantly less demanding on the system than real picking. For situations that require it, this also constrains the source drag to a plane instead of the arbitrary surface of the source object. Instead of a picking plane, other shapes could be used that are easy to intersect with the picking ray, such as a sphere.

The framework provides utilities for handling picking planes in the `Mapper` class. The `buildPickPlane` utility builds a pick plane, given a hit point and a hit node defining the plane's reference space. The `buildPickRay` utility builds a pick ray (origin point and direction vector), given a display canvas and a pick cursor position in it. This is the same utility used by `PickEngine` for picking. The `hitPickPlane` utility intersects a pick ray with a pick plane and returns the 3D hit point.

Quasi-WRM

The `QuasiWrmPlugin` subclass of `WrmPlugin` offers a variation of WRM based on use of a picking plane. It uses discrete picking to select the source node at the start of a drag, the same as for general WRM, but during the drag it uses a picking plane. The discrete pick defines a source object and the initial hit point. The picking plane is placed such that it passes through the hit point and is perpendicular to the reference source space Z axis. Depending on the plug-in constructor used, the source reference space will be defined dynamically by the discretely picked source object, or statically by the source node specified in the constructor.

19.4.3 PseudoWrmDragPlugin class

Yet another variation on WRM is pseudo-WRM. As its name implies, it is not real WRM in that no source node picking is involved, but it does work a lot like quasi-WRM. Instead of placing a picking plane relative to the picked source node, however, it is instead placed relative to a picked target node, such as the target of the manipulation itself, the actuation target object. Because no source node picking is involved, the source space reference node must be specified statically, in the constructor. Thus, the picking plane is positioned relative to the target, through its hit point, but it is oriented according to the source node's reference space, as it is in quasi-WRM.

One of the pleasant side effects of pseudo-WRM is that the dragged target object will appear to be stuck to the drag cursor, no matter where the target is dragged or how the scene is viewed. This might seem a fortunate coincidence, but it is no coincidence. Pseudo-WRM is in essence true WRM, but with a single planar source node that always passes through the initial hit point on the target object. Thus, the projection from the hit point to the reference source object, which is what was needed for real WRM sticky cursor, is zero. With zero offset, the source point under the drag cursor is the same as the hit point on the object, and thus the target appears stuck to the cursor.

A variation of pseudo-WRM, provided by one of the constructors, is to specify the target node statically instead of using a picker. In this case, a drag operation will always use the specified target node's origin as the initial hit point, with the picking plane passing through it. In this particular form of pseudo-WRM, the target object will not always appear to be stuck to the drag cursor because of the possible offset between the cursor hit position on the object and the position of the object's origin.

19.4.4   Example: WrmMapping

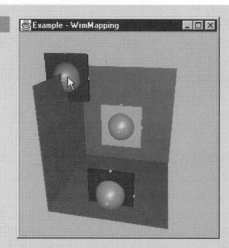

**Figure 19.7
Screen shot of the
WrmMapping example**

This example demonstrates WRM of control inputs.

> **➤ See**

The virtual world contains three target objects (red, green, blue) inside a corner space formed by three orthogonal planes (a floor and two walls). A screen shot is provided in figure 19.7.

> **➤ Do**

- Drag the mouse (left button with SHIFT) in the display or use the ARROW keys (with SHIFT) to orbit the view in heading and elevation about the world origin.
- Drag the mouse (left button) on the left (red) target to translate it along any plane beneath the mouse cursor.
- Drag the mouse (left button with CTRL) on the left (red) target to roll it relative to any plane beneath the mouse cursor.
- Drag the mouse (left button) on the middle (green) target to translate it along the plane beneath where the mouse cursor started.
- Drag the mouse (left button with CTRL) on the middle (green) target to roll it relative to the plane beneath where the mouse cursor started.
- Drag the mouse (left button) on the bottom (blue) target to translate it along the bottom *X-Z* plane.
- Drag the mouse (left button with CTRL) on the bottom (blue) target to roll it relative to the bottom *X-Z* plane.
- Repeat the drag operations from different view directions.

> **➤ Observe**

- All target operations use mouseover to enable the operation.
- The three orthogonal planes are the source objects for WRM dragging.
- The left (red) target uses full WRM coordinate mapping, meaning that target manipulation occurs relative to the source planes throughout the operation. The drag will only start and continue as long as the cursor stays over a source plane.
- The middle (green) target uses quasi-WRM coordinate mapping, meaning that target manipulation occurs relative to the source plane at the start of the operation. The drag must start over a source plane but can continue beyond it because it uses a picking plane.

The first code sample following is from the `WrmMapping` example class. It shows only those portions that pertain to WRM manipulation. Notice that absolute input dragging is used, and that the three orthogonal planes in the scene serve as the source objects. The utility building blocks `buildWrmTranslationMapper`, `buildWrmSphereMapper`, and `buildSticky WrmTranslationMapper` from the `IntuitiveBlocks` class provide WRM mapping, all of which are also shown below. The first two blocks take a `WrmPlugin` as one of its input parameters, and combine it with other intuitive mapping blocks, including source space relative origin filtering, to form modules specialized for a given type of geometric manipulation. The third block combines a target picker and a `PseudoWrmDragPlugin` in a convenient package for WRM dragging with a sticky cursor.

Notice that the WRM source picker is configured so that all hits are checked, not just the closest one. For true WRM, this allows picking during the drag to correctly determine the hit position on the underlying source planes even when the target object is dragged behind other target objects.

Setup in example for various forms of WRM mapping

Filename: J3duiBook/examples/OverEnabling/WrmMapping.java

```
...
// setup WRM
/// build source plane X
...
/// build source plane Y
...
/// build source plane Z
...
/// build source picker
ArrayList wrmSourceList = new ArrayList();
wrmSourceList.add(planeX);
wrmSourceList.add(planeY);
wrmSourceList.add(planeZ);

PickEngine wrmSourcePicker = new PickEngine(
  getWorld().getSceneRoot(), wrmSourceList);
wrmSourcePicker.setHitAll(true);

// setup manipulation controls
/// translation draggers, first button
```

```
InputDragSplitter absXlate = new InputDragSplitter();

ActuationBlocks.buildAbsoluteDragger(absXlate,
 getView(), Input.BUTTON_FIRST,
 Input.MODIFIER_NONE, Input.MODIFIER_NONE);
...
/// manipulation mappers
InputDragTarget mapper;

//// WRM: world translation, source rotation
mapper = IntuitiveBlocks.buildWrmTranslationMapper(
 affineWrm, new WrmDragPlugin(null, wrmSourcePicker),
 false, false);
absXlate.addEventTarget(mapper);

mapper = IntuitiveBlocks.buildWrmSphereMapper(
 sphereWrm, new WrmDragPlugin(wrmSourcePicker),
 true, true);
absRotate.addEventTarget(mapper);

//// Quasi-WRM: world translation, source rotation
mapper = IntuitiveBlocks.buildWrmTranslationMapper(
 affineQWrm, new QuasiWrmDragPlugin(null,
 wrmSourcePicker), false, false);
absXlate.addEventTarget(mapper);

mapper = IntuitiveBlocks.buildWrmSphereMapper(
 sphereQWrm, new QuasiWrmDragPlugin(wrmSourcePicker),
 true, true);
absRotate.addEventTarget(mapper);

//// Pseudo-WRM: picked translation, fixed rotation
mapper = IntuitiveBlocks.buildStickyWrmTranslationMapper(
 planeY, affinePWrm, getWorld().getSceneRoot(),
 true, true);
absXlate.addEventTarget(mapper);

mapper = IntuitiveBlocks.buildWrmSphereMapper(
 spherePWrm, new PseudoWrmDragPlugin(planeY,
 affinePWrm), true, true);
absRotate.addEventTarget(mapper);
...
```

Utility blocks with mapping for common WRM operations

Filename: J3duiBook/lib/j3dui/utils/blocks/IntuitiveBlocks.java
...
```
/**
Creates an intuitive drag mapper and corresponding source
drag mapper, configures them for WRM translation, and
connects them to the target object.
@param target Target object.
```

@param wrmPlugin WRM plugin with pick engine and source
object list.
@param relative True if source drag actions are relative.
Typically, use false for real WRM and true otherwise. If
false should initialize target geometry using
updateActuation() instead of initActuation().
@param cumulative True if drag actions are cumulative.
Typically, use true if relative is true.
@return New building block. Should be connected to an
absolute input drag source.
*/
public static final InputDragTarget
 buildWrmTranslationMapper(AffineGroup target,
 WrmDragPlugin **wrmPlugin**, boolean relative,
 boolean cumulative) {

   // build source drag mapper
   DirectSourceDragPlugin plugin =
    new **DirectSourceDragPlugin**(target.getTail());

   SourceDragMapper mapper = new **SourceDragMapper**(
    target.getTranslation(), plugin);
   mapper.setCumulative(cumulative);

   // build relative source filter
   SourceDragTarget filter;

   if(relative) {
     filter = new **SourceDragFilter**(
      mapper, new **RelativeSourceDragPlugin**());
   } else {
     filter = mapper;
   }

   // build input drag mapper
   return new **IntuitiveDragMapper**(filter, **wrmPlugin**);
}

/**
Creates an intuitive drag mapper and corresponding source
drag mapper, configures them for WRM spherical rotation, and
connects them to the target object.
@param target Target object.
@param wrmPlugin WRM plugin with pick engine and source
object list.
@param relative True if source drag actions are relative.
Typically, use false for real WRM and true otherwise. If
false should initialize target geometry using
updateActuation() instead of initActuation().
@param cumulative True if drag actions are cumulative.
Typically, use true for rotations in general.
@return New building block. Should be connected to an

```
absolute input drag source.
*/
public static final InputDragTarget
 buildWrmSphereMapper(AxisAngleSphereGroup target,
 WrmDragPlugin wrmPlugin, boolean relative,
 boolean cumulative) {

  AxisAngleSourceDragPlugin plugin;
  SourceDragMapper mapper;
  SourceDragSplitter splitter = new SourceDragSplitter();

  // X axis
  plugin = new AxisAngleSourceDragPlugin(target.getTail());
  plugin.setTargetMap(Mapper.DIM_NONE, Mapper.DIM_W,
   Mapper.DIM_NONE);
  plugin.setAxis(new Vector3d(-1, 0, 0));

  mapper = new SourceDragMapper(
   target.getAxisAngleX(), plugin);
  mapper.setCumulative(cumulative);

  splitter.addEventTarget(mapper);

  // Y axis
  plugin = new AxisAngleSourceDragPlugin(target.getTail());
  plugin.setTargetMap(Mapper.DIM_W, Mapper.DIM_NONE,
   Mapper.DIM_NONE);
  plugin.setAxis(new Vector3d(0, 1, 0));

  mapper = new SourceDragMapper(
   target.getAxisAngleY(), plugin);
  mapper.setCumulative(cumulative);

  splitter.addEventTarget(mapper);

  // build relative source filter
  SourceDragTarget filter;

  if(relative) {
    filter = new SourceDragFilter(
      splitter, new RelativeSourceDragPlugin());
  } else {
    filter = splitter;
  }

  // build input drag mapper
  return new IntuitiveDragMapper(filter, wrmPlugin);
}
```

```
/**
Creates an intuitive drag mapper and corresponding source
drag mapper, configures them for sticky pseudo-WRM
translation with a target picker, and connects them to the
target object.
@param source Reference source object defining the picking
plane orientation.
@param target Target object.
@param root Scene graph pick root containing the target.
@param relative True if source drag actions are relative.
Typically, use false for real WRM and true otherwise.  If
false should initialize target geometry using
updateActuation() instead of initActuation().
@param cumulative True if drag actions are cumulative.
Typically, use true if relative is true.
@return New building block.  Should be connected to an
absolute input drag source.
*/
public static final InputDragTarget
 buildStickyWrmTranslationMapper(Node source,
 AffineGroup target, BranchGroup root, boolean relative,
 boolean cumulative) {

   // build target picker
   ArrayList targetList = new ArrayList();
   targetList.add(target);

   PickEngine targetPicker = new PickEngine(
    root, targetList);

   // build mapper
   InputDragTarget mapper = buildWrmTranslationMapper(
    target, new PseudoWrmDragPlugin(source, targetPicker),
    relative, cumulative);

   return mapper;
}
...
```

19.5 SUMMARY

This chapter completes the presentation of the framework's implementation of 3D UI
control techniques. The workhorse of a 3D UI is object picking. For the purposes of
control, it forms the basis of intuitive control enabling, where user interaction is
directed only to the target object to which the mouse is pointing. Earlier chapters presented an abbreviated form of the control chain that stretches from input device to target actuator. This chapter generalized that chain by introducing several additional
links, with the result being a more intuitive interactive experience for the user. Two

new spaces were introduced: the source drag space and the target drag space. In support of these spaces, the framework provides several new building blocks, including an intuitive drag mapper and a source drag mapper, and a new filter for operating in the 3D source drag space. Examples demonstrated the control techniques of DRM and WRM that were introduced in part 2 of the book. The examples also illustrated how these techniques can be implemented using the framework core and utility building blocks.

C H A P T E R   2 0

Feedback

In terms of laying groundwork for the framework and examples, the worst is almost over. The control chain presented in the last few chapters is the most used and, to achieve a modicum of generality, one of the more extensive portions of the framework. Establishing a good control chain is a major aspect of any interactive 3D application development, so your perseverance in working through these chapters should be rewarded in your next 3D design effort.

This chapter addresses a completely different aspect of UI implementation: feedback. Feedback is the designer's opportunity to tell users what they can do and how to do it. Feedback can also keep users apprised as to what the application is doing, allowing them to verify that that is what they think it should be doing. The simplest and most used forms of feedback are tied to the interaction states, which define situations such as object selection, manipulation status, and mouseover action. Interaction states and the feedback elements that accompany them are the focus of this chapter and its examples. Most of the framework classes discussed here are located in the `j3dui.feedback` package.

20.1 INTERACTION FEEDBACK

Two fundamental requirements for implementing feedback are a mechanism for showing the feedback, and some means for detecting when feedback should be displayed and what kind that should be. For displaying feedback, chapter 5 described a technique called multi-shape, which is a convenient way to represent an object or feedback element with multiple appearances or shapes. For detecting when to display feedback, the framework offers the trigger pattern for monitoring input events and object picks that represent user interactions. For what kind of feedback to display, chapter 5 also described interaction states, which is an approach to classifying feedback based on low-level user interaction with application data objects.

20.1.1 FeedbackTarget interface

In the framework, interaction feedback is closely tied to the interaction states. Interaction states are grouped into status, selection, and action. Action states, which describe the relation of user input to objects in the scene, are described as being normal, over, pause, down, drag, drop, and cancel. Selection states include normal, auto, single, double, triple, and many. Status states include normal, disable, recommend, and discommend. These interaction states have been captured in constants and utilities provided in the `Feedback` class. This classification of feedback states is also present in the `FeedbackTarget` event interface, whose methods are `setFeedbackStatus`, `setFeedbackSelection`, and `setFeedbackAction`. Each reports feedback state changes of a given type.

20.1.2 MultiShape class

The multishape technique is a convenient way to associate interaction states with multiple appearances of a given target object or feedback element. The framework formalizes this technique in the `MultiShape` class. Although this class uses the Java 3D `Switch` class internally to manage the multiple shapes, it is a subclass of `Group` to give its internal workings a bit of privacy and, as you'll see, a more flexible role in the management of feedback geometry and events.

Shape selection is driven by input `FeedbackTarget` events, which are also relayed as output events. Relaying the feedback events allows `MultiShape` objects to be chained together forming a feedback group of sorts, with all members responding to the same feedback events. Thus, a `MultiShape` object can serve as a scene graph group, a feedback group, or both. As you'll see later in the chapter, a typical scenario is to decorate a normal data object with feedback elements, such as indicators and drag handles. Using one of the public `MultiShape` constructors, a proxy version can be made that contains no internal shapes, but which allows a normal data object to be grouped with its feedback decorations, and the decorations to be wired up to receive feedback events. The result is a single entity that encapsulates all of a target object's geometry and that responds to feedback events.

Serving as a nexus for feedback event handling, the MultiShape class breaks ranks with the general pattern for building blocks by allowing more than one event target to be registered, through its addEventTarget method. This allows feedback managers to conveniently tap into an existing feedback event chain (more on this subject in chapter 24).

20.1.3 MultiShape subclasses

In many respects, MultiShape serves as either a proxy, which is used directly for scene graph and event grouping, or as an engine for managing multiple shapes. Each subclass of MultiShape, which includes MultiStatus, MultiSelect, and MultiAction, recognizes a particular category of interaction feedback. Individual shapes in a multi-shape are added through these classes, not to MultiShape directly. For instance, in MultiAction, the method setActionNode adds a Node object as a shape, and associates it with one or more action states, specified by state flags. Each subclass has a corresponding method for adding shape nodes. If there is no shape associated with a feedback state, then nothing will appear when that state occurs.

Although nodes of any type can be added as a shape, these classes recognize MultiShape nodes, and afford them special treatment. When a MultiShape object receives a feedback event, it sets its internal switch node to show the corresponding shape, recursively scans all of its shapes looking for instances of MultiShape, and passes the event along to them. This allows MultiShape subclasses to be nested by any type, in any order, and to any depth, just so long as the initiating feedback event is sent to the root/head of the multi-shape tree/chain. By convention, the framework and examples arrange the levels in a feedback tree such that MultiStatus shapes are at the top, and MultiAction shapes are at the bottom.

Table 20.1 summarizes the classes and interfaces associated with multi-shapes, and figure 20.1 illustrates how they interrelate.

Table 20.1 Summary of classes and interfaces related to multi-shapes

Class/*Interface*	Description	Input Events	Output Events
FeedbackTarget	Event interface for reporting feedback interaction state changes		
FeedbackSplitter	Feedback event splitter	FeedbackTarget	FeedbackTarget
MultiShape	Base class for multi-shape classes, feedback proxy for scene graph and event grouping	FeedbackTarget	FeedbackTarget
MultiStatus	Multi-shape that associates shapes with feedback status states	FeedbackTarget	FeedbackTarget
MultiSelect	Multi-shape that associates shapes with feedback select states	FeedbackTarget	FeedbackTarget
MultiAction	Multi-shape that associates shapes with feedback action states	FeedbackTarget	FeedbackTarget

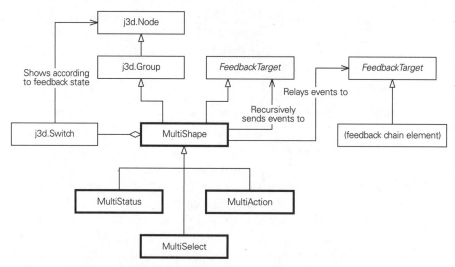

Figure 20.1   Relationship of classes and interfaces related to multi-shapes

20.1.4   FeedbackTrigger class

The `FeedbackTrigger` class and its subclasses translate input and pick events into feedback state changes. Beside serving as a base class, `FeedbackTrigger` can also act like a feedback state filter of sorts, taking in `FeedbackTarget` events and outputting only those that satisfy a specified combination of states. As with any trigger, you may need to initialize it, but only after connecting it to its event chain, which assures that it and its chain are in sync at startup.

A word of warning: Although the framework does not use multi-threading for event handling, which keeps things as simple as possible, the sequence in which events occur can be critical, problematic, and difficult to debug. To help prevent event loops, all input events are ignored while a previous event is being handled. Also, repeat action and status events are generally suppressed because they are generally not significant, whereas repeat selection events are allowed, since they can be meaningful as transient events.

Table 20.2 summarizes the classes and interfaces associated with feedback triggers, and figure 20.2 illustrates how they are related.

Table 20.2   Summary of classes and interfaces related to feedback triggers

Class/*Interface*	Description	Input Events	Output Events
FeedbackTrigger	Base class for feedback trigger classes. Also serves as a feedback state filter	FeedbackTarget	FeedbackTarget
StatusTrigger	A feedback trigger that monitors input events for status feedback state changes	FeedbackTarget EnableTarget	FeedbackTarget

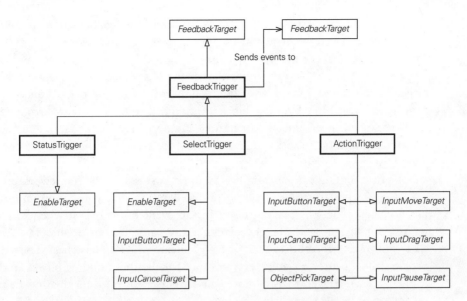

Figure 20.2   Relationship of classes and interfaces related to feedback triggers

Table 20.2   Summary of classes and interfaces related to feedback triggers (continued)

Class/*Interface*	Description	Input Events	Output Events
SelectTrigger	A feedback trigger that monitors input events for selection feedback state changes	FeedbackTarget EnableTarget InputButtonTarget InputCancelTarget	FeedbackTarget
ActionTrigger	A feedback trigger that monitors input events for action feedback state changes	FeedbackTarget InputMoveTarget InputDragTarget InputButtonTarget InputPauseTarget InputCancelTarget ObjectPickTarget	FeedbackTarget
InputPauseTrigger	A trigger that monitors input movement events for pause determination	EnableTarget InputMoveTarget	InputPauseTarget

20.1.5   FeedbackTrigger subclasses

The subclasses of `FeedbackTrigger` each handle a particular type of feedback state change detection. The `StatusTrigger` class interprets `EnableTarget` events to signify normal and disabled feedback status states. `SelectTrigger` uses `Enable-Target` as an indicator of mouseover, and `InputButtonTarget` to determine when and what kind of selection has occurred in conjunction with mouseover. `InputCancelTarget` in conjunction with mouseover signifies selection cancel (de-select).

The `ActionTrigger` is the most complex of the feedback triggers. Most feedback states are object-centric and therefore depend on mouseover status. `Action-Trigger` is capable of monitoring a list of object targets, with mouseover being true when `ObjectPickTarget` indicates that the pick cursor is over any of the action targets. `ActionTrigger` is also equipped to provide mouse-over status to the other triggers, or any other building blocks, through a collateral event output. `Input-MoveTarget` triggers updates for normal and over states; `InputDragTarget` indicates drag and drop status; and, `InputButtonTarget` indicates when the button goes down in anticipation of a drag.

Pause handling can be complicated in its own right. The framework uses a separate trigger, the `InputPauseTrigger`, to detect when a pause in input movement has occurred. The trigger's `EnableTarget` event input tells it when to recognize pausing, or to ignore it, thereby blocking any pause output events. The `Action-Trigger` uses `InputPauseTarget` to indicate when a pause has occurred, and it uses its "allow pause" collateral event output to tell other building blocks, and specifically the pause trigger, that no more pause events are needed for the time being. This separation of duties between pause detection and pause prevention is useful for group feedback management, which is addressed a bit later in the chapter.

20.1.6 Example: MultiShaping

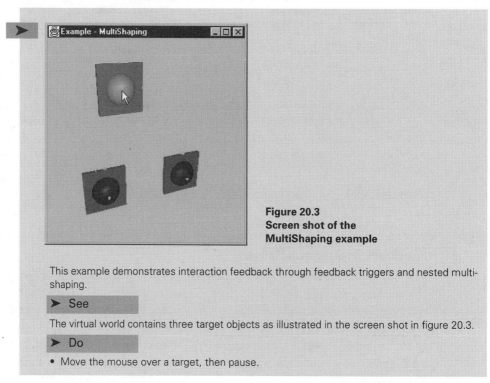

**Figure 20.3
Screen shot of the
MultiShaping example**

This example demonstrates interaction feedback through feedback triggers and nested multi-shaping.

➤ See

The virtual world contains three target objects as illustrated in the screen shot in figure 20.3.

➤ Do

• Move the mouse over a target, then pause.

Although the structure of this example borrows heavily from that of previous examples, enough has changed to warrant including most of the following example code. In this example, the utility building block `buildMultiThing` from the `FeedbackBlocks` class is used to build a hierarchical multi-shape tree, with differently colored `TestThing` objects for each of the more common interaction feedback states. The utility building blocks for this are also shown below. Each level of the multi-shape tree is broken out into a different utility block: `buildMultiThing`, `buildMultiSelectThing`, and `buildMultiActionThing`.

The example uses the utility block `buildTargetFeedbackSupport` to provide each of the multi-shape target things with a full complement of input sensors, pickers, and feedback triggers. It provides mostly event wiring, and draws upon the services of the `buildStatusTriggerSupport`, `buildSelectTriggerSupport`, and `buildActionTriggerSupport` utility blocks to handle most of the sensor and trigger details. As stated during the introduction to part 4, the framework does not shy away from using numerous input sensors. Including sensors in each trigger support utility allows it to be a self-contained building block.

You may have noticed that the example uses the utility block `buildGroupManager` to build a group manager object, which is used by `buildTargetFeedbackSupport`. This was done for expediency. It simplifies the example, and is not germane to the current discussion on multi-shapes and feedback triggering. (Management of feedback groups will be covered in the next section and example.) This example should give you a good sense for the kinds of multi-layered scaffolding that the framework provides for support of UI techniques in a somewhat general manner. Without the multi-leveled bundling of functionality that the framework core and utility building blocks provide, you can well imagine the mounds of code that would have to be packed into these examples to show even these simple control and feedback techniques.

Filename: J3duiBook/examples/MultiShaping/MultiShaping.java:

```
...
// setup multishape targets
/// target 0
MultiShape multi0 = FeedbackBlocks.buildMultiThing();
AffineGroup affine0 = new AffineGroup(multi0);

affine0.getTranslation().initActuation(
 new Vector4d(0, 2, 0, 0));
getWorld().addSceneNode(affine0);

/// target 1
MultiShape multi1 = FeedbackBlocks.buildMultiThing();
AffineGroup affine1 = new AffineGroup(multi1);

affine1.getTranslation().initActuation(
 new Vector4d(-2, -2, 0, 0));
getWorld().addSceneNode(affine1);

/// target 2
MultiShape multi2 = FeedbackBlocks.buildMultiThing();
AffineGroup affine2 = new AffineGroup(multi2);

affine2.getTranslation().initActuation(
 new Vector4d(2, -2, 0, 0));
getWorld().addSceneNode(affine2);

// setup manipulation controls
getView().getView().getViewPlatform().setCapability(
 Node.ALLOW_LOCAL_TO_VWORLD_READ);

/// manipulation draggers, first button
InputDragSplitter relDrag = new InputDragSplitter();

ActuationBlocks.buildRelativeDragger(relDrag,
 getView(), Input.BUTTON_FIRST,
 Input.MODIFIER_NONE, Input.MODIFIER_NONE);

/// manipulation mappers
InputDragTarget mapper;

//// translation
mapper = IntuitiveBlocks.buildDrmTranslationMapper(
 affine0, null, true);
relDrag.addEventTarget(mapper);

mapper = IntuitiveBlocks.buildDrmTranslationMapper(
 affine1, null, true);
relDrag.addEventTarget(mapper);
```

```
mapper = IntuitiveBlocks.buildDrmTranslationMapper(
 affine2, null, true);
relDrag.addEventTarget(mapper);

// setup manipulation feedback
/// build group manager (no multi-select)
FeedbackGroupManager groupManager = FeedbackBlocks.
 buildGroupManager(getWorld().getViewRoot());
groupManager.getSelectManager().setMultiSelect(
 Input.MODIFIER_IGNORE);

/// add targets
StatusTrigger trigger;
BranchGroup pickRoot = getWorld().getSceneRoot();

trigger = FeedbackBlocks.buildTargetFeedbackSupport(
 multi0, groupManager, relDrag, null, pickRoot);
affine0.setEventTargetEnable(trigger);

trigger = FeedbackBlocks.buildTargetFeedbackSupport(
 multi1, groupManager, relDrag, null, pickRoot);
affine1.setEventTargetEnable(trigger);

trigger = FeedbackBlocks.buildTargetFeedbackSupport(
 multi2, groupManager, relDrag, null, pickRoot);
affine2.setEventTargetEnable(trigger);

/// initialize feedback (last)
groupManager.initTargets(null, Feedback.STATUS_DISABLE,
 Feedback.SELECT_NORMAL, Feedback.ACTION_NORMAL);

// setup over management
ArrayList pickList, enableList;

pickList = new ArrayList();
pickList.add(multi0);
pickList.add(multi1);
pickList.add(multi2);

enableList = new ArrayList();
enableList.add(affine0);
enableList.add(affine1);
enableList.add(affine2);

IntuitiveBlocks.buildOverEnabler(getView(),
 getWorld().getSceneRoot(), pickList, enableList);
…
```

Filename: J3duiBook/lib/j3dui/utils/blocks/FeedbackBlocks.java

```
...
/**
Creates a MultiShape version of a TestThing whose box
and ball color are determined by the overall interaction
state.
@return New MultiShape object.
*/
public static final MultiShape buildMultiThing() {

  MultiStatus status = new MultiStatus();

  status.setStatusNode(Feedback.STATUS_NORMAL,
    buildMultiSelectThing(Feedback.STATUS_NORMAL));
  status.setStatusNode(Feedback.STATUS_DISABLE,
    buildMultiSelectThing(Feedback.STATUS_DISABLE));

  return status;
}


/**
Creates a MultiSelect version of a TestThing whose box
color is determined by the select state and whose ball color
is determined by the action state.  The box color intensity
will appear according to the status state.
@param status Status state (STATUS_NORMAL or STATUS_DISABLE).
@return New MultiSelect object.
*/
public static final MultiSelect buildMultiSelectThing(
 int status) {

  MultiSelect select = new MultiSelect();

  if(status == Feedback.STATUS_NORMAL) {
    select.setSelectNode(Feedback.SELECT_NORMAL,
      buildMultiActionThing(TestThing.BOX_NORMAL_0));
    select.setSelectNode(Feedback.SELECT_SINGLE,
      buildMultiActionThing(TestThing.BOX_NORMAL_1));
    select.setSelectNode(Feedback.SELECT_DOUBLE,
      buildMultiActionThing(TestThing.BOX_NORMAL_2));
    select.setSelectNode(Feedback.SELECT_TRIPLE,
      buildMultiActionThing(TestThing.BOX_NORMAL_3));
  } else {
    select.setSelectNode(Feedback.SELECT_NORMAL,
      buildMultiActionThing(TestThing.BOX_DISABLE_0));
    select.setSelectNode(Feedback.SELECT_SINGLE,
      buildMultiActionThing(TestThing.BOX_DISABLE_1));
    select.setSelectNode(Feedback.SELECT_DOUBLE,
      buildMultiActionThing(TestThing.BOX_DISABLE_2));
    select.setSelectNode(Feedback.SELECT_TRIPLE,
```

```
            buildMultiActionThing(TestThing.BOX_DISABLE_3));
      }

      return select;
   }

   /**
   Creates a MultiAction version of a TestThing with the
   specified box color.  The ball color will be changed
   according to the interaction state.
   @param boxColor Box color for all shapes.
   @return New MultiAction object.
   */
   public static final MultiAction buildMultiActionThing(
    Color3f boxColor) {

      MultiAction action = new MultiAction();

      action.setActionNode(Feedback.ACTION_NORMAL,
       new TestThing(boxColor, TestThing.BALL_NORMAL));
      action.setActionNode(Feedback.ACTION_OVER,
       new TestThing(boxColor, TestThing.BALL_OVER));
      action.setActionNode(Feedback.ACTION_PAUSE,
       new TestThing(boxColor, TestThing.BALL_PAUSE));
      action.setActionNode(Feedback.ACTION_DOWN,
       new TestThing(boxColor, TestThing.BALL_DOWN));
      action.setActionNode(Feedback.ACTION_DRAG,
       new TestThing(boxColor, TestThing.BALL_DRAG));
      action.setActionNode(Feedback.ACTION_DROP,
       new TestThing(boxColor, TestThing.BALL_DROP));
      action.setActionNode(Feedback.ACTION_CANCEL,
       new TestThing(boxColor, TestThing.BALL_CANCEL));

      return action;
   }
   ...
```

Utility blocks for feedback triggers

Filename: J3duiBook/lib/j3dui/utils/blocks/FeedbackBlocks.java

```
...
/**
Creates input sensors for the status trigger target.
Includes various input sensors and a select canceler.
@param target Event target.
*/
public static final void
 buildStatusTriggerSupport(StatusTrigger target) {

   // limit states to available shapes
   target.setStatusFlags(Feedback.STATUS_NORMAL|
    Feedback.STATUS_DISABLE);
```

```
}

/**
Creates input sensors for the select trigger target.
Includes various input sensors but no select canceler.
@param target Event target.
@param display Source display.  Null for all displays.
@param host Sensor host group.
*/
public static final void
 buildSelectTriggerSupport(SelectTrigger target,
 AppDisplay display, Group host) {

   // limit states to available shapes
   target.setSelectFlags(Feedback.SELECT_NORMAL|
    Feedback.SELECT_SINGLE|Feedback.SELECT_DOUBLE|
    Feedback.SELECT_TRIPLE);

   // build input sensors
   MouseButtonSensor buttoner = new MouseButtonSensor(
    target, display, host);

   /// select canceler
   InputCancelTrigger canceler =
    new InputCancelTrigger(target);

   KeyboardModifierSensor modifier =
    new KeyboardModifierSensor(canceler, display, host);
   modifier.setModifiers(Input.MODIFIER_ESC);
}

/**
Creates input sensors for the action trigger target.  The
trigger's pick targets are used for the pick engine pick
list.  Includes various input sensors, an over picker, and
a drag canceler.
@param target Event target.
@param dragSpltr An input drag splitter that supplies the
same button and modifier triggering as that used for the
target manipulation.
@param display Source display.  Null for all displays.
@param pickRoot Scene graph pick root and sensor host group.
*/
public static final void
 buildActionTriggerSupport(ActionTrigger target,
  InputDragSplitter dragSpltr, AppDisplay display,
  BranchGroup pickRoot) {

   // build input sensors
   dragSpltr.addEventTarget(target);

   InputMoveSplitter moveSpltr = new InputMoveSplitter();
```

```
    MouseMoveSensor mover = new MouseMoveSensor(moveSpltr,
     display, pickRoot);
    moveSpltr.addEventTarget(target);

    MouseButtonSensor buttoner = new MouseButtonSensor(
     target, display, pickRoot);

    // build move pauser
    InputPauseTrigger pauser =
     new InputPauseTrigger(target);
    moveSpltr.addEventTarget(pauser);
    target.getAllowPauseSource().addEventTarget(pauser);

    // build drag canceler
    InputCancelTrigger canceler =
     new InputCancelTrigger(target);

    KeyboardModifierSensor modifier =
     new KeyboardModifierSensor(canceler,
     null, pickRoot);
    modifier.setModifiers(Input.MODIFIER_ESC);

    // build over picker, use trigger's pick targets
    ObjectPickMapper picker = new ObjectPickMapper(target,
     new PickEngine(pickRoot, target.getPickTargets()));
    moveSpltr.addEventTarget(picker);
}

/**
Creates triggers and sensors for managing a target's
feedback through a common feedback group manager.  The
target's status trigger is returned so that it may be
connected to an enable source for status feedback.
@param target Pick and feedback target.
@param groupManager Feedback group manager.  Never null.
@param dragSpltr An input drag splitter that supplies the
same button and modifier triggering as that used for the
target manipulation.
@param display Source display.  Null for all displays.
@param pickRoot Scene graph pick root and sensor host group.
@return The target's status trigger.
*/
public static final StatusTrigger
 buildTargetFeedbackSupport(MultiShape target,
 FeedbackGroupManager groupManager,
 InputDragSplitter dragSpltr, AppDisplay display,
 BranchGroup pickRoot) {

  EnableSplitter overSpltr = new EnableSplitter();

  // build select trigger
  SelectManager selectManager =
```

```
    groupManager.getSelectManager();

SelectTrigger select = (SelectTrigger)
 selectManager.getTargetTrigger(target);

if(select==null) {
   select = (SelectTrigger)
    selectManager.addTarget(target);
   overSpltr.addEventTarget(select);
}

FeedbackBlocks.buildSelectTriggerSupport(select,
 display, pickRoot);

// build status trigger
StatusManager statusManager =
 groupManager.getStatusManager();

StatusTrigger status = (StatusTrigger)
 statusManager.getTargetTrigger(target);

if(status==null) {
   status = (StatusTrigger)
    statusManager.addTarget(target);

   FeedbackBlocks.buildStatusTriggerSupport(status);
}
   // build action trigger
ActionManager actionManager =
 groupManager.getActionManager();

ActionTrigger action = (ActionTrigger)
 actionManager.getTargetTrigger(target);

if(action==null) {
   action = (ActionTrigger)
    actionManager.addTarget(target);
   action.getOverTargetSource().addEventTarget(overSpltr);
}

FeedbackBlocks.buildActionTriggerSupport(action,
 dragSpltr, display, pickRoot);

return status;
}
...
```

20.2 INTERACTION MANAGEMENT

The previous section dealt with feedback mostly in terms of individual objects. Often, however, interaction must involve groups of objects, with the group itself being the target of user manipulation and the source of user feedback. Although not strictly part of feedback, group selection is included here in the framework with feedback management because of its intimate connection to interaction states and their feedback.

20.2.1 FeedbackManager class

The `FeedbackManager` class is the abstract base class for all target group feedback managers. Consistent with the rest of the framework's handling of interaction states, managers come in three flavors, each specialized for a particular type of interaction: `StatusManager`, `SelectManager`, and `ActionManager`. The role of a feedback manager is to monitor feedback on a set of target objects, and to report interaction state changes occurring to any of them, via event splitters serving as collateral event targets. Target groups can be obtained through the `getGroup` method, which returns a list of target proxies that satisfy one or more of the specified state flags.

The `MultiShape` class is used as the managed target entity because it provides a single package that can serve as the target object's geometry and feedback root. It also provides a convenient way to tap into any feedback chain connected to it. As you'll see in the following discussions and examples, the framework's feedback management model is general and powerful, but this also makes it more complicated than it otherwise would be. Table 20.3 summarizes the classes and interfaces associated with feedback management, and figure 20.4 illustrates how they interrelate.

Table 20.3 Summary of classes and interfaces related to feedback managers

Class/*Interface*	Description	Input Events	Output Events
FeedbackManager	Abstract base class for feedback managers of target groups		FeedbackTarget (target any) FeedbackTarget (trigger any)
FeedbackMinion	A proxy for a feedback target and trigger managed by a feedback manager		
StatusManager	Feedback manager that handles status interaction		FeedbackTarget (target any) FeedbackTarget (trigger any)
SelectManager	Feedback manager that handles selection interaction	InputModifierTarget	FeedbackTarget (target any) FeedbackTarget (trigger any)
ActionManager	Feedback manager that handles action interaction		FeedbackTarget (target any) FeedbackTarget (trigger any)

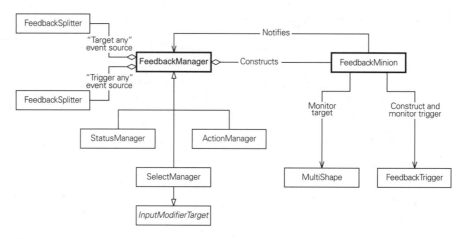

Figure 20.4   Relationship of classes and interfaces related to feedback managers

20.2.2   FeedbackMinion class

There are many reasons why a particular target's interaction state might change. The change could be the result of direct user interaction, such as an action trigger determining that the mouse is over the target. It could also be the result of indirect activity initiated through system intervention, such as when the target is a member of a selection group and the mouse passes over some other member of the group. In both cases, the desired action of the application might be to notify all selection group members of the mouseover event so that they can change their appearance accordingly. An important aspect of feedback management is being able to differentiate between these two forms of interaction: user versus system.

The approach used by FeedbackManager for differentiating between internally and externally induced state changes is to wrap each MultiShape feedback target in a FeedbackMinion class. The minion class serves as a proxy for the target object. It also acts as a factory that automatically creates a feedback trigger of the right flavor and wires it up to the target. For the feedback manager model to work reliably, the minion's trigger must be used as the target's sole interaction trigger. This allows the minion, and indirectly its host manager, to determine whether a given feedback event originated external to a target, and sent directly to it, or was the result of direct user interaction with the target, as determined by the target's trigger.

To allow maximum flexibility in defining what is a feedback target object and how interaction is detected on that object, the following procedure should be used for adding a target to a feedback manager. First, use the getTargetTrigger method on the feedback manager to get any trigger that may already be connected to the target. If none exists, as indicated by a null return, the second step is to add the target to the manager, thereby creating a new trigger for it. In either case, once the trigger has been obtained, the third step is to connect it to appropriate input and picking event sources.

The utility building block `buildTargetFeedbackSupport` follows this procedure when adding feedback support to a new `MultiShape` target.

20.2.3 FeedbackManager subclasses

The feedback manager subclasses provided by the framework perform basic group management. If your application requires different group handling, extend the subclasses and override their protected `manageFeedback` methods. The `Status-Manager` subclass of `FeedbackManager` is simply a placeholder of the correct feedback flavor in the class hierarchy; it does nothing in the way of active group management. The `ActionManager` subclass is a little more interesting. It contains two collateral event sources, one for notifying interested observers when mouseover changes on any target, and another indicating when any target changes its mind about allowing pauses.

When it comes to group-oriented activity, the `SelectManager` subclass is much more interesting than the others. It provides several modes of selection, including single-selection and multi-selection, which are controlled via the mode flags and the user's use of modifier keys, as indicated through the manager's `InputModifier-Target` input interface. The defaults are for single-selection when no modifier keys are down, and for multi-selection when the control key is down. In single-selection mode, at most one target can be selected at a time, with any previously selected target being automatically deselected. In multi-selection mode, selected targets are accumulated into a selection group. In any mode, selecting a target that is already selected deselects it. The manager can also be configured to handle only user selections, in which case the system is left to take care of any selections that it made on its own.

20.2.4 FeedbackGroupManager class

The `FeedbackGroupManager` class performs high-level feedback management on a selected group of feedback targets. It does this by relaying the feedback state from any member of the selection group to all the members of the group. The low-level group and feedback management is handled through delegation to a set of feedback managers, which do the actual work. In other words, `FeedbackGroupManager` is a meta-manager for feedback managers. Also, unlike the feedback managers, which deal exclusively with a given interaction type, this manager is equipped to handle the complete interaction state—status, select, and action.

The group manager's constructor requires a feedback manager of each type, with their "target any" collateral event outputs being internally connected to the group manager's feedback event input. Presumably, each of the feedback managers contains the same set of targets (although this is not necessary). Thus, if the mouse is over any target in the selection group, then status and action events are relayed to all the targets in the group.

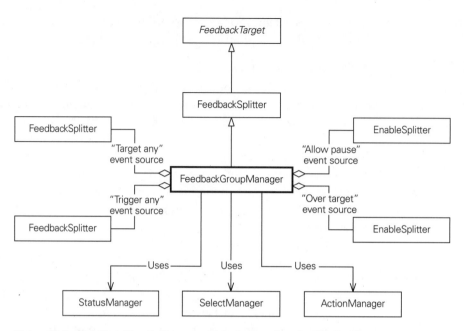

Figure 20.5   Relationship of classes and interfaces related to feedback group managers

For different group dynamics, you can extend your own group manager, but beware: There are a lot of event handling subtleties and convolutions to be dealt with. To help matters out, all input events are locked out while an event is being handled. Short of creating your own, several collateral event sources (splitters) are provided to give the application an opportunity to perform custom event handling. Table 20.4 summarizes the group manager event interfaces. Figure 20.5 illustrates how the group manager relates to its supporting classes.

Table 20.4   Summary of classes and interfaces related to feedback group managers

Class/*Interface*	Description	Input Events	Output Events
FeedbackGroupManager	Manages a selection group by relaying the complete interaction state to all group members	FeedbackTarget	EnableTarget (allow pause) EnableTarget (over any) FeedbackTarget (target any) FeedbackTarget (trigger any)

20.2.5   Example: TargetSelecting

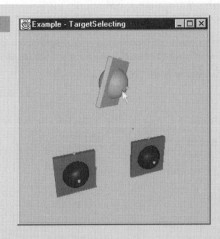

**Figure 20.6
Screen shot of the
TargetSelecting example**

This example demonstrates object and group selection for feedback and control input enabling.

> **See**

The virtual world contains three target objects. A screen shot is provided in figure 20.6.

> **Do**

- Drag the mouse (left button) on a target or use the ARROW keys to translate it relative to the display.
- Single, double, and triple-click on a target and repeat the drag.
- Select targets with the CONTROL key down, and then repeat the drag.
- Move the mouse over a selected target and press the ESCAPE key.
- Drag the mouse (left button with Shift) in the display or use the arrow keys (with SHIFT) to orbit the view in heading and elevation about the world origin.

> **Observe**

- All targets are implemented as multi-shapes, with a different shape for each feedback state combination.
- Each target is configured for DRM translation, rotation, and scale manipulation.
- Manipulation mode is determined by the target's selection state (single-red-translate, double-green-rotate, triple-blue-scale).
- Manipulation is enabled through interaction state triggering when mouse over occurs.
- Using the CONTROL key allows multi-selection.
- Feedback and manipulation affect all members of the selection group.
- Using the ESCAPE key allows de-selection.

In terms of structure, the highlights of this example are that each target requires control of three actuators, and the actuators are enabled through interaction triggering instead of an explicit over-enabler as used in the last few examples. In the example code, immediately following, the multi-shape feedback and DRM manipulation setups should be familiar, but notice the new utility block, `buildTargetSelectEnablers`, being used to handle control enabling. Notice how in this example the group manager, constructed using the `buildGroupManager` utility block, is not disabled, allowing it to do multi-selection and to perform selection group interaction management. The code for the new utility blocks is also shown below.

Setup for group manager and feedback-based enabling in TargetSelecting

Filename: J3duiBook/examples/TargetSelecting/TargetSelecting.java

```
...
// setup multishape targets
/// target 0
MultiShape multi0 = FeedbackBlocks.buildMultiThing();
AffineGroup affine0 = new AffineGroup(multi0);

affine0.getTranslation().initActuation(
  new Vector4d(0, 2, 0, 0));
getWorld().addSceneNode(affine0);

affine0.getScale().getPlugin().setTargetClamp(
  Mapper.DIM_ALL, new Vector2d(.5, 4));

/// target 1
MultiShape multi1 = FeedbackBlocks.buildMultiThing();
...
/// target 2
...
// setup manipulation controls
getView().getView().getViewPlatform().setCapability(
  Node.ALLOW_LOCAL_TO_VWORLD_READ);

/// manipulation draggers, first button
InputDragSplitter relDrag = new InputDragSplitter();

ActuationBlocks.buildRelativeDragger(relDrag,
  getView(), Input.BUTTON_FIRST,
  Input.MODIFIER_NONE, Input.MODIFIER_NONE);

/// manipulation mappers
InputDragTarget mapper;

//// translation
mapper = IntuitiveBlocks.buildDrmTranslationMapper(
  affine0, null, true);
relDrag.addEventTarget(mapper);
...
//// rotation
mapper = IntuitiveBlocks.buildDrmRotationYMapper(
  affine0, null, true);
relDrag.addEventTarget(mapper);
...
//// scale
mapper = IntuitiveBlocks.buildDrmScaleMapper(
```

```
 affine0, null, true);
relDrag.addEventTarget(mapper);
...
// setup target feedback and enable
/// build group manager
FeedbackGroupManager groupManager =
 FeedbackBlocks.buildGroupManager(
 getWorld().getViewRoot());

/// add targets
StatusTrigger trigger;
BranchGroup pickRoot = getWorld().getSceneRoot();

trigger = FeedbackBlocks.buildTargetFeedbackSupport(
 multi0, groupManager, relDrag, null, pickRoot);
FeedbackBlocks.buildTargetSelectEnablers(
 multi0, trigger, affine0.getTranslation(),
 affine0.getAxisAngle(), affine0.getScale());

trigger = FeedbackBlocks.buildTargetFeedbackSupport(
 multi1, groupManager, relDrag, null, pickRoot);
FeedbackBlocks.buildTargetSelectEnablers(
 multi1, trigger, affine1.getTranslation(),
 affine1.getAxisAngle(), affine1.getScale());

trigger = FeedbackBlocks.buildTargetFeedbackSupport(
 multi2, groupManager, relDrag, null, pickRoot);
FeedbackBlocks.buildTargetSelectEnablers(
 multi2, trigger, affine2.getTranslation(),
 affine2.getAxisAngle(), affine2.getScale());

/// initialize feedback (last)
groupManager.initTargets(null, Feedback.STATUS_DISABLE,
 Feedback.SELECT_NORMAL, Feedback.ACTION_NORMAL);
...
```

Utility block for group manager setup

Filename: J3duiBook/lib/j3dui/utils/blocks/FeedbackBlocks.java

```
...
/**
Creates a set of feedback managers and adds them to an empty
group manager.  Includes a modifier sensor for multi-
selection.  Use buildTargetSupport() to add targets to the
group manager for feedback management.
@param host Host group for sensors.
@return The feedback group manager.
*/
public static final FeedbackGroupManager
 buildGroupManager(Group host) {

   // build feedback managers
```

```
StatusManager statusManager = new StatusManager();
SelectManager selectManager = new SelectManager();
ActionManager actionManager = new ActionManager();

/// monitor all displays for modifiers
new KeyboardModifierSensor(selectManager, null, host);

// build group manager
FeedbackGroupManager groupManager =
 new FeedbackGroupManager(statusManager, selectManager,
 actionManager);

return groupManager;
}
…
```

Utility block for selection enabling

Filename: J3duiBook/lib/j3dui/utils/blocks/FeedbackBlocks.java

```
…
/**
Creates feedback enable triggers that enable target control
elements (e.g. actuators for translation, rotation, scale)
according to the selection state (single, double, triple) of
the target's multi-shape feedback source.  The target's
feedback status will be updated accordingly through its
status trigger.
<P>
Note that all triggers will be initialized "true" to permit
initialization of enable targets.  The final act of
initialization must be to initialize the multishape target
state, which in turn initializes the triggers and their
enable targets.
@param targetMulti Target's feedback source.  Never null.
@param targetTrigger Target's status trigger.  Null if none.
@param targetSingle Single-select enable target.  Null if
none.
@param targetDouble Double-select enable target.  Null if
none.
@param targetTriple Triple-select enable target.  Null if
none.
*/
public static final void buildTargetSelectEnablers(
 MultiShape targetMulti, EnableTarget targetTrigger,
 EnableTarget targetSingle, EnableTarget targetDouble,
 EnableTarget targetTriple) {

  FeedbackEnableTrigger enabler;
  int selectFlags = 0;

  // build actuator enablers by select
  if(targetSingle != null ) {
```

```
        selectFlags |= Feedback.SELECT_SINGLE;
        enabler = new FeedbackEnableTrigger(targetSingle);
        enabler.setSelectFlags(Feedback.SELECT_SINGLE);
        enabler.setActionFlags(Feedback.ACTION_IS_OVER);
        targetMulti.addEventTarget(enabler);
        enabler.initEventTarget(true);
    }

    if(targetDouble != null ) {
        selectFlags |= Feedback.SELECT_DOUBLE;
        enabler = new FeedbackEnableTrigger(targetDouble);
        enabler.setSelectFlags(Feedback.SELECT_DOUBLE);
        enabler.setActionFlags(Feedback.ACTION_IS_OVER);
        targetMulti.addEventTarget(enabler);
        enabler.initEventTarget(true);
    }

    if(targetTriple != null ) {
        selectFlags |= Feedback.SELECT_TRIPLE;
        enabler = new FeedbackEnableTrigger(targetTriple);
        enabler.setSelectFlags(Feedback.SELECT_TRIPLE);
        enabler.setActionFlags(Feedback.ACTION_IS_OVER);
        targetMulti.addEventTarget(enabler);
        enabler.initEventTarget(true);
    }

    // build status feedback enabler
    if(targetTrigger != null ) {
        enabler = new FeedbackEnableTrigger(targetTrigger);
        enabler.setSelectFlags(selectFlags);
        targetMulti.addEventTarget(enabler);
        enabler.initEventTarget(true);
    }
}
...
```

20.3 *FEEDBACK ELEMENTS*

Now that you've had enough groundwork laid to build another Mall of America, let's start putting some of it to good use. This section focuses on adding visual and audio decorations to data objects for interaction feedback. Simple but useful forms of visual feedback in a 3D UI are tooltips, indicators, and drag handles. Sound effects can be added to these to round out and reinforce the user experience. Although the multi-shape technique allows any type of object to be used for feedback decoration, the emphasis here is on the use of texture mapping. By applying transparent textures—or more accurately, textures with transparent backgrounds—to simple geometric shapes, most of the hard visual design work can be done with a paint package instead of through programming.

Table 20.5 Summary of classes and interfaces related to feedback elements

Class/*Interface*	Description	Input Events	Output Events
TextureShape	Abstract base class for transparently textured feedback elements		
TextureRect	A texture shape element with a rectangular shape		
TextureCylinder	A texture shape element with a cylindrical shape		
TextureCone	A texture shape element with a conical shape		
SoundEffect	An audio feedback element that plays once each time a "true" input event is received	EnableTarget	

Most of the classes discussed here are found in the `j3dui.feedback.elements` package. Table 20.5 summarizes the framework's feedback element classes.

20.3.1 TextureShape class

The framework provides the class `TextureShape` as an abstract base class for simple textured shapes used for feedback decorations. It is derived from `Group` so that it can contain one or more leaf shapes representing different sides of the same flat element. The object is configured for specification of color, transparency, pickability, and texture while the object is live in the scene graph. Since the object is intended for use as a feedback element and not for general object modeling, object color is set as a color attribute so that it does not depend on lighting, and the same texture is applied to all contained shapes. Note that Java 3D requires texture image dimensions to be a power of two.

Transparency

As already mentioned in the Java 3D introduction, Java 3D's handling of transparency is peculiar. For a transparent texture to appear transparent, its host shape must also be transparent, which can be set using the `setTransparency` method of `TextureShape`. The specific transparency value is unimportant as long as transparency is enabled, since it is ignored when transparent textures are involved. For this reason, if you want a transparent texture to appear on a semi-transparent background, such as for a third-person control overlaid in the display, you have to use a separate semi-transparent shape behind the transparently textured shape. For a texture to appear transparent, its image must be created with a transparent background, which can be satisfied by the GIF image format, and loaded such that its transparent qualities are preserved, which the framework utility `LoadUtils.loadTexture2D` can do.

Java 3D is also not very accommodating when transparently textured objects overlap other objects. In such situations, the shape can appear oddly. To assure correct overlap, the shapes must be non-intersecting, separate children of an `OrderedGroup`, and non-coplanar. Perhaps these requirements, which are sometimes difficult to meet, will be relaxed in future Java 3D releases.

20.3.2   TextureShape subclasses

The subclasses of `TextureShape` that are provided in this package of the framework all have similar qualities. The objects can be single or double-sided, as specified by the constants in the `Elements` class. Double-sided objects consist of back-to-back shapes with back-to-back textures. Each subclass also offers it geometry for public consumption through a utility method `buildGeometry`, which returns a Java 3D `Geometry` object.

Of the `TextureShape` subclasses, `TextureRect` has the simplest shape. It is a rectangle with arbitrary width and height lying in the *X-Y* plane and centered about the *Z* axis. The texture is stretched across the full surface of the rectangle, and is oriented correctly on the "top" side of the element, which is the one facing along the − *Z* axis. The texture on the "bottom" side will be a mirror image of that on the top side.

The `TextureCyclinder` class forms a cyclinder whose central axis is the *Y* axis. Its height can be set as well as the radius of its top and bottom edges. The texture will be stretched and wrapped width-wise around the cylinder with the side facing outward being the top.

The `TextureCone` class also uses the *Y* axis as its central axis. Its height and base radius can be set. Its rectangular texture is stretched to circumscribe the cone's circular base, and is projected down onto the cone's surface along the *Y* axis.

20.3.3   SoundEffect class

The framework provides the `SoundEffect` class for implementing audio decorations. It uses the framework's `LoadUtils.loadSound` utility to load a sound from file, and takes care of all the Java 3D boilerplate code for playing the sound. In keeping with the notion that interaction feedback sounds should be subtle, the audio gain should be kept at a low gain value, typically under 0.5. The sound effect is started/re-started whenever a true value is received via its `EnableTarget` input event interface. In the examples you may notice that the sound effects are sometimes cut off prematurely when a new sound starts before an old one finishes. The class tries to prevent this, but a Java 3D bug prevents it from working.

20.3.4   Example: TargetDecorating

Figure 20.7
Screen shot of the
TargetDecorating example

This example demonstrates object decorating with visual and audio feedback elements.

> **See**

The virtual world contains three target objects on a floor plane. A screen shot is provided in figure 20.7.

> **Do**

- Move the mouse over a target, then pause.
- Drag the mouse (left button) on a target or use the ARROW keys to translate it relative to the display.
- While dragging a target, hit the ESCAPE key.
- Single, double, and triple-click on a target and repeat the pause and drag.
- Select targets with the CONTROL key down, then repeat the pause and drag.
- Drag the mouse (left button with SHIFT) in the display or use the arrow keys (with SHIFT) to orbit the view in heading and elevation about the world origin.

> **Observe**

- The target decorations, which include tooltips, handles, and audio sound effects, are implemented as multi-shapes.
- The visual decorations use primitive shapes with transparent textures, containing arbitrary shapes and text fonts.
- Manipulation modes include WRM horizontal sliding with a sticky cursor, direct rotation, and direct vertical lifting.
- Decorations correspond to manipulation mode, which is determined by the target's selection state (single-slide, double-rotate, triple-lift).
- Selection and feedback are implemented using group management.
- As the view changes or the targets are moved, the decorations may become obscured or unreadable because of lack of visualization techniques.

This example is organized much like the previous one, except here the target manipulation modes are horizontal sliding and rotation, and vertical lifting, relative to a floor plane, which is provided by a TestPlane object. The code below from the example highlights only the new manipulation modes and the feedback decoration. Notice that sticky cursor pseudo-WRM is used for sliding, but to keep things simple, direct mapping is used for rotation and lifting. The utility building block `buildMultiFloorTarget` from the `FeedbackBlocks` class, which is also shown immediately following, is used to conveniently arrange and bundle the target decorations with a target object. Notice that this block also assembles the target's slide, rotate, and lift actuators into a control chain for constrained manipulation appropriate for a floor plane.

Separate and somewhat configurable utility blocks, also provided in the `FeedbackBlocks` class, are used to build each feedback decoration in `buildMultiFloorTarget`, which are shown highlighted. To give you a feel for how the decoration building blocks are put together, the code for the `buildMultiSlide` block is included below. This `MultiShape` feedback element is a drag handle built from a transparently textured double-sided `TextureCone` shape. For simplicity, only two versions of the shape are used: one for normal appearance, and the other for mouse-over. Notice here and in the other blocks how multi-shape proxies are used to bundle decoration geometry and feedback wiring.

Floor target construction and feedback management in *ImageDecorating*

Filename: J3duiBook/examples/TargetDecorating/TargetDecorating.java

```
...
// build floor plane
TestPlane floor = new TestPlane(
 TestPlane.PLANE_DEFAULT, 8, 8);

affine = new AffineGroup(floor);
affine.getTranslation().initActuation(
 new Vector4d(0, 0, 0, 0));
affine.getAxisAngle().initActuation(
 new Vector4d(1, 0, 0, -Math.PI/2.0));
getWorld().addSceneNode(affine);

// setup multishape targets
MultiShape thing;

/// target 0
thing = FeedbackBlocks.buildMultiThing();
AffineGroup slide0 = new AffineGroup();
AffineGroup rotate0 = new AffineGroup();
AffineGroup lift0 = new AffineGroup();
MultiShape target0 =
 FeedbackBlocks.buildMultiFloorTarget(
 thing, slide0, rotate0, lift0, getView(), 1);
getWorld().addSceneNode(target0);

slide0.getTranslation().initActuation(
 new Vector4d(0, 1, 2.5, 0));
...
```

```
/// manipulation mappers
InputDragTarget mapper;
Vector2d rotateScale = new Vector2d(.025, .025);
Vector2d liftScale = new Vector2d(.025, .025);

//// WRM slide
mapper = IntuitiveBlocks.buildStickyWrmTranslationMapper(
 floor, slide0, getWorld().getSceneRoot(), true, true);
absDrag.addEventTarget(mapper);
…
//// direct rotate
mapper = ActuationBlocks.buildDirectMapper(
 rotate0.getAxisAngle(), rotateScale,
 Mapper.DIM_W, Mapper.DIM_NONE, true);
rotate0.getAxisAngle().getPlugin().setSourceOffset(
 new Vector4d(0, 1, 0, 0));
relDrag.addEventTarget(mapper);
…
//// direct lift
mapper = ActuationBlocks.buildDirectMapper(
 lift0.getTranslation(), liftScale,
 Mapper.DIM_NONE, Mapper.DIM_Y, true);
relDrag.addEventTarget(mapper);
…
// setup target feedback and enable
/// build group manager
FeedbackGroupManager groupManager =
 FeedbackBlocks.buildGroupManager(
 getWorld().getViewRoot());

/// add targets
StatusTrigger trigger;
BranchGroup pickRoot = getWorld().getSceneRoot();

trigger = FeedbackBlocks.buildTargetFeedbackSupport(
 target0, groupManager, relDrag, null, pickRoot);
FeedbackBlocks.buildTargetSelectEnablers(
 target0, trigger, slide0.getTranslation(),
 rotate0.getAxisAngle(), lift0.getTranslation());
…
```

Utility blocks for floor target decorating

Filename: J3duiBook/lib/j3dui/utils/blocks/FeedbackBlocks.java
…
```
/**
Creates a set of MultiShape feedback decorations for a
target object that is intended to be slid, rotated, and
lifted over an X-Z floor plane.  The decorations include
tooltips, handles, and sound.
@param target Target object to be centered, offset, and
decorated.  If the target is a FeedbackTarget it will also
```

be connected as a feedback target.
@param slide Affine group used to slide the target. The
group will be connected into an internal group chain and
therefore should be supplied as new. Null if none.
@param rotate Affine group used to rotate the target. The
group will be connected into an internal group chain and
therefore should be supplied as new. Null if none.
@param lift Affine group used to slide the target. The
group will be connected into an internal target chain and
therefore should be supplied as new. Null if none.
@param view Host environment for the sound audio device.
If null then no sound.
@param height Height (+Y) of the target above its origin.
@return New MultiShape proxy target.
*/
```
public static final MultiShape buildMultiFloorTarget(
 Node target, AffineGroup slide, AffineGroup rotate,
 AffineGroup lift, AppView view, double height) {

   AffineGroup affine;
   MultiSelect select;

   String dir = Blocks.buildResourcePath("feedback/");
   double handleH = .5;
   double sliderR = 1;
   double rotateRT = .4;
   double rotateRB = .8;
   double liftW = 1;
   double liftH = .66;
   double calloutW = 3;
   double calloutH = .75;
   double margin = .1;

   // build transform chain
   MultiShape multiTarget = new MultiShape();
   Node node = target;

   if(rotate != null) {
      rotate.addNode(node);
      node = rotate;
   }
   if(lift != null) {
      lift.addNode(node);
      node = lift;
   }
   if(slide != null) {
      slide.addNode(node);
      node = slide;
   }
   multiTarget.addNode(node);

   // add pickable multi target
```

```
        PickUtils.setGeoPickable(target, true);

        if(target instanceof FeedbackTarget)
          multiTarget.addEventTarget((FeedbackTarget)target);

        // add multi sounds
        if(view!=null) {
          MultiShape sound = FeedbackBlocks.
            buildMultiSound(view);
          multiTarget.addProxyTarget(sound, sound);
        }

        // add multi handles, by selection
        select = new MultiSelect();

        select.setSelectNode(Feedback.SELECT_SINGLE,
          buildMultiSlide(true, slideR, handleH));
        select.setSelectNode(Feedback.SELECT_DOUBLE,
          buildMultiRotate(true, rotateRB, rotateRT, handleH));
        select.setSelectNode(Feedback.SELECT_TRIPLE,
          buildMultiLift(true, liftW, liftH));
        multiTarget.addEventTarget(select);

        affine = new AffineGroup(select);
        affine.getTranslation().initActuation(new Vector4d(
          0, height+margin, 0, 0));

        if(lift==null)
          multiTarget.addNode(affine);
        else
          lift.addNode(affine);

        // add multi tooltips, by selection
        select = new MultiSelect();

        select.setSelectNode(Feedback.SELECT_SINGLE,
          buildMultiTooltip(false, calloutW, calloutH,
          dir + "CalloutSlide.gif"));
        select.setSelectNode(Feedback.SELECT_DOUBLE,
          buildMultiTooltip(false, calloutW, calloutH,
          dir + "CalloutRotate.gif"));
        select.setSelectNode(Feedback.SELECT_TRIPLE,
          buildMultiTooltip(false, calloutW, calloutH,
          dir + "CalloutLift.gif"));
        multiTarget.addEventTarget(select);

        affine = new AffineGroup(select);
        affine.getTranslation().initActuation(new Vector4d(
          0, height+handleH+calloutH/2.0+margin, 0, 0));

        if(lift==null)
          multiTarget.addNode(affine);
```

```
          else
            lift.addNode(affine);

          return multiTarget;
      }
      ...
      /**
      Creates a MultiAction manipulation handle for sliding a
      target object.  The object is a cone facing up along the
      Y axis with the origin at its bottom center.
      @param pickable If true the handle will be pickable.
      @param handleR Radius of the handle.
      @param handleH Height of the handle.
      @return New MultiAction object containing the decoration.
      */
      public static final MultiAction buildMultiSlide(
       boolean pickable, double handleR, double handleH) {

          String dir = Blocks.buildResourcePath("feedback/");
          MultiAction action = new MultiAction();

          // normal shape
          Node normal = new TextureCone(pickable,
           new Color3f(0f, 0f, 0f), 0,
           dir + "NormalSlide.gif", Elements.SIDE_ALL,
           handleR, handleH);

          // over shape
          Node over = new TextureCone(pickable,
           new Color3f(0f, 0f, 0f), 0,
           dir + "OverSlide.gif", Elements.SIDE_ALL,
           handleR, handleH);

          // show actions
          action.setActionNode(Feedback.ACTION_NORMAL |
           Feedback.ACTION_CANCEL, normal);
          action.setActionNode(Feedback.ACTION_OVER |
           Feedback.ACTION_PAUSE | Feedback.ACTION_DROP, over);

          // make it visable by default
          action.setFeedbackAction(Feedback.ACTION_OVER);

          return action;
      }
      ...
```

20.4 SUMMARY

Although there is more to feedback than interaction states, using only them you can do many useful things, as shown in the examples. The three main areas of feedback covered by this chapter included multi-shapes, feedback management, and basic feedback elements. The framework includes a flexible scheme for chaining and nesting multi-shape components, and for conveniently assigning them to one or more interaction states. Feedback management includes both interaction state triggers and higher-level feedback group managers, which are capable of monitoring events occurring on a set of multi-shape target objects. To demonstrate an even higher level of management, the framework includes a meta-manager—a manager of feedback managers—that allows interactive group selection, with interaction state control enabling, and feedback occurring on the group as a whole.

High-level utility building blocks showed you how to pull together all of the low-level control and feedback building blocks and to put them to good use. The last part of the chapter demonstrated how to manipulate target objects in a constrained manner relative to a reference floor plane. The manipulation interaction states were coupled with visual and aural feedback elements, decorating the targets with tooltips, drag handles, and sound effects. Chapter 21 will show you how the decorations can be combined with visualization techniques for more convenient access and effective use in cluttered environments.

CHAPTER 21

Visualization

Typically, data objects are supposed to sit passively in the scene just being themselves. In fact, for most applications, the more the data objects are perceived as being like those of the real world they represent, the better off the designer and user will be. Feedback elements, on the other hand, often want to be anything but passive. To be effective they need to be readily seen and accessible, which means turning them to face the user, making them big enough but not too big, and overlaying them on top of their neighbors. All of these duties fall under the auspices of visualization techniques, which are demonstrated in this chapter. Other aspects of visualization that are also addressed here include display overlay, such as for creating third-person controls, and multiple displays, for showing the same scene from different vantage points.

By now you should have a fairly good feel for how the framework and utility building blocks are organized and put together. As promised earlier, the pace of the presentation will quicken now that the framework basics have been covered. This and the remaining chapters will focus just on the highlights of what the framework has to offer, and how it went about implementing them. All of the classes introduced here are located in the `j3dui.visualize` package.

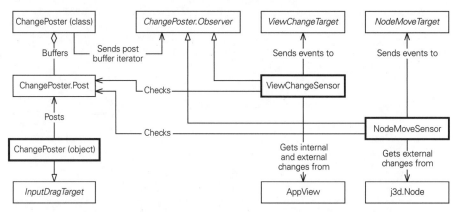

Figure 21.1 Relationship of classes and interfaces related to change detection

21.1 CHANGE DETECTION

For reasons stated in the Java 3D introduction, the framework uses geometry-only techniques to implement world and display overlay. Although such techniques offer a unified and concise way of performing overlay, they also have a tendency to expose many of the hidden flaws in a 3D API's implementation of change detection and event synchronization. Java 3D is no exception, and its flaws in this area have already been discussed in chapter 17. Due to the problems, the framework usually avoids the Java 3D behavior model for detecting and handling view and node state changes. Vestiges of the model have been left in the framework to synchronize scene graph rendering with the framework's change poster, and to serve as placeholders in anticipation of future releases that fix the current problems with behaviors.

Table 21.1 summarizes the classes and event interfaces related to view and node change detection in the framework. Figure 21.1 illustrates how the classes are related and used.

Table 21.1 Summary of classes and interfaces related to change detection

Class/*Interface*	Description	Input Events	Output Events
ChangePoster.Observer	Event interface for notifying that state changes may have occurred in an observed target object		
ChangePoster	Monitors input drag events and posts corresponding change events	InputDragTarget	Change-Poster.Observer
ChangePoster.Post	A buffered notification of possible state change		

Table 21.1   Summary of classes and interfaces related to change detection (continued)

Class/*Interface*	Description	Input Events	Output Events
NodeMoveTarget	Event interface for reporting world-relative node movement		
NodeMoveSplitter	Node movement event splitter	NodeMoveTarget	NodeMoveTarget
NodeMoveSensor	A sensor that monitors a node for world-relative movement. (Because of J3D problems, only monitors change posts)	ChangePoster.Observer	NodeMoveTarget
ViewChangeTarget	Event interface for reporting internal and external geometric changes in a view		
ViewChangeSplitter	Node movement event splitter	ViewChangeTarget	ViewChangeTarget
ViewChangeSensor	A sensor that monitors a view for internal and external geometric changes. (Because of J3D problems, only monitors change posts and AWT window events	ChangePoster.Observer	ViewChangeTarget

21.1.1   Change poster model

The visualization techniques described in part 2 of the book need to track two types of changes. They need to know when an object of interest moves, and when a view looking at the object has moved or its internal geometry has changed. Because Java 3D behaviors aren't up to the task at the time of writing, the framework has resorted to a "change poster" model independent of Java 3D for change detection and notification.

In the change poster model, changes are detected in two stages. The first stage monitors for input events, such as mouse and keyboard drags, that might cause a node or view change. Such change candidates are posted to a global post buffer by a change poster. In synchronization with the Java 3D renderer, the global post buffer notifies any interested observers that posts have been made, which starts the second stage in the change detection process. The observers, which are the change sensors, then sample the state of the source objects they are monitoring for changes, and if warranted by what they find, they generate output change events accordingly.

21.1.2 ChangePoster class

The ChangePoster class bundles together everything that is needed to provide an interim solution for change event posting. It includes a private static portion that serves as the global post buffer and a public instance portion for constructing a drag event monitor—a change poster. The ChangePoster constructor takes two parameters: a trigger object and a post ID. Post observers use these to help them decide whether or not a change in which they might be interested has occurred. The trigger object might correspond to the source node or view itself, or it could simply be some token object. The post ID is a constant provided in the ChangePoster class to narrow down the kind of change that may have occurred.

Whenever a change poster detects an input drag event, it creates a Change-Poster.Post object with the specified trigger object and post ID. The change poster then posts it to the global post buffer. Any post to the post buffer also cocks the trigger on a private behavior class so that it fires when the next rendering cycle occurs. When the behavior fires, the post buffer springs into action by notifying its observers that posts are waiting to be checked, and then clears the post buffer to wait for new posts. The ChangePoster class must be initialized before it is used. The static init method accepts a group node argument, which serves as the host for the post buffer's private synchronization behavior in the scenegraph.

The code sample below is from the buildViewOrbiter utility building block in the ActuationBlock class. It shows how a change poster is used to monitor drag inputs that affect the OrbitGroup created by the block. This is a good place for a change poster because, by its very nature, any control inputs to the view orbiter will likely cause changes to the view position and orientation—external geometry changes. Notice in the change poster constructor that the view itself is used as the trigger object, and POST_VIEW_EXTERNAL is appropriately used for the post ID.

Use of change poster in the view orbiter block

Filename: J3duiBook/lib/j3dui/utils/blocks/ActuationBlocks.java

```
...
/**
Creates an OrbitGroup, attaches the specified view to it
with a headlight, and connects it to a relative dragger.
@param view View to be attached and the source of drag input.
@param orbit Initial orbit angles.
@param dist Initial distance from view to LAP.
@param mouseButtons Mouse buttons enabling drag
(Input.BUTTON_???).
@param mouseModifiers Modifier keys enabling mouse drag
(Input.MODIFIER_???).
@param arrowModifiers Modifier keys enabling arrow drag
@return New orbit group.
*/
public static final OrbitGroup buildViewOrbiter(
  AppView view, Vector3d orbit, double dist, int mouseButtons,
```

```
                      int mouseModifiers, int arrowModifiers) {

        ...
        // build orbiter
        OrbitGroup orbitGroup = new OrbitGroup(viewGroup);
        orbitGroup.initActuation(OrbitGroup.toActuation(orbit));

        ...
        // build control
        InputDragTarget mapper = buildDirectMapper(orbitGroup,
         new Vector2d(.01, -.01), Mapper.DIM_Y, Mapper.DIM_X,
         true);

        InputDragSplitter spltr = new InputDragSplitter();
        buildRelativeDragger(spltr, view, mouseButtons,
         mouseModifiers, arrowModifiers);
        spltr.addEventTarget(mapper);

        /// change posters (kludge for Java 3D 1.1.2 view change)
        if(ChangePoster.isInit()) {
           spltr.addEventTarget(new ChangePoster(
            view, ChangePoster.POST_VIEW_EXTERNAL));
        }

        // done
        return orbitGroup;
    }
    ...
```

21.2 WORLD SPACE TECHNIQUES

The framework supports all of the basic world space techniques described in chapter 6, including display facing, constant size, world overlay, and perfect overlay. Each is implemented as an actuator group. Instead of controlling their actuators externally, however, they are controlled internally in response to view and node geometry change events. Child nodes that are added to a group exhibit the visual behavior defined by the parent group, such as constant size or overlay. The groups can be nested to perform combinations of techniques.

Each actuator group implements the `ViewChangeTarget` input event interface so that it can be notified any time a view that is looking at it changes. To simplify use, each group contains its own `NodeMoveSensor`, which allows it to update itself any time it moves. This allows the class to be self-contained. Unexpected side effects, which can occur when different visualization groups are nested, are avoided. For the internal change sensors to work, however, the application must post potential node movement changes. This will be shown in the examples below.

21.2.1 World space classes

Table 21.2 summarizes the classes related to world space visualization in the framework. Figure 21.2 illustrates how the classes are related and used.

Table 21.2   Summary of classes and interfaces related to world space visualization

Class/*Interface*	Description	Input Events	Output Events
DisplayFaceGroup	A transform actuator group that makes its children appear display facing according to input view and internal node changes	EnableTarget ViewChangeTarget	
ConstantSizeGroup	A transform actuator group that makes its children appear constant size according to input view and internal node changes	EnableTarget ViewChangeTarget	
WorldOverlayGroup	A transform actuator group that makes its children appear in world overlay according to input view and internal node changes	EnableTarget ViewChangeTarget	
PerfectOverlayGroup	An actuator group that combines the other world space visualization groups into one	EnableTarget ViewChangeTarget	

DisplayFaceGroup class

The `DisplayFaceGroup` class implements the display facing technique, where the local coordinate space of its children is oriented about its origin such that its *X-Y* plane is always parallel to and aligned with the view's display plane. Optionally, the orientation can be constrained to pivot about a fixed axis through the local space origin, similar to that allowed by the Java 3D `Billboard` class.

ConstantSizeGroup class

The `ConstantSizeGroup` class implements the constant size technique, where the local coordinate space of its children is scaled such that a child object will always appear the same size on the display screen. The apparent screen size is independent of view and group movement, as well as internal view geometry changes such as FOV, DSF, and DS. The group's scale factor is specified as a fraction of the horizontal screen (not display) width that a unit-width object will appear to fill.

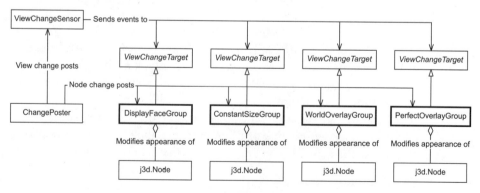

Figure 21.2   Relationship of classes and interfaces related to world space visualization

WorldOverlayGroup class

The `WorldOverlayGroup` class implements the PWO technique, which makes objects in the local coordinate space appear to overlay or underlay other objects in the world space. The group's overlay factor is expressed as a scale factor applied to the world distance between the view and the group's local space origin. Factors less than one (closer to view) produce overlay, and factors greater than one (farther from view) produce underlay. As such, to prevent overlay objects from interfering with world objects, the overlay factor should be made as large or as small as the Z-clipping planes and system performance will allow.

PerfectOverlayGroup class

The `PerfectOverlayGroup` class implements the perfect overlay technique, which is a combination of the other techniques—an actuator group of actuator groups. The techniques are conveniently configured in a group chain and wired up for view and node change detection. Flag constants from the `Visualize` class allow individual techniques to be selectively enabled for custom configuration. The order of the techniques from head to tail in the group chain is world overlay, constant size, and display facing.

21.2.2 Example: DisplayFacing

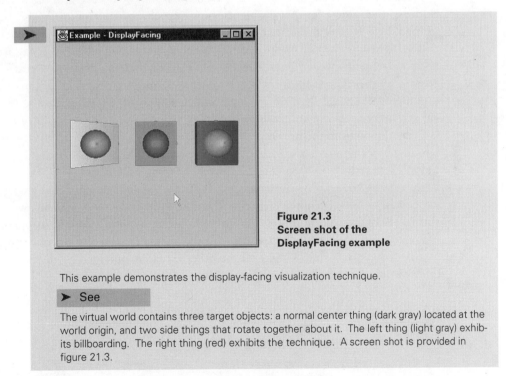

**Figure 21.3
Screen shot of the
DisplayFacing example**

This example demonstrates the display-facing visualization technique.

➤ See

The virtual world contains three target objects: a normal center thing (dark gray) located at the world origin, and two side things that rotate together about it. The left thing (light gray) exhibits billboarding. The right thing (red) exhibits the technique. A screen shot is provided in figure 21.3.

The following code sample following is from the example. It highlights those portions pertaining to change detection and the display facing visualization technique. The `DisplayFaceGroup` is created and used much like any other group node. The display-facing TestThing object is added to it as a child, and the group itself is added as a child of the *Y*-axis rotator. The `DisplayFaceGroup` already contains a `Node-MoveSensor`, so all it needs is a `ViewChangeSensor` to report view changes.

If all were normal, only the change sensors would be needed and the job would be done. Because of Java 3D problems, however, change posting must also be performed. Before using the change posting system, the `ChangePoster` is globally initialized. Then, at the end of the code, a `ChangePoster` is created to post potential node movements occurring as a result of dragging the side objects rotator. These posts use the `DisplayFaceGroup` object as the trigger, and a post ID of `POST_NODE_EXTERNAL`, indicating that the changes are affecting the node's external geometry (position and rotation).

You know from the previous code sample that the `buildViewOrbiter` utility building block already contains a view change poster. This example introduces a new way to affect the view geometry. The `buildViewFover` utility block from the `VisualizeBlocks` class constructs a dragger and custom actuator that changes the target view's internal geometry, specifically its FOV. Its code is included below to show you its use of the change poster; but, more importantly, it is a good example of how to create your own custom actuators, with the actuator target and operation defined by the `FovPlugin` class. Unlike all the other actuators provided by the framework, this one does not involve a transform group.

Filename: J3duiBook/examples/DisplayFacing/DisplayFacing.java

...

```
ChangePoster.init(getWorld().getViewRoot());

// setup orbitable view, first + shift
getView().setViewFov(Math.PI/2);

getWorld().addViewNode(
 ActuationBlocks.buildViewOrbiter(getView(),
 new Vector3d(0, 0, 0), 5,
 Input.BUTTON_FIRST, Input.MODIFIER_SHIFT,
 Input.MODIFIER_SHIFT)
);

// build sensors
ViewChangeSplitter viewSpltr = new ViewChangeSplitter();

new ViewChangeSensor(viewSpltr, getView(),
 getWorld().getViewRoot());

// build world: normal center thing
AffineGroup affine;
TestThing thing;

thing = new TestThing(TestThing.BOX_DISABLE_0,
 TestThing.BALL_CANCEL);
getWorld().addSceneNode(thing);

// build world: side rotating things
/// side thing rotator
AffineGroup affineY = new AffineGroup();
getWorld().addSceneNode(affineY);

/// side billboard thing
...
/// side display facing thing
thing = new TestThing(TestThing.BOX_NORMAL_1,
 TestThing.BALL_OVER);
DisplayFaceGroup face = new DisplayFaceGroup(thing);
viewSpltr.addEventTarget(face);

affine = new AffineGroup(face);
affine.getTranslation().initActuation(
 new Vector4d(3, 0, 0, 0));
affineY.addNode(affine);

// setup manipulation controls
InputDragTarget mapper;
InputDragSplitter dragSpltr = new InputDragSplitter();
```

```
/// side thing Y rotation, first + none
…
ActuationBlocks.buildRelativeDragger(dragSpltr,
 getView(), Input.BUTTON_FIRST,
 Input.MODIFIER_NONE, Input.MODIFIER_NONE);

/// view fov, first + control
VisualizeBlocks.buildViewFover(getView(),
 new Vector2d(Math.PI/4, Math.PI/1.5),
 Input.BUTTON_FIRST, Input.MODIFIER_CTRL,
 Input.MODIFIER_CTRL);

/// change posters (kludge for Java 3D 1.1.2)
dragSpltr.addEventTarget(new ChangePoster(
 face, ChangePoster.POST_NODE_EXTERNAL));
…
```

Custom actuator and dragger creation, in this case for view FOV control

Filename J3duiBook/lib/j3dui/utils/blocks/VisualizeBlocks.java

```
/**
Builds a FOV actuator, attaches the specified view to it,
and connects it to a relative dragger.  Increasing dragger
Y decreases FOV (zoom in).  Note that in AppView a FOV of
zero results in a parallel projection.
@param view View to be attached and the drag input source.
@param clamp Limits on the view FOV range.
@param mouseButtons Mouse buttons enabling drag
(Input.BUTTON_???).
@param mouseModifiers Modifier keys enabling mouse drag
(Input.MODIFIER_???).
@param arrowModifiers Modifier keys enabling arrow drag
@return New orbit group.
*/
public static final Actuator buildViewFover(
 AppView view, Vector2d clamp, int mouseButtons,
 int mouseModifiers, int arrowModifiers) {

   class FovPlugin extends ActuatorPlugin {
      public FovPlugin(AppView view) {_view = view;}
      public Node getTargetNode() {return _view;}
      public String toString() {return "";}

      protected void initActuation(Tuple4d value) {
         toActuationSource(value, _value);
         _state.set(_value);
         _reference.set(_state);
         toActuationTarget(_state, _state);
         _view.setViewFov(_state.y);
      }
      protected void updateActuation(Tuple4d value) {
         toActuationSource(value, _value);
```

```
            _state.y = _reference.y + _value.y;
            toActuationTarget(_state, _state);
            _view.setViewFov(_state.y);
        }
        protected void syncActuation() {
            _reference.set(_state);
        }

        private AppView _view;
        private Vector4d _reference = new Vector4d();
        private Vector4d _state = new Vector4d();
        private final Vector4d _value = new Vector4d();
    }

    // build fover
    Actuator fover = new Actuator(new FovPlugin(view));
    fover.getPlugin().setTargetClamp(Mapper.DIM_ALL, clamp);
    fover.initActuation(
     new Vector4d(0, view.getViewFov(), 0, 0));

    // build control
    InputDragTarget mapper = ActuationBlocks.
     buildDirectMapper(fover,
     new Vector2d(0, -.01), Mapper.DIM_NONE,
     Mapper.DIM_Y, true);

    InputDragSplitter spltr = new InputDragSplitter();
    ActuationBlocks.buildRelativeDragger(spltr, view,
     mouseButtons, mouseModifiers, arrowModifiers);
    spltr.addEventTarget(mapper);

    /// change posters (kludge for Java 3D 1.1.2)
    spltr.addEventTarget(new ChangePoster(
     view, ChangePoster.POST_VIEW_INTERNAL));

    // done
    return fover;
}
```

21.2.3   Example: ConstantSizing

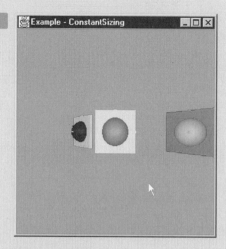

**Figure 21.4
Screen shot of the
ConstantSizing example**

This example demonstrates the constant size visualization technique.

➤ **See**

The virtual world contains three target objects: a normal center thing (dark gray) located at the world origin, and two side things that rotate together about it. The left thing (light gray) is normal. The right thing (red) exhibits the technique. A screen shot is provided in figure 21.4.

➤ **Do**

- Drag the mouse (left button with SHIFT) in the display or use the ARROW keys (with SHIFT) to orbit the view in heading and elevation about the world origin.
- Drag the mouse (left button with CONTROL) up-down in the display or use the ARROW keys (with CONTROL) to change the display field-of-view.
- Drag the mouse (left button) horizontally in the display or use the arrow keys to rotate the side things about the world Y-axis.
- Repeat the drag operations from different view directions and with different FOVs.
- Resize the display window.

➤ **Observe**

- The left (light gray) side thing gets larger as it approaches the eye and shrinks as it recedes—the latter can be seen in the screen shot.
- The right (red) side thing uses constant size to always remain the same size in spite of display re-sizing, FOV changes, or proximity to the eye—the latter can be seen in the screen shot.

The change sensor and change posting setup in this example is similar to that in the previous one. The code sample below is from the example, and shows only the portion that builds the ConstantSizeGroup object.

Setup of the visualization group in the ConstantSizing example

Filename: J3duiBook/examples/ConstantSizing/ConstantSizing.java

```
...
// build world: side rotating things
```

```
/// side thing rotator
AffineGroup affineY = new AffineGroup();
getWorld().addSceneNode(affineY);

/// side normal thing
…
/// side constant size thing
double size = 0.0235;

thing = new TestThing(TestThing.BOX_NORMAL_1,
 TestThing.BALL_OVER);
ConstantSizeGroup sizer = new ConstantSizeGroup(
 thing, size);
viewSpltr.addEventTarget(sizer);

affine = new AffineGroup(sizer);
affine.getTranslation().initActuation(
 new Vector4d(3, 0, 0, 0));
affineY.addNode(affine);
…
```

21.2.4   Example: WorldOverlaying

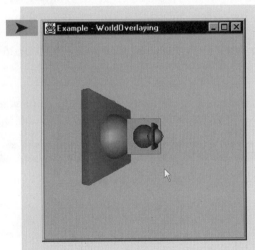

**Figure 21.5
Screen shot of the
WorldOverlaying example**

This example demonstrates the world overlay visualization technique.

➤ See

The virtual world contains three target objects: a normal center thing (dark gray) located at the world origin, and two side things that rotate together about it. The left (green) and right (red) things exhibit the technique. A screen shot is provided in figure 21.5.

➤ Do

• Drag the mouse (left button with SHIFT) in the display or use the ARROW keys (with SHIFT) to orbit the view in heading and elevation about the world origin.

The change detection setup is similar to that in the previous example. The code sample below shows how the WorldOverlayGroup objects are built. It also shows that, because there are two different instances of the visualization group involved, postings must be made to each one since each serves as its own trigger object. Change posting is indeed tedious. I hope that a future release of Java 3D will eliminate the need for it.

You may have noticed that the overlaid objects tend to jitter when any movement occurs, whether the objects are moving or the view looking at them moves. This is due to a problem in how Java 3D synchronizes scene graph updates with rendering, which was discussed in chapter 13. The jitter is not as bad if you use the ARROW keys to perform object and view drags. The jitter is also present in the other visualization techniques, only it is much more noticeable in overlay. I hope this problem too will disappear with a future release of Java 3D. Of course, an alternative would be to implement world overlay using immediate mode rendering, directly to the display, but this approach also has problems.

Visualization group and change posting setup in WorldOverlaying example

Filename: J3duiBook/examples/WorldOverlaying/WorldOverlaying.java

```
...
// build world: side rotating things
double overlay;

/// side thing rotator
AffineGroup affineY = new AffineGroup();
getWorld().addSceneNode(affineY);

/// world underlay thing
overlay = 5.0;

thing = new TestThing(TestThing.BOX_NORMAL_2,
 TestThing.BALL_OVER);
WorldOverlayGroup over0 =
 new WorldOverlayGroup(thing, overlay);
```

```
viewSpltr.addEventTarget(over0);

affine = new AffineGroup(over0);
affine.getTranslation().initActuation(
 new Vector4d(-3, 0, 0, 0));
affineY.addNode(affine);

/// world overlay thing
overlay = 0.2;

thing = new TestThing(TestThing.BOX_NORMAL_1,
 TestThing.BALL_OVER);
WorldOverlayGroup over1 =
 new WorldOverlayGroup(thing, overlay);
viewSpltr.addEventTarget(over1);

affine = new AffineGroup(over1);
affine.getTranslation().initActuation(
 new Vector4d(3, 0, 0, 0));
affineY.addNode(affine);
...
/// change posters (kludge for Java 3D 1.1.2)
dragSpltr.addEventTarget(new ChangePoster(
 over0, ChangePoster.POST_NODE_EXTERNAL));
dragSpltr.addEventTarget(new ChangePoster(
 over1, ChangePoster.POST_NODE_EXTERNAL));
...
```

21.2.5   Example: PerfectOverlaying

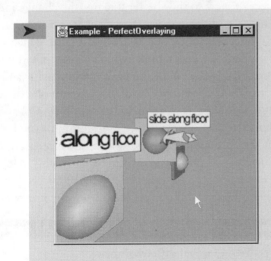

**Figure 21.6
Screen shot of the
PerfectOverlaying example**

This example demonstrates the perfect overlay visualization technique.

The code sample immediately following, from the example, shows how the `PerfectOverlayGroup` object and its decorations are built. As before, a change poster is needed for each visualization group object. Because the decorations are special, but the thing to which they are attached is normal, the decorations may not be aligned with the object after a mouse drag due to the synchronization problem. You can use the ARROW keys to nudge the object or view so they better line up (the change induced by an ARROW key is smaller and more easily controlled than that from a mouse).

While trying the example, you may notice that the world object which comes close to the eye can sometimes obscure the decorations, which are supposed to be in overlay. Although this is always an issue with PWO, the problem in these examples is much worse than it would be normally. To minimize jitter due to the synchronization problem, the overlay factors have been kept as close to 1.0 as possible—0.2 and 5.0. The ultimate limitation on the overlay scale factor is the Z resolution of the renderer and, indirectly, the position of the Z clipping planes. When these techniques are implemented in VRML (specifically Cosmo Player), even when using a low-end OpenGL display card, overlay factors on the order of 0.02 and 100.0 produce perfectly smooth results while keeping the overlaid objects away from the normal ones.

Visualization group and change posting setup in PerfectOverlaying example

Filename: J3duiBook/examples/PerfectOverlaying/PerfectOverlaying.java

```
...
/// perfect overlay side
double overlay;
```

```
double size = .025;

//// perfect callout
overlay = 0.175;

thing = FeedbackBlocks.buildMultiTooltip(false, 3, .75,
 Blocks.buildResourcePath("feedback/CalloutSlide.gif"));
affine = new AffineGroup(thing);
affine.getTranslation().initActuation(
 new Vector4d(0, 1.2, 0, 0));

PerfectOverlayGroup perfect0 =
 new PerfectOverlayGroup(affine,
 Visualize.DO_ALL, overlay, size);
viewSpltr.addEventTarget(perfect0);

affine = new AffineGroup(perfect0);
affine.getTranslation().initActuation(
 new Vector4d(3, -.5, 0, 0));
ordered.addChild(affine);

//// near perfect (over+size) handle
overlay = 0.2;

thing = new TextureCylinder(false,
 new Color3f(0f, 0f, 0f), 0,
 Blocks.buildResourcePath("feedback/OverRotate.gif"),
 Elements.SIDE_ALL, 1, .5, .75);
affine = new AffineGroup(thing);
affine.getTranslation().initActuation(
 new Vector4d(0, .05, 0, 0));

PerfectOverlayGroup perfect1 =
 new PerfectOverlayGroup(affine,
 Visualize.DO_OVER_SIZE, overlay, size);
viewSpltr.addEventTarget(perfect1);

affine = new AffineGroup(perfect1);
affine.getTranslation().initActuation(
 new Vector4d(3, -.5, 0, 0));
ordered.addChild(affine);
...
/// change posters (kludge for Java 3D 1.1.2)
dragSpltr.addEventTarget(new ChangePoster(
 perfect0, ChangePoster.POST_NODE_EXTERNAL));
dragSpltr.addEventTarget(new ChangePoster(
 perfect1, ChangePoster.POST_NODE_EXTERNAL));
...
```

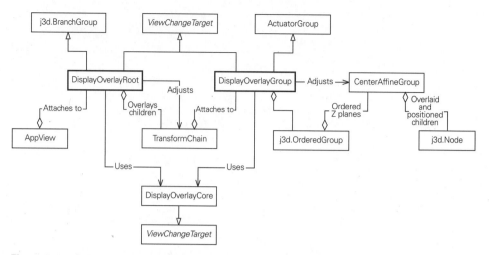

Figure 21.7 Relationship of classes and interfaces related to display space visualization

21.3 DISPLAY SPACE TECHNIQUES

Although the `WorldOverlayGroup` could in theory be used to implement display overlay, given the problems with Java 3D, the framework uses a different approach. It provides a set of classes that create a pseudo-display overlay space as a child of a view object. Being a child of the view space, external view changes are not required (but notification of internal view changes are), thereby avoiding a significant portion of the jitter. Aside from basic overlay, the framework also includes Z planes for overlap priority, and display-relative layout.

21.3.1 Display space classes

In concept, all that should be needed to implement display overlay is a "display overlay" group, similar to the `WorldOverlayGroup` class. Because of issues with how Java 3D handles overlapping transparent textures, which are used extensively in the framework for multi-shape feedback decorations, objects that may overlap must be separate children of a Java 3D `OrderedGroup`. A further complication is that `OrderedGroup` really doesn't guarantee the Z order of rendering. Instead, the overlapping children must be ordered *and* they must occupy the correct relative Z position relative to the eye. To deal with these inconveniences, display overlay has been divided into two parts: a root class and a separate group class.

Table 21.3 summarizes the classes related to display space visualization in the framework. Figure 21.7 illustrates how the classes are related and used.

DisplayOverlayRoot class

The `DisplayOverlayRoot` class handles the first part of the display overlay technique. It attaches directly to an `AppView` (one of the few uses of framework utility

Table 21.3 **Summary of classes and interfaces related to display space visualization**

Class/*Interface*	Description	Input Events	Output Events
DisplayOverlayRoot	A branch group that makes its children appear overlaid in a normalized display space	ViewChangeTarget	
DisplayOverlayGroup	An actuator group that orders, positions, and overlaps its children in display space	EnableTarget ViewChangeTarget	
DisplayOverlayCore	A helper class for normalization and layering of the display space	ViewChangeTarget	

classes in the core) and creates a normalized display overlay space for its child nodes to live in. It uses a transform chain to translate its children close to the eye, at a normalized world distance of 1.0, and to scale them down so that their apparent size and position can be expressed directly in display screen pixels. Using pixel coordinates for display-based layout is consistent with the AWT, and makes the graphic designer's job easier. The origin of the resulting pseudo-display space is also offset relative to the view space, to match the UI view model's DVO. (This is in anticipation of some future Java 3D release that will actually allow the DVO to be independently specified.)

Being a subclass of `BranchGroup` allows a `DisplayOverlayRoot` object to be conveniently used as a root for picking objects in display space, such as for manipulating third-person virtual controls. Although the display space is intended for use with flat objects that are parallel to the display plane, there is nothing to prevent objects with an arbitrary 3D shape from being added to the space. Because of their depth component, however, such objects may interfere with other objects that are in Z planes closer to the eye.

DisplayOverlayGroup class

The `DisplayOverlayGroup` class handles the second part of the display overlay technique. It attaches directly to a `DisplayOverlayRoot` and creates a local coordinate system in the display space, with provisions for placing child objects in separate overlapping Z planes. It uses an `OrderedGroup` to help make the overlap appear correctly, to which it adds a `CenterAffineGroup` for each Z plane. The individual groups are adjusted to maintain proper Z distance from the eye, to establish the local coordinate system, and to fine-tune the scaling of the local space to compensate for Z-plane position. The scaling must be performed about the local origin, not the world origin, hence the need for a center-affine group.

Adding an object to one of the predefined Z planes places it in the display space, at a given Z overlap position. The Z plane index has the same sense as the view space Z axis, with plane zero being the reference plane, planes greater than zero being closer to the eye, and planes less than zero being farther from the eye. To assist in display space layout, the class includes methods for setting the local space origin relative to the display origin, and for setting an absolute offset from that origin. Relative position is expressed as a percentage of the display dimension, and absolute position is expressed in pixels. An example will help to explain how these are used for layout.

Say you wanted to place a virtual control knob in the display space, and you wanted its lower right corner to always appear at the lower right corner of the display window, even if the window is re-sized. To achieve this, you would position the relative origin, using the setRelativeOrigin method, in the lower right corner of the display space. And, you would set the absolute offset, using the setAbsoluteOffset method, such that the center of the knob is offset from the relative origin by half of the control's width and height. Because objects in the display space are positioned and sized locally, in absolute pixels, the control remains positioned correctly with respect to the relative origin in the corner of the display. You'll see this in the next example.

DisplayOverlayCore class

The DisplayOverlayCore class is a helper function used by the display root and group. It performs most of the bookkeeping for normalizing the display space and computing Z plane positions. Unless you are developing your own display space classes, there should be no reason to use this class directly because the host classes take care of its construction and input event wiring.

21.3.2 Example: DisplayOverlaying

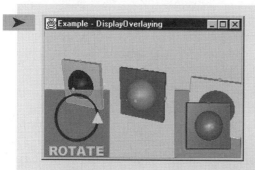

**Figure 21.8
Screen shot of the
DisplayOverlaying example**

This example demonstrates the display overlay visualization technique.

> See

The virtual world contains three target objects in world space, and two overlaid objects with semi-transparent backgrounds in display space. A screen shot is provided in figure 21.8.

> Do

- Drag the mouse (left button with SHIFT) in the display or use the ARROW keys (with SHIFT) to orbit the view in heading and elevation about the world origin.
- Drag the mouse (left button with CONTROL) up-down in the display or use the ARROW keys (with CONTROL) to change the display FOV.
- Drag the mouse (left button) horizontally in the display or use the ARROW keys to rotate the right overlay thing about its Y axis.

The code sample below shows how the lower-left display object is built in the example. The object is a nonoperational rotate control consisting of three components: an arrow-shaped mark, a control background, and a frame. Each component is placed in a different Z plane so they overlap each other correctly. A separate frame object is needed to give the control a semitransparent background because Java 3D will let only the background component, which contains a transparent texture, be either opaque or transparent—not semitransparent. (You'll see this control again in a later example, but next time it will be operational.)

You can also see in the sample how the local space origin and offset are used, and how the view change sensor is wired up. Because display overlay does not require node change sensing, posting for it is not needed. View change posting is still needed, so `ChangePoster` must be initialized.

Visualization setup and virtual control building in DisplayOverlaying example

Filename: J3duiBook/examples/DisplayOverlaying/DisplayOverlaying.java

```
...
ChangePoster.init(getWorld().getViewRoot());
...
// build sensors
ViewChangeSplitter viewSpltr = new ViewChangeSplitter();

ViewChangeSensor sensor = new ViewChangeSensor(
 viewSpltr, getView(), getWorld().getViewRoot());
...
// build display
int zPlane;
Vector2d origin = new Vector2d();
Vector2d offset = new Vector2d();

/// build display overlay root
DisplayOverlayRoot dispRoot =
 new DisplayOverlayRoot(getView());
viewSpltr.addEventTarget(dispRoot);

/// build lower-left control
origin.set(-.5, -.5);
offset.set(50, 50);
```

```
DisplayOverlayGroup disp0 =
 new DisplayOverlayGroup(dispRoot);
viewSpltr.addEventTarget(disp0);
disp0.setRelativeOrigin(origin);
disp0.setAbsoluteOffset(offset);

//// control mark
zPlane = 1;

thing = new TextureRect(true,
 new Color3f(0f, 0f, 0f), 0, Blocks.
 buildResourcePath("manipulate/NormalMark.gif"),
 Elements.SIDE_TOP, 16, 16);

affine = new AffineGroup(thing);
affine.getTranslation().initActuation(
 new Vector4d(32, 10, 0, 0));
disp0.addNode(affine, zPlane);

//// control back
zPlane = 0;

thing = new TextureRect(true,
 new Color3f(0f, 0f, 0f), 0, Blocks.
 buildResourcePath("manipulate/NormalRotateBack.gif"),
 Elements.SIDE_TOP, 100, 100);
disp0.addNode(thing, zPlane);

//// control frame
zPlane = -1;

thing = new TextureRect(true,
 new Color3f(.75f, .5f, .5f), .5, null,
 Elements.SIDE_TOP, 100, 100);
disp0.addNode(thing, zPlane);
...
```

21.4   MULTIPLE DISPLAYS

Many applications can benefit from showing the user multiple views of the same 3D scene. Incorporating multiple views into an application is straightforward: Create and position a view object for each display that is to appear in the application, and add their display canvases to the application frame the same as you would for any AWT canvas. This is the same approach used for a single-view application, only replicated for each display. The framework utility class DualFrame, which is used in the next example, is a dual-display version of the single display frame class, SingleFrame, used in all the other examples.

At the time of writing, Java 3D has problems concerning multiple displays of which you should be aware. Some of these problems are simply bugs. One is that the print image captured from the second display is always black. You can see this in an example in a later chapter, which lets you print its display images. Another bug is that the rendering of `Switch` nodes in the second display is not properly synchronized with scene graph updates, and as a result, multi-shapes appear to jump around in the second display. This can be seen in the next example.

A different kind of problem concerns the design of the API itself. Currently, techniques that depend on knowing the view position, such as `WorldOverlayGroup` and `Billboard`, can deal with only one display at a time. One solution, which was suggested earlier, is to allow the designation of the view in which an object would be rendered. Thus, a separate view-dependent object would be created for each view in an application, with the objects all being located at the same position in the world space. Until this or some functionally equivalent change occurs in the API, many of the world space techniques provided by the framework can be effectively used only in a single-display application.

21.4.1   Example: MultiDisplaying

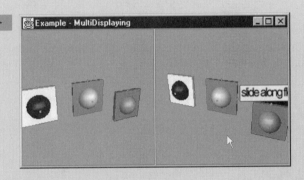

**Figure 21.9
Screen shot of the
MultiDisplaying example**

This example demonstrates the use of multiple displays and some of the problems that can ensue.

> ➤ See

The virtual world contains three target objects in world space. The left object (light gray) is a normal multi-shape object. The right object (red) is decorated with a perfect overlay callout. A screen shot is provided in figure 21.9.

> ➤ Do

- Drag the mouse (left button with SHIFT) in a display or use the ARROW keys (with SHIFT) to orbit the view in heading and elevation about the world origin.
- Drag the mouse (left button) horizontally in a display or use the ARROW keys to rotate the side things about the world Y axis.
- Move the view in one display, and then move it in the other display, while noting the appearance of the overlaid callout.
- Move the mouse over the left (light gray) or click on it to change its multi-shape appearance.

- After moving the left display, move the mouse over the multi-shape object (light gray) while noting its position in the right display.

> ➤ **Observe**

- The perfect overlay decoration appears only in the display where the view was last moved.
- If you carefully maneuver the objects and views, you may catch a glimpse of the decoration from the other view near where the first view is located in world space. This is a side effect of using pseudo-overlay instead of real overlay.
- In the second (right) display, the multi-shape object will appear to jump around when its interaction state changes because of Java 3D synchronization problems.

21.5 SUMMARY

The framework provides support for all the basic world and display space techniques described in chapter 6. Their implementation and use are complicated by several significant problems with Java 3D at the time of writing, not the least of which is the need for a change detection system independent of Java 3D, which the framework provides for both node and view change detection. The framework's world space techniques include display facing, constant size, and PWO, which are demonstrated separately and then all together in the form of perfect overlaying. For support of display space techniques, the framework defines a somewhat general system for performing PDO while wrestling with the vagaries of Java 3D ordered groups and transparency overlap. Provisions are included for Z planes, and absolute and relative layout of display space objects. Although Java 3D supports multiple displays, there are several issues to be aware of, especially when using pseudo-overlay techniques and others that require world objects to be rendered differently depending on which view is observing it.

C H A P T E R   2 2

Manipulation

Manipulation involves the combination of control, feedback and visualization techniques, and more, to assist the user in manipulating data objects in the scene. Emphasis is on allowing the user to manipulate objects in the virtual world as easily as they are manipulated in the real world. The more basic aspects of manipulation include relational feedback and manipulation personae. More advanced topics include object sticking and gluing in 3D, and PTF.

The framework provides several core building blocks for building relational feedback elements, specifically passive feelers. Such feedback helps the user to manipulate objects in a 3D world while viewing that world on a 2D display screen. This chapter also introduces a number of sophisticated utility building blocks that pull together much of what has already been presented in the framework. The core and utility blocks are combined to form application-like demonstrations of second- and third-person object manipulation, with control, feedback, and visualization.

22.1   PASSIVE FEELERS

Relational feedback helps the user to see spatial relationships among objects in the scene. *Feelers* are a type of relational feedback element used as visual aids to show how an object is situated with respect to its neighbors and surroundings. Passive feelers are a subset that does its job simply by being there for the user to see. This is distinct from active feelers, which might use in-scene ray throwing or collision detection to determine where surrounding objects are in relation to the target object. The framework provides two forms of passive feeler feedback elements as core building blocks, which are summarized in table 22.1. They are located in the `j3dui.manipulate` package.

Table 22.1   Summary of classes related to passive relational feedback

Class/*Interface*	Description	Input Events	Output Events
BoxOutline	A texture shape element consisting of lines forming the edges of a box		
BoxSkirt	A texture shape element consisting of a vertical box with filled sides		

22.1.1   Passive feeler classes

Both the `BoxOutline` and `BoxSkirt` classes are derived from `TextureShape`, which allows them to be textured, colored, made semi-transparent, and pickable. Although these shapes are typically used without texturing, if a texture is used it is stretched and wrapped horizontally around the box in a manner similar to that used for the `TextureCylinder` class. For `BoxOutline`, the texture will only appear on its lines. The geometry of both shapes is available through static utility methods.

Their geometry is quite simple. `BoxOutline` uses a Java 3D `IndexedLineStripArray` as the geometry of a box consisting of just its edge lines. Being made of lines, it only has one side for texturing. The box is intended to outline a host object. As such, the size of the host is specified using the two opposing corners of its bounding box, and a margin value can be specified that offsets the outline slightly away from the host so the outline remains distinct.

The `BoxSkirt` uses a Java 3D `IndexedTriangleStripArray` for its box geometry. The box consists of four sides, and no top or bottom. The skirt is intended to be an extension of a host object's bounding box, extending below the host along the local $-Y$ axis to a fixed length. To allow it to serve as the basis for an active version in the future, which adjusts its length according to its surroundings (as an active feeler), the shape geometry is configured for live update. Typically, a skirt feedback element is made semitransparent so that it does not obscure its neighbors.

22.1.2   Bounding box utilities

The feeler elements do not compute the extent of their host object; it must be given to them. The framework supplies several utilities for computing an object's bounding box in the `BoundsUtils` class found in the `j3dui.utils` package. Java 3D makes it as hard as possible to get an object's bounding box. It requires an object to be live in order for its bounding box to be computed automatically; to get the information from a live object, however, the object's capability bits must first be configured for live access to the information. Also, as one of its many problems in dealing with bounding boxes, at the time of writing, Java 3D can only compute the bounding box for leaf shapes.

The `allowGetBoundingBox` utility method conveniently configures a target node and its descendants for live bounding box computation. The `getBounding-Box` utility methods recursively get, transform, and accumulate a target object's bounding box from its constituent leaf shapes. One version assumes that the target object has already been configured for live access and is currently live. The other version includes an `AppWorld` host argument, which it uses to handle all live access. First, the target object is configured for live access. Then, if the object has no parent, it is temporarily attached to the world to make it live long enough for its bounding box to be computed.

22.1.3   Example: PassiveFeeling

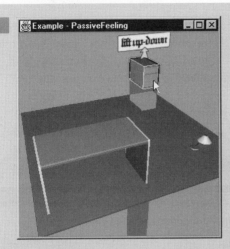

Figure 22.1
Screen shot of the
PassiveFeeling example

This example demonstrates object decorating with passive feeler feedback.

➤ See

The virtual world contains three target objects (desk, lamp, drawers) on a floor plane. A screen shot is provided in figure 22.1.

➤ Do

- Move the mouse over a target.
- Single-, double-, or triple-click on a target to select a manipulation mode.
- Move the mouse over a target, and pause.
- Drag the mouse (left button) on a selected target or use the ARROW keys to manipulate it.
- Select a target for lifting (triple-click) and lift it.
- Select targets with the CONTROL key down, and then repeat the pause and drag.
- Drag the mouse (left button with SHIFT) in the display or use the ARROW keys (with SHIFT) to orbit the view in heading and elevation about the world origin.

➤ Observe

- The target decorations include the basic feedback elements (tooltips, handles, sound effects), as well as a box outline and a semi-transparent box skirt.

The internal structure of this example is a lot like that already seen in the `TargetDecorating` example class. Here, all of the target decorations—basic and feelers—are bundled into a utility block `buildFeelerFloorTarget` from the `ManipulateBlocks` class. The first code sample, from the example, shows how the utility block is used. The second sample shows the implementation of the utility block and its helpers.

In the `ManipulateBlocks` class, the `centerFloorTarget` block computes a target object's bounding box and relocates the object's origin to the center bottom of the shape, which is appropriate for objects sitting on a floor, or on top of other objects on a floor, like a lamp on a desk. The `buildMultiOutline` and `buildMulti-Skirt` blocks build an outline and skirt, respectively, for a target object given the object's extent, such as that determined by `centerFloorTarget`. The `build-FeelerFloorTarget` block uses these other blocks to build the target's feeler decorations, and the `buildMultiFloorTarget` block from the `FeedbackBlocks` class to build its basic decorations.

Setup of desk control and feedback using a utility block in PassiveFeeling

Filename: J3duiBook/examples/PassiveFeeling/PassiveFeeling.java

```
...
// build targets with feelers
Node thing;

/// desk
thing = ModelLoader.loadModelFromName(
 Blocks.buildResourcePath("catalog/desk.wrl"));

AffineGroup slide0 = new AffineGroup();
AffineGroup rotate0 = new AffineGroup();
AffineGroup lift0 = new AffineGroup();
MultiShape target0 =
 ManipulateBlocks.buildFeelerFloorTarget(thing,
  slide0, rotate0, lift0, getWorld(), getView());
getWorld().addSceneNode(target0);

slide0.getTranslation().initActuation(
 new Vector4d(-2, 0, 2.5, 0));
...
```

Filename: J3duiBook/lib/j3dui/utils/blocks/ManipulateBlocks.java

```
...
/**
Computes the target bounds, and centers the target
horizontally and offsets it vertically so its origin is
at the bottom.
@param target Target object to be centered and offset.  If
the target is a FeedbackTarget it will also be connected as
a feedback target.
@param min Return copy of the centered target's bounding
box minimum extent.  Never null.
@param max Return copy of the centered target's bounding
box maximum extent.  Never null.
@param world Host environment for computing the target
bounds.  Never null.
@return New MultiShape proxy target.
*/
public static final MultiShape centerFloorTarget(
 Node target, Point3d min, Point3d max, AppWorld world) {

  // build centered target (before connecting it)
  MultiShape multiTarget = new MultiShape();

  /// get target bounds (before connecting target)
  BoundingBox bbox = BoundsUtils.getBoundingBox(
   target, world, new BoundingBox());

  bbox.getLower(min);
  bbox.getUpper(max);

  /// center and offset target
  Vector3d offset = new Vector3d(
   -((max.x - min.x)/2.0 + min.x),
   -min.y,
   -((max.z - min.z)/2.0 + min.z));

  AffineGroup center = new AffineGroup(target);
  center.getTranslation().initActuation(new Vector4d(
  offset.x, offset.y, offset.z, 0));

  /// center and offset bounds
  min.add(offset);
  max.add(offset);

  // connect target
  multiTarget.addNode(center);
  if(target instanceof FeedbackTarget)
     multiTarget.addEventTarget((FeedbackTarget)target);

  return multiTarget;
}
```

```
/**
Creates a MultiShape outline for a target.
@param pickable If true the outline will be pickable.
@param min   The minimum (bottom) extent of the target.
@param max   The maximum (top) extent of the target.
@param margin The distance between the target extent and the
outline itself.
@return New MultiShape object containing the decorations.
*/
public static final MultiShape buildMultiOutline(
 boolean pickable, Tuple3d min, Tuple3d max, double margin) {

   // build states
   MultiSelect select = new MultiSelect();
   MultiAction action;

   /// not selected
   action = new MultiAction();
   select.setSelectNode(Feedback.SELECT_NORMAL, action);

   action.setActionNode(Feedback.ACTION_IS_OVER &
    ~Feedback.ACTION_DRAG,
    new BoxOutline(pickable, BoxOutline.OUTLINE_DRAG,
    -1, null, min, max, margin));

   /// selected
   action = new MultiAction();
   select.setSelectNode(Feedback.SELECT_IS_SELECT, action);

   action.setActionNode(Feedback.ACTION_NORMAL,
    new BoxOutline(pickable, BoxOutline.OUTLINE_NORMAL,
    -1, null, min, max, margin));
   action.setActionNode(Feedback.ACTION_IS_OVER &
    ~Feedback.ACTION_DRAG,
    new BoxOutline(pickable, BoxOutline.OUTLINE_OVER,
    -1, null, min, max, margin));

   // make it visable by default
   select.setFeedbackSelect(Feedback.SELECT_NORMAL);
   select.setFeedbackAction(Feedback.ACTION_OVER);

   return select;
}

/**
Creates a MultiShape skirt for a target.
@param pickable If true the skirt will be pickable.
@param min   The minimum (bottom) extent of the target.
@param max   The maximum (top) extent of the target.
@param length The distance between the target extent and the
far end of the skirt.
@return New MultiShape object containing the decorations.
```

```
*/
public static final MultiShape buildMultiSkirt(
 boolean pickable, Tuple3d min, Tuple3d max, double length) {

   // build states
   MultiSelect select = new MultiSelect();
   MultiAction action;

   /// not selected
   action = new MultiAction();
   select.setSelectNode(Feedback.SELECT_NORMAL, action);

   action.setActionNode(Feedback.ACTION_IS_OVER &
    ~Feedback.ACTION_DRAG,
    new BoxSkirt(pickable, BoxSkirt.SKIRT_DRAG,
    .5, null, Elements.SIDE_TOP, min, max, length));

   /// selected
   action = new MultiAction();
   select.setSelectNode(Feedback.SELECT_IS_SELECT, action);

   action.setActionNode(Feedback.ACTION_IS_OVER &
    ~Feedback.ACTION_DRAG,
    new BoxSkirt(pickable, BoxSkirt.SKIRT_OVER,
    .5, null, Elements.SIDE_TOP, min, max, length));
   action.setActionNode(Feedback.ACTION_DRAG,
    new BoxSkirt(pickable, BoxSkirt.SKIRT_DRAG,
    .5, null, Elements.SIDE_TOP, min, max, length));

   // make it visable by default
   select.setFeedbackSelect(Feedback.SELECT_NORMAL);
   select.setFeedbackAction(Feedback.ACTION_OVER);

   return select;
}

/**
Creates a set of passive feeler feedback decorations for a
target object that is intended to be slid, rotated, and
lifted over an X-Z floor plane.  The decorations include
an outline and a skirt.  Automatically centers the object
and offsets it vertically so its origin is at the bottom.
@param target Target object to be centered, offset, and
decorated.  If the target is a FeedbackTarget it will also
be connected as a feedback target.
@param slide Affine group used to slide the target.  The
group will be connected into an internal group chain and
therefore should be supplied as new.  Null if none.
@param rotate Affine group used to rotate the target.  The
group will be connected into an internal group chain and
therefore should be supplied as new.  Null if none.
@param lift Affine group used to slide the target.  The
group will be connected into an internal target chain and
```

```
therefore should be supplied as new.  Null if none.
@param world Host environment for computing the target
bounds.  Never null.
@param view Host environment for the sound audio device.
If null then no sound.
@return New MultiShape proxy target.
*/
public static final MultiShape buildFeelerFloorTarget(
 Node target, AffineGroup slide, AffineGroup rotate,
 AffineGroup lift, AppWorld world,
 AppView view) {

   MultiShape multiTarget = new MultiShape();
   AffineGroup affine;
   double margin = .05;

   // center target (before connecting it)
   Point3d min = new Point3d();
   Point3d max = new Point3d();

   MultiShape center = centerFloorTarget(target,
    min, max, world);

   // build basic feedback decorations
   MultiShape decor = FeedbackBlocks.
    buildMultiFloorTarget(center, slide,
    rotate, lift, view, max.y);
   multiTarget.addProxyTarget(decor, decor);

   // add outline
   MultiShape outline = ManipulateBlocks.
    buildMultiOutline(true, min, max, margin);
   multiTarget.addEventTarget(outline);

   if(rotate==null)
     multiTarget.addNode(outline);
   else
     rotate.addNode(outline);

   // add skirt
   MultiShape skirt = ManipulateBlocks.
    buildMultiSkirt(false, min, max, 100.0);
   multiTarget.addEventTarget(skirt);

   if(rotate==null)
     multiTarget.addNode(skirt);
   else
     rotate.addNode(skirt);

   return multiTarget;
}
...
```

22.2 MANIPULATION PERSONAE

The following examples demonstrate how to combine the framework's techniques for application-like second- and third-person manipulation of data objects in a 3D virtual world. All data objects are endowed with a full complement of target decorations. The basic decorations—tooltips and handles—are shown in perfect overlay to keep them oriented, sized, and overlaid for optimum viewing. Perfect overlay also allows ready access to the handles, even when the target object itself may be hidden behind its neighbors.

As mentioned, the particular manner of manipulating target objects in these examples is not meant to be the paragon in 3D user interface design. Instead, it builds upon abilities developed in earlier examples, which keep the design of the code and its presentation to you as straightforward and familiar as possible. It also gives you plenty of opportunitie to improve upon the design for the specific needs of your own applications. Almost anything would be better than what is used in the examples, which require the user to multi-click on an object to select the manipulation mode.

22.2.1 A better way

Without trying to bias your application designs too much, a good rule of thumb is to make the most used and useful functions the easiest ones to access. In terms of geometric manipulation, translation (sliding an object) is usually given the highest priority. This often means that dragging on a target object moves it, without having to first select it, as in the examples. Also, multi-clicking to select manipulation modes, as in the examples, is generally a bad idea since there are few conventions for it, and multi-clicking often requires practice to perform reliably. Often, a better approach is to associate manipulation modes with specific types of drag handles.

Using these guidelines, what has worked well in the past is the following: Dragging an object automatically selects it and enables it for sliding. Alternatively, the user can single-click an object to first select it—a convention well-established in 2D GUIs. While an object is selected and not being dragged, all of its drag handles are visible, which requires careful design so they do not interfere with one another or clutter up the scene. Dragging on a particular handle performs the operation indicated by the handle, such as sliding, rotating, or lifting the object. While a drag is underway, all decorations are hidden except those for relational feedback, such as a skirt.

22.2.2   Example: SecondPerson

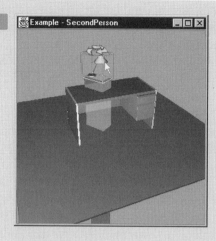

Figure 22.2
Screen shot of the
SecondPerson example

This example demonstrates second-person manipulation with target feedback in perfect overlay.

➤ See

The virtual world contains a desk with drawers on a floor plane, and a lamp on the desk. A screen shot is provided in figure 22.2.

➤ Do

- Single-, double-, or triple-click on a target to select a manipulation mode.
- Drag the mouse (left button) on a selected target or use the ARROW keys to manipulate it.
- Drag the mouse (left button with SHIFT) in the display or use the ARROW keys (with SHIFT) to orbit the view in heading and elevation about the world origin.
- Resize the display window.
- Repeat mouse pausing and dragging.

➤ Observe

- The target decorations are complete (tooltip, handle, sound effects, outline, skirt) and are in perfect overlay.
- Manipulation modes include WRM horizontal sliding with a sticky cursor, direct rotation, and direct vertical lifting.
- Decorations correspond to manipulation mode, which is determined by the target's selection state (single-slide, double-rotate, triple-lift).
- Problems with Java 3D synchronization cause the overlaid objects to jitter. Use the arrow keys for smoother manipulation.

This example builds upon the structure of the previous one, while encapsulating much of the functionality needed for second-person manipulation into utility building blocks, which are provided in the SecondBlocks class. Use of the utility blocks is shown below in the code fragments from the example class. With all the encapsulation provided by specialized floor target and room utility classes, the example code is quite straightforward and simple in comparison to earlier examples.

Room and floor

The `SecondBlocks` utility class assumes an application whose objects are confined in a floor-based environment, with a well-defined notion of up. Its objects are meant to sit on the floor, or on other objects that sit on the floor. The nested utility class `Room` includes a floor plane object, and defines the extent of a room-like space for manipulation.

The `buildPerfectFloorTarget` utility block adds decorations, with perfect overlay, to a target object. It only handles the target's feedback. The nested utility class `FloorTarget`, which is shown in the second code sample that follows, constructs actuators and mappers for manipulating a target object in a room. It uses a `Room` object to define the actuator limits, and `buildPerfectFloorTarget` to decorate the target. As in previous examples, the target manipulation is relative to a floor plane with separate actuation for horizontal sliding, horizontal rotation, and vertical lifting. Sliding uses pseudo-WRM to provide a sticky cursor drag, but rotation and lifting use direct mapping for simplicity. The class draws upon the services of several major utility building blocks, shown highlighted in the code, to perform most of the control mapping and feedback support. These blocks were described in previous chapters on control and feedback.

Utility blocks greatly simplify construction of targets in SecondPerson example

Filename: J3duiBook/examples/SecondPerson/SecondPerson.java

```
...
ChangePoster.init(getWorld().getViewRoot());

// setup orbitable view, first+shift
getWorld().addViewNode(
 ActuationBlocks.buildViewOrbiter(getView(),
 new Vector3d(-Math.PI/6, -Math.PI/8, 0), 10,
 Input.BUTTON_FIRST, Input.MODIFIER_SHIFT,
 Input.MODIFIER_SHIFT)
);

// build view change sensor
ViewChangeSplitter viewSpltr = new ViewChangeSplitter();

new ViewChangeSensor(viewSpltr, getView(),
 getWorld().getViewRoot());

// build room with floor
SecondBlocks.Room room = new SecondBlocks.Room(
 new Vector3d(8, 3, 8));
getWorld().addSceneNode(room);

// build target draggers
/// absolute draggers (for WRM slide)
InputDragSplitter absDrag = new InputDragSplitter();

ActuationBlocks.buildAbsoluteDragger(absDrag,
```

```
  getView(), Input.BUTTON_FIRST,
  Input.MODIFIER_NONE, Input.MODIFIER_NONE);

/// relative draggers (for direct rotate & lift)
InputDragSplitter relDrag = new InputDragSplitter();

ActuationBlocks.buildRelativeDragger(relDrag,
  getView(), Input.BUTTON_FIRST,
  Input.MODIFIER_NONE, Input.MODIFIER_NONE);

// build feedback manager
FeedbackGroupManager groupMgr = FeedbackBlocks.
  buildGroupManager(getWorld().getViewRoot());

/// use room for deselect
FeedbackBlocks.buildTargetFeedbackSupport(room,
  groupMgr, relDrag, null, getWorld().getSceneRoot());

// build targets
Node thing;
SecondBlocks.FloorTarget target;

/// lamp
thing = ModelLoader.loadModelFromName(
  Blocks.buildResourcePath("catalog/lamp.wrl"));

target = new SecondBlocks.FloorTarget(
  thing, room, viewSpltr, absDrag, relDrag, groupMgr,
  getWorld(), getView());
target.getSlide().initActuation(
  new Vector4d(-.45, 0, -.3, 0));
target.getLift().initActuation(
  new Vector4d(0, 1.65, 0, 0));
getWorld().addSceneNode(target);

/// desk
thing = ModelLoader.loadModelFromName(
  Blocks.buildResourcePath("catalog/desk.wrl"));

target = new SecondBlocks.FloorTarget(
  thing, room, viewSpltr, absDrag, relDrag, groupMgr,
  getWorld(), getView());
getWorld().addSceneNode(target);

/// drawers
thing = ModelLoader.loadModelFromName(
  Blocks.buildResourcePath("catalog/drawers.wrl"));

target = new SecondBlocks.FloorTarget(
  thing, room, viewSpltr, absDrag, relDrag, groupMgr,
  getWorld(), getView());
target.getSlide().initActuation(
```

```
 new Vector4d(1.2, 0, .05, 0));
target.getLift().initActuation(
 new Vector4d(0, .55, 0, 0));
getWorld().addSceneNode(target);

// initialize feedback (last)
groupMgr.initTargets(null, Feedback.STATUS_DISABLE,
 Feedback.SELECT_NORMAL, Feedback.ACTION_NORMAL);

...
```

Filename: J3duiBook/lib/j3dui/utils/blocks/SecondBlocks.java

```
...
/**
Wraps a target object for sliding, rotating, and lifting it
inside a room with an X-Z floor plane.  The wrapper
includes feedback decorations implemented with
visualization techniques, actuators that limit target
manipulation to inside a room, and mappers for WRM sliding
and direct rotation and lifting.  If the target is a
multishape it will be connected for feedback.  The target
will be centered for rotation and offset such that it sits
on the floor.
*/
public static final class FloorTarget extends MultiShape {

    // public interface =====================================

    /**
    Constructs a FloorTarget.                 .
    @param target Target object to be decorated and
    manipulated.  Never null.
    @param room Room that the target is in.
    @param viewSpltr Source for view state changes.
    Never null.
    @param absDrag Source for absolute input drags.  Used
    for target WRM sliding.  Never null.
    @param relDrag Source for relative input drags.  Used
    for target direct rotating and lifting.  Never null.
    @param groupManager Feedback group manager managing the
    target object.  Never null.
    @param world The world that the target belongs to.
    Never null.
    @param view Host environment for the sound audio device.
    If null then no sound.
    */
    public FloorTarget(Node target, Room room,
      ViewChangeSplitter viewSpltr, InputDragSplitter
      absDrag, InputDragSplitter relDrag,
```

```
        FeedbackGroupManager groupMgr, AppWorld world,
        AppView view) {

          // build floor target chain and decorations
          // (proxyTarget also serves as the poster trigger)
          Point3d min = new Point3d();
          Point3d max = new Point3d();

          MultiShape proxyTarget = SecondBlocks.
           buildPerfectFloorTarget(target, _slide, _rotate,
           _lift, min, max, viewSpltr, world, view);

          addProxyTarget(proxyTarget, proxyTarget);

          // setup manipulation actuators
          /// limit slide relative to room and bounds
          _slide.getTranslation().getPlugin().setTargetClamp(
           Mapper.DIM_X, new Vector2d(
           -room.getSize().x/2.0 - min.x,
           room.getSize().x/2.0 - max.x));
          _slide.getTranslation().getPlugin().setTargetClamp(
           Mapper.DIM_Z, new Vector2d(
           -room.getSize().z/2.0 - min.z,
           room.getSize().z/2.0 - max.z));

          _slide.getTranslation().getPlugin().setTargetClamp(
           Mapper.DIM_Y, new Vector2d(0, 0));

          /// limit lift relative to room and bounds
          _lift.getTranslation().getPlugin().setTargetClamp(
           Mapper.DIM_Y, new Vector2d(
           0, room.getSize().y - max.y));

          _lift.getTranslation().getPlugin().setTargetClamp(
           Mapper.DIM_X|Mapper.DIM_X, new Vector2d(0, 0));

          /// set rotation axis
          _rotate.getAxisAngle().getPlugin().setSourceOffset(
           new Vector4d(0, 1, 0, 0));

          // build manipulation mappers, use enablers for
          // internal control
          InputDragTarget mapper;
          Vector2d rotateScale = new Vector2d(.025, .025);
          Vector2d liftScale = new Vector2d(.025, .025);

          /// WRM slide
          mapper = IntuitiveBlocks.
           buildStickyWrmTranslationMapper(room.getFloor(),
           _slide, world.getSceneRoot(), true, true);

          EnableInputDragFilter slideEnabler =
```

```
    new EnableInputDragFilter(mapper);
   absDrag.addEventTarget(slideEnabler);

    /// direct rotate
   mapper = ActuationBlocks.buildDirectMapper(
    _rotate.getAxisAngle(), rotateScale,
    Mapper.DIM_W, Mapper.DIM_NONE, true);

    EnableInputDragFilter rotateEnabler =
     new EnableInputDragFilter(mapper);
   relDrag.addEventTarget(rotateEnabler);
    /// direct lift
   mapper = ActuationBlocks.buildDirectMapper(
    _lift.getTranslation(), liftScale,
    Mapper.DIM_NONE, Mapper.DIM_Y, true);

    EnableInputDragFilter liftEnabler =
     new EnableInputDragFilter(mapper);
   relDrag.addEventTarget(liftEnabler);

    // setup target feedback and enable
   StatusTrigger trigger = FeedbackBlocks.
    buildTargetFeedbackSupport(this,
    groupMgr, relDrag, null, world.getSceneRoot());

    FeedbackBlocks.buildTargetSelectEnablers(this,
     trigger, slideEnabler, rotateEnabler, liftEnabler);

    // build change poster (kludge for Java 3D 1.1.2)
   ChangePoster poster = new ChangePoster(
    proxyTarget, ChangePoster.POST_NODE_EXTERNAL);
   absDrag.addEventTarget(poster);
   relDrag.addEventTarget(poster);
}

/**
Gets the target manipulation slide actuator.
@return Reference to the slider.
*/
public Actuator getSlide() {
   return _slide.getTranslation();
}

/**
Gets the target manipulation rotate actuator.
@return Reference to the slider.
*/
public Actuator getRotate() {
   return _rotate.getAxisAngle();
}

/**
```

```
Gets the target manipulation lift actuator.
@return Reference to the slider.
*/
public Actuator getLift() {
   return _lift.getTranslation();
}

// personal body ========================================

/** Target slider.  Never null. */
private AffineGroup _slide = new AffineGroup();

/** Target rotator.  Never null. */
private AffineGroup _rotate = new AffineGroup();

/** Target lifter.  Never null. */
private AffineGroup _lift = new AffineGroup();
}
...
```

22.2.3 Example: ThirdPerson

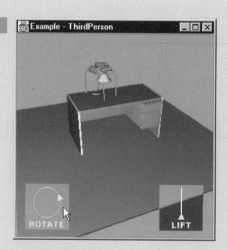

Figure 22.3
Screen shot of the
ThirdPerson example

This example demonstrates third-person manipulation, with controls in display overlay and target feedback in perfect overlay.

➤ See

The virtual world contains a desk with drawers on a floor plane, and a lamp on the desk. Two virtual controls with semi-transparent backgrounds are overlaid in display space. The screen shot is provided in figure 22.3.

➤ Do

• Single-, double-, or triple-click on a target to select a manipulation mode.

The implementation of this example class is the same as for second-person manipulation, only here a control panel with two third-person controls is added. The first code sample is from the example, and shows the high-level implementation of the control panel. The general structure of the controls should be familiar from the display overlay example in chapter 21, except here the controls are live.

Each control is constructed as three components: a movable mark, a stationary background, and a frame for the control to sit in. In the example, both frames are semi-transparent rectangles. Utility building blocks, which are found in the `ThirdBlocks` class, help in constructing and wiring up the control components. The control marks (arrows) and backgrounds are multi-shapes configured for interaction feedback, including sound effects. Their visual appearance is completely defined by transparent textures.

The second code sample below shows the `RotateControl` nested class, which is the utility block that builds the rotation control. Because of the complex nature of the event wiring between a virtual control and the target objects in the scene, the `connectRotateControl` utility block is provided as a helper. It is shown in the third code sample.

Anatomy of a virtual control

The utility blocks include several nested classes for creating virtual controls. Although they are general in nature, they make a number of assumptions about what a virtual control is and what it can do. They also make use of a number of other utility blocks, so they are included as framework utilities and not in the core.

The utility blocks `RotateControl` and `LiftControl` assemble the control components—mark, background, and frame—geometrically as well as for control and feedback. They handle the control specifics, such as defining the particular movement of the mark relative to the background, and define the manner in which its actuation value is interpreted. For example, in the rotate control, a dragger and input filter interpret the user's interaction with the control as being a circular gesture. The mark's actuator is configured to move the mark in a circle, over a specified angular range, and about a center reference point in the control. And, the *W* component of its actuation value is defined as the angle of rotation.

The base class for the control classes, `BaseControl`, handles the common aspects of virtual controls. It takes care of display positioning and overlay, with each component being placed in a separate *Z* plane. It also includes its own feedback sensing and picking. The structure of a control is complicated by the fact that it can be used as both a control and an indicator. Both input and output actuation events are handled through an actuation splitter, which is accessed through the `getActuationSplitter` method of the base class. To use the control as an indicator, the splitter is connected as an actuation target, with input events causing the mark to move accordingly. To use the control as a control, the splitter is used as an event source, with events indicating the actuation position of the mark.

Implementation of the control panel in the ThirdPerson example

Filename: J3duiBook/examples/ThirdPerson/ThirdPerson.java

...

```
// build control panel
Vector2d size = new Vector2d();
Vector2d limits = new Vector2d();
Vector2d origin = new Vector2d();
Vector2d offset = new Vector2d();
double scale;
Node mark, back, frame;

/// rotate control
size.set(66, 66);
limits.set(0, -1); // ignore limits
scale = 1.0;
origin.set(-.45, -.45);
offset.set(size.x/2.0, size.y/2.0);

mark = ThirdBlocks.buildMultiMark(true, 10, 10);
back = ThirdBlocks.buildMultiRotateBack(true,
 size.x, size.y);
frame = new TextureRect(false, new Color3f(.5f,.5f,.5f),
 .5, null, Elements.SIDE_TOP, size.x, size.y);

ThirdBlocks.RotateControl rotate = new ThirdBlocks.
 RotateControl(mark, back, frame, origin, offset,
 new Vector2d(-21, 0), new Vector2d(0, 6), limits,
 scale, viewSpltr, getView());
```

```
/// lift control
size.set(66, 66);
limits.set(0, 38);
scale = room.getSize().y / (limits.y - limits.x);
origin.set(.45, -.45);
offset.set(-size.x/2.0, size.y/2.0);

mark = ThirdBlocks.buildMultiMark(true, 10, 10);
back = ThirdBlocks.buildMultiLiftBack(true,
 size.x, size.y);
frame = new TextureRect(false, new Color3f(.5f,.5f,.5f),
 .5, null, Elements.SIDE_TOP, size.x, size.y);

ThirdBlocks.LiftControl lift = new ThirdBlocks.
 LiftControl(mark, back, frame, origin, offset,
 new Vector2d(0, 0), new Vector2d(0, -12), limits,
 scale, viewSpltr, getView());

// connect controls and targets
ActuationSplitter enabler;
FeedbackTrigger filter;
FeedbackEnableTrigger trigger;

/// interconnect control-target actuation
ThirdBlocks.connectRotateControl(rotate, lamp);
ThirdBlocks.connectRotateControl(rotate, desk);
ThirdBlocks.connectRotateControl(rotate, drawers);

ThirdBlocks.connectLiftControl(lift, lamp);
ThirdBlocks.connectLiftControl(lift, desk);
ThirdBlocks.connectLiftControl(lift, drawers);

/// enable rotate control if target selected for rotate
trigger = new FeedbackEnableTrigger(rotate);
trigger.setSelectFlags(Feedback.SELECT_DOUBLE);

lamp.addEventTarget(trigger);
desk.addEventTarget(trigger);
drawers.addEventTarget(trigger);

/// enable lift control if target selected for lift
trigger = new FeedbackEnableTrigger(lift);
trigger.setSelectFlags(Feedback.SELECT_TRIPLE);

lamp.addEventTarget(trigger);
desk.addEventTarget(trigger);
drawers.addEventTarget(trigger);
…
```

Filename: J3duiBook/lib/j3dui/utils/blocks/ThirdBlocks.java

```
...
/**
Constructs a third person "rotate" control.  The mark moves
in a circle relative to the mark and back center points in
response to internal or external actuation angle.
*/
public static final class RotateControl extends
 ThirdBlocks.BaseControl {

   // public interface =====================================

   /**
   Constructs a RotateControl.
   @param mark Control mark element.  Null if none.
   @param back Control back element.  Null if none.
   @param frame Control frame element.  Null if none.
   @param dispOrigin Position of the control origin
   relative to the display window expressed as a fraction
   of the window size.
   @param bodyOrigin Position of the control elements
   (body) relative to the control origin in pixels.
   @param markCenter Position of mark center relative to
   mark shape in pixels.
   @param backCenter Position of back center relative to
   back shape and control in pixels.
   @param markLimits Limits on the actuation range of
   the mark in radians.  Ignored if max limit less than
   min limit.
   @param actScale Scaling factor applied to the actuation
   output, and the inverse value applied to actuation input.
   @param viewSpltr Source for view change events.
   @param view Host view for the control.
   */
   public RotateControl(Node mark, Node back, Node frame,
    Vector2d dispOrigin, Vector2d bodyOffset,
    Vector2d markCenter, Vector2d backCenter,
    Vector2d markLimits, double actScale,
    ViewChangeSplitter viewSpltr, AppView view) {

      super(mark, back, frame, dispOrigin, bodyOffset,
       markCenter, backCenter, markLimits, actScale,
       viewSpltr, view);
   }

   // BaseControl implementation

   protected Node buildMarkGroup(Node mark,
    Vector2d markCenter, Vector2d backCenter) {
```

```
    /// center mark at mark center
    _markRotate = new CenterAffineGroup(mark);
    _markRotate.getTranslation().initActuation(
     new Vector4d(-markCenter.x, -markCenter.y, 0, 0));
    _markRotate.getCenter().initActuation(
     new Vector4d(markCenter.x, markCenter.y, 0, 0));

    /// connect external actuation splitter
    getActuationSplitter().addEventTarget(
      _markRotate.getAxisAngle());

    /// center mark at back center
    AffineGroup markRoot = new AffineGroup(_markRotate);
    markRoot.getTranslation().initActuation(
     new Vector4d(backCenter.x, backCenter.y, 0, 0));

    return markRoot;
}

protected InputDragSplitter buildMarkDragger(
 AppView view, ActuationTarget enabler,
 Vector2d markLimits, double actScale,
 AbsoluteInputDragPlugin plugin) {

    InputDragSplitter drag = new InputDragSplitter();

    // build drag mapper
    InputDragTarget mapper = ActuationBlocks.
     buildDirectMapper(enabler, new Vector2d(1, 1),
     Mapper.DIM_W, Mapper.DIM_NONE, true);

    // configure mark actuator
    _markRotate.getAxisAngle().getPlugin().
     setSourceOffset(new Vector4d(0, 0, 1, 0));

    /// set mark limits
    if(markLimits.x <= markLimits.y)
      _markRotate.getAxisAngle().getPlugin().
       setTargetClamp(Mapper.DIM_W, markLimits);

    /// set inverse actuation scale
    _markRotate.getAxisAngle().getPlugin().
     setSourceScale(new Vector4d(
     1, 1, 1, 1.0/actScale));

    // build drag filters
    InputDragTarget filter;

    /// relative drag
    filter = new InputDragFilter(mapper,
     new RelativeInputDragPlugin());
```

```
    /// set scale
    filter = new InputDragFilter(filter,
     new ScaleInputDragPlugin(new Vector2d(
     actScale, 1)));

    /// absolute circle drag
    filter = new InputDragFilter(filter,
     new CircleInputDragPlugin());
    filter = new InputDragFilter(filter, plugin);

    drag.addEventTarget(filter);

    // absolute drag, first button, no keyboard
    ActuationBlocks.buildAbsoluteDragger(drag,
     view, Input.BUTTON_FIRST, Input.MODIFIER_NONE,
     Input.MODIFIER_IGNORE);

    return drag;
  }

  // personal body =========================================

  /** Mark rotator.  Never null. */
  private CenterAffineGroup _markRotate;
}
...
```

Utility block for connecting a rotation control

Filename: J3duiBook/lib/j3dui/utils/blocks/ThirdBlocks.java:

```
...
/**
Interconnects the actuation of a rotate control with that
of a floor target.  The control is connected such that the
target is only affected when it is double-selected for
rotation and the mouse is over the control.
@param control Rotate control.  Never null.
@param target Floor target.  Never null.
@return Actuation splitter connected to the target and used
as an enabler.
*/
public static final ActuationSplitter connectRotateControl(
 ThirdBlocks.RotateControl control,
 SecondBlocks.FloorTarget target) {

  // connect target actuation to control input
  target.getRotate().getActuationSource().
   addEventTarget(control.getActuationSplitter());

  // build actuation enabler and connect to control
  ActuationSplitter enabler = new ActuationSplitter();
  enabler.setEnable(false);
```

```
enabler.addEventTarget(target.getRotate());
control.getActuationSplitter().addEventTarget(enabler);

// build trigger, enable on double-select and over
FeedbackEnableTrigger trigger =
 new FeedbackEnableTrigger(enabler);
trigger.setSelectFlags(Feedback.SELECT_DOUBLE);
trigger.setActionFlags(Feedback.ACTION_IS_OVER);

// connect target select and control action to trigger
FeedbackTrigger filter;

filter = new FeedbackTrigger(trigger);
filter.setStatusFlags(Feedback.STATUS_IGNORE);
filter.setActionFlags(Feedback.ACTION_IGNORE);
target.addEventTarget(filter);

filter = new FeedbackTrigger(trigger);
filter.setStatusFlags(Feedback.STATUS_IGNORE);
filter.setSelectFlags(Feedback.SELECT_IGNORE);
control.getFeedbackSource().addEventTarget(filter);

return enabler;
}
...
```

22.3   SUMMARY

This chapter completed the presentation of the framework's core with the introduction of two building blocks for building passive feeler feedback elements. Such feedback shows the relationship of a target object to its surroundings, and is especially important when viewing a 3D scene in a 2D display. Two major examples pulled together most of the framework's core and utility functionality, and presented it in application-like settings.

The first example demonstrated second-person manipulation of furniture data objects, with a full complement of in-scene control interaction and feedback. The feedback included tooltips and drag handles in perfect overlay, sound effects, bounding boxes, and box skirts indicating vertical placement. The manipulation modes included sticky cursor sliding, and direct rotation and lifting.

The second example added third-person manipulation to the second-person example. Virtual knob and slider controls were overlaid in the display, which allowed selected target objects to be manipulated indirectly. The controls were built as multishapes and used transparent textures to completely define their appearance. The controls also served as indicators, which reacted in response to direct second-person manipulation of the selected target object.

Chapter 23 will tie up a few loose ends remaining in the framework utilities, and show Java 3D working in an even larger application context, with Swing components and drag-and-drop data access.

C H A P T E R   2 3

Access

An important aspect of any application, 3D or otherwise, is getting data into and out of it. As part of the Java pantheon, Java 3D can take advantage of much of what Java has to offer in this regard. Two packages of particular interest when it comes to application data access are Swing, which offers a wide variety of full-featured 2D GUI components, and DnD, a set of classes and interfaces for performing general-purpose data drag-and-drop. Both Swing and DnD were discussed in chapter 14. Here they are demonstrated working side-by-side with Java 3D.

23.1   JAVA 3D AND SWING

The advantages of using Swing components to construct 3D application frames are many. Although there are several problems that you must contend with in trying to mix lightweight Swing components with the heavyweight Java 3D canvas, they can usually be easily resolved or avoided.

23.1.1   FancyApp classes

The following example uses Swing components to give you a feel for some of the data access ideas presented in chapter 9. The application frame consists of four panels. Two of the panels are displays of the 3D world. The third panel contains a tree widget, which provides a 1D view of the 3D world, with nodes in the tree representing the hierarchical structure of the data objects in the scene. The tree is automatically updated to reflect any changes to the contents of the scene. The fourth panel serves as an icon palette of available data objects. Double-clicking on an item causes it to be loaded into the scene. The application menus include several items that demonstrate framework utilities, including model loading and display image printing.

This example barely scratches the surface of what can be done with respect to presenting and transferring data in 2D and 3D presentations. It is simple and to the point, and should afford plenty of opportunity for improvement—you might start by connecting in-scene and out-of-scene selection so that they occur in unison. Due to their limited nature, the building blocks are not included in the framework. Instead, they can be found in the example directory itself, in `J3duiBook/examples/FancyApp`.

FancyFrame class

The `FancyFrame` example class provides the frame (top level window) for the application, and defines the virtual world and its views, using an `AppWorld` object and two `AppView` objects, one for each display. The contents of the frame is placed in a Swing `JSplitPane` object, with the two view displays in the upper portion, and the two data panels in the lower portion. The lower portion is itself a `JSplitPane`, with the tree on the left and the palette on the right. The `FancyFrame` menu bar includes entries for clearing the virtual world, through the `AppWorld` utility class, loading models, through the framework's `ModelLoader` utility class, and previewing and printing the display images, using the framework's `PrintFrame` and `AppDisplay` utility classes.

FancyTree class

The `FancyTree` example class provides the contents of the data tree panel. It extends the Swing `JScrollPane` class and uses a `JTree` object as its scrollable client. The tree is constructed by recursively walking a Java 3D scene graph starting at some root node. The `FancyFrame` class uses the `updateTree` method in `FancyTree` to update the tree whenever the scene graph changes, but only after using the `setLive` method of `AppWorld` to kill the scene graph (otherwise Java 3D would not allow the scene graph to be walked since no capability bits have been set for doing so).

FancyPalette class

The `FancyPalette` class also extends `JScrollPane`, but uses a Swing `JPanel` as its scrollable client. The content of the palette is a set of icons representing 3D models loaded from the catalog resource directory `J3duiBook/resources/catalog`. The icons are built using Swing `Jlabel` objects, with a Swing `ImageIcon` for the picture.

23.1.2   Example: FancyApp

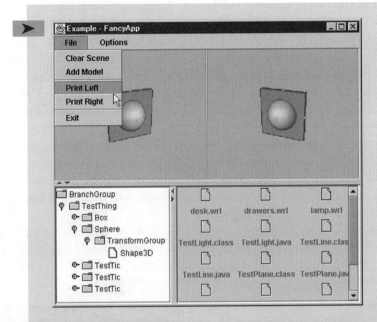

**Figure 23.1
Screen shot of the
FancyApp example**

This example demonstrates the mixing of Swing components and Java 3D, and techniques
for 1D and 2D presentation of and access to 3D data.

➤ See

The application window includes a menu bar, dual 3D displays of the world, a data tree showing the world contents as a scene graph tree, and a data palette of icons representing a data
object catalog. A screen shot is provided in figure 23.1.

➤ Do

- Drag the mouse (left button) in the display or use the ARROW keys to orbit the view in head-
  ing and elevation about the world origin.
- Use the File menu to preview and print a display image.
- Use the File menu to clear the scene and to load a new model (.wrl, .java, or .class file).
- Select a branch in the tree to expand it.
- Double-click an item in the palette to load it into the scene.

➤ Observe

- Data objects can be loaded into the scene through the menu or the data palette, and as
  VRML or Java 3D models.
- The data tree updates to reflect the actual contents of the display.
- Selecting print in the menu causes a preview window to pop up (it may come up behind the
  main window, and the right display is always blank because of a Java 3D multi-display bug).

The main example class, shown below, extends the `FancyFrame` class, which provides all of the Swing content and layout. A `buildViewOrbiter` framework utility block provides first person orbital navigation for each of the application views. A `TestThing` provides the initial scene data object. Once the frame's 2D and 3D contents have been configured, the base class `showFrame` method is called to make the scene graph live, to pack (size) the frame's contents, and to show the frame.

Several excerpts from the support classes are included below to give you a feel for how to use Swing if you are not familiar with it. The first code sample is from the `FancyFrame` base class, which includes the `showFrame` method and the class constructor. Notice in the constructor that Swing is told to use heavyweight components for displaying tooltips and pop-up menus, otherwise the Java 3D heavyweight canvas would always cover them up. The second code sample from `FancyFrame` shows how to use Swing to build menus, and how to use the framework utilities for loading models and printing the view display image.

The last code sample is the `FancyTree` class. It shows how to create a scrollable Swing pane with a `JTree` object as its client. Scrollable panes are easy to make in Swing. Just extend `JScrollable` and set its content object with the `setViewportView` method.

The Swing contents and layout in FancyApp is provided by the base class

Filename: J3duiBook/examples/FancyApp/FancyApp.java

```
public class FancyApp extends FancyFrame {

  public static void main(String[] argv) {
    Debug.loadAllProperties();
    new FancyApp();
  }

  // public interface ==========================================

  public FancyApp() {
    setTitle("Example - FancyApp");

    new HelpDialog(this, "Help - FancyApp",
      "An example of an application frame with Swing data " +
      "access components." +
      ...
    );

    // setup views
    getWorld().addViewNode(
     ActuationBlocks.buildViewOrbiter(getViewLeft(),
     new Vector3d(-Math.PI/8, -Math.PI/8, 0),
     8, Input.BUTTON_LEFT, Input.MODIFIER_NONE,
     Input.MODIFIER_NONE)
    );
```

```
      getWorld().addViewNode(
       ActuationBlocks.buildViewOrbiter(getViewRight(),
       new Vector3d(-Math.PI/8, Math.PI/8, 0),
       8, Input.BUTTON_LEFT, Input.MODIFIER_NONE,
       Input.MODIFIER_NONE)
      );

      // setup scene
      getWorld().addSceneNode(new TestThing());

      // done
      showFrame();
   }

   // personal body ===============================================
   ...
}
```

3D application frame based on Swing components

Filename: J3duiBook/examples/FancyApp/FancyFrame.java

```
...
public class FancyFrame extends JFrame {

   // public interface ==========================================

   /**
   Constructs a FancyFrame with an empty virtual world.
   */
   public FancyFrame() {
      // kill the window on close
      addWindowListener(new WindowAdapter() {
         public void windowClosing(WindowEvent winEvent) {
            System.exit(0);
         }
      });

      // build dialogs
      String catDir = Blocks.buildResourcePath("catalog");

      _selectModelDialog = new FileDialog(this,
       "Select Model", FileDialog.LOAD);
      _selectModelDialog.setDirectory(catDir);

      // tell Swing to use heavyweight popups
      JPopupMenu.setDefaultLightWeightPopupEnabled(false);
      ToolTipManager.sharedInstance().
       setLightWeightPopupEnabled(false);

      // build Swing window components
      buildMenuBar();
      buildContentPanel();
```

```
    }

    /**
    Makes the world live and sizes and shows the frame.
    */
    public void showFrame() {
       _tree.updateTree(_world.getSceneRoot());
       _world.setLive(true);

       // size contents THEN show frame
       pack();
       show();
    }
    ...
}
```

Menu items are implemented using framework application utilities

Filename: J3duiBook/examples/FancyApp/FancyFrame.java

```
...
/**
Loads a model file and updates the frame.
*/
protected void loadModel(String fileName) {
   Node node = ModelLoader.loadModelFromName(fileName);
   if(node == null) return;

   // kill the scene before adding node or updating tree
   boolean isLive = _world.setLive(false);
   _world.addSceneNode(node);
   _tree.updateTree(_world.getSceneRoot());
   _world.setLive(true);
}

// component builders

/**
Builds the window menubar and adds it to the window.
*/
protected void buildMenuBar() {

   // build the menu bar, by menu
   JMenuBar menuBar = new JMenuBar();

   JMenu menu;
   JMenuItem menuItem;
   JCheckBoxMenuItem checkItem;

   /// build the File menu, by item
   menu = new JMenu("File");

   menuItem = new JMenuItem("Clear Scene");
```

```
menuItem.addActionListener(new ActionListener() {
   public void actionPerformed(ActionEvent event) {
      boolean isLive = _world.setLive(false);
      _world.clearScene();
      _tree.updateTree(_world.getSceneRoot());
      _palette.updatePalette();
      _world.setLive(true);
   }
});
menu.add(menuItem);

menuItem = new JMenuItem("Add Model");
menuItem.addActionListener(new ActionListener() {
   public void actionPerformed(ActionEvent event) {
      _selectModelDialog.show();
      if(_selectModelDialog.getFile() == null) return;

      String fileName = new String(
       _selectModelDialog.getDirectory() +
       _selectModelDialog.getFile());

      loadModel(fileName);
   }
});
menu.add(menuItem);

menu.insertSeparator(menu.getItemCount());

menuItem = new JMenuItem("Print Left");
menuItem.addActionListener(new ActionListener() {
   public void actionPerformed(ActionEvent event) {
      new PrintFrame(new ImageCanvas(
       _viewL.getDisplay())));
   }
});
   menu.add(menuItem);
   ...
   menuBar.add(menu);

// add menu bar to frame
getRootPane().setJMenuBar(menuBar);
...
```

The scrollable tree panel is built using s JTree in a JScrollPane

Filename: J3duiBook/examples/FancyApp/FancyTree.java

```
/**
Panel showing a Java 3D scene graph or subgraph as a tree.
<P>
In order for the tree to be generated from the scene graph
either the scene graph must be dead or all the group nodes in
```

```
the tree under the specified root node must have their
capability bits set for reading children.

@author Jon Barrilleaux,
copyright (c) 1999 Jon Barrilleaux,
All Rights Reserved.
*/
public class FancyTree extends JScrollPane {

    // public interface ========================================

    /**
    Constructs a FancyTree that is empty.
    */
    public FancyTree() {}

    /**
    Constructs a FancyTree with the specified scene graph.
    @param root Root node of the scene graph.
    */
    public FancyTree(Node root) {
        this();
        updateTree(root);
    }

    /**
    Updates this object's contents with the specified scene
    graph.
    @param root Root node of the scene graph.
    */
    public void updateTree(Node root) {
        JTree tree = new JTree(buildTree(root));
        setViewportView(tree);
        tree.revalidate();
    }

    // personal body ========================================

    /**
    Builds a tree by recursively walking the scene graph.
    @param node Root node of the current scene subgraph.
    @return Tree node containing a scene subgraph.  Null if no
    tree.
    */
    protected DefaultMutableTreeNode buildTree(Node node)
    {
        if(node == null) return null;
        String name = node.getClass().getName();

        DefaultMutableTreeNode treeNode =
         new DefaultMutableTreeNode(
         name.substring(name.lastIndexOf('.') + 1)
         );
```

```
    if(node instanceof Group) {
      Group group = (Group)node;
      final int n = group.numChildren();
      for (int i = 0; i < n; i++)
        treeNode.add(buildTree(group.getChild(i)));
    }

    return treeNode;
  }

}
```

23.2   JAVA 3D AND DND

A great way for the user to move data around in an application is with drag-and-drop
(DnD). Java provides a general-purpose package for DnD that can be used with Swing
and Java 3D. As already discussed in chapter 14, the DnD package works only at the
AWT component level. To use it with Java 3D, object picking must be used to resolve
mouse movement down to an individual object in the scene. Picking is used to determine the object in the scene that the user is trying to drag or, if a drag is underway,
the object that the user is trying to use as a drop target.

23.2.1   DndApp classes

The example below sticks to the basics. Not only does this help you to better see how
Java DnD is implemented, but it is also done out of necessity. An apparent problem
with Java 3D, at least under Windows NT, is that it does not allow DnD to be used to
drag objects into a display if a Behavior class is also present in the application.

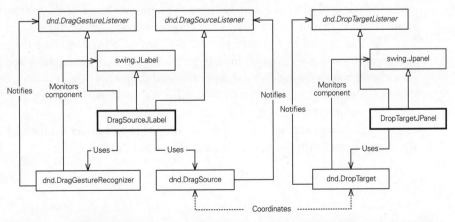

**Figure 23.2   Relationship of classes and interfaces related to Swing-based drag sources
and targets**

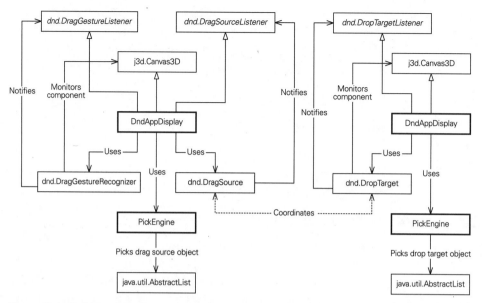

Figure 23.3 **Relationship of classes and interfaces related to Jave 3D-based drag sources and targets**

Therefore, the example uses only AWT events for input sensing, and can't use any of the framework functionality for in-scene feedback, because the framework sensors are based on behaviors.

The application frame consists of a Java 3D display and two Swing panels. The panels are extended to serve as lists and to act as drop target objects. The list items are extended to act as drag source objects. And, the display is extended to serve as a drag source and a drop target, with picking used to resolve drag and drop to an individual object in the scene. This example, like the previous one, is strictly for demonstration, and its building blocks are not included in the framework utilities. They can be found, instead, in the example directory, `J3duiBook/examples/DndApp`.

The classes used in this example and their implementation using the DnD package have already been discussed in chapter 14. Figure 23.2 summarizes and illustrates how the example's Swing-based drag source and drop target classes—`DragSource-JLabel` and `DropTargetJPanel`—utilize the DnD package. Figure 23.3 shows how the example's Java 3D display class—`DndAppDisplay`—is configured for both dragging and dropping, with a separate object picker and target list for each. For clarity, dragging and dropping are broken out separately in the figure.

23.2.2 Example: DndApp

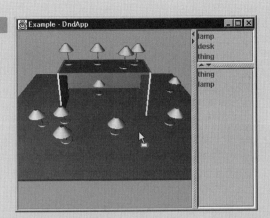

Figure 23.4
Screen shot of the
DndApp example

This example demonstrates the use of Java drag-and-drop with Swing and Java 3D.

➤ See

The application window includes a Java 3D display containing a desk and a floor plane, and two Swing panels containing several items. The screen shot is provided in figure 23.4.

➤ Do

- Drag items from one Swing list to another.
- Drag items from a Swing list to the Java 3D display.
- Drag items from the Java 3D display to a Swing list.

➤ Observe

- Data objects appear in the Swing lists in 1D, and in the Java 3D display in 3D.
- Cursor feedback indicates the suitability of an object as a drop target.
- In the 3D display, data objects can be dropped on the floor or the desk, which are designated as valid drop targets.

23.3 SUMMARY

This chapter demonstrated several of the concepts and techniques for presenting out-of-scene 3D data in an application, and for allowing the user to get that data into and out of the virtual world. The first example included a data tree and data palette, and showed how to mix lightweight Swing and heavyweight Java 3D components. It also tied up the loose ends of framework functionality by demonstrating model loading and display image printing. The second example demonstrated drag-and-drop working between Java 3D and Swing components using the Java DnD package. Data objects could be dragged into and out of the 3D display, and dropped onto other objects in the display.

C H A P T E R   2 4

Wrap-up

This ends the book's presentation and demonstration of 3D user-interface techniques. Much ground has been covered in getting from input sensors to third-person manipulation and beyond, but the journey from Java 3D to "Swing 3D" has only just begun. Even more ground would have had to be covered to get to such exotic climes as assisted navigation and PTF. Such a journey would also require making serious decisions about UI style—something that the book and examples have tried to avoid.

For some readers, necessity may spur you on to reach for some of the loftier heights discussed early on in the book. For others, you may want to take a breather, put some of what you have already learned to good use, and give the Java 3D API some time to catch up. In either case, hopefully what you have read here has been helpful and will give you a head start in developing your own next-generation 3D applications.

24.1   HINDSIGHT IS PERFECT

Beside being lightweight and incomplete, there are plenty of rough spots and plenty of areas for improvement in the framework. There are also plenty of alternative approaches for implementing the same UI techniques. In terms of the bigger picture, I feel that the framework architecture especially deserves some Monday morning quarterbacking. In trying to keep things simple, I made several architectural choices that, in hindsight, should be revisited if the framework ever evolves publicly beyond the confines of this book. I'll touch on a few noteworthy ones.

24.1.1   Event model

First and foremost in the list of what could be improved is the framework event model. The framework is firmly rooted in the notion of building blocks connected together by events. As a minimum, all event outputs should be formulated as multi-casters (splitters), the same as in the AWT event model. This would greatly facilitate delegation of duties to nodes that may be part of an existing event chain. Out of necessity, this has already been done to a few classes, such as MultiShape.

24.1.2   Event routing

An even bolder move would be to consider introducing the concept of VRML-like routes. The advantage of a route-based model is that the event wiring is much more exposed and explicit. What goes in and what comes out is clearly identified in a building block class, exposed perhaps as strongly typed member fields or through standard access methods. The event connections between the source and target event nodes are also explicit, and should help to avoid some of the confusion you may have experienced in trying to trace out event paths in the framework examples. Early prototyping (and VRML itself) has shown the merits of such an event model. From a Java perspective, however, this prior art also highlighted its unconventional and even foreign nature, which is the main reason it was not used for the book.

24.1.3   Feedback model

The model used for feedback management was expedient at the time, but seems to be overly complex in hindsight. The complexity of the model also makes it difficult to debug. This is perhaps due to the fact that it combines feedback with selection and grouping in a manner that is more intimate than it should be. For the sake of flexibility and simplicity, it might be best to separate out the selection, grouping, and/or feedback models.

24.1.4   Input sensors

It was learned late in development that input sensors can exist quite well without the Behavior class. Basing the input sensors on the AWT event model would simplify their structure and avoid the nagging little problems that showed up when using behaviors. It also avoids the hassles of hosting the class in the scene graph, and simplifies the connections between the AWT components providing the events and the framework sensors using them.

24.2 THE SOFTWARE

The framework software, including source code, examples, and documentation is available for download from the Manning Publications web site at www.manning.com/barrilleaux. You are free to use the software for personal, non-commercial use. The software is protected by copyright and all rights are reserved by the author. It comes without warranty of any kind, no liability is assumed for its use, and it is not fit to do anything in particular.

acronyms

AI	Artificial Intelligence
API	Application Programming Interface
AR	Augmented Reality
CAD	Computer Aided Design
CAVE	Computer-Assisted Virtual Environment
CMYK	Cyan, Magenta, Yellow and Black
DAG	Directed acyclic graph
DnD	Drag-and-Drop
DRM	Display-relative mapping
DS	Display size
DSF	Display scale factor
DVO	Display-view Offset
FOV	Field of view
GC	Garbage Collection
GUI	Graphical User Interface
HTML	HyperText Markup Language
HUD	Heads-up display
HSV	Hue Saturation Value
LAD	Look-at Direction
LAD-UV	Look-at Direction Up Vector
LAD-DV	Look-at Direction Direction Vector
LAP	Look-at Point
LFO	Look-from Offset
LFO_X	Look From Offset, X coordinate
LFO_Y	Look From Offset, Y coordinate
LFO_Z	Look From Offset, Z coordinate
LFP	Look-from Point
LOS	Line-of-sight
MM	Multi-user Matrix
MVC	Model View Control
PDO	Pseudo-display Overlay

POCS	Plain Old Computer System
POTS	Plain Old Telephone System
PTF	Pseudo-tactile Feedback
PWO	Pseudo-world Overlay
RGB	Red, Green, Blue
SM	Single-user Matrix
SV	Single-user Vector
TG	Transform Group
UI	User Interface
VR	Virtual Reality
VRML	Virtual Reality Modeling Language
VSF	View Scale Factor
WRM	World-Relative Mapping
WYSIWYG	What You See Is What You Get
YIQ	Luminance, In-phase, Quadrature

index